The British School at Athens

SCHOLARS, TRAVELS, ARCHIVES:
GREEK HISTORY AND CULTURE THROUGH
THE BRITISH SCHOOL AT ATHENS

We gratefully acknowledge the support of
The Alexander S. Onassis Public Benefit Foundation
in the publication of this volume

and the continued support of
Applebee's, BP Hellas, Παύλος I. Κοντέλης AEBE
and Mr and Mrs Nicholas Egon

SCHOLARS, TRAVELS, ARCHIVES:
GREEK HISTORY AND CULTURE THROUGH THE BRITISH SCHOOL AT ATHENS

Proceedings of a Conference held at
The National Hellenic Research Foundation,
Athens, 6-7 October 2006

Edited by
Michael Llewellyn Smith, Paschalis M. Kitromilides
and Eleni Calligas

BRITISH SCHOOL AT ATHENS 2009
STUDIES 17

Published and distributed by
The British School at Athens
Senate House, Malet Street, London WC1E 7HU
© The Council, The British School at Athens

Series Editor: Olga Krzyszkowska

Production Editor: Eleni Calligas

ISBN 978-090-488-760-0

Designed and typeset by POTAMOS publishers
Printed in Greece by Metropolis SA
POTAMOS publishers, 7 Fokianou St, Athens 116 35
Tel: 2107231271 Fax: 2107254629

Contents

List of figures

List of colour plates

List of maps

List of tables

List of Abbreviations

BSA — Annual of the British School at Athens
BSA AR — Annual Report of Council of the British
School at Athens for the Session
DNB — Dictionary of National Biography
Hansard — Hansard's Parliamentary Debates
BPP — British Parliamentary Papers

Abstracts / Περιλήψεις

1
Michael Llewellyn Smith and Paschalis Kitromilides

Introduction

The establishment in 1886 of the British School as one of the 'Foreign Schools' at Athens was a significant step in the development of a modern Greek state which embraced European models. From the start, archaeology held a core position at the School. But the School has also, from early days, embraced the study of Greece in all its aspects. The Introduction traces how the School's mission was defined and how scholars took advantage of its flexibility to contribute to the study of many aspects of Byzantine and modern Greek culture, art and architecture, history, language, geography, anthropology, and folklore. In introducing the scholars studied in the book, including Barnsley and Weir-Schultz, Dawkins, Wace, Thompson, Toynbee, Hasluck and Sherrard, the Introduction explores the connections and influences between the different disciplines studied at the School, in particular how the School's approach to archaeology has always had a strong anthropological element. It explores also the impact of the Greek landscape and contemporary culture on scholars raised in the classical tradition of the old British universities.

Εισαγωγή

Η ίδρυση το 1886 της Βρετανικής Σχολής ως μιας από τις «Ξένες Σχολές» στην Αθήνα αντιπροσώπευε ένα ακόμη σημαντικό βήμα στην ανάπτυξη της νεότερης Ελλάδας ως σύγχρονου κράτους που υιοθετούσε ευρωπαϊκά πρότυπα. Εξαρχής η αρχαιολογία κατείχε κυρίαρχη θέση στις δραστηριότητες της Σχολής, αν και από τα πρώτα κιόλας χρόνια, η ΒΣΑ αγκάλιασε τις ελληνικές σπουδές στο σύνολό τους. Στην Εισαγωγή εξετάζεται πως προσδιορίστηκε η αποστολή της Σχολής και πως οι ερευνητές επωφελήθηκαν από αυτή την προσφερόμενη ευελιξία για να μελετήσουν διάφορες πτυχές της Βυζαντινής και νεότερης Ελλάδος στα πεδία του πολιτισμού, της τέχνης και αρχιτεκτονικής, της ιστορίας, της γλώσσας, της γεωγραφίας, της ανθρωπολογίας και της λαογραφίας. Στην Εισαγωγή παρουσιάζονται μελετητές όπως οι Barnsley και Weir-Schultz, Dawkins, Wace, Thompson, Toynbee, Hasluck και Sherrard, ενώ διερευνάται η διασύνδεση και αλληλεπίδραση των διαφόρων επιστημών που καλλιεργήθηκαν στη Σχολή. Ιδιαίτερα επισημαίνεται το γεγονός ότι η προσέγγιση της αρχαιολογίας στη Σχολή πάντοτε εμπεριείχε ένα ισχυρό ανθρωπολογικό στοιχείο. Επίσης εξετάζεται η επίδραση του ελληνικού τοπίου και του σύγχρονου πολιτισμού σε μελετητές που είχαν ανατραφεί με τις κλασικές παραδόσεις των παλαιών πανεπιστημίων της Βρετανίας.

2
Liz Potter

'Two thousand years of suffering': George Finlay and the *History of Greece*

George Finlay's engagement with Greek affairs was both as an active philhellene and as an historian of Greece. While a student of law he became interested in themes such as civil liberty and political economy which he elaborated later in his historical writing. He was also inspired by philhellenism and after coming to fight for Greece in 1823–25, he returned in 1827 to live in the country for the rest of his life. Despite the variety of broader contexts in which Finlay can be fruitfully considered, relatively little has been written about him. This paper situates Finlay in the context of the history of ideas and aims at a better understanding of his major work, *History of Greece BC 146 – 1864 AD* (7 vols, 1877), by tracing the intellectual roots of his attitudes and the contemporary context as well as the development of Finlay's liberal philhellenism.

'Δύο χιλιάδες χρόνια παθών': ο George Finlay και το έργο του *History of Greece*

Ο George Finlay συνδέθηκε με την Ελλάδα τόσο ως δραστήριος φιλέλληνας όσο και ως ιστορικός της Ελλάδας. Κατά τη διάρκεια των νομικών σπουδών του ενδιαφέρθηκε για ζητήματα όπως η ελευθερία του πολίτη και η πολιτική οικονομία τα οποία ανέπτυξε αργότερα στο ιστορικό του έργο. Εμπνεύστηκε επίσης από τον φιλελληνισμό και, αφού έλαβε μέρος στον αγώνα για την Ανεξαρτησία της Ελλάδας στα 1823–25, επέστρεψε το 1827 για να εγκατασταθεί μόνιμα στη χώρα. Παρά τις πολλές δυνατότητες μελέτης του έργου του Finlay σε ευρύτερες συνάφειες επιστημονικής ανάλυσης, έχουν γραφτεί σχετικά λίγα περί αυτού. Η ανακοίνωση τοποθετεί τον Finlay στο πλαίσιο της ιστορίας των ιδεών και στοχεύει στην καλύτερη κατανόηση του σημαντικού του έργου *History of Greece BC 146 – 1864 AD* (7 τόμ., 1877), μέσα από την ανίχνευση των πνευματικών καταβολών των θέσεών του και του σύγχρονου ευρωπαϊκού περιβάλλοντος καθώς και της εξέλιξης του φιλελεύθερου φιλελληνισμού του ίδιου του συγγραφέα.

3

Malcolm Wagstaff

Colonel Leake's knowledge of events in Greece following Independence: the Finlay correspondence

Both sides of the correspondence between George Finlay and Colonel Leake over the period 1829–60 survive in large measure, partly in the British School at Athens and partly in the Hertfordshire County Archives. Examination of the correspondence reveals that it was dominated by three themes: Greek topography, Leake and Finlay's publications and politics (largely, but not exclusively Greek). The paper focuses on political events in Greece and Finlay's letters as a source of information for Leake, an ardent Philhellene. It deals in particular with the Cretan uprising of 1840–41 and the British claims on Greece in the 1840s culminating in the notorious Pacifico Affair. In both of these Finlay's information resulted in Leake taking political action. Leake pressed for British support for the Cretans and in a pamphlet refuted British attempts to claim the islets of Cervi (Elafonisos) and Sapienza as part of the Ionian Islands.

Η γνώση του συνταγματάρχη Leake γύρω από γεγονότα στην Ελλάδα μετά την Ανεξαρτησία: η αλληλογραφία με τον Finlay

Το μεγαλύτερο μέρος της αλληλογραφίας μεταξύ του George Finlay και του συνταγματάρχη Leake των ετών 1829–60 σώζεται σήμερα, μοιρασμένο ανάμεσα στη ΒΣΑ και τα Hertfordshire County Archives. Η μελέτη της αλληλογραφίας καταδεικνύει ότι κυριαρχούν σ' αυτήν τρία θέματα: η τοπογραφία της Ελλάδας, οι δημοσιεύσεις του Leake και του Finlay, και η πολιτική (κυρίως, αλλά όχι αποκλειστικά, της Ελλάδας). Η ανακοίνωση εστιάζεται στα ελληνικά πολιτικά γεγονότα και στα γράμματα του Finlay ως πηγή πληροφοριών για τον Leake, ο οποίος υπήρξε ένθερμος φιλέλλην. Διαπραγματεύεται ιδιαίτερα την Κρητική εξέγερση του 1840–41 καθώς και τις βρετανικές απαιτήσεις έναντι της Ελλάδας στην δεκαετία του 1840, με αποκορύφωμα τη διαβόητη υπόθεση Pacifico. Και στις δύο αυτές υποθέσεις, οι πληροφορίες του Finlay είχαν αποτέλεσμα να αναλάβει ο Leake πολιτική δράση. Ο Leake πίεσε για την εξασφάλιση βρετανικής υποστήριξης στους Κρήτες, ενώ σε δημοσίευμά του αντέκρουσε τις βρετανικές διεκδικήσεις κυριότητας επί των νησίδων Cervi (Ελαφόνησος) και Sapienza ως τμημάτων των Ιονίων Νήσων.

4

Maria Christina Hadziioannou

Like a rolling stone; R.A.H. Bickford-Smith (1859–1916) from Britain to Greece

R.A.H. Bickford-Smith is a characteristic example of a British middle class young man who was led to discover Greece and its history by his social background and studies. He compiled, among other works, a volume (1893) on Greece during the period of George I, where he aired his views and sentiments about Greek society and economy, as well as politics and British financial interests in the eastern Mediterranean during the period following the Berlin Conference of 1878. The paper attempts a biographical sketch of the author-lawyer, placing him within the context of the average educated British traveller to Greece during the last decade of the 19th century, and tracing his background and cultural models from Wheler and Byron to Macaulay.

Σαν πέτρα που κυλά: ο R.A.H. Bickford-Smith (1859–1916) από τη Βρετανία στην Ελλάδα

Ο R.A.H. Bickford-Smith αποτελεί χαρακτηριστικό παράδειγμα βρετανού αστού που οδηγήθηκε στην ανακάλυψη της Ελλάδας και της ιστορίας της λόγω της κοινωνικής καταγωγής και των σπουδών του. Ο ίδιος συνέγραψε, μεταξύ άλλων δημοσιευμάτων, ένα βιβλίο (1893) για την Ελλάδα κατά την περίοδο του Γεωργίου Α΄ εκφράζοντας απόψεις και συναισθήματα για την ελληνική κοινωνία και οικονομία, καθώς και την πολιτική και τα βρετανικά οικονομικά συμφέροντα στην Ανατολική Μεσόγειο κατά την περίοδο των ανακατατάξεων μετά το συνέδριο του Βερολίνου (1878). Η ανακοίνωση επιχειρεί ένα βιογραφικό σχεδίασμα του συγγραφέα-δικηγόρου τοποθετώντας τον στην τυπολογία του μέσου εκπαιδευμένου βρετανού ταξιδιώτη στην Ελλάδα κατά την τελευταία δεκαετία του 19ου αιώνα, ανιχνεύοντας τις καταβολές και τα πολιτισμικά πρότυπά του από τον Wheler και τον Byron μέχρι τον Macaulay.

5
Peter Mackridge

From archaeology to dialectology and folklore: the role of the British School at Athens in the career of R.M. Dawkins

Dawkins spent the greater part of the period 1902 to 1919 in Greece, which became, as he put it, 'my second *patrida*'. For twelve of these years he was a member of the British School at Athens, serving as its director from 1906 to 1914. The first two decades of the twentieth century were the heyday of the School's contribution to ethnographic and medieval studies. Although he started out there as an archaeologist, Dawkins almost immediately became interested in modern Greek dialects and other aspects of medieval and modern Greek culture, and these interests eventually superseded his concern for Classical and pre-Classical Greece. This paper focuses on Dawkins's activities in medieval and modern Greek studies while he was at the British School and on the legacy of these activities in his later career, which bore fruit in his monumental publications, from *Modern Greek in Asia Minor* (1916) to *Modern Greek Folktales* (1953).

Από την αρχαιολογία στη μελέτη των διαλέκτων και τη λαογραφία: η επίδραση της ΒΣΑ στη σταδιοδρομία του R.M. Dawkins

Ο Dawkins πέρασε το μεγαλύτερο μέρος της περιόδου 1902–1919 στην Ελλάδα, η οποία έγινε, όπως έλεγε ο ίδιος «η δεύτερη πατρίδα μου». Για δώδεκα από αυτά τα χρόνια υπήρξε μέλος της ΒΣΑ ενώ υπηρέτησε ως Διευθυντής της από το 1906 ως το 1914. Οι πρώτες δύο δεκαετίες του 20ου αιώνα ήταν η περίοδος της μεγαλύτερης συνεισφοράς της Σχολής στις εθνολογικές και μεσαιωνικές σπουδές. Αν και ο Dawkins ξεκίνησε στην Ελλάδα ως αρχαιολόγος, σχεδόν αμέσως οι σύγχρονες ελληνικές διάλεκτοι κι άλλες πτυχές του μεσαιωνικού και σύγχρονου ελληνικού πολιτισμού κίνησαν το ενδιαφέρον του, και σταδιακά υπερκέρασαν το ενδιαφέρον του για την κλασική και πρώιμη Ελλάδα. Η ανακοίνωση επικεντρώνεται στις δραστηριότητες του Dawkins γύρω από τις μεσαιωνικές και σύγχρονες ελληνικές σπουδές όσο ήταν στη ΒΣΑ, και στην επίδραση αυτών των δραστηριοτήτων στην μετέπειτα σταδιοδρομία του, που είχε ως αποτέλεσμα θεμελιώδεις δημοσιεύσεις, από το *Modern Greek in Asia Minor* του 1916 έως το *Modern Greek Folktales* του 1953.

6
Anthony Bryer

R.M. Dawkins, F.W. Hasluck and the 'Crypto-Christians' of Trebizond

Crypto-Christians are not difficult to unmask in the British School at Athens archives where George Finlay's diary of his visit to Trebizond in 1850 may have the earliest reference to a crypto-Muslim there. Do you define faith by religion, ancestry, language or Ottoman taxation? Until the Ottoman *tanzimat* reforms of 1839–56 taxation was the clue to the faith of the silverminers and -smelters of Trebizond and the Pontos who were excused tax in lieu of Muslim military service. These anomalous 'crypto-Christians' aroused interest in London and were reported on by William Gifford Palgrave (1826–88) as consul in Trebizond (1867–73). Palgrave was not impressed by them but maybe knew too much (he converted his own faith six times), with a consequence that Ottoman recognition of them, under French pressure, was postponed until 1910. R.M. Dawkins (1871–1955) was the only BSA scholar who visited them, collecting folktales, in summer 1914. But the confusion of faith, religion and language survives there, including consequent assassinations in 2006–7.

Οι R.M. Dawkins και F.W. Hasluck και οι «κρυπτο-Χριστιανοί» της Τραπεζούντας

Δεν είναι δύσκολο να αποκαλύψει κανείς κρυπτο-Χριστιανούς στα αρχεία της ΒΣΑ, όπου το ημερολόγιο του George Finlay για το ταξίδι του στην Τραπεζούντα το 1850 περιέχει την πρώτη ίσως αναφορά σε έναν «κρυπτο-μουσουλμάνο». Τίθεται το ερώτημα αν η πίστη προσδιορίζεται από τη θρησκεία, την καταγωγή, τη γλώσσα ή την οθωμανική φορολογία. Μέχρι τις οθωμανικές μεταρρυθμίσεις του *tanzimat* των ετών 1839–56, η φορολογία ήταν το κριτήριο της πίστης για τους εργάτες και μεταλλουργούς των αργυρωρυχείων της Τραπεζούντας και του Πόντου γενικά, οι οποίοι εξαιρούντο της φορολογίας εφόσον υπηρετούσαν ως μουσουλμάνοι στρατιωτική θητεία. Η ύπαρξη αυτών των «κρυπτο-Χριστιανών» κίνησε το ενδιαφέρον του Λονδίνου και αναφέρθηκε από τον William Gifford Palgrave (1826–88) τον καιρό που ήταν πρόξενος στην Τραπεζούντα (1867–73). Δεν έκαναν ιδιαίτερη εντύπωση στον Palgrave που όμως ίσως γνώριζε πολλά (είχε αλλάξει την δική του πίστη έξι φορές), με αποτέλεσμα η αναγνώρισή τους από τους Οθωμανούς – ύστερα από πίεση από την Γαλλία – να καθυστερήσει μέχρι το 1910. Ο R.M. Dawkins (1871–1955) ήταν ο μόνος μελετητής της ΒΣΑ που το καλοκαίρι του 1914 τους επισκέφθηκε και συγκέντρωσε λαϊκά παραμύθια. Όμως η σύγχυση πίστης, θρησκείας και γλώσσας εξακολουθεί να επιβιώνει στην περιοχή, καθώς έδειξαν κι οι συνακόλουθες δολοφονίες όπως αυτές το 2006–7.

7
Tom Winnifrith

A.J.B. Wace and M.S. Thompson, Nomads of the Balkans — The Vlachs

The Nomads of the Balkans by A.J.B. Wace and M.S. Thompson is still, nearly a hundred years after its publication in 1914, a standard reference work for anyone studying the Vlachs. The Vlachs can be found in scattered pockets all over the central Balkans in roughly the same areas where Wace and Thompson found them, although two world wars, two Balkan wars, various civil wars and modern civilization threaten a traditional way of life and a language derived from Latin which is in competition with Greek, Albanian and various Slav dialects. The paper deals with the career and methods of Wace and Thompson. Wace was the older man, but seems to have been the more dashing of the pair. He had already a high academic reputation and was later to have a successful, if controversial, career at the British School. Thompson spent most of his life as a tea broker, though he served faithfully as secretary of the British School in London between the wars. His academic qualifications were less impressive, but he seems to have done sterling work on the language of the Vlachs. The chapter on the Vlach language in *The Nomads of the Balkans* is still a very useful introduction to the subject, and indeed anyone studying this fascinating if obscure people must read Wace and Thompson. The work of other scholars has worn less well.

Οι A.J.B. Wace και M.S. Thompson, Νομάδες των Βαλκανίων — Οι Βλάχοι

Το έργο των A.J.B. Wace και M.S. Thompson *Nomads of the Balkans* (ελλ. μετάφρ. Π. Καραγιώργου, Θεσσαλονίκη 1989) αποτελεί μέχρι σήμερα, σχεδόν 100 χρόνια από τη δημοσίευσή του το 1914, βασικό έργο αναφοράς για κάθε μελετητή των Βλάχων. Οι Βλάχοι ανιχνεύονται σε διάσπαρτες ομάδες σε ολόκληρα τα κεντρικά Βαλκάνια, στις ίδιες περίπου περιοχές που τους επεσήμαναν και οι Wace και Thompson. Όμως, δύο παγκόσμιοι, δύο βαλκανικοί και διάφοροι εμφύλιοι πόλεμοι καθώς και ο σύγχρονος πολιτισμός απειλούν τον παραδοσιακό τρόπο ζωής και τη γλώσσα τους, η οποία προέρχεται από την λατινική αλλά βρίσκεται σε ανταγωνισμό με την ελληνική, την αλβανική και διάφορες σλαβικές διαλέκτους. Η ανακοίνωση διαπραγματεύεται τη σταδιοδρομία και τις επιστημονικές μεθόδους των Wace και Thompson. Ο Wace ήταν ο μεγαλύτερος από τους δύο σε ηλικία και οπωσδήποτε ο πιο εντυπωσιακός ως προσωπικότητα. Είχε ήδη σημαντική ακαδημαϊκή φήμη και αργότερα υπήρξε πετυχημένος — παρά τις όποιες αμφισβητήσεις — διευθυντής της ΒΣΑ. Ο Thompson αντίθετα, πέρασε το μεγαλύτερο μέρος της ζωής του ως εισαγωγέας τσαγιού, αν και υπηρέτησε πιστά τη Σχολή ως γραμματέας στο Λονδίνο μεταξύ των δύο παγκοσμίων πολέμων. Οι ακαδημαϊκές του περγαμηνές ήσαν λιγότερο σημαντικές, αλλά φαίνεται ότι πραγματοποίησε άριστο έργο στο θέμα της γλώσσας των Βλάχων. Το κεφάλαιο για τη βλάχικη γλώσσα στο *Nomads of the Balkans* παραμένει μέχρι σήμερα μια πολύ χρήσιμη εισαγωγή στο θέμα, ενώ όποιος θέλει να μελετήσει αυτόν τον τόσο ενδιαφέροντα αν και αινιγματικό λαό, πρέπει απαραίτητα να διαβάσει τους Wace και Thompson. Το έργο άλλων μελετητών έχει αντέξει λιγότερο καλά στον χρόνο.

8

Ann French

The Greek embroidery collecting of R.M. Dawkins and A.J.B. Wace

This paper seeks to provide a preliminary study of the Greek embroidery collecting of R.M. Dawkins and A.J.B. Wace, who between them collected over 1200 pieces of embroidery during their years in Greece from 1902 to 1923. Dawkins and Wace's sources of purchase, collecting methodologies, academic influences, cataloguing, research and interpretation of their embroideries are described, using contemporary archives and publications, and concluding with an account of the dispersal and disposal of their collections. Through re-evaluating Dawkins and Wace's methods and motives in collecting embroideries, another facet of the BSA's early work in Greece is examined.

Η συλλογή ελληνικών κεντημάτων των R.M. Dawkins και A.J.B. Wace

Στην ανακοίνωση αυτή επιχειρείται μια προκαταρκτική μελέτη της συγκέντρωσης ελληνικών κεντημάτων που πραγματοποίησαν οι Dawkins και Wace. Η δραστηριότητα αυτή συντελέστηκε μεταξύ των ετών 1902 και 1923 όταν και οι δύο μελετητές ήσαν στην Ελλάδα και πέτυχαν τότε τη συγκέντρωση πάνω από 1200 κεντημάτων. Με τη βοήθεια σύγχρονων αρχείων και δημοσιευμάτων εξετάζονται οι πηγές των αγορών των Dawkins και Wace, η μεθοδολογία του σχηματισμού της συλλογής, οι επιστημονικές επιρροές, η καταλογογράφηση, η έρευνα και ερμηνεία των κεντημάτων που συγκέντρωσαν. Καταλήγοντας, η ανακοίνωση αναφέρεται στη διάθεση και διασπορά της συλλογής.

Με την επανεκτίμηση των μεθόδων και των κινήτρων των Dawkins και Wace στη συλλεκτική τους δραστηριότητα, εξετάζεται μια ακόμη πλευρά του έργου της ΒΣΑ στα πρώτα χρόνια μετά από την ίδρυσή της.

9

David Shankland

Scenes pleasant and unpleasant: the life of F.W. Hasluck (1878–1920) at the British School at Athens

Hasluck, the Assistant (then Acting Director) of the School was dismissed from his post during the Great War. This article urges that the time has come to discuss this event openly, and that to do so will enable a finer appreciation of his great intellectual worth. In detail, it suggests that Hasluck's downfall should be understood as a combination of his peaceable demeanour, his possessing a formidable enemy in Wace, his inadvertently becoming caught up in the suffragette debate, and his innovative readiness to conceive of human societies in terms of their complex interaction with each other and with the past. Hasluck was unable or unwilling to defend himself; and the Committee, unaware of his intellectual significance, were manipulated into depriving the School of the most sophisticated social thinker that it has yet produced. That they did so, albeit with some qualms, meant that Hasluck's pioneering work never quite translated into the intellectual movement that it could so easily have become.

Σκηνές ευχάριστες και δυσάρεστες: η ζωή του F.W. Hasluck (1878–1920) στη Βρετανική Σχολή Αθηνών

Ο Hasluck, Υποδιευθυντής (κατόπιν Αναπληρωτής Διευθυντής) της ΒΣΑ, απολύθηκε από τη θέση αυτή κατά τη διάρκεια του Α΄ Παγκοσμίου Πολέμου. Η ανακοίνωση τονίζει ότι έχει έρθει πια ο καιρός να συζητηθεί ανοικτά το γεγονός αυτό, και ότι έτσι θα εκτιμηθεί καλύτερα η σημαντική πνευματική προσφορά του Hasluck. Λεπτομερειακά, στην ανακοίνωση υποστηρίζεται ότι η πτώση του Hasluck οφείλεται σε ένα συνδυασμό πραγμάτων όπως η πραότητα του χαρακτήρα του, η έντονη εχθρότητα του Wace, η αθέλητη ανάμειξή του στο ζήτημα της γυναικείας ισότητας και η πρωτοποριακή του ετοιμότητα να κατανοεί τις ανθρώπινες κοινωνίες στα πλαίσια των σύνθετων σχέσεων που έχουν μεταξύ τους και με το παρελθόν. Ο Hasluck δεν μπορούσε ή δεν ήθελε να υπερασπιστεί τον εαυτό του και το Διοικητικό Συμβούλιο της Σχολής, αγνοώντας την πνευματική του αξία, χειραγωγήθηκε ώστε να στερήσει τη Σχολή από τον πιο σημαντικό κοινωνικό στοχαστή που έχει αναδείξει ως τώρα. Η πράξη αυτή, παρά κάποιες τύψεις μελών, σήμαινε ότι το πρωτοποριακό έργο του Hasluck δεν μετουσιώθηκε ποτέ σε κίνηση ιδεών, όπως τόσο εύκολα θα μπορούσε να είχε συμβεί.

10
Paschalis Kitromilides

F.W. Hasluck and *Christianity and Islam under the Sultans*

This study attempts an appreciation of F.W. Hasluck's seminal contribution to scholarship on the post-Byzantine world. It opens with an appraisal of the significance of his research on the multiple expressions of religious syncretism in Asia Minor and the Balkans that went into his posthumous work *Christianity and Islam under the Sultans*. As a tribute to his pioneering contribution, instances of religious syncretism in areas surveyed by Hasluck are recorded to fill in the texture of his own imposing canvas of the phenomenon: examples of places of worship shared by Christians and Muslims in Cyprus, Asia Minor and Istanbul, not recorded by Hasluck, are briefly discussed and illustrated adducing additional evidence to his own arguments.

Ο F.W. Hasluck και το έργο του *Ο Χριστιανισμός και το Ισλάμ την εποχή των Σουλτάνων*

Η ανακοίνωση παρουσιάζει μια συνολική αποτίμηση της συνεισφοράς του F.W. Hasluck στην επιστημονική μελέτη του μετα-βυζαντινού κόσμου. Εξαίρεται η σπουδαιότητα της έρευνας των ποικίλων εκφάνσεων του φαινομένου του θρησκευτικού συγκρητισμού στη Μικρά Ασία και στα Βαλκάνια που παρουσιάζεται στο έργο του *Christianity and Islam under the Sultans* (1928, ελλ. μετάφρ. 2004). Ως εκδήλωση τιμής στην πρωτοποριακή του συμβολή καταγράφονται παραδείγματα θρησκευτικού συγκρητισμού σε περιοχές που είχαν μελετηθεί από τον Hasluck για να συμπληρωθεί η δική

του επιβλητική εικόνα του φαινομένου: παραδείγματα κοινών τόπων λατρείας που μοιράζονται Χριστιανοί και Μουσουλμάνοι από την Κύπρο, τη Μικρά Ασία και την Κωνσταντινούπολη, που δεν μνημονεύονται από τον Hasluck, αναφέρονται και εικονογραφούνται, προσθέτοντας έτσι νέες μαρτυρίες προς εδραίωση της δικής του επιχειρηματολογίας.

11
Kallistos Ware

Three different views of the Holy Mountain: Athos through the eyes of F.W. Hasluck, R.M. Dawkins and Ph. Sherrard

The British School at Athens has included among its members a number of eminent specialists in Byzantine and Modern Greek Studies, three of whom wrote books about the Holy Mountain of Athos. F. W. Hasluck's account, *Athos and its Monasteries* (published posthumously, 1924), is largely factual, and gives special attention to continuity and change in Athonite governance over the centuries. R. M. Dawkins, in his book, *The Monks of Athos* (1936), deals in much greater detail with the inner life of the monks, their legends, corporate memory and self-perception; this is based in part on personal conversations that he had during his visits to the Holy Mountain. The work of Ph. Sherrard, *Athos the Mountain of Silence* (1959–60; revised edition, 1982), has an important and original concluding section on the spiritual aim of monasticism, based largely on texts in *The Philokalia*, and emphasizing the meaning of repentance, freedom and silence in the experience of the Athonite monks.

Τρεις διαφορετικές όψεις του Αγίου Όρους: ο Άθως μέσα από την οπτική των F.W. Hasluck, R.M. Dawkins και Ph. Sherrard

Μερικοί εξέχοντες ειδικοί στις βυζαντινές και νεο-ελληνικές σπουδές υπήρξαν μέλη της ΒΣΑ και τρεις από αυτούς έγραψαν βιβλία για τον Άθω, το Άγιο Όρος. Το έργο του Hasluck *Athos and its Monasteries* (που δημοσιεύθηκε μεταθανάτια, το 1924) είναι κυρίως μια αποτύπωση πραγμάτων και τονίζει ιδιαίτερα τη συνέχεια και τις αλλαγές της αθωνικής διοίκησης μέσα στους αιώνες. Ο Dawkins στο βιβλίο του *The Monks of Athos* (1936) διαπραγματεύεται με πολύ μεγαλύτερη λεπτομέρεια τον εσωτερικό κόσμο των μοναχών, τις πεποιθήσεις τους, τη συλλογική μνήμη και τον αυτοπροσδιορισμό τους. Η μελέτη αυτή προέκυψε εν μέρει από προσωπικές συζητήσεις του ίδιου με μοναχούς κατά τις επισκέψεις του στο Άγιο Όρος. Το έργο του Sherrard *Athos the Mountain of Silence* (1959–60, αναθεωρημένη έκδοση το 1982) περιλαμβάνει ένα σημαντικό και πρωτότυπο τμήμα στο τέλος σχετικά με τον πνευματικό σκοπό του μοναχισμού. Το τμήμα αυτό βασίζεται κυρίως στο έργο *Η Φιλοκαλία* και τονίζει την έννοια της μετάνοιας, της ελευθερίας και της σιωπής στην εμπειρία των αθωνιτών μοναχών.

12
Amalia G. Kakissis

The Byzantine Research Fund Archive: encounters of Arts and Crafts architects in Byzantium

At the turn of the 19th century, the British School at Athens brought Byzantium to Britain. As the vital link between classical and modern Greece, Byzantium captured the imagination of British architects influenced by the Arts and Crafts movement. Their studies of gothic and byzantine architecture in Italy, Greece and Asia Minor, played a major role in the gothic and neo-byzantine revival buildings built in Britain from the 1880s on — a prime example being Westminster Cathedral. In 1888, two students of the Royal Academy of Arts — Robert Weir Schultz and Sidney H. Barnsley – arrived in Greece to begin their studies of Byzantine architecture. They, and the many architects who followed them, used the newly-founded British School as their home base. They travelled from the School to undertake the study and measurement of Byzantine monuments throughout Greece and neighbouring countries. Each monument was carefully recorded through a series of drawings, plans and photographs. Some monuments were captured at critical moments in their history, as the expansion of the Greek state brought churches back into Christian use after centuries, while other monuments were subsequently to be lost to us through catastrophes such as the Great Fire in Thessaloniki in 1917. The collected result of these labours is today known as the 'Byzantine Research Fund Archive', a unique collection of over 1500 drawings and 1000 photographs, created between 1888 and 1949.

To Byzantine Research Fund Archive, όπου συναντώνται οι αρχιτέκτονες του κινήματος των Arts and Crafts με το Βυζάντιο

Στα τέλη του 19ου αιώνα η ΒΣΑ έκανε γνωστό το Βυζάντιο στη Βρετανία. Το Βυζάντιο, ως συνδετικός κρίκος μεταξύ της κλασικής και της σύγχρονης Ελλάδος, κίνησε τη φαντασία των βρετανών αρχιτεκτόνων που ήσαν επηρεασμένοι από το κίνημα Arts and Crafts. Η μελέτη της γοτθικής και βυζαντινής αρχιτεκτονικής στην Ιταλία, την Ελλάδα και τη Μικρά Ασία συνέβαλε ουσιαστικά στην ανέγερση στη Βρετανία κτηρίων νεογοτθικού και νεο-βυζαντινού ρυθμού κατά τη δεκαετία του 1880 και μετέπειτα — κύριο δείγμα αυτής της αναβίωσης είναι ο καθεδρικός ναός του Westminster στο Λονδίνο. Το 1888, δύο φοιτητές της Royal Academy of Arts, ο Robert Weir Schultz και ο Sidney H. Barnsley, ήλθαν στην Ελλάδα για να μελετήσουν την βυζαντινή αρχιτεκτονική. Όπως και άλλοι πολλοί αρχιτέκτονες που ακολούθησαν, χρησιμοποίησαν την πρόσφατα ιδρυμένη Βρετανική Σχολή ως βάση τους. Ταξίδεψαν σε όλη την Ελλάδα και στις γειτονικές χώρες για να μελετήσουν και να αποτυπώσουν βυζαντινά μνημεία. Κατέγραφαν λεπτομερειακά κάθε κτίσμα με σειρά σχεδίων, αποτυπώσεων και φωτογραφιών. Μερικά μνημεία καταγράφηκαν σε μια καίρια στιγμή της ιστορίας τους, καθώς η επέκταση του ελληνικού κράτους επανέφερε ορισμένες εκκλησίες στη χριστιανική λατρεία ύστερα από αιώνες. Άλλα μνημεία χάθηκαν αργότερα εντελώς λόγω φυσικών καταστροφών, όπως η μεγάλη πυρκαγιά της Θεσσαλονίκης το 1917. Το σύνολο του έργου αυτών των αρχιτεκτόνων, που σχηματίστηκε μεταξύ των ετών 1888 και 1949 και είναι σήμερα γνωστό ως 'Byzantine Research Fund Archive', αποτελεί μια μοναδική συλλογή πάνω από 1500 σχεδίων και 1000 φωτογραφιών.

13
Eugenia Drakopoulou

British School at Athens research into Byzantine Attica

The archive of the British Archaeological School includes altogether 268 drawings of 23 Byzantine monuments of Attica and especially Athens, from 1890 to 1903, 100 photographs of the decade 1890–1900, and the notebooks of the research groups. This rich and unpublished material adds valuable pieces to a puzzle which is difficult to reconstruct, that of the buildings of Athens in the Byzantine era and during the Ottoman occupation. At the same time, however, it reveals the influences of Byzantine architecture and decorative art on British architects of the 19th century and the beginnings of the 20th century.

Η ΒΣΑ στην έρευνα της βυζαντικής Αττικής

Στα αρχεία της ΒΣΑ περιλαμβάνονται συνολικά 268 αρχιτεκτονικά σχέδια εικοσιτριών βυζαντινών μνημείων της Αττικής και κυρίως των Αθηνών, που συντάχθηκαν μεταξύ των ετών 1890 και 1903, εκατό φωτογραφίες της δεκαετίας 1890–1900, και τα σημειωματάρια της ερευνητικής ομάδας. Το πλούσιο και αδημοσίευτο αυτό υλικό εμπλουτίζει τις περιορισμένες μας πληροφορίες για τα αθηναϊκά μνημεία κατά τη διάρκεια της βυζαντινής περιόδου και της οθωμανικής κυριαρχίας. Συγχρόνως όμως φανερώνει και την επίδραση της βυζαντινής αρχιτεκτονικής και των διακοσμητικών τεχνών στους βρετανούς αρχιτέκτονες του 19ου και των αρχών του 20ου αιώνα.

14

Paul Hetherington

William Miller: medieval historian and modern journalist

The paper assesses the career, works and character of William Miller. He was born in 1864, and after a successful university career, qualified as a lawyer. He never practised, but embarked instead on two parallel careers: as a journalist and as an academic historian. He pursued the first of these for some three decades, writing mainly for the *Morning Post*. As a historian he published a succession of books on the medieval and modern history of the Balkans, Greece and Turkey. Best known of these are *The Latins in the Levant* (1908) and *Essays on the Latin Orient* (1921). Miller's academic reputation was such that in 1916 he received, but rejected, requests to become the first holder of the Koraes Chair at King's College, London. He lived in Rome from 1903 to 1923, then moved to Athens, where he was a frequent visitor at the British School. He left Athens in 1941 on the German invasion, and died in Durban, South Africa in 1945.

Ο William Miller ως ιστορικός του μεσαίωνα και σύγχρονος δημοσιογράφος

Η ανακοίνωση πραγματεύεται την σταδιοδρομία, το έργο και την προσωπικότητα του William Miller. Ο Miller γεννήθηκε το 1864 και ύστερα από επιτυχημένες πανεπιστημιακές σπουδές διορίστηκε δικηγόρος. Δεν εξάσκησε όμως ποτέ το επάγγελμα του δικηγόρου αλλά αντίθετα ξεκίνησε παράλληλα δύο άλλες σταδιοδρομίες, του δημοσιογράφου και του ιστορικού. Ως δημοσιογράφος εργάστηκε για σχεδόν τρεις δεκαετίες, αρθρογραφώντας κυρίως στην εφημερίδα *Morning Post*. Ως ιστορικός δημοσίευσε μια σειρά βιβλίων σχετικά με τη μεσαιωνική και τη νεότερη ιστορία των Βαλκανίων, της Ελλάδος και της Τουρκίας. Τα γνωστότερα έργα του είναι *The Latins in the Levant* (1908, ελλ. μετάφρ. Σπ. Λάμπρου *Ιστορία της Φραγκοκρατίας εν Ελλάδι* 1909–10) και *Essays on the Latin Orient* (1921). Η επιστημονική απήχηση του έργου του Miller ήταν τέτοια ώστε του προτάθηκε το 1916 να αναλάβει πρώτος τη νέα έδρα «Κοραής» στο King's College του Λονδίνου, πρόταση όμως που αυτός απέρριψε. Έζησε στη Ρώμη από το 1903 έως το 1923 και στη συνέχεια ήλθε στην Αθήνα, όπου ήταν συχνός επισκέπτης στη ΒΣΑ. Εγκατέλειψε την Αθήνα με την εισβολή των Γερμανών το 1941, και πέθανε το 1945 στο Durban της Νοτίου Αφρικής.

15

Richard Clogg

Academics at War: the British School at Athens during the First World War

The fact that Greece did not enter the First World War until June 1917 posed problems for the foreign archaeological schools in Athens and created difficulties for the Greek authorities. As the Great Powers sought to put pressure on Greece to enter the war on their side or, at least, to maintain neutrality, they sought to harness the schools to their war effort. In the age of total war, this was perhaps inevitable but it necessarily led to the compromising of Greece's neutrality. It was likewise inevitable that countries on both sides of the conflict should make use of the linguistic skills and knowledge of the culture and geography of Greece of archaeologists and classical scholars to further their political, intelligence and military objectives in the country. This paper looks at the wartime activities of scholars associated with the BSA during the critical years of the First World War.

Ακαδημαϊκοί σε πόλεμο: η Βρετανική Σχολή Αθηνών κατά τον Α΄ Παγκόσμιο Πόλεμο

Το γεγονός ότι η Ελλάδα δεν μπήκε στον Α΄ Παγκόσμιο Πόλεμο μέχρι τον Ιούνιο 1917 δημιούργησε προβλήματα στις ξένες αρχαιολογικές σχολές στην Αθήνα και δυσκολίες στις ελληνικές αρχές. Καθώς οι Μεγάλες Δυνάμεις πίεζαν την Ελλάδα να μπει στον πόλεμο στο πλευρό τους ή τουλάχιστον να παραμείνει ουδέτερη, προσπαθούσαν επίσης να δέσουν τις Σχολές στο πολεμικό τους άρμα. Στην εποχή του ολοκληρωτικού πολέμου αυτό πιθανόν να ήταν αναπόφευκτο, αλλά οδήγησε αναγκαστικά στην υπονόμευση της ελληνικής ουδετερότητας. Κατά τον ίδιο τρόπο, ήταν αναπόφευκτο ότι κράτη και από τα δύο μέτωπα θα χρησιμοποιούσαν τις γλωσσικές ικανότητες και τη γνώση του πολιτισμού και της γεωγραφίας της Ελλάδος που είχαν αρχαιολόγοι και μελετητές των κλασικών σπουδών για να προωθήσουν τις πολιτικές, κατασκοπευτικές και στρατιωτικές τους επιδιώξεις στη χώρα. Η ανακοίνωση εξετάζει τις σχετικές δραστηριότητες των μελετητών που συνδέονταν με τη ΒΣΑ κατά τα κρίσιμα πρώτα χρόνια του Α΄ Παγκοσμίου Πολέμου.

16
Roger Just

The Archaeology of Greek Ethnography

From the 1960s onwards the anthropology of Greece (and of the Mediterranean) has produced a very significant body of ethnographic work. At the same time, Mediterranean anthropology appears to have made little impact within the discipline of anthropology as a whole and is seldom mentioned in historical accounts of its development. This paper argues that Mediterranean anthropologists of the 1960s to the 1980s made substantial ethnographic innovations that prefigured many of the later theoretical developments within anthropology, but that these innovations went rhetorically unannounced and failed to attract wider scholarly attention because Mediterraneanists continued to write as if they adhered to the very paradigms that their work was subverting.

Η αρχαιολογία της ελληνικής εθνολογία

Από τη δεκαετία του 1960 και πέρα, η επιστήμη της ανθρωπολογίας της Ελλάδος (και της Μεσογείου) έχει παρουσιάσει πολύ σημαντικό έργο σχετικά με την εθνολογία. Συγχρόνως όμως, η ανθρωπολογία της Μεσογείου μοιάζει να έχει επιδράσει ελάχιστα στη μελέτη της ανθρωπολογίας γενικά και σπάνια αναφέρεται σε ιστορικές αναδρομές της εξέλιξής του κλάδου. Η ανακοίνωση υποστηρίζει ότι οι μελετητές της μεσογειακής ανθρωπολογίας των δεκαετιών 1960 έως και 1980 εισήγαγαν σημαντικές εθνολογικές καινοτομίες οι οποίες προανήγγειλαν πολλές από τις μεταγενέστερες θεωρητικές εξελίξεις στη μελέτη της ανθρωπολογίας. Οι καινοτομίες όμως αυτές δεν υποστηρίχτηκαν ως τέτοιες και απέτυχαν να προσελκύσουν την προσοχή του ευρύτερου επιστημονικού κόσμου γιατί οι ερευνητές της Μεσογειακής ανθρωπολογίας συνέχισαν να γράφουν ωσάν να υποστήριζαν θέσεις που η ίδια τους η έρευνα κατέρριπτε.

17
Renée Hirschon

'Home from home': the role of the British School at Athens in anthropological fieldwork

The unexamined assumption that the BSA would provide a congenial home base for anthropologists ignored the fact that the BSA is structured on particular educational institutions in Britain. This assumption is challenged on the basis of a minor piece of ethnographic research involving interviews with some foreign anthropologists with a particular focus on John Campbell. They had conducted fieldwork in Greece from the 1950s–80s, which revealed that the experience of the role of the BSA varied widely, depending on factors such as place of origin, class, gender, and personality. Since anthropology was not seen as a central activity of the School, and because its methodology (participant-observation) requires knowledge of the language and involvement in the local society, the BSA was sometimes seen as providing little more than an institutional base. In the period since the 1980s, the development of anthropological research by Greek scholars has created a new context in which the contribution of foreign anthropologists is being re-evaluated, while the BSA continues to provide a secure base for them.

'Ένα σπίτι στα ξένα': η συμβολή της ΒΣΑ στην ανθρωπολογική έρευνα

Η υπόθεση ότι η ΒΣΑ θα παρείχε φιλόξενη στέγη σε μελετητές της ανθρωπολογίας, παραγνώριζε το γεγονός ότι η Σχολή έχει θεμελιωθεί πάνω σε συγκεκριμένα πρότυπα βρετανικών εκπαιδευτικών ιδρυμάτων. Η ανακοίνωση όμως αμφισβητεί αυτήν την υπόθεση, ύστερα κυρίως από την πραγματοποίηση μικρής εθνολογικής έρευνας σε μερικούς ξένους ανθρωπολόγους με επίκεντρο τον John Campbell. Οι μελετητές αυτοί είχαν διεξαγάγει επιτόπια έρευνα στην Ελλάδα μεταξύ του 1950 και 1990. Στην ανακοίνωση υποστηρίζεται ότι η εμπειρία της συμβολής της ΒΣΑ διέφερε σημαντικά και βασίζονταν σε παράγοντες όπως ο τόπος καταγωγής, η κοινωνική τάξη, το φύλο και η προσωπικότητα. Καθότι η μελέτη της ανθρωπολογίας δεν αντιμετωπίζονταν ως μια από τις κύριες δραστηριότητες της Σχολής και επειδή η μεθοδολογία της (παρατήρηση του συμμετέχοντος) απαιτούσε γνώση της γλώσσας και συμμετοχή στην τοπική κοινωνία, η ΒΣΑ έμοιαζε να παρέχει σχεδόν μόνο υπηρεσιακή βάση για τις σπουδές αυτές. Αλλά από την δεκαετία του 1980, η ανάπτυξη των ανθρωπολογικών μελετών από έλληνες ερευνητές έχει δημιουργήσει ένα νέο πλαίσιο μέσα στο οποίο η συνεισφορά των ξένων ανθρωπολόγων επανεκτιμάται και όπου η ΒΣΑ συνεχίζει να παρέχει μια σταθερή βάση.

18
Paul Halstead

Studying the past in the present: archaeological engagement with modern Greece

For prehistorians active in Greece, modern farmers and craftsmen have been a rich source of 'analogical' insight into the distant past. For example, studies of modern field- and garden-weeds, threshing-floor residues, dental microwear in sheep, and growth rings in 'shredded' trees have provided reliable methods for determining how people managed crops, animals and woodland in the past, both in Greece and further afield. Analogical study has also highlighted how recent practices, such as cereal-olive-vine polyculture or seasonally transhumant pastoralism, are contingent on factors (urban markets, unequal land ownership)

of questionable relevance to the distant past. With the shift from *what* past people did to *why*, the use of analogy becomes more contentious. Recent agricultural decision-making in rural Greece, however, suggest that the thorny opposition between 'practical' and 'cultural' reason is unnecessary and less productive than an integrated approach.

Ερευνώντας το παρελθόν στο παρόν: αρχαιολογικοί δεσμοί με τη σύγχρονη Ελλάδα

Για τους ερευνητές της προϊστορίας που εργάζονται στην Ελλάδα οι σύγχρονοι γεωργοί και τεχνίτες παρέχουν μια πλούσια πηγή «αναλογικής» γνώσης του μακρινού παρελθόντος. Για παράδειγμα, μελέτες των φυτών σύγχρονων αγρών και κήπων, των καταλοίπων αλωνιών, της φθοράς των δοντιών προβάτων καθώς και των κύκλων ζωής υλοτομημένων δένδρων, παρέχουν βάσιμες μεθόδους για να προσδιορίσουμε πως χειρίζονταν στο παρελθόν καρπούς, ζώα και δάση, τόσο στην Ελλάδα όσο κι αλλού. Η αναλογική μελέτη έχει επίσης φωτίσει το πως σύγχρονες πρακτικές, όπως οι πολυκαλλιέργειες σιτηρών, ελιάς και αμπέλου ή η εποχιακή νομαδική κτηνοτροφία, εξαρτώνται από παράγοντες (αστικές αγορές, άνιση κατοχή γης) οι οποίοι έχουν αμφισβητούμενη σχέση με το μακρινό παρελθόν. Όταν το ερώτημα *τι* έκαναν οι άνθρωποι του παρελθόντος μεταβληθεί στο *γιατί* το έκαναν, η χρήση αναλογιών γίνεται πιο προβληματική. Παρόλα αυτά, διεργασίες για τη λήψη πρόσφατων γεωργικών αποφάσεων στην ελληνική ύπαιθρο υποδηλώνουν ότι η ακανθώδης αντιπαράθεση μεταξύ «πρακτικών» και «πολιτισμικών» αιτίων είναι περιττή και όχι τόσο παραγωγική όσο μια συνθετική προσέγγιση.

British School at Athens, view from the Finlay balcony looking towards Lycabettus hill, photograph by F.W. Hasluck, ca 1904; BSA Photographic Archive: BSAA8–2 (SPHS–6265).

1
Introduction

Michael Llewellyn Smith and Paschalis Kitromilides

The establishment of the so-called 'Foreign Schools' in Athens, starting with the French School in 1846, followed by the German (1882), the American (1883), and in 1886 the British, was a significant step in the development of a modern Greek state which embraced European models, locating Greece within a European network of intellectual and cultural institutions. It answered to the need of foreign students of the material culture of ancient Greece to have their own base in the country. The Schools immediately became, and have remained, a part of the intellectual life of Athens. Their establishment marked the beginning of the end of the period of the casual appropriation of antiquities by foreign travellers, and the beginning of a process of negotiation of the terms and conditions of excavation between the Schools and the sovereign — albeit limited — power of Greece.[1]

From the start, the relatively new discipline of archaeology held a key position in the missions of these Schools. The reason is clear enough: the archaeology of Greece depends on material remains, which are for the most part available only in Greece and Greek lands. You do not need a School in Athens in order to study classical languages and literature. Foreigners had done this satisfactorily for centuries in Oxford, Cambridge and other universities of Europe. Archaeology by contrast requires a physical presence, such as a School, from which to negotiate with Greek authorities, launch excavations, store sherds. Some other disciplines which flourished in Britain also required a physical presence in the landscape of Greece: travel and topography, geography, the study of folklore, ethnography, the

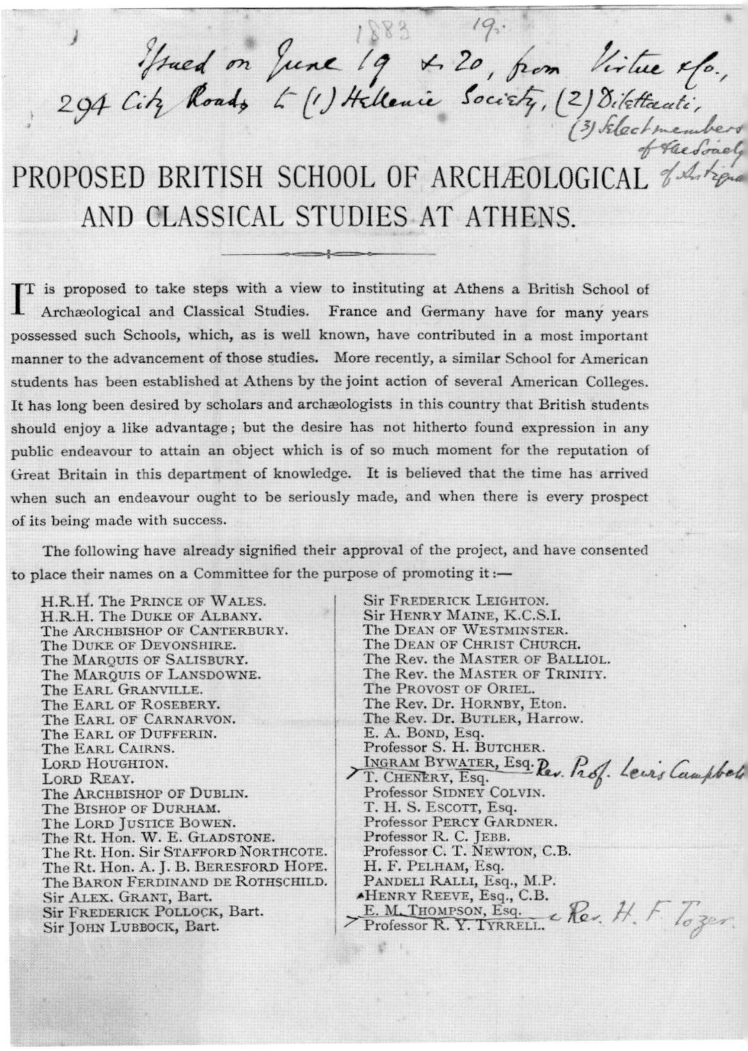

1883 19.
Issued on June 19 & 20, from Virtue & Co., 294 City Road, to (1) Hellenic Society, (2) Dilettanti, (3) Select members of the Society of Antiq

PROPOSED BRITISH SCHOOL OF ARCHÆOLOGICAL AND CLASSICAL STUDIES AT ATHENS.

It is proposed to take steps with a view to instituting at Athens a British School of Archæological and Classical Studies. France and Germany have for many years possessed such Schools, which, as is well known, have contributed in a most important manner to the advancement of those studies. More recently, a similar School for American students has been established at Athens by the joint action of several American Colleges. It has long been desired by scholars and archæologists in this country that British students should enjoy a like advantage; but the desire has not hitherto found expression in any public endeavour to attain an object which is of so much moment for the reputation of Great Britain in this department of knowledge. It is believed that the time has arrived when such an endeavour ought to be seriously made, and when there is every prospect of its being made with success.

The following have already signified their approval of the project, and have consented to place their names on a Committee for the purpose of promoting it:—

H.R.H. The Prince of Wales.
H.R.H. The Duke of Albany.
The Archbishop of Canterbury.
The Duke of Devonshire.
The Marquis of Salisbury.
The Marquis of Lansdowne.
The Earl Granville.
The Earl of Rosebery.
The Earl of Carnarvon.
The Earl of Dufferin.
The Earl Cairns.
Lord Houghton.
Lord Reay.
The Archbishop of Dublin.
The Bishop of Durham.
The Lord Justice Bowen.
The Rt. Hon. W. E. Gladstone.
The Rt. Hon. Sir Stafford Northcote.
The Rt. Hon. A. J. B. Beresford Hope.
The Baron Ferdinand de Rothschild.
Sir Alex. Grant, Bart.
Sir Frederick Pollock, Bart.
Sir John Lubbock, Bart.
Sir Frederick Leighton.
Sir Henry Maine, K.C.S.I.
The Dean of Westminster.
The Dean of Christ Church.
The Rev. the Master of Balliol.
The Rev. the Master of Trinity.
The Provost of Oriel.
The Rev. Dr. Hornby, Eton.
The Rev. Dr. Butler, Harrow.
E. A. Bond, Esq.
Professor S. H. Butcher.
Ingram Bywater, Esq. Rev. Prof. Lewis Campbell
T. Chenery, Esq.
Professor Sidney Colvin.
T. H. S. Escott, Esq.
Professor Percy Gardner.
Professor R. C. Jebb.
Professor C. T. Newton, C.B.
H. F. Pelham, Esq.
Pandeli Ralli, Esq., M.P.
Henry Reeve, Esq., C.B.
E. M. Thompson, Esq. Rev. H. F. Tozer
Professor R. Y. Tyrrell.

Fig. 1.1: 'Proposed British School of Archaeological and Classical Studies at Athens'; BSA Corporate Records—Athens: Athens Property, Correspondence: R. Jebb 1882–86, no. 19.

1. For the early history of the British School at Athens see Waterhouse 1986, esp. chs. 1 and 5, and Calligas and Whitley 2005. For recent debate about the role of the Foreign Schools see Hamilakis 2007, 48–51. Hamilakis rightly rejects the view that Greek archaeology has simply been a victim of 'colonialism' (represented by the Foreign Schools), arguing that it is partner in an exchange relationship where archaeology and colonialism meet.

modern language and dialects, even politics. These also stood to benefit by the presence of a British School.

The Foreign Schools each had and has its own individuality. From the start the mission of the French School extended more widely than archaeology, into philology, architecture and art, classical studies and the modern Greek language. The more narrowly focussed missions of the American and German Schools are reflected in their names ('American School of Classical Studies' and 'German Institute of Archaeology'). The British School at Athens, like the French, spread its net more widely. Here are the Objects of the School as set out in the 'Rules and Regulations of the British School at Athens' drafted in 1894–95:[2]

> I. The first aim of the School shall be to promote the study of Greek archaeology in all its departments. Among these shall be (i) the study of Greek art and architecture in their remains of every period; (ii) the study of inscriptions; (iii) the exploration of ancient sites; (iv) the tracing of ancient roads and routes of traffic.
>
> II. Besides being a School of Archaeology, it shall be also, in the most comprehensive sense, a School of Classical Studies. Every period of the Greek language and literature, from the earliest age to the present day, shall be considered as coming within the province of the School.
>
> III. The School shall also be a centre at which information can be obtained and books consulted by British travellers in Greece.
>
> IV. For these purposes a Library shall be formed and maintained of archaeological and other suitable books, including maps, plans and photographs.

Much of the ethos and future direction of the School is reflected in this statement. Although the primacy of archaeology is asserted, there is sufficient flexibility to permit the study of any aspect of Greek culture in any period,

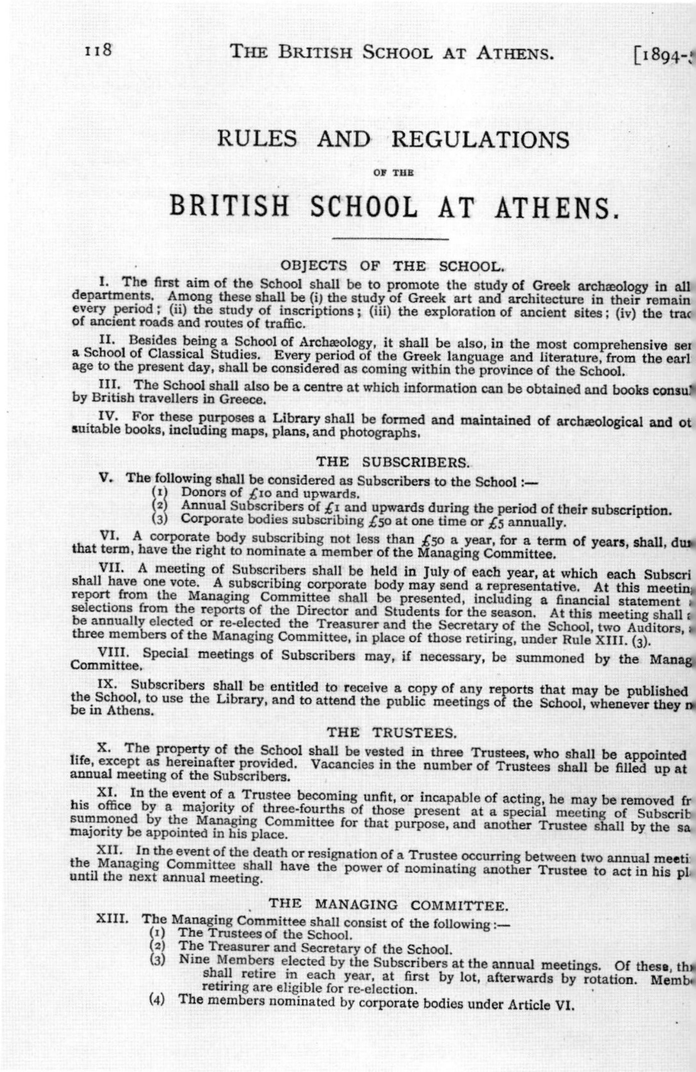

118 THE BRITISH SCHOOL AT ATHENS. [1894-

RULES AND REGULATIONS

OF THE

BRITISH SCHOOL AT ATHENS.

OBJECTS OF THE SCHOOL.

I. The first aim of the School shall be to promote the study of Greek archæology in all departments. Among these shall be (i) the study of Greek art and architecture in their remain every period; (ii) the study of inscriptions; (iii) the exploration of ancient sites; (iv) the trac of ancient roads and routes of traffic.

II. Besides being a School of Archæology, it shall be also, in the most comprehensive ser a School of Classical Studies. Every period of the Greek language and literature, from the earl age to the present day, shall be considered as coming within the province of the School.

III. The School shall also be a centre at which information can be obtained and books consu by British travellers in Greece.

IV. For these purposes a Library shall be formed and maintained of archæological and ot suitable books, including maps, plans, and photographs.

THE SUBSCRIBERS.

V. The following shall be considered as Subscribers to the School:—
(1) Donors of £10 and upwards.
(2) Annual Subscribers of £1 and upwards during the period of their subscription.
(3) Corporate bodies subscribing £50 at one time or £5 annually.

VI. A corporate body subscribing not less than £50 a year, for a term of years, shall, du that term, have the right to nominate a member of the Managing Committee.

VII. A meeting of Subscribers shall be held in July of each year, at which each Subscri shall have one vote. A subscribing corporate body may send a representative. At this meetin report from the Managing Committee shall be presented, including a financial statement selections from the reports of the Director and Students for the season. At this meeting shall be annually elected or re-elected the Treasurer and the Secretary of the School, two Auditors, three members of the Managing Committee, in place of those retiring, under Rule XIII. (3).

VIII. Special meetings of Subscribers may, if necessary, be summoned by the Manag Committee.

IX. Subscribers shall be entitled to receive a copy of any reports that may be published the School, to use the Library, and to attend the public meetings of the School, whenever they n be in Athens.

THE TRUSTEES.

X. The property of the School shall be vested in three Trustees, who shall be appointed life, except as hereinafter provided. Vacancies in the number of Trustees shall be filled up at annual meeting of the Subscribers.

XI. In the event of a Trustee becoming unfit, or incapable of acting, he may be removed fr his office by a majority of three-fourths of those present at a special meeting of Subscrib summoned by the Managing Committee for that purpose, and another Trustee shall by the sa majority be appointed in his place.

XII. In the event of the death or resignation of a Trustee occurring between two annual meeti the Managing Committee shall have the power of nominating another Trustee to act in his pl until the next annual meeting.

THE MANAGING COMMITTEE.

XIII. The Managing Committee shall consist of the following:—
(1) The Trustees of the School.
(2) The Treasurer and Secretary of the School.
(3) Nine Members elected by the Subscribers at the annual meetings. Of these, th shall retire in each year, at first by lot, afterwards by rotation. Memb retiring are eligible for re-election.
(4) The members nominated by corporate bodies under Article VI.

Fig.1.2: Statutes, BSA 1, 1894–95, 118.

and there is an openness to the amateur traveller as well as the professional academic. The mission of the School has been modified since 1896, to put all scholarly disciplines on a footing of equality, within the general purpose 'to promote the study of Greece in all its aspects.'[3]

2. Note the name of the School (in Greek, Βρεταννική Σχολή Αθηνών). It later changed its name to 'British School of Archaeology' (Αγγλική Αρχαιολογική Σχολή). As pointed out by Whitley, all three words of that title in Greek are misleading, since the School is British not English, it is not exclusively 'archaeological', nor is it a School in the sense of a primarily teaching institution —rather a research institute. The School has changed its name back to British School at Athens. Calligas and Whitley 2005, 11.

3. Statute no 1 of the current statutes is as follows: 'The purpose of the British School at Athens shall be to promote the study of Greece in all its aspects. It shall be its aim in particular to provide facilities for those engaged in research into the anthropology, archaeology, archaeometry, architecture, art, environment, geography, history, language, literature, religion and topography of Greece in all periods to modern times...' The alphabetical order seems consciously designed to avoid privileging any discipline, although in practice archaeology remains pre-eminent.

XIV. The Committee shall have control of all the affairs of the School, and shall decide any dispute that may arise between the Director and Students. They shall have power to deprive any Student of the use of the school-building.

XV. The Committee shall meet as a rule once in every two months; but the Secretary or Treasurer may, with the approval of two members of the Committee, summon a special meeting when necessary.

XVI. Due notice of every meeting shall be sent to each member of the Committee by a summons signed by the Secretary. Three members of the Committee shall be a quorum.

XVII. In case of an equality of votes, the Chairman shall have a second or casting vote.

XVIII. In the event of vacancies occurring among the officers or on the Committee between the annual elections, they may be provisionally filled up by the Committee until the next annual meeting.

STUDENTS.

XIX. The Students shall consist of the following :—
(1) Holders of travelling fellowships, studentships, or scholarships at any University of the United Kingdom or of the British Colonies.
(2) Travelling Students sent out by the Royal Academy, the Royal Institute of British Architects, or other similar bodies.
(3) Other persons who shall satisfy the Managing Committee that they are duly qualified to be admitted to the privileges of the School.

XX. Students attached to the School will be expected to pursue some definite course of study or research in a department of Hellenic studies, and to write in each season a report upon their work. Such reports shall be submitted to the Director, shall by him be forwarded to the Managing Committee, and may be published by the Committee if and as they think proper.

XXI. Intending Students are required to apply to the Secretary. No person shall be enrolled as a student who does not intend to reside at least three months in Greek lands.

XXII. Students shall have a right to use the library of the School, and to attend all lectures given in connexion with the School, free of charge.

XXIII. So far as the accommodation of the house permits, Students shall be admitted to reside at the school building, paying at a fixed rate for board and lodging. Priority of claim to such accommodation to be determined by the Managing Committee.

XXIV. The Managing Committee may elect as honorary members of the School any persons actively engaged in study or exploration in Greek lands, or such persons as they may from time to time think desirable.

THE DIRECTOR.

XXV. The Director shall be appointed by the Managing Committee, on terms which shall be agreed upon at the time, for a period of not more than three years. He shall be eligible for re-election.

XXVI. He shall have possession of the school-building as a dwelling-house; but Students of the School shall have a right to the use of the library at all reasonable times.

XXVII. It shall be his duty to guide and assist the studies of Students of the School, affording them all the aid in his power, and also to see that reports are duly furnished, in accordance with Rule XX., and placed in the hands of the Secretary before the end of June.

XXVIII. (a) Public Meetings of the School shall be held in Athens during the season, at which the Director and Students of the School shall read papers on some subject of study or research, and make reports on the work undertaken by the School. (b) The Director shall deliver lectures to Students of the School. At least six of such meetings and lectures shall be held in the course of each session.

XXIX. He may at his discretion allow persons, not Students of the School, to use the library and attend his lectures.

XXX. He shall be resident at Athens from the beginning of October in each year to the end of the following May, but shall be at liberty to absent himself for short periods for purposes of exploration or research.

XXXI. At the end of each season he shall report to the Managing Committee—(i) on the studies pursued during the season by himself and by each Student; (ii) on the state of the School-premises and the repairs needed for them; (iii) on the state of the Library and the purchases of books, &c., which he may think desirable; and (iv) on any other matter affecting the interests of the School.

XXXII. In case of misconduct the Director may be removed from his office by the Managing Committee by a majority of three-fourths of those present at a meeting specially summoned for the purpose. Of such meeting at least a fortnight's notice shall be given.

PUBLICATION.

XXXIII. No publication whatever, respecting the work of the School, shall be made without the previous approval of the Committee.

THE FINANCES.

XXXIV. All money received on behalf of the School beyond what is required for current expenses shall be invested in the names and at the discretion of the Trustees.

XXXV. The banking account of the School shall be placed in the names of the Treasurer and Secretary, who shall sign cheques jointly.

XXXVI. The first claim on the revenue of the School shall be the maintenance and repair of the School-building, and the payment of rates, taxes, and insurance.

XXXVII. The second claim shall be the salary of the Director, as arranged between him and the Managing Committee.

XXXVIII. In case of there being a surplus, a sum shall be annually devoted to the maintenance of the library of the School and to the publication of a report; and a fund shall be formed from which grants may be made for travelling and excavation.

REGULATIONS FOR THE LIBRARY.

XXXIX. The first Director shall, on commencing residence at Athens, draw up regulations as to the management of the library, its use by Students, and the like, and submit them to the Managing Committee, on whose approval they shall become binding on Director and Students. These regulations may afterwards be modified by the Managing Committee.

Fig.1.3: Statutes, BSA 1, 1894–95, 119.

Fig.1.4: Statutes, BSA 1, 1894–95, 120.

From the earliest days scholars at the School have taken advantage of the flexibility of this remit. In the second year of the School's existence, the arrival of the architects S. Barnsley and R. Weir-Schultz as Royal Academy Travelling Students signalled that Byzantine art and architecture was within the scope of the School. The interests of early School members such as R.A.H. Bickford-Smith, D.G. Hogarth, J.L. Myres, R.M. Dawkins, A.J.B. Wace and M.S. Thompson included aspects of modern Greece, its society, physical features and language.

The conference 'Scholars, Archives, Travels' which gave rise to this book was conceived jointly by the editors as a way of illuminating what the British School and its scholars have done to further the study of Byzantine history and culture, and the 'modern' period in Greece in disciplines other than archaeology. We wanted also to explore connections and influences between these disciplines, in particular anthropology and archaeology.

The conference was a joint project of the British School at Athens and the Institute for Neohellenic Research of the National Hellenic Research Foundation, and was held at the L. Zervas amphitheatre of the Institute. The papers read at the conference, which took place on 6–7 October 2006, are reproduced in this book, with one exception (John Koliopoulos's paper on Finlay's Disenchanted Progeny) and one addition (Ann French's paper on Wace and Dawkins as collectors of Greek embroideries).

The best account of the intellectual currents which swirled around the British School in its early years is given by James Whitley, Director of the School at the time of the conference, in the book *On Site: British Archaeologists in Greece.*[4] Two connected things seem to have happened. First, British archaeology developed around the turn of the century a strong ethnographic content, which it has never lost. Second, scholars emerging mainly from the 'old' British universities, and coming to Athens to pursue the study of the history, archaeology and culture of ancient Greece, were seduced by the powerful impact of the Greek landscape[5] and contemporary culture, and drawn into other, and more contemporary, pursuits.

Whitley notes how in the first decade of the 20th century, largely under the influence of Arthur Evans's work at Knossos in Crete, the School developed a corner in the archaeology of the bronze age and a bias towards prehistory which has persisted to this day. He noted also the anthropological and comparative perspective which Evans brought to his material. Evans himself was not of the British School, but profoundly influenced the ethos and intellectual interests of the School, and became its greatest benefactor. He brought to his investigations in Crete both a wide range of comparative experience including in Celtic archaeology, and practical liberal engagement as a journalist in the politics of the south eastern European states still under Ottoman rule. Other scholars at the School followed Evans in taking a close and informed interest in the societies around them. Some, such as A.J.B. Wace, were able to do so without at any point abandoning their main commitment to bronze age archaeology. Others, such as R.M. Dawkins, shifted their focus of interest from archaeology to other fields, in Dawkins's case to modern Greek dialects and folk tales. Both Dawkins and Wace developed an interest in Greek folk embroideries which went far beyond amateurish dabbling, to the extent that their meticulously catalogued collections now enrich museums in the UK.

To those conventionally educated in the classics, the impact of the Greek landscape and culture threw up questions about Greek history, society and geography, and about possible connexions and continuities, of language, cult or custom, between the ancient and the modern worlds. Such themes had been debated by Greek and foreign historians and thinkers since the 18th century. To these questions, scholars from the British School made a distinctive contribution, such that when during the First World War it was proposed to set up a new Koraes Chair of Modern Greek and Byzantine History, Language and Literature at King's College London, the School was seen as the natural recruiting ground for the first incumbent. Those seriously considered as candidates, R.M. Dawkins, A.W. Gomme, F.W. Hasluck, C.A. Scutt, A.J.B. Wace and Arnold Toynbee all had close connections with the School.[6]

The successful candidate, Arnold Toynbee, had spent nine months of the years 1911–12 as a student of the British School, much of the time walking in the Greek countryside (something of a passion among many students at the School). Later, after taking part in propaganda work during the First World War, he was elected in 1919 as the first Koraes Professor. The appointment led to an acrimonious row on account of his reporting on the Greco-Turkish war of 1919–22, and in particular his book *The Western Question in Greece and Turkey*, published in 1922. In the end Toynbee resigned his Chair. His graduation from the classical to the modern, and the modern political, was traumatic for himself and for the subscribers to the Chair, but resulted in a book that has stood the test of time. Toynbee went on, with his voluminous publications about Hellenism and history, to become one of the acknowledged great men of 20th century historiography. Even if time has eroded his reputation he retains his interest as representing one sort of outcome of the exposure of Greek scholars and 'philhellenes' to 'Greek reality'. He is not considered further in this book, but has been studied in lively detail by Richard Clogg.[7]

---

4. Calligas and Whitley 2005.

5. An example of an Oxford scholar profoundly affected by the impact of Greece and its physical environment is Alfred Zimmern, author of *The Greek Commonwealth*, which he wrote during his at the BSA in 1909–11; see Millett 2007, 168–202.

6. Clogg 2000, 20.

7. Clogg 2000, in particular the chapters 1, 'Anglo-Greek Attitudes: an Introduction'; 2, 'The British School at Athens and the Modern History of Greece'; and 3, 'The "ingenious enthusiasm" of Dr Burrows and the "unsatiated hatred" of Professor Toynbee'. See also Clogg 1986.

Although British School students pursued a wide range of interests, ranging from Byzantine art and architecture to folk tales, embroideries, travel and topography, and ethnography, these remained for the most part at the periphery of the School's activities. The reason is clear. The classics were the core of the British education system until the 19th century. The Byzantine and the modern were regarded as a side show.[8] Byzantium had to struggle against the prejudices of Gibbon and Lecky. The interest of the Arts and Crafts movement, happening to coincide in time with the foundation of the School, gave Byzantine art and architecture a toehold at the School. The modern had to struggle against the disillusion of philhellenes with the development of the new Greek Kingdom, fostered by men such as Edmond About (an early fellow of the French School). Classical Greek therefore ruled the university curriculum in Britain, progressively supplemented by archaeology. The study of Byzantium and of the history, geography, language, literature and anthropology of the modern country had to fight for a place.

They were helped to do so by the man who should be seen as a founding father of the School, though he died before it was established. This was the Scottish historian George Finlay, who followed Byron to Greece, settled in Athens, wrote a series of books about the history of the country, quarrelled with the Greek government, and corresponded about Greek affairs with British politicians and writers. The particular importance of Finlay to the British School is his library, which was donated, with his papers, to the School in 1900. It is a wonderful collection of books about Greece and the Levant, European history, English and Scottish literature and other subjects. The Finlay papers are a main part of the School's archive.[9] By personal example as well as by his books and papers Finlay is a continuing presence and influence, though a paradoxical one, in that though devoted to the study of Greek history throughout the ages, he was himself responsible for some of the disillusion felt in Britain with the development of the Greek state. The 'Finlay Library' which contains many of his books, and a marble bust of him, is also the School's common room.

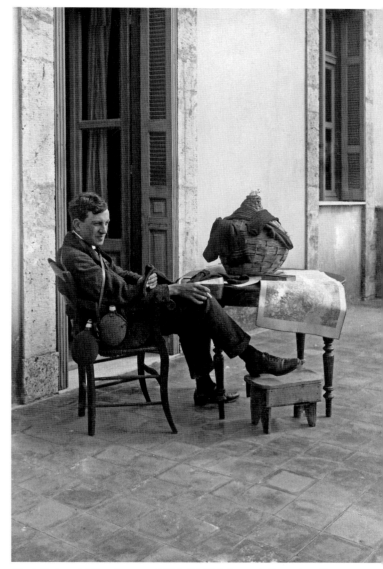

Fig.1.5: Arnold Toynbee, ca. 1911-12; This is part of a series of photographs for which students and officers of the School posed in the same setting but surrounded by a different collection of objects. The photographs seem to be part of a, now undecipherable, inside joke. BSA Photographic Archive: BSAA7–61.

Finlay lived in Athens at the time when the great Greek historian Konstantinos Paparrigopoulos was reclaiming Byzantium and its history as an integral part of the history of the Greek people.[10] Finlay contributed to the same end by his books, for example *A History of Greece: From its Conquest by the Romans to the Present*

---

8. For Byzantium, see Cameron 2006.
9. Hussey 1973.

10. Paparrigopoulos 1886–87; Kitromilides 1998.

Fig.1.6: The BSA Hostel, ca. 1900; BSA Photographic Archive: BSAA3–69.

Time.[11] His career and his influence are considered by Liz Potter in her paper 'George Finlay and the *History of Greece*'. Malcolm Wagstaff explores Finlay's correspondence with the great traveller, topographer and observer Colonel Martin Leake, a correspondence bearing on British-Greek relations.

It is worth looking more closely at the path taken by the early members of the School, from upbringing in England and education in the classics to archaeology and thence to other pursuits: a path from the ancient to the modern, in some cases from the classical to the ethnographic. These early members were almost all men. Although women were admitted as student members from 1890, it took time, and some agonising, for them to be accepted fully into the School's community. They were admitted to accommodation in the School hostel only in 1920, and as David Shankland describes in his paper, when in 1912 F.W. Hasluck married the young Margaret Hardie, a student at the School, and requested that they be accommodated in the hostel, the refusal of his request was disruptive, obliging him and his new wife to move out of the School into their own accommodation.

Of the scholars described in this book, R.M. Dawkins was the first to be Director of the School, in 1906–13. His career path illustrates the contingent and

zig-zag way in which he came to realise the true focus of his life. Always passionately interested in languages and literature, especially ancient ones, he trained as an engineer, stumbled into the classics at Cambridge at the age of 27, and was thus already 30 when he arrived at the British School in 1902. He thereupon acquired the skills of archaeology, supervising the excavation of Palaikastro in eastern Crete, and studying the local dialects of Crete and the islands whenever he got the chance. Travelling with A.J.B. Wace in the Cyclades in 1906 and 1907, he acquired an impressive collection of Greek embroideries. He travelled prodigiously to most parts of the Greek world including Cappadocia in Asia Minor and Pontos. An aspect of Pontos which attracted Dawkins's interest was the phenomenon of the 'crypto-Christians', which is examined by Anthony Bryer, the eminent historian of the area. Bryer's paper offers an explanation of the phenomenon which deserves and requires close reading.

Peter Mackridge writes that Dawkins reckoned to have visited all the Greek islands except Chalki, a record which if true, which we doubt, must have been unique. During the war he served in the RNVR in Crete, which gave him a further opportunity to study the dialects and customs of the islanders. Mackridge's comment on Dawkins's approach to archaeology is an indication of the direction that others at the School were to take: 'what interested him in archaeology was its anthropological and ethnographic aspect: the way to reconstruct the way of life, the belief system, the thought-world and the mentality of the people whose material remains were being examined'. He ended as a dialectologist and folk-lorist, tracing the folk tales of Greeks in Asia Minor, the legends of the monks of Mount Athos, and the dialects of those with whom he came in contact.

Dawkins illustrates better than any other the successful progression or broadening of intellectual endeavour which the School, and the Greek environment, made possible. He made a major contribution to the understanding of the prehistoric civilisation of Crete and of the classical period in Sparta, before going on to explore the philology of the Greeks of Asia Minor, at first for purely linguistic purposes, and finally for the meaning of the folk tales, poems and legends he collected, and their illustration of the mentality of the

---

11. Finlay 1877. Also Finlay 1844; 1861 and 1856.

people who produced them. He flourished in the hospitable atmosphere of the British School.

Alan Wace succeeded Dawkins as Director of the School and served in the eventful period from 1913–23. Wace is best known for his archaeological work, first his collaboration with Maurice Thompson on prehistoric Thessaly in the early years of the century, later at Mycenae in the 1920s and 30s. But his interests were much wider. Apart from his collection of embroideries, during his season of work in Thessaly he became interested in the way of life of the Vlach transhumant shepherd communities which wintered in the plains of Thessaly, returning to Samarina and other Vlach villages in the high Pindus for the summer pasturage. The outcome was the classic account of the Vlachs of Greece, *Nomads of the Balkans,* in which Wace and Thompson, without submitting the Vlachs to the systematic ethnographic analysis of a modern social anthropologist, nevertheless went about as far as it was possible to go in all-round description of the language, culture, origins and way of life of this unusual community of mysterious origins - all illustrated by their own photographs.[12] Tom Winnifrith, who has made a long and loving study of the Vlachs, describes in his paper how often he found that Wace and Thompson had been there before him.

Dawkins's closest friend and intellectual stimulus was F.W. Hasluck, Assistant Director and Librarian at the School, a quiet man of charm and great learning who died at the age of forty two in 1920. His life and career, including his differences with Wace, are considered by David Shankland; and both Shankland and Paschalis Kitromilides assess his contribution to historical thought. Hasluck has won much attention recently, in large part owing to Dr Shankland's own efforts. He calls him, controversially, 'by far the greatest scholar it [i.e. the British School] has had'. Shankland argues that Hasluck was doing something new and different, in applying historical, archaeological and anthropological skills to pre-modern societies in such a way as to show the connections, continuities and discontinuities between them. For Kitromilides, Hasluck's thought 'tries to rescue pre-national pluralism which is directly threatened by the agenda of nationalism'. Even if the

Fig.1.7: The Penrose Library; BSA Photographic Archive: SPHS–6340.

prime interest of the School remained a more conventional archaeology of the ancient world, the currents explored by Hasluck continued to flow beneath the surface and to break out in later work up to this day.[13]

Some of these scholars come together in two other contexts, those of the First World War, and of Mount Athos. Richard Clogg's paper on the School in the First World War explores the role of the School in the political and military history of Greece, a subject about which he has written extensively.[14] He describes the parts played by Wace, Hasluck, Dawkins, Myres and others in the British military and intelligence effort in Greece. It is not surprising that these people, knowledgeable about the country, its culture and (to different degrees) its language, should have played an important role, as was to happen again in the Second World War. Clogg's account makes clear that the School was caught up, willingly, in the British war effort and in the violations of Greek sovereignty which it involved. In the light of this story, it is hardly surprising that in the early 1950s, at a time of rising tension between Greece and Britain over Cyprus, Greeks should have assumed that

---

12. Wace and Thompson 1914.

13. For an example, influenced by Hasluck's demolishing of unsound theories of cultic continuities, see Nixon 2006.
14. Clogg 2000.

Fig.1.8: Kafeneio in Attica; BSA Photographic Archive: SPHS–3408.

the fair haired British anthropologist doing fieldwork in the Zagorochoria near the border with Albania must be up to no good. This was John Campbell, innocent of politics but rumoured to be scouting out landing fields for parachute drops.

A second context in which scholars of the British School converged was Mount Athos. Metropolitan Kallistos in the keynote address to the October 2006 conference considered 'three different views' of the Holy Mountain, those of Hasluck, Dawkins, and the scholar poet Philip Sherrard, who was Assistant Director of the School in the 1950s (1950–52 and 1958–61). Here the Metropolitan confronts what we have called the 'powerful impact of the landscape' and the people who inhabit it. Mount Athos demands visiting if one is to understand and appreciate Eastern Orthodox monasticism. His paper shows how different facets of

Athonite monasticism are filtered through the imaginations of these three scholars, all sensitive and all linguistically competent. Hasluck's particular object of study was the history of the monastic establishments and their governance; Dawkins's was the legends of the monks and what they reveal of the monks' mental world; Sherrard's, the inner life of the monks, and the new challenges of balancing the pressures of modernity with the spiritual need to preserve silence and stillness. It is not difficult to see which approach is for Kallistos the most fruitful; but he skilfully extracts the useful and valuable from all three.

The question of how Byzantium fitted into the British School's conception of its mission, which as we have seen is to explore every aspect of Hellenism then and now, arose early in its life, and was resolved empirically. It was only one year after the establishment of the

School that Robert Weir Schultz and Sidney Barnsley came to the School, with travelling scholarships from the Royal Academy's School of Architecture, and started to explore and illustrate the Byzantine monuments of the Hellenic world. Their mission arose as part of a growing interest on the part of British architects from the Academy and the Royal Institute of British Architects, which were closely associated with the Arts and Crafts movement. There followed a series of architects, including Walter George who recorded St Demetrios Church in Thessaloniki before the great fire of 1917; Ramsay Traquair who documented churches in Laconia and Constantinople; and Harry H. Jewell who studied the church of Our Lady of the Hundred Gates (*Ekatontapyliani)* in Paros.

The Byzantine Research and Publication Fund was established in 1908 with the aim of sponsoring and publishing the work of these British architects. The Fund responded to a mixture of aesthetic and practical needs. Byzantine art and architecture were forcing themselves on western European taste and scholarship. At the same time the monuments, churches and paintings were in need of recording and conservation. (Many still are.) After many vicissitudes the Fund's holdings of drawings and photographs have found a permanent home at the School under the new title Byzantine Research Fund Archive. They were presented in February 2008 in an exhibition at the Hellenic Centre, London: 'The Byzantine Research Fund: Encounters of British Arts and Crafts Architects in Byzantium'. Amalia Kakissis, the archivist at the School, has charge of the conservation, cataloguing and digitisation of the archive, and tells in her paper the story of the Fund and its connexion with the Arts and Crafts movement. In view of its importance and new accessibility, we hope that this archive will serve as a resource for further scholarly research.

It may seem inevitable, in the light of the growth of social anthropology in the UK, that Greece should have become a field for anthropological fieldwork by British scholars. It did not seem so in the early post-war years. The first into the field in Greece was John Campbell, with his fieldwork on the value system of the Sarakatsani of Epirus, carried out (with his wife Sheila) in 1954–55. Campbell was not primarily a British School scholar. He was an anthropologist trained at Cambridge and then Oxford. The factors which led him to northern Greece were his war experiences in 1944–45 in Greece, and the influence of his teachers, especially Professor E. Evans-Pritchard of Oxford. But once launched on his course, he found the School a helpful 'home from home' particularly after he was obliged to leave the Zagorochoria because of tensions over Cyprus.

The School however played a large part in the subsequent story, of scholars, many of them taught or influenced by Campbell, who enlarged and enriched the practice of anthropology in Greek lands. This wider story is told by Roger Just, himself a student of Campbell, and Assistant Director of the School from 1982–84. His conclusion is that in developing an ethnography of values as opposed to social structures, the early ethnographers of Greece, such as Campbell, Juliet du Boulay, Renée Hirschon, Michael Herzfeld, Charles Stewart — and I would add Just himself — achieved ground-breaking work the theoretical content of which was not sufficiently appreciated at the time, or since.

Paul Halstead opens up another aspect of ethnography in which the School has been active, in his paper 'Studying the Past in the Present: Archaeological Engagement with Modern Greece'. Ethnoarchaeology aims to use the present as a key to the past by the use of analogy. Halstead concentrates particularly on the analogical investigation of farming and land use practices. He outlines the different approaches required in exploring the 'what' and the 'why' of ancient farming practices, and despite cautionary words about the use of evidence, he notes that important conclusions can be drawn. In developing the science of ethnoarchaeology, Halstead and others have been following the footsteps of earlier generations at the School, such as Stanley Casson (pottery) and John Pendlebury. The prominence of survey work in the School's activities, with its line of descent from the 19th century travellers' observations, is another area in which the anthropological and the archaeological come together.

This cross-disciplinary ferment of ideas is in tension with the tendency, with increasing professionalisation and compartmentalisation, for archaeologists and social anthropologists to constitute themselves as separate tribes. Renée Hirschon bends her anthropologist's eye on the School itself through the personal experiences of anthropologists who have worked there. Her title 'Home from Home' — a title that on close inspection rings somewhat ironically — brings out the ambivalence of anthropologists about some aspects of the School: its old fashioned ethos, reflecting the Old Universities and public schools; its finicky rules, 'like a British boarding school'; the sometimes self-absorbed world of archaeology; the English speaking environment unsuited to anthropologists who have to work with Greek speaking people. All these made the School a less than ideal place for students of anthropology especially if they came from other than British middle-class backgrounds. And yet...the School also inspired affection, it led to lasting friendships, it served as a source of credentials and respectability, it had a good library, and it had baths and showers. For most, it was some sort of a home from home.

From its inception, the very features of the School which anthropologists have found strange made it a comfortable and familiar home for the amateur, the man of letters, generally of middle class background, who does not quite fit into the category of professional university scholar. Two examples are explored in this book. R.A.H. Bickford-Smith, whom Maria Christina Chatziioannou likens to the rolling stone that gathers no moss, was not a particularly important writer nor an original scholar. He was a law graduate who came to Greece almost by accident on the way to Constantinople, and stayed. The interest in Maria Christina Chatziioannou's paper lies in the scrupulously researched anatomy of a 'generalist' subscribing member of the School in its early years. Bickford-Smith represented distrust of ideas, enthusiasm for facts, and the propensity of British visitors to be carried away by the experience of Greece. In him, the School was carrying out its function as expressed in the original Statutes, of serving the interests of travellers. The result, Bickford-Smith's book *Greece under King George,* was a work of taxonomy on the state of the Greek polity and economy in the time of King George I which has served historians well.

The second case is William Miller, a more intriguing figure. Far from amateurish in his approach to his material, indeed a professional writer and journalist to the

core, he nevertheless did not fit the profile of a British School academic, except in that he had had a classical education at Oxford. Like Bickford-Smith he then read for the bar, but never practised. Like Arthur Evans, he travelled extensively in the Balkans as a young man. He spent twenty years, between 1903 and 1923, in Rome, working as a journalist, and the following eighteen years, 1923–41, in Greece. When he settled in Greece he was already nearly sixty years old. He held no university post, rejecting the attempt of Ronald Burrows, Principal of King's College London, to persuade him to take up the newly established Koraes Chair. Miller preferred to stick to his amiable, gentlemanly life in Athens, writing a series of well-informed and stimulating books about Greece and the Balkans and about medieval Greece, of which the cream are *Greek Life in Town and Country, The Latins in the Levant* and *Essays in the Latin Orient.* The Millers were forced to leave Greece by Hitler's invasion of April 1941, and he spent his declining years in South Africa, dying in 1945.

Paul Hetherington throws much light on this amiable figure, who played a notable part in the movement for animal welfare in Greece, a cause in which expatriate British people remain active today. His eccentricities included an obsession with accurate numeration which drove him to count and record the strokes he swam every day of every year (taxonomy again!). His importance, in Hetherington's account, is his ability to apply to the study of history a journalist's ability to delve for facts, and to apply his knowledge of history to the task of reporting and interpreting the current political scene, in Italy and Greece.

These examples show the School as a garden in which many different flowers can grow and blossom. Openness to the non-university scholar and the amateur continues.

As James Whitley remarked in his introductory remarks at the conference, the 'modern Greece' which has been the object of study continually changes, through the effects of war, migration, tourism and economic development.[15] Some of these changes are reflected in this book. The papers which follow are part of the history

---

15. 'Greeks are always in the process of becoming.' (J.L. Myres)

Fig.1.9: Athens from Lycabettos hill; BSA Photographic Archive: SPHS–1076.

of the British School at Athens, but part also of the wider history of Britain's engagement with Greece. The first feeds into the second in, for example, Finlay's correspondence with Leake about Britain's relations with Greece, as described by Wagstaff. That larger story is considered in an epilogue by Professor Roderick Beaton, who concluded the 'Scholars, Archives, Travels' conference with some stimulating thoughts arising from it.

Many people have contributed in various ways to the making of this book and the conference which gave rise to it. We wish to thank the sponsors of the conference and of this book, Applebee's; BP Hellas; Pavlos I. Condellis AEVE; and Mr and Mrs Nicholas Egon for their generous support; the British Hellenic Chamber of Commerce for their assistance; the Alexander S. Onassis Public Benefit Foundation for generous support for the publication of this book. We thank also the Council of the British School at Athens; the National Hellenic Research Foundation for the use of its amphitheatre as our conference venue and other support. We should also like to thank the contributors themselves for their work; the BSA archivist Amalia Kakissis for her expert help with illustrations; and our fellow editor Eleni Calligas, without whose patient work neither conference nor book would have been possible.

REFERENCES

Bickford-Smith, R.A.H, 1893. *Greece Under King George*. London.

Calligas, E. and Whitley, J. (eds), 2005. *On Site: British Archaeologists in Greece*. Athens.

Cameron, A., 2006. *The Byzantines*. Oxford.

Campbell, J.K., 1964. *Honour, Family and Patronage: A Study of Institutions and Moral Values in a Greek Mountain Community*. Oxford.

Clogg, R., 1986. *Politics and the Academy: Arnold Toynbee and the Koraes Chair*. London.

—, 2000. *Anglo-Greek Attitudes: Studies in History*. London.

Dawkins, R.M., 1916. *Modern Greek in Asia Minor*. Cambridge.

—, 1936. *The Monks of Athos*. London.

—,1953. *Modern Greek Folk Tales*. Oxford.

Finlay, G., 1844. *Greece under the Romans: a Historical View of the Condition of the Greek Nation*. Edinburgh.

—, 1856. *History of the Byzantine Empire from 717 to 1057*. Edinburgh.

—, 1861. *History of the Greek Revolution*. London and Edinburgh.

—, 1877. *A History of Greece: From its Conquest by the Romans to the Present Time*. Oxford.

Hamilakis, Y., 2007, *The Nation and its Ruins: Antiquity, Archaeology and National Imagination in Greece*. Oxford.

Hasluck, F.W., 1924. *Athos and its Monasteries*. London.

—, 1926. *Letters on Religion and Folklore*. London.

—, 1929. *Christianity and Islam under the Sultans*. Oxford.

Hussey J. (ed.), 1973. *The Finlay Papers: a Catalogue*. Oxford.

Kitromilides, P., 1998. 'On the Intellectual Content of Greek Nationalism: Paparrigopoulos, Byzantium and the Great Idea', in D. Ricks and P. Magdalino (eds), *Byzantium and Modern Greek Identity*: 25–33. Aldershot.

Miller, W., 1905. *Greek Life in Town and Country*. London.

—, 1908. *The Latins in the Levant: a History of Frankish Greece (1204–1566)*. London.

—, 1921. *Essays on the Latin Orient*. Cambridge.

Millet, P., 2007. 'Alfred Zimmern's *The Greek Commonwealth Revisited*', in C. Stray (ed.), *Oxford Classics: Teaching and Learning 1800-2000*. London.

Nixon, L., 2006. *Making a Landscape Sacred: Outlying Churches and Icon Stands in Sphakia, Southwestern Crete*. Oxford.

Paparrigopoulos, K., 1886–87. Ιστορία του Ελληνικού Έθνους. 2 edition, vols 1–3: 1886, vols. 4–5: 1887). Athens.

Sherrard, Ph., 1959. *The Greek East and the Latin West*. Oxford.

—, 1960. *Athos, the Mountain of Silence*. Oxford.

Wace, A.J.B. and Thompson, M.S., 1914. *The Nomads of the Balkans: an Account of Life and Customs among the Vlachs of Northern Pindus*. London.

Waterhouse, H., 1986. *The British School at Athens: the First Hundred Years*. London.

Zimmern, Alfred, 1911. *The Greek Commonwealth: Politics and Economics in Fifth-Century Athens*. Oxford.

2
'Two thousand years of suffering': George Finlay and the *History of Greece*
Liz Potter

INTRODUCTION

In a volume devoted to the contribution made by the British School at Athens to Byzantine and Modern Greek Studies, George Finlay has a claim on our attention in a number of respects. He was a philhellene who fought for modern Greek liberty, who then settled in the country and became an historian of Greece in her Roman, Byzantine, Ottoman and Modern periods. He was also, in both guises, inescapably negotiating a relationship with the classical past. Research in his archive, which is based at the School, has deepened my understanding of the many facets of that relationship.[1]

Born in 1799, to a family of Protestant merchants and bureaucrats, he was raised largely in Scotland. He studied law at Glasgow and Göttingen, when he became actively involved in various liberal societies.[2] Papers contained in his archive include some of the essays he read to these societies, which demonstrate an early interest in many themes he would elaborate in his *History of Greece*, prominently those of civil liberty and political economy.[3] It was at this time too that he developed an interest in philhellenism, and he came to fight for Greece in 1823–25. Returning in 1827, he was to live in the country for the rest of his life.

Fig.2.1: George Finlay; BSA George Finlay Personal Papers: A20, p.84.

He was active in Greek politics (especially in the development of the new capital at Athens in the 1830s and 40s), as a journalist and an historian, as a collector and a traveller. As such, he was connected not only with many prominent Greeks and foreigners in Athens, but also with a wide range of British travellers, writers and intellectuals. Likewise, intellectually he was in touch with a range of British, Greek and Western European periodical writing and historical scholarship.[4]

Finlay is thus of interest, and could be studied, from a number of points of view — as a philhellene, a traveller, a scholar with diverse connections, a collector, an

---

1. I was given permission to read in the archive by the Director of the British School at Athens. I am extremely grateful to the Librarian, Archivist and staff at the British School for the many ways in which they have helped my work.

2. For biographical information, see esp. Hussey 1975, Arnakis 1960 and Frazee 1964.

3. 'On the Progress of Civil Liberty in Modern Europe', read to the Speculative Society on 26 March 1821, and 'Some Observations on the Commercial Situation and Policy of Great Britain', read to the Literary and Commercial Society of Glasgow on 18 April 1821 (*Finlay Papers* A.1(19) and (20)). All references to Finlay's archive in this piece are given according to the reference system used by J.M. Hussey to catalogue the archive: see Hussey 1973.

---

4. His archive contains his correspondence with a great many travellers, writers and scholars.

historian, a liberal, for instance. Yet scholars have paid him little attention. There was a brief wave of interest in the early twentieth century, when Alan Wace and William Miller marked the importance of his archive; both however emphasised his disappointment with Greece and his sense of pessimism.[5] In a second wave of interest, in the 1970s, Joan Hussey highlighted instead the warmer, more romantic and adventurous sides of his character, 'a genial, if sardonically inclined, companion' to the many British visitors to Athens who sought him out (including Gladstone and J.S. Mill). Hussey also made a greater effort to see Finlay's intellectual proclivities in context, appreciating some of the Victorian roots of his depiction of the 'healthy polity'.[6]

Finlay's ideas bear further investigation. What *kind* of liberal philhellene was he in his twenties, and did he later become a thorough pessimist — even a 'mishellene', as one reviewer suggested in 1861?[7] The sheer variety of British liberalism is justly a prominent theme in current scholarship, and a recent contribution to the history of British philhellenism emphasises precisely the *range* of liberalisms embedded within it.[8] In this piece, I use these and other ideas to enliven our understanding of Finlay's *History of Greece BC 146 — 1864 AD*, tracing the intellectual roots of its attitudes and its contemporary context.[9] My aim is to situate Finlay in the context of the history of ideas as part of a broader interest in British Hellenism and its intellectual affinities. My focus in this piece thus lies principally in depicting broader contexts in which Finlay can be fruitfully considered.

Briefly setting out contemporary British interest in the classical past, and its relevance as the context in which Finlay was working, I concentrate largely on

Finlay's account of the build-up to 1821 in the first five volumes of his *History*. In particular, I consider his debts to, and his reconstructions of, the traditions of republican thinking, 'philosophic' and conjectural history and contemporary liberalism. Seen in broader contexts, as an historian responding to the urgent intellectual and political issues of his time, I argue that Finlay is a more complex and interesting thinker than has previously been suggested. It is also important to see his 'optimism' or 'pessimism' in terms of intellectual heritage as well as personal character. This reading enables a richer appreciation of Finlay's involvements with Greece: they were the fruits of a deep personal engagement with those centuries-long battles over the uses of the past which remain our heritage.

THE SHADOW OF THE CLASSICAL PAST

The classical past was a source of fascination to Western Europeans of Finlay's time. Viewed in broad terms, the roots of this fascination are traceable to the 're-birth' of classical learning in the Renaissance. If Latin literature and the example of Rome had exercised more attraction until the mid-eighteenth century, that emphasis would change. With the stimulus of German literary, historical and philological activity, and the European stirrings of liberal democracy, the perceived relevance of the Greek past rose dramatically. Nurtured by education systems which devoted a majority of their time to the classics, it is hard to overestimate how much educated nineteenth-century Europeans thought about Greece.

But *which* Greece? Most interest focused on the heroic age depicted by Homer and on the literature, buildings and sculpture of the classical period. In Britain, specifically, Classical Athens would come to be valorised as a democracy which was also imperially successful, which had high levels of citizen participation and high cultural standards, produced works of intellectual 'genius', and embodied social cohesiveness and a 'moral' fibre capable of being maintained without Christian revelation. Almost all of the prominent public figures of the Victorian age reflected on how Athens had managed this, and how her achievement might be replicated in the large-scale representative democracy in Britain. In the fields of historical and socio-political thought — the relevant contexts for Finlay — Grote's

---

5. See Miller 1924*a*, Miller 1924*b*, Miller 1923–25, Miller 1926. Also Wace 1916–18. On his disappointment, see esp. Miller 1924*a*, 397f and Wace 1916–18, 130f.

6. Hussey 1994; 'Introduction' (xiii–xxxiii) to Hussey 1995.

7. *The Critic* (28 December 1861) said that, far from showing the 'frantic enthusiasm of many Philhellenes', Finlay's tone 'frequently disposes us to believe that he has a tendency to mis-Hellenism.'

8. Rosen 1992. Rosen does not discuss or reference Finlay.

9. Finlay's works were originally published discretely (Finlay 1844; 1851*a*; 1852; 1854; 1856; 1861). They were edited as the seven volumes of a single history for their posthumous publication (Finlay 1877). All references in this piece are to the 1877 edition.

monumental history of archaic and classical Greece and the works of J.S. Mill and Matthew Arnold are just some of the most prominent outputs of this British absorption in Greece.[10]

This veneration of the classical past had also been an important component in British philhellenism in the 1820s (with liberalism, nationalism, romanticism and Christian fellow-feeling also playing prominent roles). This was the background against which Finlay would present his work. The characterisation of ancient Greece as the 'childhood' of Europe had generally meant that 'later' Greece was simply seen as less interesting or relevant in itself. Byzantium, where it had been considered at all, was generally treated as a 'hanger on' to arguments about the decline and fall of Classical Rome. Here Edward Gibbon was Finlay's crucial predecessor.

GIBBON AND FINLAY

Gibbon's focus had been Rome and its 'decline', rather than Byzantium as such. His impatience with the quantity of Byzantine material his topic requires him to digest often comes across.[11] Byzantium is included to help him teach the lesson of his 'philosophic' history. Philosophic history took a variety of forms, but all of its practitioners were interested in the past for the purposes of present instruction, and the crucial contrast was always with the antiquarians or *érudits*, chroniclers of facts or events for their own sake. What mattered to the philosophic historian was the wider significance of events — the knowledge they implied of man, morality and politics, the patterns they suggested of cause and effect, progress and decline. For Gibbon, the organising

pattern of the past could be discerned in the fortunes of the classical values of Rome — that *humanitas* which, together with a healthy military readiness, endowed the Roman citizen with *virtus*. Following the idea of Voltaire and the *philosophes* that history peaked in a number of 'happy ages', Gibbon portrayed the Antonine period as a climax, an age abundant in civilised values: at this time, as he saw it, the *pax Romana* had brought internal peace and good government to the empire, fostering material affluence and the cultivation of learning.[12] Indeed, many other Enlightenment thinkers also saw this as a period of 'enlightened absolutism', with rule by benevolent despots.

Gibbon used this 'happy period' as the acme from which to draw down his tale of the decline and fall of classical values, which would only resurface in the Renaissance. He charted how the forces of barbarism and religion, in particular, compounded the decline in Rome's classical virtues, depicting an escalating decay in patriotism, virtue and military discipline, and thus liberty.[13] Byzantium's function in this scheme was largely to exemplify the state in its enervated form.[14] Presenting this picture of the past — from Rome through Byzantium to the Renaissance — he delivered his readers to the Enlightened present with a sense of reassurance that this, once again, was a period of Progress.

Under the confident surface, however, lurks a distinct unease. While Gibbon admired the 'Enlightened absolutism' of the Antonine period, the reader cannot quite get away from the fact that it was based on the Augustan settlement, which offered only a precarious freedom to its citizens — never quite the robust,

---

10. Grote 1846–56; Arnold 1960–77; Mill 1963–91. (All of Arnold's works are informed by his Hellenism. Of Mill's phenomenal output, little can justly be regarded as un-informed by his interest in classical education and in classical Greek history and political thought; his most *direct* reflections on Greek history are contained in his review essays on Grote. Sections of *Considerations on Representative Government* and *On Liberty* are also important for the uses they make of the Athenian model of democracy.) See further Potter 2004.

11. See esp. Gibbon 1909, I, xli and his plan for his last two (quarto) volumes: he merely presses on into Byzantine history because it is '*passively* connected with the most splendid and important revolutions which have changed the state of the world' (Gibbon 1909, V, 180ff; this quote, p.182, original emphasis).

12. The 'happy ages', for the *philosophes*, were Periclean Athens, Classical Rome, Renaissance Italy and the Age of Louis XIV (merging into the Enlightenment). We note that Gibbon's 'happy period' was not 'Classical Rome', exactly, but the period from Nerva to Marcus Aurelius.

13. These are the key themes in Gibbon's account of decline, and attract most of his interest and his energy. Some causal role in decline is also given to increases in taxation and disease, and to decreases in population numbers and agricultural efficiency (themes on which Finlay would expand).

14. Indeed, Finlay's editor criticized Gibbon precisely for having treated Byzantium 'rather as a peg on which to hang his general survey of the history of the time, than as deserving of study for its own sake'. Finlay 1877, I, vii.

'rational' liberty, backed by military fervour, of the Republican period. This inherent, structural weakness was only obviated in the Antonine period by the personal qualities of the emperors. Further, beneath the depiction of the 'happy' *pax Romana*, there lurked the suspicion that the state of peace was in itself akin to a state of stagnation: citizens in this sort of state would soon lose that courage which would match the warlike vigour of barbarians.

Finlay wrote in Gibbon's shadow.[15] The similarities as well as the differences are crucial. Finlay's very focus was Greece and Byzantium, not Rome. But his too was conceived as a philosophic history, aiming to instruct.[16] In this fundamental sense, Finlay's work was a conceptual descendant of Gibbon's.

Yet within that broad framework, the particular 'instruction' he wished to offer was strikingly different to that of his predecessor, and he often categorically set his arguments against those of Gibbon.[17] First, he saw both periods of 'decline' and of 'resurgence' (some more significant than others): his Byzantium was one of 'rises and falls', whereas for Gibbon Byzantium *was* 'decline and fall' in absolute terms. Second, for Finlay — crucially in contrast to Voltaire and Gibbon — no 'absolutism' could ever be 'enlightened': he disagreed with the very concept. No government could be enlightened with an emperor and without a separation of powers, and with no place for the effective operation of public opinion.[18] Third, he differs entirely from his predecessor in the feature that had been so striking in Gibbon's work, that is, his treatment of Christianity.

Fourth, we see in Finlay a different formulation of an argument about virtue, which crucially affects his conception of 'liberty'. This difference belies a deeper similarity. That is, to develop their own views on the nature of politics and freedom, both men are fluidly re-working traditions of political thought which are rooted in classically-derived notions of 'civic virtue'. To appreciate this, we need first to understand Finlay's *History*, and the political uses made of historical schemes by other important figures of the Scottish Enlightenment.

FINLAY'S HISTORY

FINLAY'S HISTORICAL SCHEME

Finlay opens his *magnum opus* with these sentences, from which I have taken the title for this piece:

> The history of Greece under foreign domination records the degradation and the calamities of the nation which attained the highest degree of civilization in the ancient world. Two thousand years of suffering have not obliterated the national character, not extinguished the national ambition.[19]

Both decline and character will be key themes throughout the work. The 'civilization' of antiquity will cast a long, dark shadow over later periods, which represent 'degradation'. Nevertheless, Finlay was determined that even the 'calamities' of two millennia had not destroyed his subject — the Greek 'national character'. As we shall see, neither 'decline' nor 'character' are quite the simple and clear-cut concepts they might appear in this bald opening.

We also apprehend, in this opening, a duality that is central to Finlay. He devoted his life to Greece, was active in her cause and did not, like many British philhellenes, return home to fan disillusion after the War of Independence; but at the same time he remained a relentless critic of the developing country. He was never slow to highlight the corruption of the government and the desperate need for social reform. He was, about the Greek past and present, both ardent supporter and harsh judge at one and the same time.

---

15. Less kindly, one reviewer put it that Finlay's relation to Gibbon was as a 'pigmy fighting under the shade of a giant's shield'; *Finlay Papers* E1.

16. For Finlay's most direct comments about the instruction offered by the past, see his prefatory remarks (Finlay 1877, I, xv–xx), his conclusion (Finlay 1877, VII, 332f) and his Royal Society pamphlet (Finlay 1851*b*, 64).

17. See esp. Finlay 1851*b*, 1 and Finlay 1877, II, 8f. His Preface has a more self-effacing tone (Finlay 1877, I, xxiii).

18. The idea of a *total* contrast between our two authors here is complicated somewhat by Finlay's readiness to concede that, even if Byzantine absolutism has not been admirable in itself, and was not a good *exemplum* for nineteenth-century Britain, one could nevertheless admire its effectiveness. See esp. Finlay 1851*b* — where he significantly adds that this imperial effectiveness 'may serve as a lesson to the rulers of India' (64).

---

19. Finlay 1877, I, xv.

This fundamental paradox is evident in all his writings, and is crucial to understanding his thought.

It might seem at this stage that Finlay is shackled to the idea of classical Greece as the glorious pinnacle of civilization from which later periods declined.[20] Yet although the *History* has its share of references to the 'high civilization' of the classical era,[21] there is a revealing difference in some papers in his archive. Strikingly, he says:

> We must also remember that the history of Greece is the history of a declining nation in morals and politics. The decline commenced at the period when history began to be written. The period of true greatness of the greek nation precedes history. We know little of the time when the greeks filled the Mediterranean and the Black Sea with their colonies. We know nothing of the causes which led to the rapid increase of the greek race. The light of history falls strongly only on the causes of Hellenic decline.[22]

Finlay thus envisages not only a general decline from the classical past, but a rather more monumental fall. Somewhere in the back of his mind, he feels that the truly 'ideal' period was in fact pre-classical, stretching into pre-history. It is tempting to link this with Finlay's Presbyterian morality: the reader often has the sense that he regards the 'decline' he depicts as part of a fall from grace from which divine providence alone might save us.

Although characterizing his story broadly as one of degradation and decline, Finlay does *not* offer a straightforwardly linear picture of 'a fall'. Within the overall framework, periods of rise and fall were envisaged. There are many examples of this.[23] Most strikingly, though, within the 'Byzantine' period (which he

defined as 716–1204 AD), Finlay argued that the iconoclast era (716–867 AD) had in fact offset decline.

It was Finlay's admiration for Leo III that led him to attach such significance to 716.[24] As the first iconoclast emperor, the commissioner of an important legal code, and the author of successes in foreign policy against the East, Finlay found Leo III an impressive figure in various respects. However, he is clear that it is, above all, the union of commerce under the aegis of law that 'saved the Roman and constituted the Byzantine empire'.[25] Leo thus infused new life into Byzantium — effectively countering Gibbon's charge that the empire lacked the capacity to renew itself.

This era was followed, in Finlay's view, by the Byzantines' 'highest pitch of external power and internal prosperity', 867–1057 AD.[26] At this period, it was the law that was pre-eminent:

> But it was neither the success of the Byzantine armies, nor the extent of the Greek commerce, nor the orthodox of the Greek church, which gave the empire its power and durability, and formed the historical character of this glorious period. It was the power of Roman law. These two centuries are pre-eminently the reign of the judicial system.[27]

It was only after this that 'the true period of the decline and fall of the Eastern Empire' followed, under the Comneni, in 1057–1204 AD. At this point, the nobles 'wrenched the administration out of the hands of a trained body of officials, whose systematic proceedings

---

20. Certainly Finlay's reviewers overwhelmingly accepted the idea of Byzantine decline from the classical past, brandishing metaphors of senility, decay and disease. (See *Finlay Papers* E1, *passim*.)

21. See, for example, Finlay 1877, I, xv and 9; Finlay 1877, II, 198.

22. *Finlay Papers* E58.

23. See, for example, Finlay's treatment of Hadrian and Herodes Atticus in the Roman period, and of the century from 408 AD onwards (where it is probably safe to assume that a large part of Finlay's admiration for the period is owed to the Theodosian Code). See esp. Finlay 1877, I, 171ff.

---

24. This is worth emphasizing not least because Finlay's periodization is not one which many scholars would follow today. The majority would now see a break in continuity with the upheaval under Phokas (602–10 AD), and there is less of an emphasis on 716 as a major 'turning point'. (Treadgold for example would date 'revival' from 780: see Treadgold 1988.) As for 'decline', many scholars probably now see a break in continuity at 1025, with the death of Basil II. The fourth crusade of 1204, on the other hand, is still, and presumably always will be, one of the most significant chronological breaks for Byzantinists.

25. See esp. Finlay 1851*b*.

26. It is entirely clear, however, that Finlay has greater preference and respect for the Isaurian than the Basilian dynasty — there is a strong sense that the 'rise' is more impressive than the full flourishing (a point to which we shall return).

27. Finlay 1851*b*, 37ff.

had tempered the imperial despotism'.[28] The centuries from 1204 all the way through to the end of the Otto-man period were then, for Finlay, utterly abject. Only in the Revolution and the modern period could one discern the signs of a 'regeneration' which, nevertheless, he found regrettably slow and beset with corruption.

PHILOSOPHIC HISTORY AND THE CAUSES OF DECLINE

This brief overview of the build-up to 1821 leaves unanswered the questions which will drive the *History*. For, in the tradition of the philosophic historian, Finlay aimed not only to chart the history of political decline, but to diagnose its causes. If he did not agree with Gibbon's diagnosis, why *did* Greece decline? How was revival possible, either on a small scale, or in 716, or in the eighteenth century?

Although Finlay considered external factors in Greek decline — the kinds of enemies she encoun-tered, for instance, and their characteristic vices[29] — he was emphatic that internal factors were always more important: 'The misfortunes of nations are generally the direct consequence of their own vices, social or political'.[30] Through his seven volumes, he charged the Greeks with being responsible for their own decline, under Roman, Byzantine and Ottoman rule.

Those internal factors included, most fundamentally, the very structure of the empire. As we have said, for Finlay there was no such thing as 'enlightened' absolut-ism. He regarded the Eastern Roman Empire as a vir-tual despotism, which the Byzantines made absolute. It combined all the legislative, executive and administra-tive powers in the person of the emperor. Government was increasingly performed by unaccountable imperial placemen, with no regard for public opinion, further divorcing 'the people' from 'the government'.

This meant that, although the *systematic* nature of Roman law was admirable, it could never operate well without its own independence, in the absence of a sep-aration of powers. This could have saved the empire: he commented in a notebook, 'Had an independent

judicial system been formed the Roman empire would probably never have fallen'.[31] Nevertheless, if there is something that accounts for the sheer persistence of Byzantium, through this long tale of decline, it is the glimmer of hope offered by the systematic administra-tion of Roman-derived law.

Law was especially important, for Finlay, in the com-mercial sphere. Justice and commerce together were crucial bulwarks of liberty and their erosion was at the root of 'degeneration'. His interest in the economic realm stemmed from the time he had spent in Scotland in the care of his uncle, the MP Kirkman Finlay, who was well-read in political economy in particular.[32] Fin-lay's early essays attest a knowledge of Smith, Ricardo and Malthus, among others.[33] He identified financial maladministration and fiscal oppression throughout his work. The taxation of the imperial government was rapacious, making the people merely the 'slaves of the imperial treasury'.[34] Its effects were far-reaching: 'fiscal rapacity was the incurable canker of the Byzantine, as it had been of the Roman government. From it arose all those measures which reduced society to a station-ary condition'.[35] Greece was thus drained by successive emperors — Constantine,[36] Justinian,[37] Nicephorus I,[38] the Comneni[39] — and by this process she lost not only money, capital and population, but was morally dev-astated: 'Poverty produced barbarism.'[40]

The imperial system thus arrogated power to the cen-tre, oppressing the provinces. It failed to allow popular control of public servants, and the robust exercise of public opinion. There was little of that popular involve-ment in central government which was, for Finlay, essential to political morality. Local institutions were important because they *involved* people in the political

---

28. Finlay 1877, I, xviiff; Finlay 1877, II, 9ff; see also Finlay 1851*b*.
29. See, for example, his treatment of Roman 'greed' in Vol. I.
30. Finlay 1877, V, 136.

31. *Finlay Papers* D12.
32. Finlay 1877, I, xl.
33. 'Some Observations on the Commercial Situation and Policy of Great Britain', *Finlay Papers* A.1.
34. Finlay 1877, I, 195.
35. Finlay 1877, II, 202.
36. Finlay 1877, I, 102ff.
37. Finlay 1877, I, 193ff.
38. Finlay 1877, II, 93 and 97.
39. Finlay 1877, II, 11.
40. Finlay 1877, I, 195.

process; people were thus more likely to turn to debate, and less likely to revolt, in order to effect change. These institutions also stimulated material and commercial benefits for the people, and made them more likely to defend themselves against external threats.[41] Their absence was serious, a point which is made frequently in the text, but never more emphatically than in the account of 1204 in these terms:

> Never was the national imbecility which arises from the want of municipal institutions and executive activity in local spheres more apparent. Had the towns, cities, corporations, districts, and provinces, inhabited by a Greek population, possessed magistrates responsible to the people and accustomed to independent action, there can be no doubt that thousands of Greek citizens would have rushed forward to defend their country.[42]

There is an important link between localism and the citizen's readiness to fight. Finlay follows the argument he had made so doggedly in his earlier (and more widely read) pamphlet on the Byzantine empire, that the absence of a citizen militia, and an unwillingness to arm the middle classes, had been crucial in its decline:

> Here [then] we find the principal cause of that unwarlike disposition, which is made a standing reproach of the wealthy classes in the Roman and Byzantine empires. They could not become soldiers if they had wished it … The meek spirit of Byzantine society, which has been generally attributed exclusively to the influence of the doctrines of Christianity, originated, in part, in these fiscal and military arrangements of the pagan emperors.[43]

This emphasis on a citizen militia links Finlay firmly with traditional depictions of 'civic virtue'.

Religion became an additional factor in decline, in Finlay's account, roughly from the tenth century onwards (whereas in the earlier periods, in contrast to Gibbon, he saw moments when Christianity had in fact helped to stimulate social renewal).[44] However, by the Ottoman period, he had become excoriating about corrupt monastic influence.[45]

These internal causes of decline are thus both structural and governmental — 'top down', and also related to citizens' character — 'bottom up'. Ultimately Finlay insists that 'the people' had to accept the responsibility for what he calls their 'moral' decline. He was emphatic, too, that the political decline of the Greeks was the *result* of moral decline.[46] This emphasis on the moral sphere as the single most important feature of a polity — the wellspring of its successes and its failures — is perhaps now the most striking feature of the work. The point is pressed home in the grand conclusion of the *History*:

> Those who have long studied the history of Greece never fail to observe that, *until the people undergo a moral change* as well as the government, national progress must be slow, and the surest pledges for the enjoyment of true liberty will be wanting.[47]

Finlay's characterization of this 'morality' needs to be carefully unpacked. This is a complex task which is crucial to my argument. It becomes clearer if we consider first Finlay's prescription for Greece's recovery from decline.

ENABLING RESURGENCE

For Finlay is concerned not only with narration and explanation, but also with providing an account of how to stimulate 'resurgence'. The case history requires not just a diagnosis but a cure.

To flourish, he makes clear, a state would certainly need those things whose decline were charted above — a strong centre, which operated alongside local institutions and a well-informed public opinion[48];

---

41. See especially Finlay 1851*b*.
42. Finlay 1877, III, 282; Finlay 1877, IV, 264; Finlay 1877, V, 228f.
43. Finlay 1851*b*, 39.

44. Finlay 1877, III, *passim*.
45. Finlay 1877, V, 132f.
46. See eg. Finlay 1877, I, 57; Finlay 1877, II, 319ff.
47. Finlay 1877, VII, 332 (my emphasis).
48. Thus he says that, if the Eastern Empire offered a lesson in the dangers of centralization, nevertheless it survived as long as it did, unlike the Western, because the Greeks had local institutions: Finlay 1877, I, xxif.

the systematic administration of law, particularly in its relation, and as a stimulus, to commerce; martial readiness and order. There is also an important role for Providence — in his description of the decline of the Ottomans and in particular the build-up to 1821, Finlay often had recourse to a notion of inevitability, events being portrayed as part of the inexorable tide of what he significantly calls 'human progress'.[49]

Yet in themselves these are not enough. A flourishing state needs a 'morality' whose character was emphatically *public*. How could this be achieved or renewed? Finlay stresses the importance of the family and local religious organization in particular in inculcating a drive towards such public-spiritedness, which could in turn be the motor of larger improvements. He argues that the English moved from the Norman Conquest towards liberty because of improvements fostered at the level of 'the family, the parish, the borough and the county; not [in] parliament and … central government'.[50] The argument is that Greece needs to 'use' *her* experience of national conquest, by the Ottomans, by attending to social, religious and moral issues at the level of the individual. In addition, a type of education was required which instilled respect for the public realm, and which would thus be a stimulus to participation — a far cry from the current type of education which he saw as 'pedantic', private- rather than public-oriented.[51]

An involvement in local institutions would further instill morality in the public realm, helping to generate that 'energy' and 'vigour' — two key terms — which would sustain liberty. Yet, even adding this, we still do not have a complete recipe for a healthy 'moral polity'. This is because local institutions could be perverted to manipulate the people, instead of being the instruments of a public-oriented civic virtue that Finlay had in mind. Even in Constantine's time, for example, he saw the local curia partly as a vehicle for

extorting taxes.[52] Likewise, later, he argued that those municipal institutions which persisted in Greece in the Ottoman period in fact became the instruments of Turkish oppression and tax-collecting, and hence 'this vaunted institution protected the liberties of the people by accident'.[53] Similarly, in the nineteenth century, he criticized the king and his 'oligarchical elective college' for effectively making local officials an instrument of the central government.[54]

We shall return to the importance of this, but at this stage it is worth pressing this rather vague term 'morality'. It is clear that Finlay has in mind wider and deeper concerns than could ever be met by the sorts of things outlined above. It also becomes evident that the text uses 'morality' virtually interchangeably with 'character'. He is disdainful not only about declining public morality in Greece, but about 'Greek character' — frequently the Greeks are depicted as 'selfish', 'vain' and 'presumptuous' in terms of individual and national character. Indeed, his comments about Greek 'national character' are one of the reasons he is little read today.

However, sensitivity to contemporary uses of the term 'character' is essential. Stefan Collini's recent work on the nineteenth-century use of the concept of character has argued that it was a new articulation, in a different register, of that 'civic virtue' which was the keystone of eighteenth-century political discourse.[55] 'Morality' and 'character', I suggest, were Finlay's terms for encouraging this sort of public-spirited 'virtue' in citizens. His comments on Greek character are not quite the straightforwardly chauvinistic criticism they might appear to us now.[56] They are rooted in a language and a logic which stresses the importance of the cultivation of individuals' civic virtue.

---

49. He saw 1821 as a 'clear manifestation of God's providence in the progress of human society' (Finlay 1877, VII, 181; cf. Finlay 1877, VI, 103). See also Finlay 1877, V, 3 on the role of 'Divine Providence' in the decline of the Ottomans.

50. Finlay 1877, IV, 227f.

51. See esp. Finlay 1877, II, 4 and Finlay 1877, IV, 43.

52. Finlay 1877, I, 109.

53. Finlay 1877, VII, 102.

54. Finlay 1877, VII, 120f.

55. Collini 1991, esp. ch.3.

56. It might be added, too, that Finlay's disparaging comments about 'national character' were certainly not confined to the Greeks. His journals and papers contain a number of such remarks about the national characters of others. Indeed, Charles Frazee aptly captured Finlay's critical temper when he said that Finlay 'did not spare those whom he felt did not measure up to his ideals. Within this group could be placed the overwhelming majority of mankind.' Frazee 1964, 195.

CIVIC VIRTUE IN THE MORAL POLITY

Virtue was the key component of the 'civic tradition' of political thought, which had close affinities with republicanism, its modern roots in Machiavelli's Roman-inspired vision. Virtuous citizens participated in the running of government, and fought in person on behalf of their homeland: this is how they maintained their liberty. The tradition of civic virtue, and its role in the freedom of the state and in good government, was crucial to British political thinking from the sixteenth to the eighteenth centuries.

Finlay's formulation of 'morality' and 'character' stem from these civic and republican traditions. Equally important is the fact that they have been calibrated through Scottish Enlightenment thinking. For the *type* of virtue required of the modern citizen, and thus the type of liberty that characterised modern society, had become an object of intense debate among the Scots. Here we need to address the uses made of the past by philosophic historians other than Gibbon.

David Hume and Adam Smith made the most trenchant use of philosophic or conjectural history in arguing for the progress of the modern world. For them, developments in the means of subsistence — from hunting, to pasturage, to agriculture and finally to commerce — represented stages in the development of civil society, or, in their new coinage, 'civil-isation'. Modernity was thus 'commercial society', and they used the idea of progress to argue that this 'civil-ised' (modern, commercial) stage was society in its 'best' form.

To support this argument, they denigrated antiquity and the type of civic virtue associated with it. Essentially the view of ancient republics offered by Hume and Smith — and this held, at the time, for both Greece and Rome — was that they were small communities in which slaves did the essential work, thus enabling the extensive participation of citizens in the political and military spheres.[57] In this they were perceived, by the Scots as well as by many other 'moderns', to be engaged in a 'public' or 'community-oriented' kind of liberty, at the expense of freedoms in the private sphere.[58] This view of the ancient world was set against a view of the 'developed', modern world where the majority of citizens were free enough from military duties to devote their energies to the production of material wealth, with little time or inclination for political or military life (thus having little need of that 'civic virtue' which upheld this sort of citizen participation).[59]

On the other hand, there was another, more pessimistic side to the Scottish Enlightenment. Lord Kames, John Millar and Adam Ferguson were less confident about the moral beneficence of the fourth stage of social development — 'modern' or 'commercial society'. Ferguson, for example, less convinced that the moderns were so unequivocally 'progressing' beyond the ancients, continued to advocate ancient civic virtue and a citizen militia.[60]

Gibbon represents a related view, but with an emphasis which is more cyclical than linear. For him, classical values and the *pax Romana* had enabled a 'happy period' to which we might aspire again (and to which the Enlightenment had some claim to aspire), if those classical values could genuinely be reasserted (about which we noted the element of doubt).

Lists of Finlay's reading material, as well as his notebooks, amply attest what is evident anyway from the text — that he had been deeply influenced by these Scottish thinkers. With his commitment to political morality, he clearly has something in common with what is usually called the 'pessimistic' strain of Enlightenment thinking, with its stress on citizens' virtue, and especially on their military readiness. However, his confidence in the mechanism of the market gives him more in common with Smith, (quotations from whose works he was often copying in to his notebooks), even though his admiration for the more 'republican' aspects of citizenship fit less well with Smith's view of antiquity

---

57. Hume's essays 'Of the populousness of ancient nations' and 'Of Commerce' are particularly relevant here; see also 'Of Refinement', 'Arts and Sciences' and 'Of Civil Liberty'. (Many of these essays can now be found in Haakonssen 1994.)

58. The classic later formulation of this was Constant's 'The Liberty of the Ancients Compared with that of the Moderns' published in 1819 (Fontana 1998). Isaiah Berlin later schematised ancient and modern liberties as 'positive' and 'negative' respectively. This view has come under attack in recent years.

59. For Smith on the ancient world, see esp. the fifth volume of The Wealth of Nations (Smith 2000).

60. Ferguson 1767.

and modernity. Overall, he should be situated some-where between the optimism of the Hume-Smith view and the more pessimistic outlook of a Ferguson. Relating Finlay's language of morality and character, and his deep concern with citizen's virtue, to these traditions shows us that his attitudes — 'morose' or otherwise, mishellenic or philhellenic — are crucially influenced by his intellectual background, and bequeathed to him not least by those traditions.

FINLAY'S LIBERALISM

If we situate Finlay in the tradition of civic and republican virtue in this way, and in the context of Scottish thinking about the nature and effects of 'progress', there are important implications for how we think about his liberalism. It has long been recognised that his general commitments to civil, commercial, political and religious freedoms make him broadly speaking 'a liberal'.[61] His tendency to ally law and commerce, and to see the role of government in civilized society as most importantly to ensure the security of person and property, sounds like a classic liberal formulation of minimal government; and in his anti-central and pro-local views, Finlay was echoing a key liberal formulation.

However, his attitude to character, morality and virtue, and his application of these ideas to the Greek context, significantly alters the character of his 'liberal' pedigree. Here the most useful point of reference is J.S. Mill. Probably the most significant liberal thinker of the nineteenth century, he was deeply interested in the question of how the modern world could regenerate the virtues of ancient Athens, and how its achievements could be replicated in modern, representative democracy. Building on Tocqueville, he had recourse to classical Athens not least because he was concerned that commercial society would result in the 'tyranny of the majority' and passive individualism.[62]

Finlay was deeply influenced by liberalism and by J.S. Mill, (and was even visited by him in Athens).[63] But he did not share his concerns about *restraining* the effects of 'commercial society': for him, the majority were so oppressed in Greece that they had not yet developed the sort of 'tyranny' that Tocqueville and Mill had in mind. Further, he did not view the tendency to individualism and an over-concern with the private sphere as the result of 'commercial society' and its political counterpart, 'democracy'. He believed he saw apathy in the public realm in all the stages of the Greek past (as we saw above). Although he had a liberal-inspired stress on local institutions as cultivators of civic virtue, he also had to confront a belief that these had existed for years and that they had not been effective.

This, I believe, explains his recourse to republican traditions of thought: their emphasis on the *active* involvement of citizens in government enabled him not only to insist, with contemporary liberals, that local institutions were important, but also that they must be organized in such a way as to allow the active flourishing of virtue. This stress on the importance of individual character and virtue in politics accounts for the notion that he developed that there was a 'moral' realm, crucially connected to the family, local religion and 'civic education', which was *prior* to politics, but was what healthy politics relied on.

Finlay's combination of liberal and republican strains of thinking is particularly interesting in the light of recent scholarship in the history of political thought. It was until fairly recently held that liberalism and republicanism were more or less antithetical impulses, characterizing 'freedom' in divergent ways. However, the neat polarization of 'republicanism' with 'positive' liberty and 'liberalism' with 'negative' liberty has recently come under increasing attack. Prominent examples include Quentin Skinner's argument that the republican tradition in fact included a significant emphasis on liberal individualism, and — conversely — Eugenio Biagini's contention that Gladstonian pop-

---

61. Cf. the Introduction to this piece.
62. See esp. Biagini 1996, Urbinati 2002 and Potter 2004 (ch.3).

63. Finlay transcribed quotations from Mill's articles into his notebooks as he was reading them. His papers also contain some correspondence pertaining to Mill's visit to Athens, but overall he seems to have recorded frustratingly little about this (*Finlay Papers* B.6 (73), (138); B.9 (Q. 7. 12)).

Fig.2.2: Athens University and Lycabettus hill; BSA Photographic Archive: BSAA2–13.

ular liberalism — supposedly 'negative' liberty — in fact had a considerable attachment to community and 'positive' liberty.[64] Finlay's position, as I have drawn it out, amply supports the argument that the two traditions intertwined. His *History* can help us to elucidate the complex relationship between these sets of ideas, and to test the liberal model against a different set of empirical data (that is, the history of a country outside Western Europe and America).

GREEK HISTORIOGRAPHY

The other key context for Finlay's thought is contemporary *Greek* interest in their own past. In general, there is a dramatic contrast between British responses to mediaeval and modern Greece and those of contemporary Greeks. It is true that eighteenth-century Greek thinking had had something in common with British Hellenism in its Western-inspired animus against Byzantium: Greek intellectuals also had looked decisively to the ancient world as the defining pole of national exist-

64. Skinner 1990; Biagini 1992.

ence.[65] Byzantium was triumphantly reclaimed, however, with Paparrigopoulos. His ground-breaking history was published in five volumes between 1860 and 1874. It emphasised both the continuity of the Greek nation, and, crucially, the importance of the Byzantine tradition within that. Paschalis Kitromilides has characterized this text as 'the most important intellectual achievement of nineteenth-century Greece'. Its importance lay not only in the historiographical field, but in the ways in which it was used to legitimate new political ideology, encouraging national unity at a crucial moment for the emerging Greek nation state.[66]

Finlay shared with Paparrigopoulos an emphasis on 'continuity' in Greek history, and a particular interest in the iconoclast emperors. Both thus refuted Gibbon's charges that Byzantium lacked enterprise and the capacity for self-renovation.[67] However, Finlay's tale did not offer the ebullient confidence in national unity which was the key-note of Paparrigopoulos' work. Finlay was more acerbic, and although there was something of a sense of Greek achievement, the tale was overwhelmingly less positive about continuity and unification.[68]

CONCLUSION

Having arrived in Greece an optimistic philhellene, Finlay certainly came to know disillusion. In part this was a general effect of having experienced the bruising realities of political engagement. It was also surely related to his view that good government was so rare and so exceedingly hard to achieve. Nevertheless, he remained in Greece, committed to the cause of national liberty and to the study of the whole range of her past — even if he was also a severe critic of his own work.[69] It seems to me more accurate and realistic to acknowledge that, as a result of his practical and scholarly engagements with Greece, he tended to both pessimism and optimism, disillusionment and enthusiasm. To restrict oneself to focusing on his 'morose' character, or to asking whether he should be seen as simply either 'philhellene' or 'mishellene', is a reductive approach.

We enrich our understanding of his thought if we draw out his intellectual inheritance. He reflected on both the optimistic and pessimistic strains of Scottish thought, and tempered them in the light of his study of the history of Greece. He also chose to weld a republican-inspired idea of 'civic virtue' with contemporary liberal propensities in order to meet the challenge of applying liberal thinking beyond the context of Britain. It is not enough simply to label Finlay as a 'liberal': recent scholarship having emphasized how complex a phenomenon nineteenth-century liberalism was, we need to attend to the particular contours of Finlay's case.[70] The attempt to do so rewards us with a closer understanding of an unusual and rather misunderstood figure.

It also helps us to understand more fully the power exerted by the classical past on the nineteenth century, and the uses that were made of it. It is clear that it was always hard for later Greece to emerge from the shadow of the classical period. The Roman Empire is also clearly in the bloodline of Byzantine and Modern Greece. Less obvious at first sight, but equally important from the point of view of this paper, was the example of the Roman republic. Its influence was carried through traditions of political thought which spanned centuries and crossed national boundaries. It remains alive in any meaningful attempt to understand what it means for modern citizens to have civic virtue.

---

65. See Politis 1998, Huxley 1998 and Kitromilides 1998.

66. On Paparrigopoulos, see esp. Kitromilides 1998 and 1982. Also Hatzidimitriou 1982.

67. On this aspect of Paparrigopoulos, see esp. Huxley 1998, 17.

68. Stephenson is thus unjust in saying that Finlay repackages Paparrigopoulos. I hope that further consideration of Finlay's relationship to Greek historians will be a focus of future work.

69. He often described his work as a 'melancholy' task (eg Finlay 1877, VII, 125f,), and in his papers he calls it a 'thankless and dispiriting task' (*Finlay Papers* E.58). For his harsh judgements of his own achievements, see eg. the Preface to Finlay 1877, I and the conclusion in Finlay 1877, VII.

70. As part of this, more should be said than there is space for here about the Finlay's romanticism, Christianity and knowledge of developments in Greek historical and political thought.

REFERENCES

MANUSCRIPTS

Finlay Papers (British School at Athens).

PUBLICATIONS

Arnakis, G.G., 1960. *The Historical Work of Samuel G. Howe and the Historian George Finlay*. Athens.

Arnold, M., 1960–77. *The Complete Prose Works of Matthew Arnold*. 11 Vols, R.H. Super (ed.).

Biagini, E., 1992. *Liberty, Retrenchment and Reform. Popular Liberalism in the Age of Gladstone, 1860–1880*. Cambridge.

—, 1996. 'Liberalism and direct democracy: John Stuart Mill and the model of ancient Athens' in E. Biagini (ed.), *Citizenship and Community: Liberals, Radicals and Collective Identities in the British Isles, 1865–1931*. Cambridge.

Collini, S., 1991. *Public Moralists. Political Thought and Intellectual Life in Britain 1850–1930*. Oxford.

Constant, B., 1998 [1819]. *The Liberty of the Ancients Compared with that of the Moderns*, ed. B. Fontana. Cambridge.

Ferguson, A., 1996 [1767]. *An Essay on the History of Civil Society*, ed. F.Oz-Salzberger. Cambridge.

Finlay, G., 1844. *Greece under the Romans B.C. 146 to A.D. 716*. Edinburgh and London.

—, 1851*a*. *Medieval Greece and Trebizond*. Edinburgh and London.

—, 1851*b*. 'Observations on the Characteristic Features of Byzantine History', *Transactions of the Royal Society of Literature*.

—, 1852, 1854. *History of the Byzantine Empire*, 2 Vols. Edinburgh and London.

—, 1856. *The History of Greece under Othoman and Venetian domination*. Edinburgh and London.

—, 1861. *The History of the Greek Revolution*, 2 Vols. Edinburgh and London.

—, 1877. *A History of Greece from it Conquest by the Romans to the Present Time BC 146 to AD 1864*. 7 Vols. Oxford.

Frazee, C.A., 1964. 'The Historian George Finlay and Correspondence with Cornelius C. Felton (1854–1859)', *Südost-Forschungen* 23: 179–214.

Gibbon, E., 1909 [1776-88]. *The History of the Decline and Fall of the Roman Empire*. 7 Vols., ed. J.B. Bury. London.

Grote, G., 1846–56. *History of Greece*. 12 Vols. London.

Haakonssen, K. (ed.), 1994. *Hume. Political Essays*. Cambridge.

Hatzidimitriou, C., 1982. 'From Paparrigopoulos to Vacalopoulos: Modern Greek Historiography on the Ottoman Period', in A.L. Macrakis and P.N. Diamandouros (eds), *New Trends in Modern Greek Historiography*: 13–24. Hanover.

Hussey, J.M., 1973. *The Finlay Papers. A Catalogue*. London.

—, 1975. 'George Finlay in Perspective — a Centenary Reappraisal', *BSA* 70: 135–44.

—, 1994. 'The Historian George Finlay — Readjustments', *Jahrbuch der Osterreichischen Byzantinistik* 44: 179–86.

— (ed.), 1995. *The Journals and Letters of George Finlay*, 2 Vols. Surrey.

Huxley, G., 1998. 'Aspects of modern Greek historiography of Byzantium', in D. Ricks and P. Magdalino (eds), *Byzantium and the Modern Greek Identity*: 15–24. Aldershot.

Kitromilides, P.M., 1982. 'Historiographical Interpretations of Modern Greek Reality: An Exploratory Essay', in A.L. Macrakis and P.N. Diamandouros (eds), *New Trends in Modern Greek Historiography*: 7–12. Hanover.

—, 1998. 'On the intellectual content of Greek nationalism: Paparrigopoulos, Byzantium and the Greek idea' in D. Ricks and P. Magdalino (eds), *Byzantium and the Modern Greek Identity*: 25–34. Aldershot.

Mill, J.S., 1963–91. *The Collected Works of John Stuart Mill*, 33 vols., ed. J.M. Robson and subsequently F.E.L. Priestley. Toronto.

Miller, W., 1923–25. 'The Finlay Library', *BSA* 26: 46–66.

—, 1924*a*. 'The Finlay Papers', *English Historical Review* 39: 386–98.

—, 1924*b*. 'George Finlay as a Journalist', *English Historical Review* 39: 552–67.

—, 1926. 'The Journals of Finlay and Jarvis', *English Historical Review* 41: 514–25.

Politis, A., 1998. 'From Christian Roman emperors to the glorious Greek ancestors', in D. Ricks and P. Magdalino (eds), *Byzantium and the Modern Greek Identity*. Aldershot.

Potter, E.J., 2004. 'Confronting Modernity. Ancient Athens and Modern British Political Thought'. PhD Thesis. London.

Rosen, F., 1992. *Bentham, Byron and Greece. Constitutionalism, Nationalism, and Early Liberal Political Thought*. Oxford.

Skinner, Q., 1990. 'The Republican Idea of Political Liberty', in G. Brock, Q. Skinner and M. Viroli (eds), *Machiavelli and Republicanism*. Cambridge.

Smith, A., 1999 [1776]. *The Wealth of Nations*. 2 Vols. London.

Stephenson, P., 2001. Review of Encyclopaedia of Greece and Hellenic Tradition (2 vols), ed. Graham Speake, London and Chicago Fitzroy Dearborn Publishers, 2000. *Bryn Mawr Classical Review* 2001.09.22.

Treadgold, W., 1988. *The Byzantine Revival 780–842*. Stanford.

Urbinati, N., 2002. *Mill on Democracy. From the Athenian Polis to Representative Government*. Chicago and London.

Wace, A.J.B. 1916–[17, 1917–1]8. 'Hastings and Finlay', *BSA* 22: 110–32.

3

Colonel Leake's knowledge of events in Greece following Independence: the Finlay correspondence

Malcolm Wagstaff

INTRODUCTION

The 'Eastern Question' framed political events in Greece during the nineteenth century. A weakening Ottoman Empire struggled with an expanding Czarist Empire for dominance in south-eastern Europe and the wider Near and Middle East. At the same time various national groups claimed their independence, while powerful individuals sought to extend their own power. The other major European states intervened in pursuit of their own interests. Contingency was important to how events actually unfolded, while both the circumstances under which Greek independence was secured and the conditions under which it was maintained were significant for the political evolution of the country.

Christians living on the Balkan peninsula south of a line from the Gulf of Arta to the Gulf of Volos and in the Aegean islands of the Sporades, Euboea (Evvia) and the Cyclades secured their independence from the Ottoman Empire in 1829–30 after a bloody uprising involving the 'ethnic cleansing' of the Muslim population. Britain, France and Russia guaranteed the independence of the new state. In May 1832, with the general agreement of the Greek leaders, they imposed a young prince, Otto, the second son of King Ludwig of Bavaria, on the new state as King. His father appointed Otto's advisers and even when he gained his majority in 1835, most of his counsellors were foreigners, while several of his ministers were Phanariotes[71] or had lived abroad. Neither set had much experience of conditions in the new country, but they had strong ideas of what a modern European state should be like. Centralisation of power and decision-making continued the policy of Ioannis Kapodistrias (1776–1831), the President of the provisional government (1828–31), which had preceded Otto's accession. Conflict with the old ways and vested interests continued. Inefficiency, nepotism and corruption, unrestrained even nominally by a constitution, eventually resulted in a *coup d'état* in 1843. Although this produced a constitution, Otto was able to continue his autocratic ways until he was finally deposed in 1862. Throughout Otto's reign, popular attention was diverted from the short-comings of his government by populist moves to extend the frontiers of the country to include more and eventually, it was hoped, all of the Greek Orthodox Christians of the Ottoman Empire into a single Greek state. Although there was continual friction along an unsatisfactory frontier, major crises were seized upon to try to expand the state, as in 1840–41 when the *enosis* of Crete seemed possible.

Crete had joined in the uprisings of 1821, which created the Greek state, but the movement there was put down with great brutality in 1824 by the European-style army of Mehmet Ali/Muhammad Ali Pasha, an Albanian adventurer from Kavalla, who had seized power in Egypt and become recognised as its governor by the Sultan. His help in Crete and that of his son, Ibrahim Pasha, in the Morea (1825–27) was rewarded with the government of the island. Muhammad Ali was not satisfied with his reward and sought to seize more territory from the Sultan. Under the command of Ibrahim Pasha, the Egyptian army moved into the Syrian provinces in 1832, and pushed across Anatolia as far as Kütahya and Bursa the following year. Russian military support for the Sultan halted the advance, and diplomatic pressure confined Muhammad Ali's rule to

---

71. Greeks from the Phanar (Fener) district of Istanbul, where the Oecumenical Patriarch lived, who were often employed in the Ottoman central administration.

Fig.3.1: Colonel Martin Leake; National Portrait Gallery, London.

Syria and the Çukorova. The Sultan's attempt to recover his territories beyond the Taurus Mountains failed at Nezib, north-east of Aleppo (24 June 1839). Alarmed by the possible ramifications, and despite French support for Muhammad Ali, the other European powers sought to preserve the Ottoman Empire. Austrian and British pressure in 1840 involved the naval blockade of the Syrian and Egyptian coasts, as well as the bombardment of Beirut and Acre. Ibrahim Pasha was forced to withdraw. The resulting settlement saw Muhammad Ali deprived of Syria and Crete, but confirmed as the Sultan's viceroy in Egypt.

Sea power supported British diplomacy in the Near East from the battle of Navarino (1827) onwards, but Britain had a territorial presence in the region as well. She was the protector of the Septinsular Republic, the constituent islands of which virtually enclose the western and southern sides of Greece and whose inhabitants were largely Greek speaking and Orthodox in religion, despite generations of rule by Venice. The Czar ruled territories contiguous with the Ottoman Empire around the northern and eastern shores of the Black Sea, some of them comparatively recently con-

quered in the seemingly endless wars between the two empires. The southwards advance of Russian control and influence in the Balkans and across the Caucasus was a constant element in the Eastern Question. Concern about it in London and Paris led eventually to the Crimean War (1854–56). France began colonising the Maghreb, while retaining important commercial and political interests in the eastern Mediterranean. Austria had territories adjacent to those of the Ottoman Empire in the Balkans and sought both to expand these and also to contain plan-Slavism.

COLONEL LEAKE

Colonel Martin Leake (1777–1860), the soldier, traveller and topographer of ancient Greece, was familiar not only with the wider political context in which independent Greece existed, but also with conditions on the ground in the Near East. As a young artillery officer he had been seconded to the British Military Mission to Turkey (1799–1802). This took him to Istanbul, Syria, Egypt and, for the first time, to Greece (July-September 1802). Between 1804 and 1807, he travelled widely in Greece as a military advisor to the Ottoman authorities. With French complicity he was arrested as a British spy at Salonica in February 1807, and spent nine months in confinement. In 1808–10, Leake was British resident at the court of one of the most powerful of the semi-independent governors in European Turkey, Ali Pasha of Ioannina, and travelled in Epirus and Thessaly. One of his more onerous duties was to look after Lord Byron and John Cam Hobhouse, and to arrange the famous meeting between the pasha and the poet.

Service with the Ottoman Army during the 1801 invasion of Egypt almost certainly brought acquaintance with Muhammad Ali, who commanded a contingent of Albanian irregulars in the campaign. Leake's travels in Greece a decade or so before the outbreak of the Greek Revolution brought contact with many of the local Greek leaders who came to prominence during the war and remained significant players on the political stage after independence. Active military service ended for Leake in 1816, when he returned from duty with the Swiss army in the Jura during Napoleon's 'Hundred Days', though he did not retire from the British army until 1823. Although Leake devoted himself to research and publication about ancient Greece, he also played important roles on the Publications' Committee of the Society of Dilettanti, in the foundation of the Royal Geographical Society and the Royal Society of Literature, and in the establishment of the Travellers' Club. Leake never returned to the Near East after 1810, but he retained a lively interest in the region and specifically in Greece.

Leake was a Philhellene. His first book, *Researches in Greece*, was designed to promote knowledge of the 'vernacular tongues' used in Greece, particularly Modern Greek, because this would lead to 'a better understanding of the physical and natural peculiarities of Greece and its inhabitants'.[72] Leake's *An Historical Outline of the Greek Revolution* provided background to the Greek uprising and was intended to counter both 'those mixed compilations of truth and error called Histories or Memoirs of the Revolution' and also 'the streams of misrepresentation reaching London and Paris from various quarters'.[73] Even Leake's massive travel books, so often quarried for information on ancient topography, aimed to present a picture of the Peloponnese and Northern Greece as they were when 'no more than the thinly peopled province[s] of a semi-barbarous empire, presenting the usual results of Ottoman bigotry and despotism',[74] and to show — sadly, as Leake evidently thought — how little conditions had been changed 'by the new political state of a part of Greece'.[75]

Leake noted, however, the efforts of the Greeks under Ottoman rule to lift themselves from the state of degradation into which they had been plunged by the folly of Ottoman administrators and the laziness of the Muslim population. Wealthy individuals, often merchants, founded and endowed schools, sponsored translations into modern Greek and supported compilations of western philosophical and scientific work. Leake's later political pamphlet, *Greece at the End of Twenty-three Years of Protection*,[76] is a bitter condemnation of British policy towards independence in which he accused governments of all hues of showing 'a preference of incurable barbarism to progress and civilisa-

Fig.3.2: George Finlay; Finlay 1877, vol. I, frontispiece.

tion' which resulted in 'the abasement of Greece'.

His letters to George Finlay (1800–75), the Scottish historian of Greece, display the same sentiments. Leake hoped that Greece could become 'an improved and flourishing state'[77] and was concerned about its 'misgovernment' under Otto.[78] As he also wrote to Finlay, he had 'always conceded a good opinion of the peasantry and had hoped for their improvement physical and moral as one of the principal benefits to be derived from the regeneration of Greece'.[79] The northern frontier was 'bad' because it excluded 'the peaceful, industrious, and the entirely-free-from-Turks districts of Agrafa and Mount Pelion'[80] and he believed that 'there must at last be an independent Greek state, extending as far North as the language is spoken',[81] but warned that the Greeks' 'modest proposal' in claiming Constantinople as the capital of a state 'comprehending European

72. Martin Leake 1814, i and ii.
73. Martin Leake 1825, 6–7.
74. Martin Leake 1830, I, v.
75. Martin Leake 1835, I, vi.
76. Martin Leake 1851.

77. *Finlay Papers* A42(11); Hussey 1995, 537–40.
78. *Finlay Papers* A42(44, 76); Hussey 1995, 631–3, 753–5.
79. *Finlay Papers* A42(47); Hussey 1995, 649–50.
80. *Finlay Papers* A42(47); Hussey 1995, 714–5.
81. *Finlay Papers* A42(70); Hussey 1995, 723–5.

Turkey' was 'folly' since it would require all Europe to go to war with the Turks'.[82] Leake's philhellenism is confirmed in two other ways. First, Finlay dedicated the third volume of his *History of Greece under Foreign Occupation* to Leake, 'whose long and laborious exertions cleared the ancient history of Greece from obscurity and the modern from misrepresentation'.[83] Second, shortly after Leake died, Spyridon Trikoupis (1788–1873), an important politician and historian of the Greek War of Independence, then in his third term as Greek Ambassador to London, wrote to Finlay

> Our lamented friend died as he lived an ardent Philhellene. His last words to the public, I mean the preface to the third volume of Numismata Hellenica, are exclusively dictated by his noble sympathies for Greece. No Greek will read them without feeling a great respect for his memory.[84]

Leake's correspondence with Finlay reveals the variety of sources upon which he drew for information about events in Greece. From time to time Leake received Greek bulletins and newspapers[85] and he read the *Spectateur de l'Orient.*[86] Letters and reports in the London newspapers, specifically *The Times* and *The Morning Chronicle*, were other sources, as were articles in journals like the *Edinburgh Review,* including some by Finlay.[87] Leake clearly read more substantial publications as well, for example, Robert Pashley's *Travels in Crete* (1837) and Frederick Strong's *Greece as a Kingdom* (1842), both specifically mentioned in his correspondence. The *Blue Books*, official publications containing the papers called for by the Houses of Parliament, were another source, at least at particular times and on specific issues such as British claims against Greece in the 1840s. More anecdotal information came from Leake's personal acquaintances among the increasingly numerous travellers to Greece. There is some evidence that Leake also met visiting Greeks, including Spyridon Trikoupis, at least on

those occasions when he was ambassador in London (1835–38, 1841–43, 1850–61). Leake may have known the Trikoupis family from his visit to Mesolonghi in March 1809.[88] Finally, Leake had a network of correspondents, of whom the most important in Greece was George Finlay. He kept Finlay's letters, and clearly valued them. In 1854, he even wrote specifically to Finlay that 'he was much obliged for your communications'.[89] Finlay's letters provided information which Leake could not easily acquire otherwise.

George Finlay was settled in Athens. Following illness while serving in the Greek War of Independence (1823–24), he had returned to Britain to complete his legal studies, but went to Greece again in 1826, and made his home there. Finlay acquired a country estate at Liosia and property in the Athens area, some of which was subsequently expropriated to build the royal palace and army barracks. His town house was in Adrianou Street in the Plaka district of the city. Finlay was well informed about a range of events in Greece — archaeological, economic and political — partly as a natural consequence of prolonged residence in the country, but also from the employees on his estates. In the 1830s he travelled in the Peloponnese, toured the islands and went on a military expedition to central Greece. During 1834, he was briefly one of the commissioners involved in the planning of Athens. Hussey noted Finlay's 'genius' for picking up information and his alertness to political developments.[90] The historian William Miller pointed out that Finlay's personal grievances against the government 'should be considered in estimating his impartiality as a historian of his own time' and noted that he became increasingly embittered.[91] Petropulos observed that Finlay was severely critical of 'virtually every element that played an influential role in Greek politics', attributing inadequate performance by the authorities almost entirely to moral failings and a lack of statesmanship.[92]

The surviving correspondence between Finlay and Leake begins with a letter from Finlay dated 1–2 April

82. *Finlay Papers* A42(67); Hussey 1995, 705–7.
83. *Finlay Papers* B7(37); Hussey 1995, 679.
84. *Finlay Papers* A42(81).
85. *Finlay Papers* A42(68); Hussey 1995, 714–5.
86. *Finlay Papers* A42(70, 71); Hussey 1995, 723, 725–6.
87. *Finlay Papers* A42(2, 72); Hussey 1995, 468–9, 729–31.

88. Leake 1835, III, 531–2, 540–1.
89. *Finlay Papers* A42(68); Hussey 1995, 714–5.
90. Hussey 1995, xxiv, xxx.
91. Miller 1924.
92. Petropulos 1968, 596.

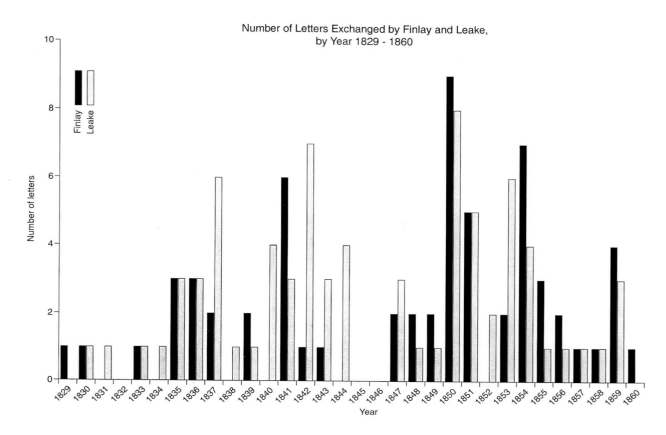

Table.3.1: Number of Letters exchanged by Finlay and Leake, by year; 1829–60.

1829, and ends with one from him dated 5 January 1860, a day before Leake died, which the Colonel obviously could not have seen. They span about thirty years. There are 144 letters altogether, of which 79 (54.9 per cent) are from Leake. The great majority (123 or 85.4 per cent) are in the archives of the British School at Athens, to which they were donated in 1899.[93] The remaining 21 letters from Finlay (14.6 per cent of the total) are amongst the Leake, or strictly the Martin Leake, papers in the County Archives at Hertford and consist of letters from Finlay to Leake beginning on 27 July 1852. The whole collection was transcribed and edited by Professor Joan Hussey.[94] As Hussey noted, evidence in the surviving letters shows that we do not have a complete run of the entire correspondence (TABLE 3.1). At least nine letters do not appear

to have survived, eight of them from Finlay to Leake.[95] There are other gaps, too. In some cases Finlay and Leake simply did not write to each other and neither offered any explanation, for example during eight and a half months in 1837–38. The long break in the correspondence between 1845 and the first half of 1847 Leake attributed to his own 'negligence',[96] while Finlay said the thirteen month gap between 22 July 1856 and 13 August 1857 resulted from 'the lazy routine of the business life here' (in Athens) which 'made me of late neglect my correspondence with England. When I thought of writing, it always appeared to me that I had nothing to say of the slightest interest'.[97] The lack of let-

93. Hussey 1995, xii.
94. Hussey 1995, xvi–xvii, 459–773.

95. *Finlay Papers* A42(3, 19, 21, 22, 36, 43, 67); Hussey 1995, 470–2, 577–9, 581–3, 583–4, 611–2, 623–4, 705–7; *Finlay Papers* B7(41); Hussey 1995, 692.
96. *Finlay Papers* A42(42); Hussey 1995, 621–2.
97. *Leake Papers* 85708; Hussey 1995, 744–5.

ters between 30 August 1838 and 17 August 1839, on the other hand, was explained, at least in part, because Leake was on his wedding tour in Italy,[98] while Finlay explained two other breaks in the correspondence as the result of his being ill from a long and troublesome liver complaint.[99]

Hussey remarked that the letters 'afford an admirable illustration of the two men's far reaching interests and activities',[100] while simple content analysis shows that, though they wrote about the economy and society of modern Greece, as well as Greek archaeology and history and ancient Greek coins, which Leake collected, three topics dominated their correspondence — Greek topography (13.6 per cent), their publication activities (25.8 per cent) and Greek politics (31.1 per cent). Discussion of topography tended to dominate in the early days when Leake was preparing his *Travels in the Morea* and *Travels in Northern Greece*, and again when he was working on the second edition of his *Topography of Athens*. They commented on each other's publications and described progress with their own work, making it possible to trace developments from initial idea to final publication, as with the second edition of Leake's *Topography of Athens*. Leake first mentioned it to Finlay on 28 November 1836 and then told him on 2 November 1840 that the printing of the first part, on Athens, was complete.[101]

Politics, however, was the most recurring topic — particularly, but not exclusively, Greek politics. Although various developments are covered, perhaps the four most important are

1. the build-up to the bloodless *coup d'état* of 3 September 1843,
2. the Cretan Uprising of 1840–41,
3. British claims on Greece, culminating in the Pacifico Affair, and
4. the Crimean War.

To unravel exactly what Leake knew of these events and how much information he derived from Finlay compared with other possible sources is complicated and may ultimately prove to be impossible, though my research is still incomplete. I will, therefore, focus on just two sets of events where Leake's knowledge of events in Greece led him to try to shape British policy.

THE CRETAN UPRISING, 1840–41

Finlay wrote to Leake on 5 April 1841 to say that he had been asked 'by the chief Cretans residing in Greece' to draw his 'attention to the position and demands of their countrymen now in arms' and to entreat him 'to take an interest in the cause of the inhabitants of the island'.[102] He had also been asked to write to 'Mr. Pashley' in similar terms. As far as we know, Leake never visited Crete. Robert Pashley (1805–59), however, had travelled in the island eight years before and in 1837 published his *Travels in Crete*, which described the atrocities and destruction brought about when the 1821 uprising was suppressed.

Finlay attributed the 1840–41 uprising to the decision of Mustapha Pasha, Muhammad Ali's governor in Crete, to arm the Christians to counter the strength of the Muslims, so that his own position would be secured following the recent defeat of the Ottoman army at Nezib in June 1839. When the Egyptians were forced to evacuate Syria, Mustapha Pasha was surprised to find himself confirmed as governor of Crete by the Sultan. He immediately set about trying to disarm the Christians, but they were unwilling to surrender their weapons and demanded 'a legal settlement of their rights under the stipulations of the triple alliance. The rebels called on their countrymen then in Greece for assistance and collected military supplies. They recognised, though, that their real hope lay not in military action but in the intervention of the allies. Their demand for independence, though 'far beyond their hopes', Finlay thought, was made precisely with the intent of securing outside support. The rebels' Manifesto, which Finlay enclosed for Leake, was cast in terms of the rights of man, and claimed that they wished to establish

98. *Finlay Papers* A42(17); Hussey 1995, 568–9; *Finlay Papers* B7(15); Hussey 1995, 569–71. Leake married Mrs Elizabeth Wray Marsden on 18 September 1838.

99. *Finlay Papers* A42(17); Hussey 1995, 568–9; *Finlay Papers* B7(15); Hussey 1995, 569–71.

100. Hussey 1995, xvii.

101. *Finlay Papers* A42(10, 24); Hussey 1995, 519–21, 584–7.

102. *Finlay Papers* B7(18); Hussey 1995, 588–91.

a national union, to secure domestic peace, to promote the general happiness, to prevent injustice and violence, to establish equal laws throughout all Crete, to promote the long-neglected education of our children, and to consolidate all the benefits arising from these institutions, as well as for ourselves as for our descendents. We desire that all the inhabitants of Crete, of whatever sect or religion they may be, shall be partakers of these same advantages, and particularly the Ottomans, whom, as natives of Crete, we consider to be Hellenes as well as ourselves.[103]

Leake was aware of recent developments in the eastern Mediterranean, and had even written to Finlay on 14 August 1839, before British intervention forced the Egyptian withdrawal from Syria, that if Muhammad Ali's principal demands were secured, the allies should guarantee them only on condition of liberating Crete. But how much Leake already knew about events in Crete itself following its return to the Sultan in 1840 is not clear, though a few more or less detailed reports appeared in the British press, often taken from foreign newspapers. Finlay's letter arrived on 9 May 1841, 'an unpropitious moment' in Leake's view because both Parliament and public were yet again preoccupied with the 'Corn question'. Nonetheless, Leake undertook to do what he could for the Cretan cause. His actions are outlined in letters dated 21 and 30 May 1841.[104]

First, Leake gave the Foreign Secretary, Lord Palmerston (1784–1865), 'an abstract' of the information which he had received from Finlay so that he would be aware of the real expectations of the insurgents and in the hope that it might prevent him from taking 'severe measures … for doubtless he is not a little displeased at the insurrection, as *per contra* to the successful termination of his Syrian policy'. Second, Leake wrote an article which, with Pashley's help, was inserted in *The Morning Chronicle* for 15 May 1841, a day after an article headed 'The Greeks in Crete (latest intelligence)' appeared in its rival, *The Times*. Leake and Pashley thought this was 'the best mode of publica-

tion' since the Whig-orientated *Morning Chronicle* was considered to be the 'Go[vernmen]t paper'. Doubtless they hoped that the government would support the rebels. Under the title 'Insurrection in Crete (from a correspondent)', Leake's article regretted 'the revival of even the semblance of that cruel war of the revolution' and then drew on Finlay for an account of how the insurrection had started, before outlining the Cretans' objectives. He went on to argue that the Cretans should obtain the necessary support from 'our own cabinet, as well as from those of our allies, in the Eastern Question' and reminded his readers that, but for British intervention in 1830, Crete would 'never have been again subjected either to the Sultan or to Mehmet Ali' and that the Turks would 'either have abandoned the island or have perished in it'. Leake concluded by reminding his readers how assurances had been given to the Christians, especially by England, that the rule of law would prevail in the island, and reminding them that these had not been honoured under Muhammad Ali and would be achieved 'under the restored domination of the Porte only through the intervention of the European powers'.

The third step which Leake took, was to translate the Cretan manifesto and have it published in *The Morning Chronicle* on 18 May 1841, without the multiple epithets and repetitions but with some explanatory notes from Pashley's book. Finally, Leake 'attacked' (his word) his friends in Parliament. He persuaded Lord Teignmouth, the MP for Marylebone where Leake lived, to interrogate the Foreign Secretary in the House of Commons, but 'we have not yet quite decided how this question is to be framed. The doubt is whether the Resolution of the London Conference of 20th February 1830 can be made applicable to the present state of Crete'. Leake thought it could apply.

Teignmouth raised the question in the House on Friday, 28 May 1841, but he got no answer since Palmerston was not present.[105] Leake interpreted this to mean that the Cabinet was 'not yet agreed on the orders to be given on the subject to ministers and other officers in the Mediterranean' and that the Allies were being consulted. Teignmouth tried again on the following Friday,

103. Leake's translation, *Morning Chronicle*, 18 May 1841.
104. *Finlay Papers* A42(25, 26) Hussey 1995, 591–4.

105. Hansard, 28 May 1841, 891–2.

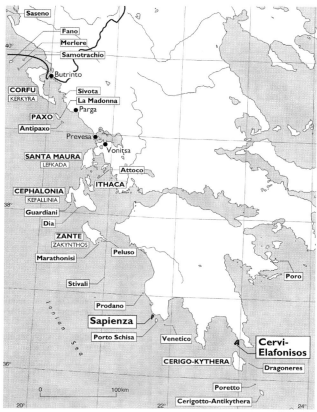

Map.3.1: Map showing position of Cervi and Sapienza relative to Greece and the Ionian Islands.

That was virtually the end of the matter. The newspapers duly reported what Palmerston said,[107] but they did not pressure the Government for urgent action, as Leake had hoped. Leake also failed to persuade Lord Aberdeen, whom he knew socially through the Society of Dilettanti, to take the subject up in the Lords. Meanwhile, the British press began to carry fuller and more frequent reports on events in Crete.

A further letter from Finlay dated 8 June 1841 told Leake that British intervention had now become urgent.[108] He seemed to be optimistic in his next letter of 22 July 1841, reporting that a considerable subscription had been raised in Greece and four ships had been bought in Hydra to help the Cretans, though there had been problems in getting them off.[109] A week later, however, Finlay wrote: 'I regret to inform you that the Cretan insurrection is at an end'.[110] The basic reason, accordingly to Finlay, was that the Turks had 'displayed a good deal of energy' — more than had been expected. They had acted rapidly, brought a large force to the island and put pressure on the Greek frontier in Thessaly, while the local and Greek forces in Crete had simply been too few. King Otto had failed to deliver on his promises of assistance. The Cretans, for their part, had put 'too great hopes on the immediate interference of the Allies'. Critically, Finlay thought, Lord Ponsonby, the British Ambassador to the Porte, had failed to put pressure on the Ottoman government and had been too easily persuaded by its assurances about the future governance of the island. In fact, Ponsonby had simply followed Palmerston's instructions. The integrity of the Ottoman Empire was to be preserved, and Palmerston was reluctant, in Petropulos' words, to strengthen 'a state which appeared to serve Russian interests in the Near East'. Instead, Ponsonby proposed that Crete should have autonomy within the Ottoman Empire under a Christian ruler, a regime similar to that enjoyed by Samos at the time. In Petropulos' view, this would have amounted to a British protectorate, given Britain's naval supremacy in the eastern Mediterranean.[111]

4 June 1841, when he saw the Foreign Secretary in his place. He asked Palmerston directly if he had 'taken any measures, in conformity with the declaration of the Allied Powers, to prevent the perpetration by the Turks, of cruelties on the Christian inhabitants of Candia'. Palmerston replied that he did not know to what declaration Teignmouth referred, but that as soon as the government had received information about the 'troubles' in Candia, the British Ambassador in Constantinople had been directed to prevail upon the Turkish government 'to enter into some arrangement with the Greek population of Candia, which, while on the one hand it should be satisfactory to the Turkish Government, should, on the other, give the Greek population of Candia full security for their persons and properties'. The Ambassador had also been directed 'to urge the Turkish Government not to have recourse to measures more severe than should be absolutely necessary'.[106]

---

106. Hansard, 4 June 1841, 1120–1.

107. *Finlay Papers* A42(27); Hussey 1995, 596–7.
108. *Finlay Papers* B7(19); Hussey 1995, 594–5.
109. *Finlay Papers* B7(20); Hussey 1995, 597–8.
110. *Finlay Papers* B7(21); Hussey 1995, 598–601.
111. Petropulos 1968, 350–1.

BRITISH CLAIMS ON GREECE

Following Palmerston's return to the Foreign Office in 1846 the British government made a number of claims on Greece for compensation and apologies on behalf of a few of its own subjects, together with a handful of Ionian Islanders. The claims included one by Finlay himself. He wanted indemnifying for the seizure in 1836 of some of his property in Athens by the builders of the royal palace. Another claim, the most notorious of all, was put forward on behalf of David Pacifico for damage to his house by an anti-Semitic Athenian mob at Easter 1847, and the consequent loss of documents connected with a legal case in which he said he was engaged. Pacifico maintained that he was born a British subject, despite being a naturalised citizen of Portugal and a former Portuguese consul in Athens.

Linked with these personal claims was a territorial one. Britain declared that the offshore islands of Cervi (now known as Elafonisos) near Cape Malea and Sapienza (Sapientza), which lies to the south of Modon (Methoni), belonged to the Ionian States and not to Greece. In the view of *The Times* this was 'the most important and dangerous of the demands made in the name of this country'.[112]

Leake published a pamphlet, which refuted the British case. The Greek government refused to concede sovereignty over the islands, would not apologise (except in the Pacifico case) and was reluctant to pay compensation. On 3 December 1849 Palmerston ordered the British Ambassador to Athens, Thomas Wyse (later Sir Thomas), to use the British Mediterranean fleet to pressure the Greek government in whatever manner he saw fit. The fleet arrived on 15 January 1850 and next day Wyse delivered an ultimatum, demanding the whole compensation sum within twenty-four hours. Failure to comply would lead to naval action. The Greek requests for arbitration and time to pay were refused. Piraeus was closed to Greek vessels, and then the blockade was extended to Patras and other Greek ports. At the end of January, Wyse ordered the seizure of Greek merchant ships. Protests came from the ambassadors of the other powers in Athens and London.

On 12 February 1850 Palmerston agreed to French arbitration, and Wyse was ordered to suspend the blockade and negotiate with the French ambassador in Athens. The negotiations in Athens proved difficult and eventually broke down. In London, however, an agreement was reached on 19 April. Wyse was informed that a deal was nearing conclusion, but he ordered the resumption of the blockade before official confirmation arrived. Greece capitulated two days later. A major diplomatic row with France ensued, and there was the possibility of war. British public opinion was divided. The government lost a vote of censure in the House of Lords on 17 June 1850, but narrowly won in the Commons just over a week later, following a long speech by Palmerston defending British foreign policy in the East with its rousing peroration:

> as the Roman, in days of old, held himself free from indignity when he should say *Civis Romanus sum*; so also a British subject, in whatever land he may be, shall feel confident that the watchful eye and strong arm of England will protect him against injustice and wrong.[113]

Although the detail of what happened during the dispute was contained in the official correspondence published by the two governments, Finlay's letters not only provided Leake with the background to his own claim for indemnity, but also gave him the Greek reaction to the claims and the bullying tactics employed by Britain to get its way.

Immediately after the imposition of the blockade, 'the patriotic cry against England was very violent for a few days', Finlay told Leake on 28 January 1850. 'Indeed yesterday', he continued, 'was the first day that a dawn of reflection began. A snow storm that I never saw equalled in violence with the thermometer at 26 has done more damage than the blockade and made the people think that heaven joins the barbarians'. The Greek Parliament had not called for a vote of confidence in the government, and ministers had not been blamed for the situation. On the whole, the Greek press was 'by no means very violent'.[114] In general, according

---

112. *The Times*, 15 April 1850, 4, a–b.

113. Hansard 1850, quoted Ridley 1972, 524.
114. *Finlay Papers* B7(29); Hussey 1995, 646–9.

to Finlay, the Greek public knew little about the issues in the dispute but had their attention directed to the progress of the 'quarrel' rather than to its causes. He thought, however, that Britain cut 'a wretched figure' in Greece.[115] The court hated Britain, Finlay reported, and was looking for an alliance to annoy it.[116] After the indemnities had been settled, he told Leake that King Otto had no wish to 'conciliate' Britain or to establish friendly relations.[117]

Surprisingly, Finlay had virtually nothing to say specifically about the local reaction to the Pacifico affair, though he summarised for Leake the settlement agreed in Athens.[118] Leake thought the claims were exaggerated.[119] Finlay was fairly reticent about how his own case was perceived, preferring to outline the development of the dispute over the previous decade. He thought the Greek authorities had tried throughout to avoid reaching a settlement or had offered what he considered to be inadequate terms. After the claims had been settled he commented that, considering how his affair was unavoidably linked with that of Pacifico, 'he had escaped wonderfully well from the press in England and was treated with great liberality and respect by the press in Greece which never said an insulting word concerning me'.[120]

The claim to the islands of Cervi and Sapienza was not pressed by Britain. To do so, Finlay thought, would make Britain look 'ridiculous' and Palmerston had plenty of good grounds for a quarrel without taking up a bad one like this.[121] Palmerston's geography was as bad as his statesmanship, Finlay wrote, for he placed Salamis, Aegina and Hydra in the Cyclades. Nonetheless, Finlay thought it worthwhile having Leake's pamphlet on the question translated into Greek for publication in the *Athena*. He commented:

> It is of some political importance that we have your name on this subject, as it enables the liberals to keep this an open question

and oppose the claim of England without joining France or Russia.[122]

Leake produced the first edition of his pamphlet, *On the Claim to the Islands of Cervi and Sapienza*, before 16 February 1850.[123] He argued that since both islands were within gunshot of the mainland they would normally be considered to be attached to it under international law, unless specific exceptions had been made by particular treaty. No exceptions had been made by the relevant international treaties, though Leake admitted that there was an ambiguity because it was not clear exactly which islands were actually possessed or claimed by Venice as constituting the Ionian Islands before the Treaty of Campo Formio of 1797, when the Ionian Islands passed to France. He argued that the act of the supreme legislative body of the Septinsular Republic of 22 January 1804, which named Cervi and Sapienza as components of the Ionian Islands and on which the British government's case ultimately rested, had no validity. It was not an international treaty but had only local application; the Ottoman government was not a party to it and probably did not know of its existence; Venice did not *bestow* the islands of Cervi and Sapienza and they had not been specifically ceded to the Serene Republic by the Treaty of Passarowitz (1699), which was based on the principle of *uti possidetis*; and that, in any case, the 1804 act had been made under Russian pressure when Russian troops garrisoned the Ionian Islands.

Finlay was not the only one to think that Leake had 'well exposed' the lack of foundation for the British claim. *The Times* did so as well.

> On this subject we have now the testimony of a witness whose authority is above all dispute on such a point, if it is to be decided by geography and justice, and not by petulance and men-of-war. We have before us a short statement of this case, drawn up and published by Colonel Leake, whose personal Knowledge of the territory of Greece, and whose profound researches into the ancient and modern topography of that country, are

115. *Finlay Papers* B7(32); Hussey 1995, 662–4.

116. *Finlay Papers* B7(36); Hussey 1995, 672–5.

117. *Finlay Papers* B7(30); Hussey 1995, 651–4.

118. *Finlay Papers* B7(32); Hussey 1995, 662–4.

119. *Finlay Papers* A42(50); Hussey 1995, 656–7.

120. *Finlay Papers* B7(34); Hussey 1995, 668–9.

121. *Finlay Papers* B7(32); Hussey 1995, 668–9.

122. *Finlay Papers* B7(33); Hussey 1995, 666–7.

123. *Finlay Papers* A42(47); Hussey 1995, 649–50.

familiar to the whole world. Expressed with no political bias, but with scientific precision, Colonel Leake's opinion carries with it the greatest possible weight, and it annihilates the pretensions rashly based on the loose statements of the Ionian authorities by both the Colonial and Foreign departments of the home Government.[124]

There is an irony here for the hare was set running in 1839 by General Sir Howard Douglas (1776–1861) following an inspection of the 'Southern Islands' during his time as High Commissioner in the Ionian Islands (1835–41).[125] He and Leake formed a life-long friendship while they were cadets at the Royal Military Academy, Woolwich.[126]

CONCLUSION

Finlay and Leake believed that Britain, as one of the guarantor powers, had a right to intervene in Greece. It was the manner and objectives which concerned them. Both were disappointed at the way things evolved following independence, and thought that Britain should have played a more constructive role in the country. Finlay was on the spot, a participant observer, and his correspondence with Leake gave the London-based scholar a personal commentary on economic, social and above all political developments in Greece during the 1840s and 1850s. Finlay's comments informed Leake's view of the situation in Greece and the interventionist roles of successive British ambassadors, as well as the part played by the King and his ministers. Admiral Sir Edmund Lyons, claimed Finlay in 1844, was 'even more ignorant of administrative business than the King'.[127] Five years later, after Lyons had been recalled, he pointed out that the over-restless ambassador was 'more hostile to Greece than the Turkish Minister' and that 'his furious conduct … induced his party to do the constitution more harm than either the

King or Coletti could have effected'.[128] Thomas Wyse was a 'complete contrast'.[129] More circumspect than his predecessor, he saw matters in Greece in what Finlay thought was 'the right light'. However, he was 'very slow and lazy to a considerable degree', but no less bullying than Lyons.[130]

Leake drew on Finlay's material for his pamphlet, *Greece at the End of Twenty-three Years of Protection*, published early in 1851.[131] The debt is particularly noticeable in Leake's comments on the neglect of agriculture and the failure to attract Greek labourers from the Ottoman provinces, as he acknowledged in a subsequent letter to Finlay.[132] Ambassador Trikoupis in London, however, objected to Leake's assertion, based upon Finlay's information, that agriculture was less productive than before the War of Independence and instanced the great increases in currant and silk production, though — as Leake pointed out — he said nothing about 'the great natural productions corn, wine and oil'.[133] Finlay replied a month later that Trikoupis knew well that the Greek government had done 'all the damage possible both to the currant trade and the silk',[134] alluding no doubt to his view that the fiscal system was destructive of agriculture.[135]

Finlay also informed Leake that George Psyllas (1794–1879), journalist and politician, had read the pamphlet and pronounced

> strongly in its favour as a correct view of the state of Greece. The currant trade was a present from Lord P[almerston] when he took off the differential duty and as for silk production, it is a disgrace to the gov[ernment] that it is not ten times as much as it is.[136]

---

124. *The Times*, 15 April 1850, 4, a–b.
125. *British Parliamentary Papers* 1863, 932–73.
126. Marsden 1864, 2.
127. *Finlay Papers* B7(24); Hussey 1995, 625–7.

128. *Finlay Papers* B7(28); Hussey 1995, 641–3. Ioannis Kolettis (1773–1847), Prime Minister of Greece, 1844–47.
129. *Leake Papers* 85695; Hussey 1995, 701–3.
130. *Leake Papers* 85706; Hussey1995, 737–9.
131. *Finlay Papers* A42(57); Hussey 1995, 685–6.
132. *Finlay Papers* A42(57); Hussey 1995, 685–6.
133. *Finlay Papers* A42(57); Hussey 1995, 685–6.
134. *Finlay Papers* B7(39); Hussey 1995, 688.
135. See for example, *Leake Papers* 85695; Hussey 1995, 701–3.
136. *Finlay Papers* B7(39); Hussey 1995, 688.

In a subsequent letter he told Leake that he thought Psyllas, one of the few 'political men' who consider truth of primary importance, would probably publish the pamphlet, but 'not one of the leading political newspapers', whatever party it supported, would publish a translation.[137] Leake, then, accepted Finlay's information and used it to criticise the Greek government, though he must have thought that it agreed with material coming from his other sources. Finlay, in turn, used Leake — his authority, letters and publications — in the Athenian struggle against the Greek government and in support of the 'English' party. Both men gained benefit from their correspondence, as indeed from their long friendship.

REFERENCES

MANUSCRIPTS

Finlay Papers (British School at Athens). A42 Leake's letters to Finlay. The number in brackets is the number of the letter. B7 Finlay's letters to Leake

Leake Papers (Hertfordshire County Archives, Hertford). 85695–85711: Finlay's letters to Leake

PUBLICATIONS

British Parliamentary Papers 39 (1849–50). London.

Hansard (ed.) *Parliamentary Debates.* 1841, 28 May and 4 June.

Hussey, J.M. (ed.), 1995. *The Journals and Letters of George Finlay.* Camberley.

Marsden, J.H., 1864. *A Brief Memoir of the Life and Writings of the Late Lieutenant-Colonel Leake.* London.

Martin Leake, W., 1814. *Researches in Greece.* London.

—, 1825. *An Historical Outline of the Greek Revolution.* London.

—, 1830. *Travels in the Morea.* London.

—, 1835. *Travels in Northern Greece.* London.

—, 1841. *The Topography of Athens.* London.

—, 1850. *On the Claim to the Islands of Cervi and Sapienza.* London.

—, 1851. *Greece at the End of Twenty-three Years of Protection.* London.

Miller, W., 1924. 'The Finlay papers', *English Historical Review* 34: 386–398.

Morning Chronicle, (15 and 18 May 1841).

Pashley, R., 1837. *Travels in Crete.* London.

Petropulos, J., 1968. *Politics and Statecraft in the Kingdom of Greece, 1833–1843.* Princeton N.J.

Ridley, J., 1972. *Lord Palmerston.* London.

Strong, F.,1842. *Greece as a Kingdom. Or, A Statistical Description of that Country from the Arrival of King Otho, in 1833, Down to the Present Time.* London.

The Times, (20 April 1841; 3 May 1841; 15 Apr. 1850).

---

137. *Finlay Papers* B7(41); Hussey 1995, 692.

4

Like a rolling stone, R.A.H. Bickford-Smith (1859–1916) from Britain to Greece

Maria Christina Chatziioanou

How does it feel
To be on your own
With no direction home
Like a complete unknown
Like a rolling stone?

Bob Dylan, 1965

The phrase 'rolling stone' became very popular in the 1960s, in the music world of the west; a music group and a magazine were named after it, and Bob Dylan wrote his famous song *Like A Rolling Stone*.[1] This expression derives from the proverb *a rolling stone gathers no moss*, which indicates that a person who moves about a great deal and never settles down will not do well. People pay a price for being always on the move, in that they have no roots in a specific place (the original meaning); or people who keep moving avoid picking up responsibilities and obligations. After some 300 years of this interpretation, in the mid–1800s the value of gathering moss (and staying put) began to be questioned, and in current usage the phrase is most often used without any particular value judgement.

What Roandeau Albert Henry Bickford-Smith has to do with rolling stones is not immediately obvious. Victorian scholar, Fellow of the Society of Antiquarians and barrister, he is known for his book *Greece under King George* (translated into Greek in 1993),[2] a work that almost all historians studying the Greek nineteenth century have consulted. In searching through *Google* to find information about him, I was directed via various links to the chat room of Bob Dylan fans. There, to my great surprise, I discovered that the phrase *a rolling stone gathers no moss* was attributed to Pub-

lilius Syrus,[3] a Latin writer of mimes, active in the 1st century BC. All that remains of his works is a collection of Sentences (*Sententiae*), a series of moral maxims in iambic and trochaic verse.[4] R.A.H. Bickford-Smith is one of the main editors of this Latin writer. Why did he butt into Roman literature? And, more to the point here, why did a Victorian barrister write about modern Greece? In order to understand his scholarly initiatives, we have to comprehend Bickford-Smith's cultural background, as well as his intellectual patterns and sources of inspiration.

There is no British biographical dictionary to my knowledge with an entry under his name. Bickford-Smith was not a conspicuous man, his career did not intersect with dramatic events in British or Greek history and it is difficult to get him into perspective. The constants in Bickford-Smith's intellectual make-up that influenced his actions were his education and his cultivation in a late Victorian milieu.

The only biographical data available hint at an affluent family background that provided Roandeau Albert Henry with a good education. He was born on 3 May

---

1. BobDylanTalk.com
2. Bickford-Smith 1893; the copy in the BSA is signed by the author. Greek translation edited by Lydia Papadaki.

3. A native of Syria, he was brought as a slave to Italy and, by his wit and talent, won the favour of his master who freed and educated him. His mimes, which he acted himself, enjoyed great success in the provincial towns of Italy and at the games given by Caesar in 46 BC. Publilius (less correctly Publius) was perhaps even more famous as an *improvisatore*, and received from Caesar himself the prize in a contest where he vanquished all his competitors, including the celebrated Decimus Laberius.
4. In the course of time the collection was interpolated with sentences drawn from other writers, including many pithy sayings like 'Pecunia una regimen est rerum omnium'. Each maxim is composed in a single verse and the verses are arranged in alphabetical order according to their initial letters. The best texts of the *Sentences* are those of E. Wolfflin (1869), A. Spengel (1874) and W. Meyer (1880), with complete critical apparatus and index verborum; recent editions with notes by O. Friedrich (1880), Bickford-Smith (1895), see also Edward Bensly, 'Authors of quotations wanted', in Bickford-Smith 1908, 229.

Fig.4.1: R.A.H. Bickford Smith; BSA Photographic Archive: BSAA7–4.

1859, eldest son of William Bickford-Smith (1827–99), who was Member of Parliament for Trevarno, at Helston, Cornwall. William Bickford-Smith was elected in 1885 with the Liberals and in 1886 was re-elected with the Liberal Unionists,[5] obviously following the defenders of the union of Britain and Ireland and dissenting from W.E. Gladstone. Roandeau Albert Henry was admitted to Trinity College, Cambridge in 1878, where he read Law, graduating in 1883 and taking his Masters of Arts in 1886.[6] He became a member of the Inner Temple in 1882 and was called to the bar in

1886.[7] According to the Inner Temple archives, his professional address in 1889 and 1891 was 1 Elm Court, an upper middle class neighbourhood of London.[8] In 1891, he married Caroline Louise Marianne Skinner (1873–1936), and three children followed, John Allan, William Nugent Venning, Aubrey Luis.

Bickford is a name of ancient Anglo-Saxon origin (becca and ford = a type of axe and a shallow place in a river) and is encountered as a toponym in several places in England. It is first found in Devonshire in a maritime region in the southwest of the county, not far from Cornwall where Trevarno, Bickford-Smith's birthplace, is located. Trevarno is an important manor and garden dating back to 1296. The estate of c.750 acres was bought in 1874 by R.A.H. Bickford-Smith's father and remained in the family until 1994.[9]

Following searches in various directions — local archives and internet sites — information was found associating R.A.H. Bickford-Smith with a prominent figure in nineteenth-century British technological innovation related to the industrial revolution. The person in question is William Bickford (1774–1834), a native of Cornwall who was a leather seller by trade and an inventor. He had combined gunpowder and flax yarn into a reliable slow-burning fuse, which he patented in 1831 as the 'Safety Rod', to be changed later to the 'Safety Fuze'. After his death, his factory, producing fuse by the mile, became *Bickford-Smith & Co.* The company underwent many changes of name and was registered as a limited liability company in 1888 when it became Bickford, Smith and Co. Ltd. Safety fuse continued to be made there with numerous changes and alterations until 1961. This company was the biggest British manufacturer of safety fuses and was taken over by Nobel Industries in 1921 and closed in 1962. A tin tablet set into the wall of the works commemorates William Bickford's invention.[10] This important invention was initially motivated by the local tin-mining

---

5. Craig 1974, 243.

6. In his time the Master of Trinity College was an enlightened scholar of classics, William Hepworth Thompson (1866–86). His tutor was the mathematician J.M. Image, in line with Trinity's great tradition in Mathematics (Isaac Newton).

---

7. Venn 1940, pt II, vol. I, 257.

8. See Booth Poverty Map (1898–99) (Charles Booth Online Archive) http://booth.lse.ac.uk.

9. Ellory-Pett 1998, 72–3.

10. For William Bickford see http://www.devonlife.co.uk, http://www.themagicofcornwall.com and http://www.cornish-mining.org.uk/status/status. htm.

industry, which was plagued by many accidents at the time, due to the intensification of extraction and inadequate safety measures.

William Bickford-Smith was the inventor's grandson through his mother's line, and the one who bore both surnames of his parents, George Smith and Elizabeth Burrall Bickford. R.A.H. Bickford-Smith, therefore, is closely related to the innovative tradition emerging from the British industrial revolution. Furthermore, strong links with the Cornish mining industry and British political life appear through his family history. There is no doubt that a network of personal acquaintances from relevant circles would be important in his life. It is not unrelated that two chapters of *Greece under King George* had been published in England a year earlier, in a leading radical newspaper, the *Newcastle Daily Chronicle*.[11] The newspaper was owned by Joseph Cowen (1831–1900), politician, journalist and mine owner of Newcastle-on-Tyne, son of a liberal MP. Through his publications he vigorously advocated reform of the mine industry in the colliery villages in his area and was well known for his ardent concern for the welfare of the miners. Joseph Cowen came from a background similar to that of Bickford-Smith, and could have very well been acquainted with him through common social and political circles.[12]

For Britain, the last decades of the 19th century were marked by a major territorial expansion. British imperialism and colonial expansion were at their peak with serious economic, social and cultural transformations taking place in the country and the colonies. A devotion to the idea of progress had been encouraged by a most important figure in Victorian Britain, Thomas Babington Macaulay (1800–59), who had a profound impact on certain circles. Bickford-Smith was driven by the same restlessness that drove many young Victorian men and women of rank and wealth to the ends of earth, like Rolling Stones. They escaped from the dull ease and elaborate conventions of rigid 19th century society to the exciting and challenging simplicities of travel, exploration and mountaineering, in remote and primitive places. An example was the Irishman John

Palliser, a brilliant amateur geographer and adventurer fascinated by the Great Plains who persuaded the Royal Geographical Society to back his exploration of Western Canada (1857–59).[13] The Palliser expedition was financed by the Colonial Office, which was interested in all British inroads in North America. John Palliser, his brothers and friends succumbed to the fever of expedition. They were ardent sportsmen, wrote diaries and memoirs, spoke languages and adopted a literary style. A good number of these young men who did not head for tours of 'imaginative geography'[14] as narrated in books or described in letters, choose instead the Grand Tour and its variations. This was a travel route that provided education and entertainment and, to a lesser degree, conquest and domestication of the wild. The Grand Tour was popular among British upper-class young men, serving as an educational rite of passage for wealthy university graduates. Its primary value lay in the exposure to the cultural artifacts of Antiquity and the Renaissance, as well as to the aristocratic and fashionable society of the European Continent. Its length varied from several months to several years. Parallel to, and sometimes as an extension of, the European tour to Italy, these travels led to Constantinople, the great international capital of the East. The impressions and opinions formed in the course of these travels of the Balkans, the East and the Levant, were recorded in personal writings (diaries, memoirs), as well as in books and European newspaper articles. Newspaper stories in particular reached a large public, because they were short and had a wide circulation.

In April 1890, R.A.H. Bickford-Smith came to Greece for 'archaeological travelling' and the British School at Athens became his natural point of reference and residence. At that time, British archaeological interests were focused on the Peloponnese. James Frazer had completed an extensive tour in Greece whilst preparing his edition of Pausanias.[15] Excavations in Megalopolis were at their peak, with G.C. Richards, W.J. Woodhouse, W. Loring believing that they had discovered there the first fairly complete 'proscenium' (stage) of

---

11. Bickford-Smith 1893, xx.
12. http://www.1911encyclopedia.org/Joseph_Cowen

13. Foran 1982, 35.
14. Chard 1999, 10.
15. For Frazer's project on Pausanias see Henderson 2001, 213.

the 'Greek period'. So it is most likely that Bickford-Smith was inspired by the fervour of his countrymen and visited the newly discovered archaeological site of Megalopolis. One of the urgent demands of the School's Managing Committee that year was to secure grants for sustaining the promising British institution in Greece. They referred to the advantage of finding in Athens a good library and guidance of competent scholars. If only by endowment or by annual subscription a permanent income of 600 or 700 pounds a year could be assured, no one need doubt that the British School at Athens would amply justify its foundation.[16]

Bickford-Smith 'Esquire' was supporting the British School at Athens with his 1 pound and 1 shilling annual subscription up until 1893, in which year he probably ceased to reside there. Besides the contributions of other individual subscribers, the BSA received donations from the Society of Antiquaries and the Society for the Promotion of Hellenic Studies.[17] Not all the students who came to the BSA as holders of travelling fellowships at any university in the UK or the colonies or as travelling students of the Royal Academy or other similar bodies became annual subscribers.[18] Becoming a subscriber implied a sufficient personal income as well as a strong interest in the School's objectives: 'the promotion of classical studies and every period of the Greek language and literature, from the earliest age to the present day'.[19]

It is obvious that the BSA was trying to establish itself in Greece, somewhat delayed in relation to the existing foreign schools in Athens: the French, the German and the American. In its early stages, it followed the example of the Society for the Promotion of Hellenic Studies, founded in 1879. The inspiration of the Hellenic Society of London was 'to advance the study of Greek language, literature, and art, and to illustrate

the history of the Greek race in the ancient, Byzantine and Neo-Hellenic periods by the publication of memoirs and unedited documents or monuments'. According to one of the leading classicists of the Victorian era, R.C. Jebb, Professor of Greek at Glasgow and later Cambridge, these objectives would be promoted in the most direct and effective manner 'by the creation of a permanent agency at a central point of the Hellenic countries', as he wrote in 1883.[20] Ideological support for the establishment and expansion of the BSA was not difficult to find among British scholars of classical studies and restless young Victorians. However, finding financial support for the whole project was the most difficult task for the Managing Committee of the early years. Since the financial position of the School was very precarious, depending solely on a limited number of grants and subscriptions, many of those who wished to take part in the project had to support themselves, or find their own means of support. A close set of British scholars supported the School, made their acquaintances in the emerging Greek social scene, studied and wrote extensively about ancient Greece and 'the continuity of Greek life'.

Following the travelling habits of his countrymen, Bickford-Smith, a young barrister in his early thirties, chose the route to Constantinople and, on his way to the imperial capital, decided to stop over in Greece. The story of his decision, prompted by the captain of the ship on which he was sailing, is charming and one of the few really spontaneous and original experiences that Bickford-Smith relates in *Greece under King George*.[21] Everyone reading his lines is aware of a strong and motivated control of feelings:

> But as a personal experience, it was of some value in backing up my already-made determination to beware of sentiment… At any rate, I made up my mind to observe facts, and each day I found some new items which seemed worthy to be added to the stock from which I might eventually evolve an opinion.[22]

16. *BSA AR* 1889–90, 7–17.

17. Pandelis Ralli, from the London Ralli Bros was one of the trustees of the BSA and actually visited the School during that time, *BSA AR* 1891–92, 15.

18. Of the eighteen students of the period 1886–90 only Bickford-Smith and David Hogarth, Fellow and Tutor of Magdalen College Oxford, were subscribers to the BSA according to the lists of 1892–93, *BSA AR* 1893, 23.

19. See objectives in 'Rules and Regulations of the British School at Athens', published in all BSA Annual Reports of the period.

20. Jebb 1883, 3–4.
21. Bickford-Smith 1893, ix–x.
22. Bickford-Smith 1893, xi.

We are in the realm of the 'Empire of Fact' and, as Peter Gay has pointed out, 'the industrial revolution was a revolution in knowledge that the Victorian century would master more completely and would need more urgently than any of its predecessors'.[23] This knowledge was based on facts generated by modern sciences that influenced a large number of British scholars.

Facts apart, there is little doubt that Bickford-Smith was swept off his feet by the sentiments he experienced during his three-year stay in Athens. This is not expressed explicitly anywhere, but it is implicit in his writings about modern Greece and the Greeks. He liked everything, he justified everything and he praised everything: he saw the cheating habits in everyday dealings as integrally linked to more appealing characteristics. Greek students with their lively participation in their tutorial courses were compared to the 'listless air' prevalent in British schools. The Greeks were deemed more polite than the French. Even the fact that one might be invaded in his bedroom by a whole Greek family was justified by the fact that the English wear 'such very funny clothes'. Greeks were 'fully alive to the Epikurean pleasure', but never got drunk. A series of incidents narrated in the introduction of his book reveals strong positive sentiments for modern Greece, sentiments that Bickford-Smith wanted to share with his countrymen back in England. The main aim of his book was to enlighten his countrymen, in the hope that they would favour 'the Hellenic factor in the Eastern Question'. His vision of assigning Constantinople to Greece as the natural successor of Turkey, after the expulsion of the Turks from Europe, confirms his vigorous support of panhellenism;[24] a scheme inspired by classical times, with the aspiration of uniting all Greeks in one political body and which in modern times acquired the visionary aspect of a *Megali Idea*. Panhellenism was one of the polymorphous poly-ideologies that were born in the 19th century, like panslavism and pan-Turkism, expressing a nationalistic interest in the unity of an ethnic group; a movement of irredentism characterized by cultural and political trends.

Bickford-Smith became a follower of panhellenism, praised modern life and progress in Greece in the time of King George I, and made a plea for the Greek cause. Bickford-Smith's sojourn in Greece coincided with a strengthening of the liberal parliamentary regime and conspicuous economic development.[25] However, we know that the Greek economy had entered a phase of successive crises, the most serious being the financial crisis of 1893 and the collapse of the currant trade. There is evidence that Bickford-Smith was aware of the critical situation of Greek public finances. The dedication of his book to Charilaos Trikoupis (Χαριλάῳ Τρικούπηι τιμής ένεκα) denotes Bickford-Smith's appreciation of the anglophile Greek politician, who was probably a personal acquaintance.

Bickford-Smith's cultural and educational background informs the way he structures his book. As an observant barrister he declares his sources and lays out his chapters in a way more or less analogous to that of other descriptive essays: the population, the natural resources, industry and commerce, entrepreneurial activities, communications, public finances, public order, education, culture, archaeology, religion, the army, the constitution, politics, society, charity, miscellaneous, Panhellenism. The political strife between Trikoupis and Deliyiannis was a major topic during Bickford-Smith's time in Greece. However, he was ill-prepared to understand the structure of modern Athenian society and its relation to Greek politics. Old families were socializing with heroes from the Greek Revolution of 1821, as well as with diaspora Greek entrepreneurs and politicians.[26] Social mobility on a large scale was abolishing notions of class structure such as would have been familiar to a Victorian man. Still, it seems that Bickford-Smith thought that the presentation of Greek politics and society to the English newspaper-reading public would be of major interest.

Why did Bickford-Smith write a book about Greece, a relatively new, foreign state? One reason was the fact that this new state represented continuity with Greek

23. Gay 1993, 447.
24. Bickford-Smith 1893, ix–xviii.
25. For an overview of the reign of King George I, see Carabott 1997.
26. Bickford-Smith 1893, 285–94.

antiquity. His own presence in Greece, the BSA milieu and his Greek acquaintances were other reasons, which enabled him to express a political view of the Eastern Question in its geopolitical dimension. But it is difficult to ascertain his ideological equipment for confronting this subject. Bickford-Smith learnt Greek and had compiled a handwritten, and hitherto unpublished, Greek-French 'vocabulary'.[27] We know that some of his books and papers somehow ended up in the library of King's College London (Anglo-Hellenic League fund). They include his Greek-French vocabulary, cuttings from English newspapers concerning the situation in Greece in 1877, 1878, etc., C. Fauriel, *Chants populaires de la Grèce moderne* (1824–25), J. Sibthorp, *Flora Graecae prodromus* (1806) — personal readings indicating that Bickford-Smith was following the history of modern Greece from the time he was at Trinity, when the Treaty of Berlin was concluded (1878).

Bickford-Smith's aim in writing *Greece under King George* was to inform enlightened tourists who wanted a deeper insight into and understanding of modern Greece than that offered by Baedeker's *Handbook for Travellers*.[28] His intention was not to compile an original scientific work, for he was well aware that he was an amateur in archaeology and history. His suggestion that the prospective traveller to Greece should bring with him photographic apparatus, so as to be able to take away a comprehensive set of images of the country, is interesting.[29] A good sense of taxonomy, an invaluable resource for a Victorian barrister and traveller, is evident from the way he deploys his second-hand sources and personal interpretations about late 19th century Greece. He presents demographic data, catalogues of plants, data of agricultural production, catalogues of professions, public revenues and expenses, imports and exports, lists of industries accompanied by their horsepower; series of numerical data that shed light on modern Greece's progress in the last decades of the nineteenth century.

In *Greece under King George* one can detect the author's political ideas, his engagement in favour of Greek irredentism. It has been argued that there was more than one concept of patriotism in Britain in the late 19th century, in connection to growing national consciousness.[30] Bickford-Smith contrasts modern Greek patriotism with the British Victorian concept:

> I noticed that whereas in England patriotism was not generally looked on as a virtue of quite the front rank, and was, indeed, treated rather as a vice by our most advanced school as well as by the little band of millennial cosmopolitanists, while in one part of the United Kingdom the accentuation of the word differed, here in Greece the idea embraced in the word was the staple of conversation and the master-soul of all politics.[31]

Here Bickford-Smith attacks cosmopolitanism as a major factor in undermining patriotism in late Victorian Britain.

Recent historiography has placed Bickford-Smith among the first historiographers of modern Greece to whom the term *philhellene* properly applies. These philhellenes had come to study modern Greece via the classics and most of them were interested in contemporary Greece mainly because they hoped to find in its customs and mores surviving traces of the classical past. This was an approach that found confirmation in the 'survivals' theory popularized by 19th century anthropologists and folklorists. Travellers and amateur scholars of classical Greece wandered through the Greek countryside, searching for the remnants of classical tradition.[32] *Greece under King George* has been characterized as 'a mine of information on the kingdom of Greece in the last decade of the nineteenth century that retains its value to the present day'.[33] This assessment was valid for several decades, for want of empirical evidence. Bickford-Smith's numbers on Greek industry were used and reproduced by Greek

---

27. I consulted the Bickford-Smith Vocabulary at the Archives of KCL. A detailed publication of the document is planned.

28. Baedeker 1889.

29. Bickford-Smith 1893, 316. A French companion book is also cited, here identified as S. Reinach (1858–1932), *Conseils aux voyageurs archéologiques en Grèce et dans l'orient héllenique,* Paris 1889.

30. Varouxakis 2002, 21–2 quoting Julia Stapleton's views on the subject.

31. Bickford-Smith 1893, xiv.

32. Fleming 2001.

33. Clogg 2000, 20.

economic historians of the interwar period up to the recent decades without much question as to the identity of the author and his intentions.[34]

Three years after his first publication, Bickford-Smith published his second book, the annotated edition of Publilius Syrus, the collection of *Sentences* already mentioned. After his return to England, Bickford-Smith handed in his manuscript for printing, in early 1894. He did not search for new manuscripts and although he had consulted nearly a hundred editions of Publilius Syrus he defined his work as 'the attempt of an amateur'. The main goal of his initiative was taxonomy:

> the only merit I might lay claim to, if comparison must be made with these Teutonic giants [previous German editors], is that of giving a rather more orderly account of the manuscripts and editions. The collecting of information on these heads has been a most delightful recreation.[35]

On the other hand, we must not forget that Latin sentences with pithy meaning were widely used in prose and writings, especially in eloquent speeches of entertainment, or professional use. The other reason for editing Publilius Syrus was to lessen the Latin dominance,

> in giving English surroundings to Publilius… In this I have been guided mainly by the prevailing custom in this country and further by the hope that some will be tempted to gain an introduction to my author who might have been frightened away by the Latin setting.[36]

In 1898, Bickford-Smith published his last book, *Cretan Sketches*, a year after the Cretan uprising of 1897, led by Manousos Koundouros, himself a jurist. Bickford-Smith had long before declared that he would prefer to be 'a returned tourist' rather than 'an unreturned candidate for Parliament'.[37] It is most probable that he visited Crete in his status of 'Late Commissioner of the Cretan Relief Committee', during or soon after the insurrection. In this book Bickford-Smith quotes some of the insurgent leaders and several residents there, implying strong personal acquaintances in Crete, where he most probably compiled his Greek-French vocabulary since the French language was much more widespread.[38] As expounded in the brief preface, the aim of publishing *Cretan Sketches* 'is merely to enable the newspaper-reader to fill in the gaps in his mental panorama of Cretan struggles by a few rough etchings mostly taken from life'[39]. The fact is that Bickford-Smith fails all expectations to give an original view of Crete or the Cretan struggle. Crete is dealt with in much the same way as Palliser dealt with western Canada, as a remote place full of natural beauties and peculiarities, with a valued local history and tradition. Among the oddest impressions from the island are those recorded under the title 'The terrible undead', where the savageness of the Sfakia region is revealed:

> The Society for Psychical Research ought to send a committee of investigation to the region of the White Mountains…But their country is the home of the vampire, and the vampire is the most interesting and bloodthirsty of all spooks…His habits are well known; the only oath that binds him is by his winding-sheet; articles arranged crosswise disconcert him; he amuses himself by rolling stones down a cliff; human liver is the dainty he is keenest on; he has a whole holiday on Saturdays.[40]

Casual scenes from everyday life in Crete are intermingled with historical and scientific information. Nonetheless, Bickford-Smith remains faithful to his linguistic researches and, under the poetic title 'A legacy of words', publishes a list of words from the Cretan dialect translated into English.[41]

---

34. His main sources on the Greek economy are Lewis Sergeant, *New Greece*, London 1878; Πανελλήνιος Σύντροφος; Joseph D. Beckman, *Les finances de la Grèce, Etude composée sur la base de documents authentiques,* Athens 1892; Bickford-Smith 1893, xix. Agriantoni 1990.

35. Bickford-Smith 1895, viii, Preface, written at The Cottage Blackwell, in February 1894.

36. Bickford-Smith 1895, viii.

37. Bickford-Smith 1893, xviii.

38. Bickford-Smith 1898, 79.

39. Bickford-Smith 1898; the preface was written at 98 Palace Gardens Terrace, 17 November 1897.

40. Bickford-Smith 1898, 52–3.

41. Bickford-Smith 1898, 154–8.

Three factors help to elucidate Bickford-Smith's partiality for Greece: sentimental predilection, national trade interests and politics. Bickford-Smith's panhellenism might be related to the 'survivals' theory of the 19th century. Nonetheless, it is evident that his political views were shaped after the Treaty of Berlin and the weakening of the Turkish presence in Europe, followed by the growth of the power of Russia. His anti-Turkish sentiments and his sympathies for Greek irredentism were accompanied by political views of British origin. Bickford-Smith's strong sentiments for his own country can be found throughout his books, and the slogan 'Rule Britannia' actually appears as a chapter subtitle in *Cretan Sketches*.[42] The view that a strong and independent Greece would be a good trade partner for England is expressed openly in *Greece under King George*. He presumed that Britain and the Triple Alliance could become better clients for Greece than France and Russia. Still, his main concern was strengthening the British presence in Greece, to the point of proposing specific governmental measures, such as the abolition of British import taxes on Greek currants and silk; the financing of the British School at Athens so as to boost the prestige of Britain in the Greek capital; the implementation of British-Greek diplomatic friendship in Athens; a British naval presence at Piraeus, and a Greek-English royal marriage. As he saw it, these apparently dissimilar measures should be accompanied by a personal dedication to that cause, which could be realised by publicly declaring philhellenic views and by purchasing Greek products.[43] British dominance in Greek foreign trade had been unquestioned in previous decades, based mainly on the export of currants from Patras. British manufacturers from the north west of England were impatiently waiting for their products to be consumed also in Greek cities. However, other trading partners were endeavouring to strengthen their presence in Greek economic life such as Russia and Austria-Hungary, as well as Turkey, which had always been present.

At the end of *Greece under King George* Bickford-Smith mentions his intellectual predecessors, who stim-

ulated his commitment to this small nation, Greece. The first was George Wheler,[44] the English traveller who accompanied Dr Jacob Spon to Greece in 1675–76, and was especially interested in botany and topography. His publication remained the standard English book on Greece for many years. The second source of inspiration was Lord Byron, who introduced Greece to the broad public of the middle classes.[45] Wheler's book offered information and a taxonomic approach to Greece in the geography of the eastern Mediterranean, while Byron's romantic writings evoked strong feelings for the Greek cause in the long run. Besides these acknowledged sources of inspiration Macaulay is, in my opinion, an archetype who profoundly influenced Victorian scholars and who was not mentioned by Bickford-Smith as he was a near contemporary.

Macaulay was educated at the University of Cambridge; he was called to the bar in 1826, though he practised little, preferring to follow his extensive literary pursuits and politics. His residence in India set its seal on his cultural and professional ideal. In 1842, he finalized his *Lays of Ancient Rome*, a collection of poems in ballad form, retelling legends of the beginnings of the Roman Republic. Three volumes of his *Essays* were published in 1843. His ongoing major historical work was envisaged to become eventually a comprehensive history of England from the accession of King James II to 1832, the year of the Parliamentary Reform Act. The first two volumes of the *History of England from the Accession of James II* were published in December 1848 and were at once a huge success, running through numerous editions in both Britain and the United States. His work contributed substantially to the development of social history, by presenting an extensive survey of English society in the year 1685, in terms of such topics as population, cities, classes and tastes. Macaulay's masterwork was an unprecedented best-seller. His approach was that of a positive promoter of 'progress' and his *History of England*, with its wealth of material, its use of vivid details, and its rhetorical, narrative style combined to

---

42. Bickford-Smith 1898, 88.
43. Bickford-Smith 1893, 341–5.

44. Wheler 1682.
45. Bickford-Smith 1893, 320. On Byron's influence on travel writing see Dritsas 2006.

Fig.4.2: From this photograph, which is captioned 'Photographers on Delos', it would appear that Bickford Smith's advice was taken by later travellers; BSA Photographic Archive: Members, Schoolmasters' Trip 1910–12, M. Scott, Islands–1.

make it one of the most popular literary works of the 19th century.

Macaulay, a barrister with — like Bickford-Smith — a Trinity college Cambridge education, and a preference for Roman literature and the history of his own country, offered a multifaceted cultural model that was dedicated to progress and was much followed in Victorian Britain. Macaulay and the Anglicists promoted English language and culture throughout the continent and the colonies.[46] Roman literature and history were particularly appreciated by jurists and politicians of the time. Accumulating information and data, discovering and narrating the history of a country were also part of the British travelling tradition. All these factors were helpful to travellers who ventured beyond the continent, enabling them to appropriate new countries.

The life and career of Roandeau Albert Henry Bickford-Smith evolved on a Victorian pattern that could be delineated in Britain, or any other destination of similar restless Victorians. Their writings reflect the adaptations of these patterns to different surroundings and circumstances.

During the turbulent years of World War I, Bickford-Smith died in 1916, at the age of 57. His death was announced in *The Annual of the British School at Athens*,[47] but no obituary was published in *The Times* or the *Telegraph*, an expected after death remembrance and praise. In the waning years of the long 19th century, Bickford-Smith with his written anxieties signalled the type of a Victorian bourgeois traveller. He combined in his travellings to Greece political and literary pur-

---

46. Lawson 1998, 149–53.

47. *BSA* XXII, 217; see also obituary in the *Royal Cornwall Gazette*, 21/12/1916.

suits with personal freedom and independence from work and social restrictions. Visual impressions from travelling would not be expressed only in historical accounts and sketches. A new ground to express feelings and impressions was opened up in his time, that of photography: 'They have eyes but they see not and is meant even more for the ambitious traveller, whether specialist or encyclopaedist. He is especially strong on the advantages of photography, and in these Kodak days neither the luggage nuisance nor the expense need frighten anyone out of taking a little trouble, which will be more than compensated by the possession of such mementoes in after years.'[48] Who knows, maybe in the near future someone might come across a photographic album of Bickford-Smith, mementos from his travels in Greece.

ACKNOWLEDGEMENTS

I am grateful to Dr Alexandra Dumas for her support and assistance, to Professor Malcolm Wagstaff and the Cornwall Records Office in the UK for providing information from British libraries. I would also like to thank the BSA Archivist Amalia G. Kakissis and Mr Stathis Finopoulos.

REFERENCES

MANUSCRIPTS

Bickford-Smith, R.A.H., [n.d.]. 'Vocabulary'. unpublished manuscript in the Anglo-Hellenic League Archives, Kings College London.

PUBLICATIONS

Agriantoni, Chr., 1990. «Η βιομηχανική απογραφή του 1889: ανατομία μιας ατελούς και ημιτελούς στατιστικής απόπειρας», Ίστωρ 2: 35–50.

Baedeker, K., 1889. *Handbook for Travellers*. London.

Beckman, Joseph D., 1892. *Les finances de la Grèce, Etude composée sur la base de documents authentiques*. Athens.

Bensley, Edward, 1908. *Notes and Queries*. London.

Bickford-Smith, R.A.H., 1893. *Greece under King George*. London.

—, (ed.), 1895. *Publilii Syri Sententiae*. London.

—, 1898. *Cretan Sketches*. London.

Carabott, Ph. (ed.), 1997. *Greek Society in the making, 1863–1913. Realities, Symbols and Visions*. London.

Chard, Chloe, 1999. *Pleasure and Guilt on the Grand Tour: Travel Writing and Imaginative Geography 1600–1830*. Manchester.

Clogg, R., 2000. *Anglo-Greek Attitudes. Studies in History*. London.

Craig, F. W.S. (ed.), 1974. *British Parliamentary Election Results 1885–1918*. London & Basingstoke.

Dritsas, Margarita, 2006. 'From Travellers'Accounts to Travel Books and Guide Books: the Formation of Greek Tourism Market in the 19th century', *Tourismos* 1/1: 29, 32–3.

Ellory-Pett, D., 1998. *The parks and Gardens of Cornwall: A Companion Guide*. ed. Alison Hodge, Pezance, Cornwall.

Fleming, K.E., 2001. 'The Paradoxes of Nationalism: Modern Greek Historiography and The Burden of the Past', *Bulletin for the Royal Institute for Inter-Faith Studies* 3/2.

Foran, M. and McEwan, H., 1982. *Calgary, Canada's Frontier Metropolis*. Windsor.

Gay, P., 1993. *The Bourgeois Experience: Victoria to Freud, v. 3 The Cultivation of Hatred*. London.

Henderson J., 2001. 'Farnell's Cults. The Making and Breaking of Pausanias in Victorian Archaeology and Anthropology', in S. Alcock, J. Cherry, J. Elsner (eds), *Pausanias, Travel and Memory in Roman Greece*. New York.

Jebb, R.C., 1883. 'A plea for a British Institute at Athens', *Fortnightly Review* 33ns, no. 197 (May): 705-14.

Lawson, Ph., 1998. *The East India Company: A History*. London.

Royal Cornwall Gazette 21/12/1916.

Sergeant, Lewis, 1878, *New Greece*. London.

Varouxakis, G., 2002. *Victorian Political Thought on France and the French*. London.

Venn, J. A. (ed.), 1940. *Alumni Cantabrigienses*. Cambridge.

Wheler, G., 1682. *A Journey into Greece ... in company of Dr Spon of Lyons. In six books. Containing I. A voyage from Venice to Constantinople. II. An account of Constantinople and the adjacent places. III. A voyage through the Lesser Asia. IV. A voyage from Zante through several parts of Greece to Athens. V. An account of Athens. VI. Several journeys from Athens, into Attica, Corinth, Boeotia, &c. With variety of sculptures*. London.

---

48. Bickford-Smith 1893, 316.

From archaeology to dialectology and folklore: the role of the British School at Athens in the career of R.M. Dawkins

Peter Mackridge

As R.M. Dawkins himself would have been the first to point out,[1] chance (or perhaps I should say providence) played a significant role in his career — certainly a more significant role than either ambition or forward planning. It is characteristic that one of his unpublished memoirs, written in 1950, on which I have drawn in preparing this paper, is entitled not 'What I did' but 'What happened to me'.

Dawkins was born in 1871 into what he calls 'a fairly prosperous family of the middle class'.[2] Having been sent by his father to King's College, London, to read electrical engineering — a subject profoundly alien to his nature —, he dropped out of the course after two years and found a job, first as an apprentice and then as a designer, at the Arc Works in Chelmsford ('Arc' as in arc lamps); the company, started by Colonel R.E.B. Crompton, later became, after a merger, the famous firm of Crompton Parkinson. Throughout this period Dawkins devoted his spare time to studying languages and reading literature, including Greek, Latin, Sanskrit, Old Norse, Icelandic and even Finnish. His parents died within a short period in 1896–97, leaving him an income of £160 a year, and soon afterwards he fulfilled a life-long desire to travel by touring Spain, France, Switzerland and Italy for nine months. At the end of this period he applied on impulse to become an undergraduate student at Emmanuel College, Cambridge, with no clear idea of what subject he would pursue, and he was immediately accepted to read Classics as a mature student of 27. This time he completed his undergraduate course with a Double First. Having successfully made a fresh start in life, he was awarded a Craven Scholarship to the British School at Athens from 1902 to 1903.

Although he could not have foreseen it at the time, Dawkins was to spend the greater part of the next sixteen and a half years in Greece, which became, as he put it, 'my second patrida'.[3] For twelve of these years he was a member of the British School at Athens. Although he had specialized in comparative philology at Cambridge, Dawkins soon mastered the practical techniques of archaeology in the field, where his familiarity with the design and use of machinery, his talent as a draughtsman and his experience of dealing with workmen must have been a considerable advantage.[4] His archaeological career began at the Minoan site of Palaikastro in eastern Crete, where he spent his spare time collecting material on the local dialect. As early as Dawkins's second season at the site (1904), R.C. Bosanquet, with whom he got on very badly, placed him in charge of the excavations. In his periods of annual leave from the School, he used to travel to the Greek islands and Asia Minor in search of dialect material. Even during his tenure of the Craven Studentship in 1903, he travelled to Karpathos (then still in the Ottoman Empire) to study the local dialect and compare it with the East Cretan dialect he had learned at Palaikastro, and he continued to work on modern Greek dialects throughout his years at the School. While touring the Dodecanese and the Cyclades with A.J.B. Wace in 1906 and 1907, he amassed a rich collection of Greek embroider-

---

1. 'It has sometimes occurred to me that the more important actions of my life have been to all appearances directed by the merest chances' (Dawkins 1938, 21). Dawkins 1938 and Dawkins 1950 are his two typed autobiographical accounts.
2. Dawkins 1938, 5.

---

3. Dawkins 1950, VII, 19.
4. For an instance of Dawkins's success in dealing with restive Cretan workmen at Palaikastro in 1905, see Hood 2000, 211.

Fig.5.1: Dawkins and the Abbot of St Barlaam, Meteora, 1903; BSA Photographic Archive: BSAA1–58.

ies, some of which are now proudly displayed at the Victoria and Albert Museum in London. While he was at the British School, Dawkins travelled to Mani, Yannina, Thessaly, Mount Athos, Constantinople and many parts of Asia Minor and Italy (including the Greek colonies in Calabria and the Terra d'Otranto), as well as Albania, Dalmatia, Egypt, Syria and Palestine; he also reckoned to have visited all the Greek islands except Chalki.

In 1906 Dawkins succeeded Bosanquet as Director of the British School, a post he held till his resignation in the summer of 1914. As well as Palaikastro and other sites in Crete, he directed the important excavation of the shrine of Artemis Orthia at Sparta (1906–10). But in 1907 providence struck again: his relative John Doyle, a fellow of All Souls College, Oxford, died, leaving him a substantial legacy that derived from Sir John Easthope, Dawkins's great-grandfather, a member of parliament, railway magnate and proprietor of the *Morning Chronicle* newspaper. This legacy included a property called Plas Dulas near Colwyn Bay in North Wales, which at that time was sufficiently grand — but has since become sufficiently dilapidated — to feature in a recent BBC programme.[5] The receipt of this legacy enabled Dawkins to resign from the British School without

a thought for his personal future, save to devote himself to the study of modern Greek dialects, particularly those of Pontos (north-east Turkey). The next stage of his life was once again decreed by chance. No sooner had he left the School and begun his researches in Turkey than the First World War broke out, and he was forced to return to Athens. After a few months in Wales and a spell back in Athens, where he worked with F.W. Hasluck as a cipher expert in the Intelligence Department of the British Legation and carried out dialect research in the archives of the Historical Dictionary of the Greek Language in 1915–16, Dawkins was commissioned as a lieutenant in the Royal Naval Voluntary Reserve and sent to Crete, where he spent the rest of the War travelling all over the island from his base on the depot ship HMS Pelorus in Suda Bay and gathering not only intelligence about the political leanings of the local people but also a wealth of linguistic and ethnographic material.

Dawkins kept voluminous notes in Crete, from the time he first worked there in the winter of 1902–03 to the period of his service with the RNVR in 1916–19. In 1918–19 he was preparing to put together a book about Crete in the crucial period before and after its incorporation into the Greek state, when the population still consisted of a mixture of Christians and Muslims. This book was never completed. Dawkins describes the content of his 'Cretan book' in a letter to Hasluck as follows:

> I find my material includes an account with sketch plans of nearly every monastery in Crete with the local accounts of the foundation and copies of the inscriptions which date the buildings; Descriptions of roads and the scenery and remarkable objects passed by them; A good deal of folklore and local traditions of the Politis kind;[6] Notes on animals plants trees and ideas connected with them; Notes on the different kinds of houses with sketches of the plans of older Venetian houses; Note on Venetian remains. Notes on churches (all of which as far as it is Vene-

---

5. For details see the web page http://www.bbc.co.uk/wales/just-thejob/followyourdream/time/h_getstarted.shtml

6. Dawkins is referring to Politis 1904.

tian will be in Gerola[7]). Notes on trades and handicrafts etc. A fine mixed bag.[8]

Later he refers to the layout of the projected book as

my Cretan notes which are now nearly all typewritten and arranged according to area which will be how I shall write it finally. There will be little bits in which a real journey will be described, but for the most part it will be a mosaic of many journeys presented as such.[9]

While he was still in Crete in 1917–19 Dawkins was already writing to Hasluck about the new posts in Byzantine and Modern Greek that were being set up at King's College, London, and the University of Oxford. He rejected the idea of the Koraes Chair at King's out of hand, but frequently expressed interest in the Bywater and Sotheby Professorship of Byzantine and Modern Greek Language and Literature at Oxford — though he often said he would have far preferred to teach at Cambridge.[10] A few months after he returned to England to be demobilized in April 1919 with no clear idea whether or how he should take up some useful occupation, he successfully applied for the chair at Oxford, a post he held from the beginning of 1920 until

his retirement in 1939. The story of Dawkins's Oxford period, which lasted for 35 years until his death in 1955, falls outside the limits of this paper. From now on I want to concentrate on his activities while he was at the British School and on the legacy of these activities in his later career.

I have a feeling that Dawkins was a somewhat reluctant archaeologist. If this is so, it is all the more remarkable that he should have directed excavations that have proved so significant for the understanding of both prehistoric Cretan civilization and the culture of ancient Sparta. He has recently been hailed, together with Arthur Evans and others, as one of the discoverers of Cretan Bronze Age civilization.[11] Despite Dawkins's deep interest in and knowledge of geology and botany, he was more interested in language and literature than in material culture — though this did not stop him, while he was in Crete and elsewhere, from recording details of churches, monasteries, ovens, water-mills, beehives, looms, olive-oil presses, wells, bells and *simandra*. As far as archaeology is concerned, he was more taken by the prehistoric than by the Classical. Classical archaeology did not engage his interest, he wrote, since the Classical Greeks themselves had told us in writing how they lived, thought and felt.[12] What interested him in archaeology was its anthropological and ethnographic aspect: the attempt to reconstruct the way of life, the belief system, the thought-world and the mentality of the people whose material remains were being examined. Even though much of the sanctuary of Artemis Orthia dates to the Hellenistic and Roman periods, it especially interested Dawkins — as it did the contemporary Greek poet Angelos Sikelianos — both because the Spartans had left little in the way of literary remains and because the rituals that had been practised at the sanctuary were based on traditions stretching back into prehistoric times. None the less, after the completion of the Sparta dig, the activities of the School in terms of excavations seem to have hit a lull from 1911 onwards, for whatever reason — perhaps not only because of the political situation in the Balkans. Dawkins was granted

---

7. Dawkins means Gerola 1905–32.

8. Dawkins to Hasluck, 18 March 1919, p. 1. Dawkins's letters to Hasluck are in the Dawkins Archive, deposited in the Taylor Institution Library, shelfmark f.Arch.Z.Dawk.15. He eventually abandoned his plan to write the Cretan book, but the typescript drafts of sections of it, with pencilled annotations by John Pendlebury and additions by Dawkins based on information provided by Patrick Leigh Fermor, are also deposited in the Taylor Institution Library (f.Arch.Z.Dawk.12). While in Crete, Dawkins also took a lot of photographs, not only of monuments but also of street scenes, which are likewise preserved in his archive.

9. Dawkins to Hasluck, 20 Nov. 1919, pp. 3–4.

10. In Dawkins's first reference to these posts in his extant letters to Hasluck he writes, 'I do hope I get that Oxford job: it would do me so very proud', and he even plans the topic of his inaugural lecture (Dawkins to Hasluck, 3 Oct. 1917, p. 4). Dawkins explains his rejection of the King's post by the fact that 'evening classes, college meetings are to be an important part of the work, and most awful of all the professor or the reader but probably both must keep in touch with the Greek community in London and then there is the Anglo hell league [Anglo-Hellenic League] and as a principal ramping Ronald [Burrows] a great light of the same league; so altogether thanking God for my private means I think no thank you' (Dawkins to Hasluck, 20 Aug. 1918, p. 1). After this, his references to the Oxford chair are frequent.

11. Whitley, in Calligas and Whitley 2005, 109.

12. Dawkins 1950, X, 1–2.

a year's leave of absence for the period 1911–12. Until this point his unmarried sister Annie had been keeping house for him in Athens, but she then became ill and decided to move back to Britain. Dawkins's leave of absence was probably intended to enable him to help his sister settle into the house in Wales and to get on with his own research and writing. But this situation may have been related to Dawkins's realization by 1914 that his time as director was up; much later he simply wrote that he had resigned because 'I began to feel that I had been long enough away from England'[13] — an ironic statement in view of the fact that he spent most of the next five years in Greece.

Like Hasluck, and unlike many British classicists who visited Greece at that time, Dawkins seems not to have approached the modern Greeks with strong preconceptions or with some kind of agenda. For this reason, he did not experience any disillusionment with contemporary Greece, as Arnold Toynbee notoriously did. On the contrary, the medieval and modern Greek world seems to have been an altogether pleasant surprise for Dawkins, who remained fascinated by a culture whose existence he seems not to have previously suspected — and which has now largely disappeared, save for the traces recorded by scholars such as he.

Dawkins showed no interest at all in Greek politics and very little in contemporary Greek literature, C.P. Cavafy being a significant exception.[14] He seems not to have been personally acquainted with members of Greece's political and literary classes, although he maintained good relations with a few academic colleagues. Even while he was based at the British School, Dawkins always seems to have been in a hurry to escape from Athens, and indeed from continental Greece as a whole, preferring to head for the more eastern parts of the Greek-speaking world, many of which lay beyond the frontiers of the modern Greek state. As I have written elsewhere, he was more attracted by the Greece of Herodotus, with its Oriental legends, than by the more rationalist Greece of Thucydides.[15] Moreover, Dawkins

realized that in order to know Greece — past as well as present — it was not sufficient to dig below the surface of the earth; it was also useful and interesting to dig beneath the surface of modern life by studying the language and lore of the contemporary rural inhabitants. Yet, as we shall see, his search for remains of the past in the present had little to do with naïve survivalism.

The monumental volume *Modern Greek in Asia Minor* (1916) has been said to be Dawkins's most significant work. It is the fruit of his three visits to Cappadocia in the summers of 1909, 1910 and 1911. As I have written in an earlier article, Dawkins decided to carry out his fieldwork just at the right time, since working on Greek dialects in Turkey would have become problematic (to say the least) once the Balkan Wars began in 1912. After ten years of almost continuous war in the region, the Christian inhabitants of Cappadocia were expelled to Greece under the terms of the Lausanne Treaty of 1923. In their new home these displaced people were less successful than the Pontians in preserving their language and culture and in establishing it in the consciousness of other Greeks. In fact, the Cappadocian dialects of Greek were reported to have died out in the 1960s. However, the contemporary relevance of Dawkins's work on Cappadocian Greek became evident in 2005, when Mark Janse of the Roosevelt Academy in Holland and Dimitris Papazachariou of the University of Patras discovered people still speaking the Misti variety of Cappadocian in Larisa and near Kavala. Their discovery was prompted by linguistic studies of Cappadocian that Janse had been publishing on the basis of material contained in Dawkins's book.[16]

After his Cappadocian project, Dawkins decided to carry out a similar study of the Greek dialects spoken in Pontos, beginning in the summer of 1914. He had been in Pontos for little more than a month when he was forced to abandon his project by the outbreak of the First World War. 'When I was caught by the outbreak of the war in 1914,' he later reminisced, 'I was beginning what I hoped to be a series of visits to Pontos for the purpose of a similar book [to his Cappadocian one] on Pontic; it has always been a deep regret to me that

---

13. Dawkins 1950, VIII, 15.

14. A paper by Dawkins on Cavafy delivered at Exeter College, Oxford, in 1939 is preserved in the Dawkins Archive and was published as Dawkins 1990.

15. Mackridge 1990, 207.

---

16. For this information I am indebted to a lecture given by Mark Janse at the Classics Centre, University of Oxford, on 26 May 2006.

this was made impossible.'[17] Nevertheless, in this single month in 1914 Dawkins was able to collect no fewer than sixty-six folk-tales and other material useful for the study of the dialect.[18] Dawkins was one of the few — and one of the last — scholars to carry out fieldwork on the language and folklore of the Greek-speaking Christians of Pontos before they were expelled from their homeland as a result of the Treaty of Lausanne. At his home in Wales in 1919 he carried out some work on what he called his 'Pontic book', which was to consist of a grammar and vocabulary together with folk-tale texts. Sadly, he had to abandon it in order to prepare his lectures for his Oxford job; yet at the time he was planning to get it published 'inside the next three years'.[19]

His work on modern Greek dialects led to a number of publications over the following two decades or so, culminating in a general survey of the dialects in the form of an important article published in 1940. Here he took the view, first proposed by Albert Thumb and espoused by Manolis Triantaphyllides and later by Nicolaos Contossopoulos, that the most fundamental division within the modern Greek dialects is between east and west — the opposite of the north-south division proposed earlier by G.N. Hatzidakis.[20] I believe Dawkins is right in this. In another article, on the language of the Cypriot chronicle of Machairas, he writes:

> there was in the middle ages a western popular Greek as well as an eastern; [...] the former forms the base of the general common Greek of to-day, and had a progressive tendency very likely due to the great influx of strangers into the Greek mainland, whilst the eastern Greek of mediaeval times has retained more of its old character, perhaps again due to the greater purity of Greek blood in the east.[21]

By 'the great influx of strangers' Dawkins is clearly alluding to the controversial question of the influence

Fig.5.2: Dawkins and Webster on top of Pentelicus, 1903; BSA Photographic Archive: BSAA1–31.

exerted on Greek language and culture by the Slav invasions of the Greek mainland around the seventh century A.D. and by the later Albanian settlements. Medieval Greek texts show that there was a common medieval written vernacular in which it is usually impossible to detect regional features. With the help of his researches on the eastern dialects of Cappadocia, Pontos and Cyprus, Dawkins tried to penetrate beyond the texts in order to investigate what might have been the actual spoken language in various parts of the Greek-speaking world in the Middle Ages.

The first two decades of the twentieth century were the heyday of the School's contribution to ethnographic and medieval studies. Of his years as Director, Dawkins writes:

---

17. Dawkins 1938, 31.

18. For further details of the Pontic stories collected by Dawkins see Mackridge 1990–1, 107–22.

19. Dawkins to Hasluck, 2 Jan. 1920, p. 2.

20. Dawkins 1940, 1–38. For more details of Dawkins's contribution to the study of Greek dialects see Mackridge 1990.

21. Dawkins 1925–30, 320–1.

Fig.5.3: Peasants on the road to Eleusis; BSA Photographic Archive: BSAA1–22.

I always seemed to have an abundance of leisure to do very much what I wanted to do, whereas my predecessors and my successors seemed always to be much more fully occupied and often overworked. I think that was due to the very high quality of the students in my time. Most of them in fact were men who struck out each his own line and to attempt any kind of guidance would have been absurd.[22]

While at the School, Dawkins was perfectly capable of getting on with his dialectological studies on his own. But in other fields of study he was very much influenced by some of the colleagues and students that he met there. Among these were A.J.B. Wace and M.S. Thompson, whose researches into the life, language, customs and lore of the Vlachs of the northern Pindus began while they were looking for inscriptions and other antiquities in southern Thessaly in the winter of 1909–10 — shortly before the Balkan Wars resulted in the placing of new national boundaries that put an end to the traditional life of many of these transhumant shepherds.[23] In addition, Wace provided Dawkins with much modern Greek dialect material, especially from areas that he himself had not visited, while the archaeological survey of Cyprus that Dawkins and Thompson carried out in the winter of 1908–09 enabled him to gain an intimate knowledge of that island, which bore fruit in 1932 in his monumental edition of the fifteenth-century Cypriot *Chronicle* of Machairas.[24] Already in January 1918 Dawkins was writing to Hasluck about his desire to translate Machairas and the need for a new edition of this work, about which he says, 'I have seldom seen a book which delighted me more'.[25] By the

22. Dawkins 1950, VIII, 16.

23. These researches culminated in Wace and Thompson 1914.
24. Makhairas 1932.
25. Dawkins to Hasluck, 22 Jan. 1918, p.2.

time he left Crete in the spring of 1919 he had already translated half of Machairas.[26]

Dawkins's interest in Machairas' *Chronicle* was prompted less by its value as a source of historical facts than as a source for linguistic information, for the legends and the popular story-telling techniques used by the author, and for the insights provided by the text into the collective mentality of the Cypriots under Lusignan rule. For Dawkins, as I have written elsewhere, living legend was

> the organic and constantly developing mediation between past and present, a reflection of what people think and believe in the present about the past, and as such a kind of knowledge about the past, different from the knowledge contained in historical documents, but equally valid and valuable.[27]

Hasluck was chief among the scholars Dawkins befriended at the School, and it was Hasluck that awakened his interest in Balkan and Anatolian folklore and popular religion. We can only imagine the conversations between Dawkins and Hasluck during their years together at the school, but their continuation is conveniently provided in the form of the letters they exchanged between Dawkins's departure from the School in 1914 and Hasluck's tragic death from consumption in 1920. 'I must count this correspondence,' Dawkins reminisced thirty years later, 'and our close though always very limited friendship as one of the most profitable to my mental development that has ever come my way.'[28] Hasluck's encyclopaedic knowledge of and sensitive insight into Greek and Turkish culture and of popular Christianity and Islam in the Balkans and Asia Minor complemented Dawkins's knowledge of the Greek language in all its historical stages and his interest in medieval popular religion in the West. As Dawkins wrote in his unpublished memoir,

> Hasluck's knowledge of the mentality of the people about whose beliefs he was writing [i.e. in his articles, his letters to Dawkins and in his projected books] showed me that no

study of savages and still less of prehistoric peoples can ever lead to results as solid as can a study of people nearer to ourselves with whom we can come into personal contact.[29]

In this passage we can clearly discern Dawkins's view, aided by hindsight, of prehistoric archaeology and of anthropology as they tended to be practised during his lifetime. Both the study of prehistoric peoples and the study of modern peoples who are geographically and culturally remote from ourselves seemed to him to be less satisfying and less worthwhile than the study of peoples with whom one could feel one had much in common and with whom one could communicate on a more equal level. The information such people provided about themselves could also be interpreted by the scholar in terms that they themselves would understand. Such an attitude, shared by both Hasluck and Dawkins, adumbrates later developments in the human sciences, such as the historical study of collective mentalities by the *Annales* School and the anthropological studies of Mediterranean cultures pioneered by John Campbell and others.

All this is connected with the redirection of Dawkins's endeavours from philology to folklore, though he never abandoned his first love. When he carried out his fieldwork on the Greek dialects of Cappadocia in the summers of 1909, 1910 and 1911, one of his chief methods was to establish a corpus of oral narratives that he could then analyse linguistically in order to establish the grammar and vocabulary of each dialect. Just as Yannis Psycharis and his pupil Hubert Pernot had already done in Chios, Dawkins collected stories for linguistic purposes.[30] (It is characteristic of Dawkins that, despite his background in electrical engineering, he did not follow Pernot's example by recording Greek dialects with the aid of a phonograph.) These linguists chose to record folk-tales because they were likely to contain more traditional linguistic features and a wider range of vocabulary and structure than were to be found in everyday conversation — and precisely because they did *not* involve the dialogue between scholar and

---

26. Dawkins to Hasluck, 26 March 1919, p.5.
27. Mackridge 2000, 192.
28. Dawkins 1950, IX, 8.

29. Dawkins 1950, IX, 7.
30. Similarly, the Danish philologist Jean Pio, the first person to publish a collection of Greek folk-tales in Greek in 1879, did so for linguistic reasons (Olsen 2006, 50–1).

informant that is the procedure preferred in more recent linguistic fieldwork.

As Dawkins writes in his memoir, he was at the time so uninterested in the content of the folk-tales he collected in Cappadocia that he got his younger colleague W.R. Halliday (a student at the School, who accompanied him on his third field trip) to write an account of it for the publication of the material in *Modern Greek in Asia Minor*.[31] He later planned to get Halliday to contribute a similar chapter to his 'Pontic book'.[32] Much earlier, while in Palaikastro in 1904, Dawkins had written down 953 *mantinades* which were recited to him by a couple of local men during the course of three evenings, but he seems to have been interested in them purely as material for linguistic study rather than in terms of their content and their social context.[33] In this way he came to amass considerable knowledge of folklore 'partly insensibly', as he put it himself.[34] While in Crete, he collected oral narratives, but these were accounts relating to the history of the previous hundred years, with no connection to folk-tales.[35] It was only later that he came to see that the oral narratives he had collected in Cappadocia were of interest as folktales, which could be analysed in terms of their structure, their style and their motifs; these in turn could be compared and contrasted with folk-tales from other cultures and could thence offer an insight into the collective thought-world of the people who told them.

Unlike N.G. Politis, the pioneer of folklore studies in Greece and one of the leading proponents of Greek cultural nationalism, Dawkins was not so much interested in tracing modern Greek folklore back to ancient Greek mythology as he was in comparing it with the folk traditions of other contemporary cultures. This was perhaps another of Hasluck's legacies, survivalism being one of the many errors and falsehoods that Dawkins's friend subjected to ruthless but gleeful rationalist scrutiny.[36] Neither Hasluck nor Dawkins approved of the book entitled *Modern Greek Folklore and Ancient Greek Religion: a Study in Survivals* by another former student at the British School, J.C. Lawson.[37] This may be one of the reasons why Dawkins is only mentioned on a single page (and then not by name) of Lawson's entertaining account of skulduggery and derring-do in Crete during the First World War (which included assisting Venizelos' revolution in 1916), even though the two men worked together in the Intelligence branch of the RNVR.[38]

Dawkins believed in the unity of medieval and modern Greek culture rather than in the continuity of Greek culture from antiquity to the present day.[39] This is why the phrase 'Medieval and Modern Greek' is appropriate not only as the title of the collection of articles by the linguist G.N. Hatzidakis,[40] but also as the title of the subject taught for the Final Honour School in Medieval and Modern Languages at Oxford.

In 1919 Dawkins claimed that Greek folktales belong to the Balkan rather than the Turkish family, while Hasluck argued that they are 'oriental' (i.e. related to Persian and Arabic).[41] Later, however, Dawkins main-

---

31. Dawkins 1950, XI, 3–4. Halliday's contribution to *Modern Greek in Asia Minor* is chapter III, 'The subject-matter of the folk-tales' (pp. 215–83), a comparative study containing references to Near Eastern and Oriental folklore. Before this, Halliday (1886–1966) had published the book *Greek Divination: a Study of its Principles* (1913) as well as some articles on folklore in Greece and Asia Minor. He went on to become one of the leading British folklorists, combining the study of ancient and modern culture.

32. Dawkins to Hasluck, 3 Aug. 1919. Halliday spent some time working with Dawkins in Crete during the First World War.

33. These texts are to be found in the Dawkins Archive, Arch.Z.Dawk.7(1).

34. Dawkins 1950, X, 12.

35. See Dawkins 1919–20 for some of these narratives of oral history.

36. For Hasluck's antipathy towards survivalism see, e.g., Hasluck 1926, 13, 14. This volume consists of the letters Hasluck wrote to Dawkins. Halliday too wrote that 'it cannot be too strongly insisted that there is no special connexion at all between ancient mythology and modern Greek folk-tales. […] That close and peculiar connexion between modern Greek folk-lore and ancient Greek mythology […] is in reality an article of faith rather than a matter of fact' (Halliday, in Dawkins 1916, 216–7).

37. Lawson 1910.

38. See Lawson 1920, 154. I am indebted to Clogg 2000, 31, for introducing me to this book. Dawkins describes Lawson 1910 as 'not a good book' (Dawkins to Hasluck, 3 June 1919, p.3) and writes that Lawson 'has not an imaginative mind. It is odd that such an unsuitable person got hold of such a subject' (Dawkins to Hasluck, 2 Feb. 1919, p.1).

39. Mackridge 2000, 195.

40. Hatzidakis 1905–7.

41. Halliday had argued that Greek folk-tales belong to the Turkish family (Halliday, in Dawkins 1916, 219). For Dawkins's disagreement with Halliday see Hasluck 1926, 229, and Dawkins to Hasluck, 9 Nov. 1919.

tained that Greek folktales have many common features with those from Armenia, the Caucasus, Persia and even India.[42] It is probable that Hasluck influenced this apparent change of view.

Dawkins devoted the last twenty-five years of his life to the edition, translation, annotation and codification of Greek folk-tales. Since Birgit Olsen has recently written about this aspect of Dawkins's work, I need not say much here on this topic.[43] Nevertheless, I cannot resist making some remarks that connect his work on folk-tales with other aspects of his career.

The American folklorist Robert Georges described Dawkins as 'one of the giants of folk-tale studies of this century'.[44] In her recent book on Greek folktales, Chrysoula Chatzitaki-Kapsomenou writes that 'Dawkins's research into the Greek folk-tale remains unsurpassed today and undoubtedly represents a high point in Greek folklore studies.' She adds that it was Dawkins that 'raised the study of the Greek folk-tale to a science'.[45] The same writer praises Dawkins for avoiding speculation about the origins of folk-tales in earlier ages and for concentrating instead on their meaning for the community that tells them, arguing that a community sheds features of folk-tales that no longer correspond with its thought-world. Greek folklorists of his time, inspired by nationalist ideology, tended not only to trace the origins of folk-tales in ancient culture, but also to present the tales as being panhellenic, ignoring regional differences. By contrast, not only did Dawkins avoid survivalism, but he concentrated on tales from particular regions[46] and tried to find specifically regional patterns in them. Here we can trace the influence of his work on dialects and embroideries, in which one of the paramount aims is to define the synchronic semeiotic system that is inherent in the local particularity.

Fig.5.4: Dawkins, chapel on top of Mt Stroumboulas, Crete, Jan. 1903; BSA Photographic Archive: BSAA3–4.

The British School was, in the Cavafian sense, Dawkins's Ithaca, in that it 'gave him the lovely journey' to Greece. During the course of this long journey, like Cavafy's Odysseus, Dawkins visited harbours, Phoenician emporia and Egyptian cities, where he enjoyed many adventures and gathered varied knowledge from the uneducated folk of Greek and Turkish islands and villages. After he had lingered there for twelve years, the School 'had no more to give him'. Yet the wealth of information, knowledge, insight and wisdom that he gained during those years from his travels, from his researches and from his contacts with his colleagues provided him with enough material and inspiration to last him for the rest of his scholarly career.

I will close with the following words that Dawkins wrote to Hasluck in 1919:

> I don't believe that I shall ever have better years than those I spent at the school when you and your Missis kept house with me, or perhaps I should say with gratitude to her, kept house for me.[47]

42. Dawkins 1953, v.

43. Olsen 2004 and 2006.

44. Georges 1965, 202–12.

45. Chatzitaki-Kapsomenou 2002. The author devotes pp. 140–6 to a survey of Dawkins's work on Greek folk-tales and pp. 146–62 to what Dawkins's studies left out.

46. Chatzitaki-Kapsomenou 2002, 142.

47. Dawkins to Hasluck, 14 Feb. 1919. Dawkins was lodging with the Haslucks after his return from Wales in 1912, while Hasluck was Acting Director and living with his wife Margaret in the Director's lodgings. At that time, living with one's spouse in the British School was a privilege normally granted only to the Director.

REFERENCES

MANUSCRIPTS

Dawkins, R.M., 1938. 'The story up to 1938'. Unpublished typescript, Dawkins Archive, Slavonic and Greek Section, Taylor Institution Library, University of Oxford, shelfmark f.Arch.Z.Dawk.6(2).

Dawkins, R.M., 1950. 'What happened to me'. Unpublished typescript, Dawkins Archive, Slavonic and Greek Section, Taylor Institution Library, University of Oxford, shelfmark f.Arch.Z.Dawk.6(3).

PUBLICATIONS

Calligas, E. and Whitley, J. (eds), 2005. *On Site: British Archaeologists in Greece*. Athens.

Chatzitaki-Kapsomenou, C., 2002. *Το νεοελληνικό λαϊκό παραμύθι*. Thessaloniki.

Clogg, R., 2000. *Anglo-Greek Attitudes: Studies in History*. Basingstoke.

Dawkins, R.M., 1916. *Modern Greek in Asia Minor*. Cambridge.

—, 1919–20. 'Some stories from Crete', *Emmanuel College Magazine* 22.1: 12–21.

—, 1925–30. 'The vocabulary of the mediaeval Cypriot Chronicle of Leontios Makhairas', *Transactions of the Philological Society*: 300–30.

—, 1940. 'The dialects of Modern Greek', *Transactions of the Philological Society*: 1–38.

—, 1953. *Modern Greek Folktales*. Oxford.

—, 1990. 'The poems of Constantine Petrou Cavafi (1863–1933)', *Μολυβδο-κονδυλο-πελεκητής* 2: 7–26.

Georges, R.A., 1965. 'Richard M. Dawkins: a commemorative essay on the tenth anniversary of his death', *Folklore* 76: 202–12.

Gerola, G., 1905–32. *Monumenti veneti nell'isola di Creta*. Venice.

Hasluck, F.W., 1926. *Letters on Religion and Folklore*. London.

Hatzidakis, G.N., 1905–7. *Μεσαιωνικά και νέα ελληνικά*. Athens.

Hood, R. and Hood, S., 2000. 'Artists and craftsmen', in D. Huxley (ed.), *Cretan Quests: British Explorers, Excavators and Historians*: 208–19. London.

Lawson, J.C., 1910. *Modern Greek Folklore and Ancient Greek Religion: a Study in Survivals*. Cambridge.

—, 1920. *Tales of Aegean Intrigue*. London.

Mackridge, P., 1990. '"Some pamphlets on dead Greek dialects": R.M. Dawkins and modern Greek dialectology', *BSA* 85: 201–12.

—, 1990/91. 'Unpublished Pontic stories collected by R.M. Dawkins', *Δελτίο Κέντρου Μικρασιατικών Σπουδών* 8: 107–22.

—, 2000. 'R.M. Dawkins and Byzantium', in R. Cormack and E. Jeffreys (eds), *Through the Looking Glass: Byzantium through British Eyes*: 185–95. Aldershot.

Makhairas, L., 1932. *Recital concerning the sweet land of Cyprus, entitled 'Chronicle'*, (ed. and trans. R.M. Dawkins). Oxford.

Olsen, B., 2004. 'R.M. Dawkins and Greece', in D. Shankland (ed.), *Anthropology and Heritage in the Balkans and Anatolia: the Life and Times of F.W. Hasluck, 1878–1920*: 105–20. Istanbul.

—, 2006. 'Richard M. Dawkins: a pioneer in the field of Modern Greek folk-tales', *Κάμπος: Cambridge Papers in Modern Greek* 14: 47–64.

Politis, N.G., 1904. *Μελέται περί του βίου και της γλώσσης του ελληνικού λαού. Παραδόσεις*. Athens.

Wace, A.J.B. and Thompson, M.S., 1914. *The Nomads of the Balkans: an Account of Life and Customs among the Vlachs of Northern Pindus*. London.

6

R.M. Dawkins, F.W. Hasluck and the 'Crypto-Christians' of Trebizond

Anthony Bryer

The classic dilemma was faced by Naaman the Syrian who converted to the God of Israel and asked Elisha what to do when his master took him to worship Baal in the House of Rimmon. He was told to 'Go in peace' (2 *Kings v*, 19). When in 1338 the citizens of Ottoman Nicaea put the same question to patriarch John XIV Kalekas, they were told that 'As many as wish to live in secret practising and keeping in their heart the Christian way, because of fear of punishment against them, shall also attain salvation'.[1] The patriarch was more explicit than the prophet, but now asked for trouble, for reversion from Islam meant death until the *Tanzimat* reforms which began in 1839. One of the last neo-martyrs was St George of Ioannina in 1838.[2] Under various terms the civil mark of a Muslim was military service, and a head tax defined a Christian. Christians lost their daughters, language and faith to Islam, not necessarily in that order. There were anomalies. After the Ottoman conquest of Cyprus in 1571, the Orthodox replaced the Roman as the established church. What happened to the papists? Are the descendants of the Lusignans to be found either among Turkish Cypriots, or what they called the *linovamvakoi* ('linen-cotton' '*meso-meso*')? More significantly, why did such 'crypto-Christians' survive after 1878 when (as in the Pontos) their limbo was no longer necessary?[3]

Political definitions divide cultural spheres, particularly in the Pontos. Here the Akampsis (Çoruh) river has separated Byzantine and Ottoman Anatolia from the Caucasus since the sixth century, leaving some identities by language stranded on the west bank. Interest taken in them by outsiders, amid contemporary concepts of nationalism, has not been wholly welcome

Fig.6.1: Dawkins and local boy; BSA Photographic Archive: BSAA4–43.

in modern Turkey. The Armenian-speaking Hemshinli have only recently resurfaced in scholarly discussion.[4] Since Procopius, the Georgian-speaking Laz have been more numerous and better known.[5] But from the 1960s Wolfgang Feuerstein of Germany started giving the Laz an alphabet, textbooks and written language. By 1992 there were Laz posters in Istanbul pastry-shops and Mingrelian *natashas* crossed the Akampsis border expecting a welcome from their lost cousins in Trebi-

---

1. Bryer 1983, 13; Photiades 2001, 66.
2. Vaporis 2000, 352-7.
3. Michell 1908.

4. Simonian 2007.
5. For example Dumézil 1967.

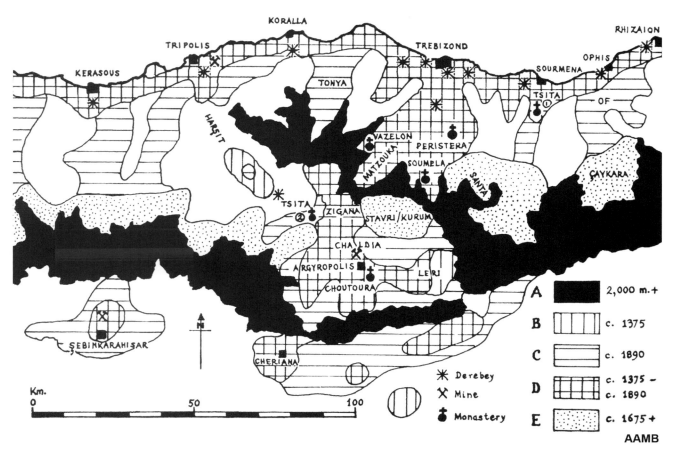

Map.6.1: Key to Pontic Greek-speaking areas.

A Summer Pastures over 2,000 m.
B c.1375
C c.1890
D c.1375–1890
E from c.1675

zond.[6] This was not wholly reciprocated. Ömer Asan, born in 1961 in Ophis (Of), was curious about the Pontic Greek spoken there, but his account of a Pontic culture has had a mixed reception in Turkey.[7] The common feature of these examples is that those whose spoken language is not standard Turkish try harder, mostly as Sunni Muslims. A happy explanation in Ophis was that Oflus had converted with the prophet in seventh-century Mecca, had returned home to wait as crypto-proto-Muslims, until Alexander bishop of Ophis became Iskender *pasha* and took his flock over to Islam in the seventeenth century. None of this is corroborated in Ottoman registers which show a gentler rate of conversion, leaving numbers of Muslim Pontic Greek speakers in Turkey in 1923 at the exchange of populations, where they stayed at home with the Pontic Hemshinli and Laz.[8] (MAP 6.1)

Pontic Greeks who left Turkey in 1923 are somehow still 'returning', but sometimes to New Soumela in Greece, by way of Samarkand or Canberra. They are pursued by a new school of anthropologists, led most recently by Eftihia Voutira.[9]

It depends on what you are looking for. R.M. Dawkins (1871–1955) was the only scholar from the British School at Athens who visited Pontic Greek

---

6. Ascherson 1995, 203-9.

7. Asan 2000.

8. Umur 1951; Bryer 1970, 30, map; Bryer and Winfield 1985, I, 323-4; Mackridge 1987, 115-9.

9. Voutira 2006.

speakers in the field, on the eve of the First World War, recording 66 folktales in Ophis, Sourmena, Santa and Imera (Stavri/Kurum) between 11 July and 14 August 1914.[10] When I first climbed into the Santa valley from Imera in 1967 I was told that 'This is Rum country: they spoke Christian', and that an Englishman 'like a goat' had come before the Russians in 1916. Peter Mackridge had more precise prey: he hunted down the ancient pre-verbal negative particle 'ou' in Sourmena. We are both grateful to Chrysostomos Savvides of Bradford, grandson of the headmaster of the then new central school at Sourmena/Tsita in 1914, where a new recording was planned in 1985, but the students opted for television — *Trabzonspor* is said to be in local Laz hands.[11]

F.W. Hasluck (1878–1920) did not visit Trebizond, but his posthumous article on its 'crypto-Christians' has much to answer for.[12] Some of Hasluck's wider related themes are now being re-explored by Michel Balivet.[13] Meanwhile Konstantinos Photiades of the Pontic diaspora in Greece has greatly expanded the study of its lost Christians.[14]

These scholars agree with Dawkins: that following the advice of patriarch John XIV Kalekas in 1338, the crypto-Christians had earnestly secreted their true faith, with complicated consequences of double names, festivals, even circumcisions and funerals. Dawkins found that in Stavri and Kurum they were 'most earnestly Christian. These people felt that they represented a remnant of the high civilisation of their country and that only by concealment could they be kept together'.[15] In Imera in 1914, he noted that Ottoman officials had only just arrived, but published an archontic house dated 1825, apparently equipped for both faiths. This is apparently the Phosteropoulos house, but I have only known its ruins since 1962. Who are we to question Dawkins of its dual functions of faith? I can only comment that it had the common *selamlik/haremlik*, public/private quarters of such a notable house. More

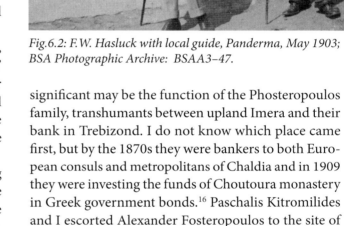

Fig.6.2: F.W. Hasluck with local guide, Panderma, May 1903; BSA Photographic Archive: BSAA3–47.

significant may be the function of the Phosteropoulos family, transhumants between upland Imera and their bank in Trebizond. I do not know which place came first, but by the 1870s they were bankers to both European consuls and metropolitans of Chaldia and in 1909 they were investing the funds of Choutoura monastery in Greek government bonds.[16] Paschalis Kitromilides and I escorted Alexander Fosteropoulos to the site of the bank in Trabzon in 1997. It was hardly a crypto-Christian affair: Fr Fosteropoulos is Orthodox chaplain to King's College London. Maybe we should look for a simply economic clue to the secrecy of some Pontic Christians.

I venture a more mundane thesis: that Pontic crypto-Christians only entered their twilight world after 1829, and were reluctant to re-emerge in the sunlight after 1856. This was to do with the silver-mining and smelting economy of Gűműşhane — which was only called Argyropolis by Athens-trained schoolmasters after 1846. The earliest Ottoman silver *akçes* were struck there at Tzanicha (Canca) from 1520, and the first mining agents were Armenian. But from 1654 to 1841, both the mining concessionaries (*archimetallourgoi*) and a new metropolis of Chaldia were in Greek hands, principally the dynasty of Phytianos — which

10. Dawkins 1931; Mackridge 1990/1991.

11. Bryer and others 2002, xvii; iv, 133-42.

12. Hasluck 1921.

13. Hasluck 1929; Balivet 1994, 100-3.

14. Fotiadis 1985; Photiades 2001.

15. Dawkins 1933, 274.

16. Bryer and others 2002, I, 269-83; IV, 142-51, 238-41.

was to provide miners and bishops all over Anatolia and the Caucasus, and a patriarch of Antioch. Ignatios Phytianos founded the cathedral of St George in Gŭmŭşhane in 1723.[17] Its codex of donors and much of its silver is now in the Benaki Museum, Athens. The handsome episcopal palace is dated 1749, where in 1829 the metropolitan of Chaldia welcomed count Paskevich-Erevansky and Russian invaders, who soon retreated, escorting a part of the local population. The scene was repeated in 1916, but the Russians left again by 1918. On 17 December 1919, colonel (Sir) Alfred Rawlinson of the British Army of the Black Sea, five men and a dog (George) met Lavrentios Papadopoulos, last metropolitan of Chaldia and All Metal-Bearing Lands. The colonel and the bishop seem to have been unaware that Mustapha Kemal had landed at Amisos (Samsun) on 19 May 1919 — now variously observed as Atatŭrk Memorial Youth and Sports Day in Turkey and Pontic Genocide Day in Greece. A consequence was that Rawlinson was incarcerated in Erzurum and Lavrentios ended up as metropolitan of Drama.[18]

The events of 1829 led to the treaty of Adrianople and the appointment of James Brant as first British consul in Trebizond in 1830. He and Robert Curzon were to be partly responsible for the long-negotiated Anglo-Persian trading treaty at Erzurum in 1843, by which time the summer road from Trebizond to Tabriz was busy.[19] Locally the real crux also came in 1829, when it was a question whether the silver mines of Chaldia or the charcoal for smelting from Imera (Stavri/Kurum) through which the summer road passed, would be exhausted first. Western travellers now monitored its route through the crypto-Christian areas. None of twenty-five whom I find to have left a record between 1796 and 1832 mention them. The first reference to Pontic crypto-Christians comes from an American missionary in 1833, followed by W.J. Hamilton in 1836 and two French travellers in 1840.[20]

In 1850 comes the first report of the reverse phenomenon, a crypto-Muslim in Trebizond, appropri-

ately in George Finlay's journals, deposited in the British School at Athens. Finlay

> engaged a man called Demetri as my guide & servant. He spoke a kind of Greek and was something as I found out afterwards neither Mussulman nor Christian called Krumledhes [i.e. from Kurum]. I asked one day as we were looking down on Trebizond … to point out to me the parish church. After wondering at his ignorance I asked him with some contempt if he was not a christian, to which he composedly replied "No! but my fathers were." Then what is your name pray? Omar was his plain reply. He then explained the whole mystery, telling me that as the[y] considered [him] not quite a Mussulman & he lived more with the christians than the Turks, he began to consider himself *almost a christian* & answered to the name of Demetri. I thought the conversation worth his wages.[21]

Things became clearer in 1856. Sultan Abdul Mecit neatly anticipated the Treaty of Paris of 30 March with the *Hatti-Hŭmayun* of 18 February, concluding the *Tanzimat* and granting freedom of religion. On 14 May 1856, Petros Savvas Sideropoulos of Kurum presented himself in Trebizond and lived to tell the tale. On 15 July 1857, the Kurumli crypto-Christians presented a petition to the pasha and western consuls (such as consul G.A. Stevens, who had looked after Finlay) in Trebizond on behalf of 55,755 inhabitants of 58 settlements, of whom 52% were claimed to be open Christians, 33% 'Kurumlis' and 17% Muslims;[22] Through Stevens the crypto-Christians appealed to Queen Victoria for protection, but no consul seems to have questioned the figures. The most intensive crypto-Christian areas had been economically dependent on silver-mining and (especially) charcoal burning for smelting. They also counted the fewest Muslims. For example, of the villages known to Dawkins in 1914, the settlements of Stavri had only ten Muslim households, Kurum six, Imera (of the Phosteropoulos family) two,

---

17. Bryer and others 2002, III, 324-50; IV, 151-76, 219-27.

18. Bryer and others 2002, xxi-xl.

19. Erkut and Mitchell 2007.

20. Smith 1833, II, 319-20; Hamilton 1842, 340; Flandin and Coste 1851, I, 38 as 'meso-meso'; actual travel dates naturally precede publication.

21. Hussey 1995, 289-91.

22. Bryer 1983, 35-41; Photiades 2001, 72-81.

Fig.6.3: Trebizond, St John the Theologian, subsequently Mum Hane Camii, finally (here) an Ottoman police station, in the northeast corner of the Lower city; BSA Photographic Archive: SPHS–2904.

and Santa none at all in 1857. Here the 330 open Christian households outnumbered the 285 secret Christian, while Tzanicha (Canca), the original Ottoman mine and mint of Gűműşhane, counted 50 households in 1857 — all crypto-Christian. Other smaller crypto-Christian elements are listed near alum mines to which the *archimetallourgoi* of Argyropolis turned after 1829, when their own silver failed. Neither Dawkins nor Hasluck asked why crypto-Christians were keeping their identity secret in places where there were so few declared Muslims.

The Orthodox church was more reluctant than the Ottoman state to recognise the situation after 1856. By 1863 its solution was to combine the monastic exarchates of Soumela, Vazelon and Peristereota into the final Orthodox Anatolian eparchy, misnamed Rhodopolis. Its cathedral of St George was built at Livera/Doubera where the winter and summer roads south of Trebizond divide in Matzouka/Maçka at the turnoff to Soumela. According to the petition of 1857 the 14,525 inhabitants of the new diocese were 53% open Christian, 37% secret Christian and 10% Muslim. Here, if their landlord was one of the three ruling abbots, one must ask from whom the crypto-Christians were keeping their identity secret.

In Trebizond consul G.A. Stevens was succeeded by his brother F.J. Stevens in 1859, who by 1867 had quite enough and was invalided. The crypto-Christians were arousing interest in London and Stevens was replaced from 1867 to 1873 by a new kind of consul, William Gifford Palgrave (1826–88), partly to report on them. Palgrave did not foresee that the opening of the Suez Canal in 1869 was to lead to the decline of the overland Trebizond route east and reduce the consulate to

Fig.6.4: Trebizond, east ravine, looking south, between St Eugenios (left) and citadel (right); BSA Photographic Archive: SPHS–2907.

a backwater. His despatches just missed Austen Henry Layard (1817–94), who left the desk of the Under-Secretary for Foreign Affairs in 1867. Layard would have been exceptionally qualified to assess them, for he had ridden through Kurum and the summer road in 1849, and reported no crypto-Christians — though he may have been distracted by other members of his party who included Muslims and Anglicans, a Catholic Syrian, an unspecified Armenian, a Yezidi divine and a Nestorian Christian agent, who was also to be known to Palgrave.[23] But Palgrave had his own connections. In England he was related to, or on dining terms with, more liberal academics and parliamentarians than was perhaps good for him.[24]

Palgrave was first to observe that Ottoman mining and smelting service in the Pontos was in lieu of mili-tary service, so Kurumlis carried arms as Muslims who were somehow excused the call-up, yet also somehow did not pay poll tax as Christians. After the decline of the mines after 1829, they clung to the best of both worlds. His *Report concerning the treatment of the Greek and other Christian subjects of the Sultan*, Trebizond, 17 April 1867, concludes: 'The complaints of the Christians, and especially of the Greeks, are unjust. They do not aim at equality, which they have already got, but at mastery'.[25] Privately he found 'the Kurumlis are apostates beneath contempt … simply the most disagreeable, quarrelsome, bigoted, narrow-minded set I have ever had to deal with'.[26] He proposed that they were descendants of Xenophon's Ten Thousand:

> The Greeks, plundering brigands that they were by their own avowal, I don't wonder

---

23. Layard 1853, 1-8.
24. Allen 1972, 205-20.

25. Bryer 1983, 67; Photiades 2001, 116.
26. Bryer 1983, 28.

that the 'natives' objected to their visit. Had they behaved like gentlemen, matters would doubtless have gone very differently.[27]

In Trebizond, Palgrave's own concern was a courtship doomed by distance with Clara Jekyll (later Lady Henley). In a letter to her (now in St Antony's College, Oxford), he wrote on 16 June 1867: 'There is an Eastern proverb: "He who changes his religion has none at all"'.[28] Palgrave's problem was that he had too many religions. In 1867 he was a professed Anglican but converted at least six times. Palgrave was otherwise Fr Sohail S.J., *alias* Selim abu Mahmud el Eys; his father was born Cohen. Palgrave's publications caught the Victorian imagination, but his own imagination colours his reports from Trebizond, which the Foreign Office, parliament and his biographer did not compare with the more workaday despatches of the Stevens brothers. A consequence was that recognition of the 'crypto-Christians' of Trebizond, under French pressure, was postponed until 1910, just before Dawkins met them.[29]

Things should be quieter now, after Rose Macaulay's visit to *The Towers of Trebizond*.[30] By 1969 I used to serve for Fr Tarsicio Succi OFM in Santa Maria Trapezuntis, the only church open in town.[31] My task was to distribute blessed water in Coca-Cola bottles to people in need at the back — not crypto-Christians or even Pontic Greek speakers, but simply coming with ailments and the understanding of local *imams,* to try anything once. But here on 5 February 2006, Fr Andrea Santoro was shot after mass by Oğuzhan Akdin, born in 1990 in Tonya. On 19 January 2007, the Turkish Armenian editor Hrant Dink was killed in Istanbul by Oğün Sumart, born in 1990 in Duzköy. The connection is that these teenage assassins were born within a mountainous six miles of each other and one (I do not know of the other) is Pontic Greek speaking. The region lies south-west of Trebizond and Matzouka. Byzantine documentary and archaeological evidence for the area

ends in 1384 and the first evidence of Çepni (Alevi) settlement begins in 1402, before the Ottoman conquest of 1461.[32] No crypto-Christian claim for it was made in 1857 and the Trabzon *salname* (provincial almanac) of 1869 made it one of two areas wholly Muslim, with no Christians at all — let alone silver miners or smelters. Yet numbers speak Pontic Greek, untouched by any schoolmaster. Some Tonyalis evidently try harder to be Turkish.

Travellers and scholars have a happier colleague in these parts. He is Ilyas Karagöz, born in Tonya in 1933. In Germany he read Fallmerayer and may be the only subscriber to the *Archeion Pontou* in the Pontos. His family moved from Tonya to Livera/Doubera in Matzouka/Maçka well after Gervasios Sarasites, last resident metropolitan of Rhodopolis, left. Papa Eftim I, 'patriarch' of the 'Turkish Orthodox Church' (1923–62), supposedly claimed the cathedral, now mosque of the village, but found no local support.[33] But this valley is home to Turkish scholars who refer to Dawkins for its language, such as Kudret Emiroğlu.[34] Ilyas Karagöz was more concerned when the watchtower above his library and village, recorded in the bull for Soumela of 1364 as warning to Turkmans, was dynamited by treasure seekers on 17 July 1993. It had been known to countless travellers and scholars and marks the birthplace of Maria of Doubera, stepmother of sultan Selim (1512–20) and a home of the Amoiroutzes family. People here know of scholarship, language and conversion.[35] Ilyas Karagöz sends me tea from Ophis and his own hazelnuts. I wish we could have shared them with Dawkins. But I recommend Ilyas's latest study of the region[36] to the BSA library — and have promised to send him the papers of this conference in exchange.

27. Bryer 1983, 28.
28. Bryer 1983, 28.
29. Janin 1912.
30. Macaulay 1956.
31. Succi 1973, 325.

32. Bryer and Winfield 1985, I, 160-4.
33. Sarasites 1935.
34. Emiroğlu 1989.
35. Frangedaki 1984/85.
36. Karagöz 2006.

REFERENCES

Allen, M., 1972. *Palgrave of Arabia. The Life of William Gifford Palgrave, 1826–88.* London.

Asan, Ő., 2000. *Pontos Kűltűrű.* Istanbul.

Ascherson, N., 1995. *Black Sea.* London.

Balivet, M., 1994. *Romanie Byantine et pays de Rûm Turc. Histoire d'un espace d'imbrication Gréco-Turque.* Istanbul.

Bryer, A., 1970. 'The *Tourkokratia* in the Pontos: some problems and preliminary conclusions', *Neo-Hellenika* I: 30–54.

—, 1983. 'The crypto-Christians of the Pontos and Consul William Gifford Palgrave of Trebizond', Δελτίο Κέντρου Μικρασιατικών Σπουδών 4: 13–68, 363–5.

— and Winfield, D., 1985. *The Byzantine Monuments and Topography of the Pontos* I–II. Washington D.C.

— and others, 2002. *The Post-Byzantine Monuments of the Pontos: A Source Book.* Aldershot.

Dawkins, R.M., 1931. 'Folk tales from Sourmena and the valley of Ophis', Αρχείον Πόντου 3: 79–122.

—, 1933. 'The Crypto-Christians of Turkey', *Byzantion* 8: 247–75.

Dumézil, G., 1967. *Documents Anatoliens* IV: *Récits Lazes en Dialecte d'Arhavi.* Paris.

Emiroğlu, K., 1989. *Trabzon-Maçka Etimoloji Sőzlűğű.* Ankara.

Erkut, G. and Mitchell, S. (eds), 2007. *The Black Sea: Past, Present and Future. Proceedings of the international, Interdisciplinary conference. Istanbul 2004.* London.

Flandin, E. and Coste, P., 1851. *Voyage en Perse.* Paris.

Fotiadis, K., 1985. *Die Islamisierung Kleinasiens und die Kryptochristen des Pontos.* Tübingen.

Frangedaki, A., 1984/85. 'On fifteenth-century Cryptochristianity: A letter to George Amoiroutzes from Michael Apostolis', *Byzantine and Modern Greek Studies* 9: 221–4.

Hamilton, W.J., 1842. *Researches in Asia Minor, Pontus, and Armenia.* London.

Hasluck, F.W., 1921. 'The Crypto-Christians of Trebizond', *Journal of Hellenic Studies* 41: 199–202.

—, 1929. *Christianity and Islam under the Sultans.* Oxford.

Hussey, J.M. (ed.), 1995. *The Journals and Letters of George Finlay.* I *The Journals.* London.

Janin, R., 1912. 'Musulmans malgré eux. Les Stavriotes', *Echos d'Orient* 13: 81–6; 15: 495–505.

Karagőz, I., 2006. *Trabzon Yer Adlari.* Trebizond.

Layard, A.H., 1853. *Discoveries in the ruins of Nineveh and Babylon; with travels in Armenia, Kurdistan and the Desert: being the result of a second expedition.* London.

Macaulay, R., 1956. *The Towers of Trebizond.* London.

Mackridge, P., 1987. 'Greek-speaking Moslems of north-east Turkey: prolegomena to a study of the Ophitic sub-dialect of Pontic', *Byzantine and Modern Greek Studies* 11: 115–37.

—, 1990/91. 'Unpublished Pontic stories collected by R.M. Dawkins', Δελτίο Κέντρου Μικρασιατικών Σπουδών 8: 107–22.

Michell, R.L.N., 1908. 'A Muslim-Christian sect in Cyprus', *The Nineteenth Century and After* 63: 751–62.

Photiades, K.E., 2001. Πηγές της Ιστορίας του Κρυπτοχριστιανικού Προβλήματος. Thessaloniki.

Sarasites, G., 1935. 'Επαρχία Ροδοπόλεως', Αρχείον Πόντου 6: 68–85.

Simonian, H.H. (ed.), 2007. *The Hemshin: History, Society and Identity in the Highlands of Northeast Turkey.* London.

Smith, E., 1833. *Researches of the Rev. E. Smith and the Rev. H.G.O. Dwight in Armenia.* Boston.

Succi, T., 1973. *Trebisonda. Porta d'Oriente.* Istanbul.

Umur, H., 1951. *Of Tarihi.* Istanbul.

Vaporis, N.M., 2000. *Witnesses for Christ. Orthodox Christian Neomartyrs of the Ottoman Period 1437–1860.* New York.

Voutira, E., 2006. *Pontic Greeks of the Former Soviet Union: Diaspora and Final Repatriation.* Cambridge.

7
A.J.B. Wace and M.S. Thompson, Nomads of the Balkans — The Vlachs

Tom Winnifrith

In the Pindus mountains and other remote redoubts of the Central Balkans, there are communities which speak among themselves a dialect derived not from Greek or Slav or Albanian or Turkish, but Latin. The Greeks call them Kutsovlachs, the Serbs Tsintsars, they often call themselves Aroumanians, but I shall call them, as Wace and Thompson do, Vlachs. The term is slightly unsatisfactory, as Vlach can have a derogatory meaning or alternatively can mean a shepherd. Wace and Thompson also call the Vlachs nomads, a rather misleading title for the regular transhumance between summer and winter quarters in the plains which

many Vlachs undertook until very recently, although journeys by foot with vast flocks of sheep and goats declined after 1912, having been made more difficult by wars which created frontiers and destroyed flocks. Vlachs still today make journeys between mountain and plain, but by car rather than on foot, and to summer country cottages and winter flats rather than summer or winter pastures.

Studying the Vlachs without using Wace and Thompson is a bit like studying Greek literature without using Liddell and Scott. The former were a more lively pair, hunting together like hounds, in their contemporary

Fig.7.1: M.S. Thompson; BSA 1936 Exhibition: no.147a Sparta 1908 team, detail.

Fig.7.2: A.J.B. Wace; BSA 1936 Exhibition: no.147a Sparta 1908 team, detail.

Arnold Toynbee's phrase. Wace was definitely the senior partner. He came from an academic Cambridge family, had scored highly in Cambridge examinations, and was already a fellow of Pembroke College before he embarked on his Greek adventures. His career is admirably summarized in the new Dictionary of National Biography. The article on Wace gives an insight into the many-sided nature of his contributions, such as his interest in textiles, his invention of passports in the First World War, his flitting between the British School at Athens and Rome in his early career, his work in American universities when he had retired from Cambridge, and his sense of humour, a great asset in Balkan travel. The annual report of the British School at Athens gives a great deal of space and credit to Wace in the years between 1907 and 1923.

In contrast, Thompson's life apart from the Vlachs seems to have little to offer. The BSA gives him less attention than Wace in the years before the First World War when the two were working in Thessaly, although the reports of these years are interesting. Our two authors produced a book on ancient Thessaly in which articles by the pair are quoted. Quite apart from *The Nomads of the Balkans* Thompson, albeit in conjunction with Wace, had a good publication record while still only in his twenties. Observing that he had published nothing after 1914, I once foolishly thought that he had perished in the First World War. In fact he came through the war with distinction, winning the OBE and a Serbian military medal on the Salonica front, and served as the Secretary of the BSA in London from 1920 to 1927. He was on the Council of the School as representative of the Hellenic Society until 1939 but then, though still a subscriber from his home in Redhill (a place in suburban Surrey very unlike the Vlach hills), he appears to have severed contact with academic life, preferring instead to work at the family firm of Thompson and Thompson, tea brokers, not a very romantic occupation. Thompson gave two lectures on Ancient Geography at Oxford in 1912 and took a post in Ancient History in the embryo University of Newcastle in the same year, but otherwise seems to have eschewed the groves of academe in spite of his work in the hills of the Balkans.

Rachel Hood's account of Thompson's life suggests that it was family pressure which led him to eschew academic life in favour of tea broking.[1] An unpublished memoir written for his grandchildren forms the basis of this account, in which caricatures by Piet de Jong show Thompson in a pinstriped suit smoking a pipe, a marked contrast to the more dashing Wace who is colourfully attired in a striped old Salopian blazer. But de Jong had met Thompson in the twenties and Wace at a much earlier period. Thompson's acceptance of the post of secretary to the BSA and his retirement from it are noted laconically in the Society's reports and, after reading the fulsome praise of Hasluck and Wace, one assumes that both the appointment and the resignation of Thompson were entirely uncontroversial.

Another reason for preferring tea broking to university teaching may have been that Thompson's academic career got off to a bad start when he obtained a humble third class in Honour Moderations, that examination in Greek and Latin language (14 papers in 10 days) which concludes the first part of the Oxford Classical course. Perhaps he wrote Latin prose like the Vlachs. Thompson did obtain a second class in 'Greats' (Literae Humaniores), the final exam, as well as two travelling scholarships from Oxford, and was clearly a valued member of the British School at Athens. In any case the work of Wace and Thompson passed a stiffer test than that of Honour Moderations, the test of time which has ruined the reputation of many scholars, now either totally forgotten or remembered only as an object of scorn. Modern scholarship on the Vlachs, whether English, German, Romanian or Greek, mentions Wace and Thompson as a matter of course. Their book *The Nomads of the Balkans* was translated into Greek in 1989. They are mentioned in surprising places, for instance in Noel Malcolm's book on Kosovo, because the Vlachs, now unfortunately for themselves assimilated with the Serbs, form a fourth factor in that disputed land besides Albanians, Serbs and Turks. Tim Salmon, in *The Unwritten Places*, mentions Wace (unfortunately not Thompson) in describing the last *dhiava*, the annual pilgrimage with sheep and goats from Samarina to Thessaly.

Wace and Thompson explained in the introduction to *The Nomads of the Balkans* how they came to study

---

1. I am grateful to Ann French, Wace's granddaughter, for drawing my attention to Rachel Hood's work (1998) and to Thompson's unpublished memoirs.

Fig.7.3: Samarina Church of Great St Mary; Wace and Thompson 1914, plate XIV.

the life and customs of the Vlachs of northern Pindus. Their acquaintance with the Vlachs began by chance. In the winter of 1909–10 they were travelling in Southern Thessaly in search of inscriptions and other antiquities. In an area where there were a number of Albanian Vlachs they employed one as a muleteer, and began to learn a few words of Vlach. Attracted by the stories they heard from this man, and from another Vlach muleteer from the village of Samarina, they decided to visit the Pindus villages the following summer. The obvious course was to travel up there with the Vlach families of transhumant shepherds who leave for the hills each year about the same day. This first visit in 1910 to Samarina and the Pindus villages led to others, and to exploration of Vlach villages in southern Macedonia. They wrote that their book could have no claim to be a complete account of all the Vlach settlements; its aim was rather to give a 'detailed description of Samarina and the adjacent villages on Pindus together with some account of the Balkan Vlachs as a whole'.[2]

Most of the first eight chapters of *The Nomads of the Balkans* concern the life and customs, environment and history, of Samarina. There are chapters on Life at

Samarina; the Costumes of Samarina; Government and Trade, Churches and Houses; Birth, Baptism, Betrothal, Marriage and Burial Customs; Festivals and Folklore; and the History of Samarina. It might be thought a failure of Wace and Thompson that they concentrate on Samarina and, moreover, do so at a particular point of time, the early twentieth century, before two Balkan wars, two World Wars and one civil war changed the shape of the landscape. I have only been to Samarina once for two days about thirty years ago, and it did not seem to have changed much: the tree shown in Wace and Thompson's photograph was still growing out of the church of Great St Mary's.[3] Staying for longer periods in or near Metsovo, I was able to see and hear the same customs and songs which appear in *The Nomads of the Balkans*. But the last time I went in 1994 there were discos in Metsovo and tourist shops in the smaller village of Anilion (*Nkiare* in Vlach) which now has a bus service, whereas in 1974 I arrived by mule.

Right on the Albanian border is the appropriately named Kephalovrison, *Migidia* in Vlach, often spoken about in Vlach story and song. In 1974 it seemed impossibly remote, but in 1998 we drove along beautifully tarmaced roads to find prosperous cafés where

2. Wace and Thompson 1914, 5. See also maps of 'Northern Pindus' and of 'The Territory of Samarina', facing p. 60.

3. Wace and Thompson 1914, PL. XIV, facing p. 86 - see FIG. 7.3.

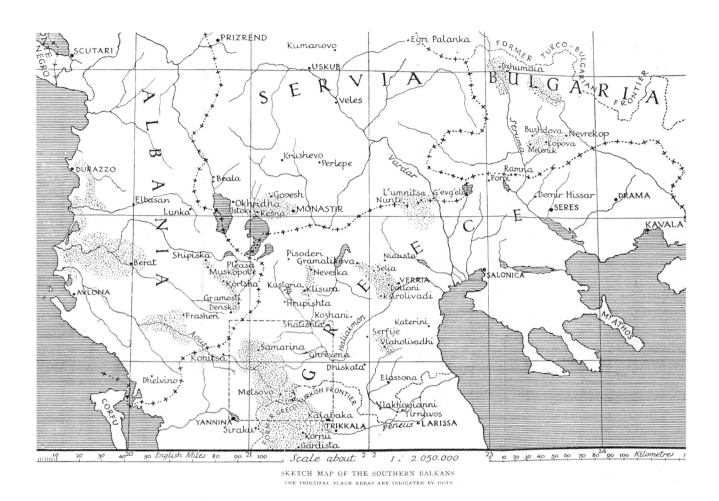

SKETCH MAP OF THE SOUTHERN BALKANS
THE PRINCIPAL VLACH AREAS ARE INDICATED BY DOTS

Map.7.1: Wace and Thompson 1914, 206.

Vlachs, having done their time as *Gastarbeiter*, were now serving up *Wienerschnitzel* and forgetting their Vlach customs in the process. Over the border in Albania there are no roads, but the Vlach villages are deserted because the inhabitants have left for Greece. It is premature to say of the Vlachs, as Byron mistakenly says of the Greeks, that all except their sun is set; indeed manful efforts are being made all over the Balkans but especially in Greece to preserve Vlach folklore, dances and songs. But the first eight chapters of *The Nomads of the Balkans* describing life in Samarina describe a vanished age. I doubt if one could find and photograph now, as I and Wace and Thompson did, a Beetling Mill in full working order.[4] This is the *batale*, an extraordinary Heath Robinson apparatus, involving wooden

hammers bashing sheepskins into *flokati* carpets with the aid of Vlach streams.

Chapters 9 and 10 of the *Nomads of the Balkans* describe more briefly the Vlach villages round Samarina and then throughout the Balkans. These chapters are amazingly valuable in tracking down where the Vlachs can be found today, since they have held on to their nineteenth century settlements with great tenacity. My map, composed after studying the Vlachs in the 1970s and 1980s, is not very different from that of Wace and Thompson.[5] Perhaps this is not surprising, since my empirical method of investigating the Vlachs was to catch a bus from Ioannina or Trikala to

---

4. Wace and Thompson 1914, PL XIII, facing p. 84.

5. Wace and Thompson 1914, 206 and Winnifrith 1987, 161. Both maps are frequently reprinted, often without permission and sometimes without acknowledgement.

a village mentioned by Wace and Thompson, to see if it was Vlach, as it usually was, to make enquiries about customs, language, other villages, and then catch the bus back. There was the occasional disappointment of getting a bus at 4 in the morning, being told there were no Vlachs at 8, and that the bus back did not leave until 6 in the evening. More thorough investigators like the German Theodore Kahl and the Greek Asterios Koukoudis give more elaborate maps, but do little to suggest that Wace and Thompson are unreliable guides to the whereabouts of the Vlachs.[6]

Kahl marks villages which are totally Vlach, largely Vlach, have a minority Vlach population, or were once inhabited by Vlachs although none live there any more. Even he, however, is no longer up to date, due to massive emigration from Albania. Koukoudis is very useful in showing how, for hundreds of years, Vlach communities have shrunk and grown as people have either settled in new winter or summer quarters or have decided to abandon one Vlach village for another. It is extremely difficult to know just how many Vlachs there are in the Balkans, let alone in the world where I know of flourishing Vlach communities in Bridgeport, Connecticut, and Melbourne, Australia.

There are also difficulties in establishing just who is a Vlach. Does the term mean someone with some vague consciousness of Vlach ancestry or even identity, in which case I and most Presidents of the United States are Irish, or does it mean regular use of the Vlach language in the home? Even this latter criterion is hardly watertight. In Wace and Thompson's time most of the Vlachs, whom they numbered rather imprecisely as half a million, would have spoken Vlach at home in all three generations in a household. In the 1970s travelling around Vlach villages with my children, I observed the old men speaking Vlach, people of my generation understanding it, and children eager to practise their English abandoning their Vlach altogether.

Wace and Thompson's penultimate chapter is on the Vlach language. There is some evidence that Thompson, who spent a summer at Samarina for the purpose of learning the language, is the main author of this chapter, although due acknowledgements are made in the pref-

VLACH VILLAGES TODAY

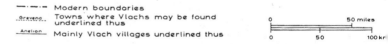

—·—·—	Modern boundaries
Graveno	Towns where Vlachs may be found underlined thus
Anilion	Mainly Vlach villages underlined thus

Map.7.2: Winnifrith 1987, 161.

ace to linguistic help from Cambridge experts. Possibly Dawkins helped in suggesting that a visitor to remote communities should ask members of these communities to tell their tales, and work out the grammar afterwards. Vlach folk tales are not very exciting, and even Vlach songs, though remarkably durable, are not literary masterpieces. As Wace and Thompson acknowledge, they have drawn upon the work of the great Balkan ethnologist Gustav Weigand for some of their examples.[7]

The chapter is like Kennedy's Latin grammar, clear, authoritative and slightly boring. We have declensions and conjugations, verbs regular and irregular. It is nice to see old friends in *suntu* (they are), *earam* (I was being) and *fui* (I was). Sound changes from Latin (o to

---

6. Kahl 1999, 26–34 and Koukoudis 2003, 47–75.

---

7. Weigand 1888, unfortunately not translated into English, is very good on Vlachs outside Greece.

Fig.7.4: 'Wallachs — Gypsies of Greece'; BSA Photographic Archive: Members, Schoolmasters' Trip 1910–12, M. Scott, Misc–1.

u) (qu to ts) hence *bun* (good), *durnire* (to sleep), *tsintsi* (five), *tsi* (who) are clearly explained. But I have to acknowledge that I find Vlach a very hard language. If one wants to learn it, Wace and Thompson is an excellent primer, providing texts in the shape of Vlach songs and some rather simplistic stories, as well as a rudimentary Vlach vocabulary, again with some comforting old friends. *Multi ani* (many years) is what people say on your birthday. Other Vlach grammars, Greek or Romanian, and even an English-Vlach dictionary with grammar prepared by the American Vlachs generally fail through being too prescriptive.[8] Wace and Thomp-

son are remarkably good, if we bear in mind that they were largely based on Samarina, in distinguishing different dialects among the Vlachs. As well as the totally distinct form of the language known as Meglen Vlach spoken in a few villages north of Salonica, there are different forms of Vlach in different areas of the Balkans, with the Vlachs on Mount Olympus lisping *sti* for *shti* and the Vlachs of Krusevo adding an extra 'sh', *shtshii*, to what I knew as *scivi*.

Some work has been done on Vlach dialects by a team of German philologists who in the 1970s went out recording words and phrases in various Vlach villages.[9] More work is, I believe, being done by Romanian scholars preparing a gigantic linguistic atlas and, naturally

8. Papahagi 1974, Koltsidas 1976, and Vrabic 2000 all give their different versions of the Vlach Kennedy and even the Vlach Lewis and Short but Wace and Thompson are perfectly adequate for basic grammar and vocabulary.

9. Kramer 1976 and 1977 record work mainly done in Greece.

Fig.7.5: Samarina marketplace; Wace and Thompson 1914, Plate VI.

and controversially, claiming the Vlachs as Romanians. I have tried to do a little on this score, hoping to find some historical insights through linguistic differences, but soon gave up, realizing that, as Koukoudis points out, the Vlachs are always on the move, sometimes bringing their linguistic quirks with them, sometimes adapting to the norms of their new environment. Wace and Thompson do not mark on their maps two groups of Vlachs who were almost permanently nomadic at the time. Some are now cattle breeders located west of Skopje, near Kozani, almost on the Bulgarian border, while others settled in the largely Greek villages of northern Epirus in south Albania after the Second World War. The latter have a linguistic peculiarity which I mention because it is not mentioned by Wace and Thompson. The word for a horse in most Vlach villages, derived from *caballus*, French *cheval*, is *calu*.

Among Albanian Vlachs the 'l' is dropped. If you want a horse in Albanian Vlach villages, and you often do, ask for a *cau*, pronounced 'cow'.[10]

With this sage piece of advice, not as sage as that of Wace and Thompson who end their chapter on language with a Vlach sentence meaning 'our language is the most upside down of all', I pass to their last chapter: 'The History of the Balkan Vlachs'. They had discussed various aspects of history in the chapters concerning Samarina, in particular the Turkish period and the

---

10. In 1999 I travelled in a jeep from Pogradec to the Vlach village of Llengë. As the crow flies the distance is about 15 miles but the journey took 3 hours. A young Vlach on his *cau* easily overtook us. Ninety years earlier there would have been no jeeps, and roads and political conditions in Albania, not exactly easy now, would have been even harder.

rise of two parties, one supporting Greece, the other Romania. Briskly our authors go through the evidence attesting Latin speaking populations in the Balkans. There are the Latin names in Procopius's *De Aedificiis*, that baffling road map of the Balkans where names are plentiful, but matching names with places is almost impossible. Then there is the *torna/torna* incident where a Byzantine muleteer, in some sources addressing a fellow muleteer as *fratre*, says that his baggage is slipping (*torna* in one sense) and the army takes this as a sign of retreat (about turn).[11] This linguistic confusion seems appropriate for introducing the Vlachs, but never seemed to me very useful for determining Vlach history. The incident took place in the East Balkans, rather far from Vlach settlements. We know that Latin persisted in military commands when it had vanished elsewhere, and though *fratre* is definitely Latin, *torna* is not.

We then have a gap of 400 years before we get any mention of anything that looks like Vlach. In 976, the brother of the Bulgarian emperor Samuel was killed between Prespa and Kastoria by some Vlach *hoditai*. The area is prime Vlach territory, and Vlachs have always been connected with roads, although in this instance it is not clear whether they were muleteers or highwaymen, armatoles or klephts. Wace and Thompson hint at the possibility that Samuel, a powerful force at the beginning of the eleventh century, may have been himself a Vlach, and in discussion of the Second Bulgarian Empire point out that our Byzantine sources call these Bulgarians Vlachs. After the Fourth Crusade, Vlachs turn up all over the Balkans, and Wace and Thompson trace some of the appearances, noting that quite often they are mentioned as being on the move, as befits transhumants. The Ottoman invasion made transhumance easier, and the way of life described by Wace and Thompson in their earlier chapters seems to go back only as far as the sixteenth century, when most of the famous Vlach villages were founded.

As well as demonstrating an admirable knowledge of Byzantine sources not on the usual Classical syllabus, Wace and Thompson showed in their scholarly pursuits, as in their lives, considerable courage in entering the controversial area of Vlach origins. Their conclusion, reached after a long historical discussion, is that the Balkan Vlachs 'are for the most part the Romanised tribes of the Balkan peninsula, reinforced perhaps at times by tribes from over the Danube'.[12] The Bulgarians cannot have been pleased at the remarks about their early empires, and our authors' conclusions about the origins of the Vlachs could not have satisfied either Greek or Romanian historians, although wisely Wace and Thompson do not ascribe the various theories of Vlach origins to particular nationalistic groups. I am less wise, and I have noted the weaknesses of the theory that the Vlachs split off from the Romanians as late as the tenth century, and thus are really Romanians; or that the Vlachs are descendants of Roman legionaries married to Greek girls, and thus are really Greek, learning their language —improbably— at their fathers' knees. Wace and Thompson also deal with a third theory, that the Vlachs are the descendants of a wild nomadic tribe which crept into the Balkans at the time of the Slav invasions, by pointing out that this theory has no evidence to back it up.

Wace and Thompson's conclusion is that, though much of the history of the Balkan Vlachs is obscure, one fact stands out clearly, that from the time when they first appear in history they have been allowing themselves to be absorbed gradually by the larger nations that surround them. 'Their numbers have been steadily, but slowly diminishing, and they themselves have helped this by their lack of national feeling, their dispersion and their power of self-effacement.'[13]

Studying the Vlachs over forty years has brought me in touch with many writers who lack Wace and Thompson's objectivity, wide knowledge and outstanding energy and courage. It is possible that their work may not find favour with modern social anthropologists, being written as it is in clear intelligible English, refreshingly free from pretentious theoretical academic jargon. As a callow schoolboy I heard Wace lecture on Mycenae, and wish I had met Thompson as I lived near Redhill. Aware that my greyhound days are over I am eager to find some enthusiastic researcher into the Vlachs who can carry on the torch of Vlach studies better than I have done.[14]

---

11. Wace and Thompson 1914, 257.

12. Wace and Thompson 1914, 272.
13. Wace and Thompson 1914, 273.
14. I am grateful to Metropolitan Kallistos Ware, Professor P. Mackridge and Dr D. Shankland for suggesting improvements to this paper.

REFERENCES

Gill, D., 2004. 'Wace, Alan John Bayard' in *The Dictionary of National Biography* 56: 632–5. Oxford.

Hood, R., 1998. *Faces of Archaeology in Greece. Caricatures by Piet de Jong*. Oxford.

Kahl, T., 1999. *Ethnizität und Raumliche Verteilung der Aromunen in Südosteuropa*. Münster.

Koltsidas, A., 1976. *Γραμματική και Λεξικό της Κουτσοβλαχικής Γλώσσας*. Thessaloniki.

Koukoudis, A., 2003. *The Vlachs: Metropolis and Diaspora*. Thessaloniki.

Kramer, J. et al, 1976. 'Dialektologische Forschungen bei den Aromunen in Frohjahr 1976', *Balkan-Archiv* 1: 7–78.

— et al, 1977. 'Dialektologische Forschungen bei den Aromunen in Frohjahr 1977', *Balkan-Archiv* 2: 91–180.

Malcolm, N., 1998. *Kosovo: A Short History*. London.

Papaphagi, T., 1974. *Dictionarul Dialectul Aroman*. Bucarest.

Salmon, T., 1995. *The Unwritten Places*. London.

Vrabic, E., 2000. *An English-Aromanian Dictionary*. Mississipi.

Wace, A.J.B. and Thompson, M.S., 1912. *Prehistoric Thessaly*. Cambridge.

— and Thompson, M.S., 1914. *The Nomads of the Balkans: an Account of Life and Customs among the Vlachs of Northern Pindus*. London.

— and Thompson, M.S., 1989. *Οι Νομάδες των Βαλκανίων*, trans. P. Karayorgos. Thessaloniki.

Weigand, G., 1888. *Die Aromunen*. Leipzig.

Winnifrith, T.J., 1987. *The Vlachs: the History of a Balkan People*. London.

8

The Greek embroidery collecting of
R.M. Dawkins and A.J.B. Wace

Ann French

The academic work and publications of those who studied and worked at the British School at Athens (BSA) during its early years have been well studied and remain the basis of much on-going work. Less well studied has been the collecting, by these same people, of archaeological and other objects which are now in UK museums.[1] Those who collected include R.C. Bosanquet, R.M. Dawkins, G. Dickins, F.W. Hasluck, M. Hasluck, J.L. Myres, E.W. Tillyard and A.J.B. Wace. Museums cannot but reflect the interests of those who collected and donated objects, and the study of collectors provides new insights and perspectives. This approach also illuminates the early history and work of the BSA and its students.

The purpose of this paper is to provide a preliminary study of the Greek embroidery collecting of R.M. Dawkins and A.J.B. Wace. Between them they collected over 1200 pieces of embroidery, which are largely still intact as collections. Dawkins bequeathed his entire collection to the Victoria and Albert Museum (V&A) in 1950, and Wace's collection is divided amongst three institutions; the V&A, Liverpool Museums and the Textile Museum, Washington D.C. While the embroideries themselves have been well studied in various publications,[2] Dawkins and Wace's methods and motives for collecting have been less thoroughly examined, and the wealth of existing archive material has not been fully utilised. While Dawkins and Wace concentrated on embroidery collecting, they also collected a variety of other contemporary Greek 'ethnographic' material such as shadow puppets, café posters,

amulets, and accessories for performing at carnivals, in addition to a considerable amount of archaeological material. They were also not the only acquirers of Greek embroideries. Bosanquet, Dickins and Tillyard all bought embroideries in the same period, but they did not choose to study, interpret and exhibit them. This approach makes Dawkins and Wace's embroidery collecting significant.

METHODS OF COLLECTING

Various clues as to how Greek embroideries came to be collected by BSA members can be found in letters, publications and catalogues. Bosanquet wrote to his wife Ellen in December 1901:

> I am so glad V. likes her sash. It came from Rhodes, brought by our pet Rhodian vagabond: it was dyed in the old days from some local herb, which was very scarce according to the old woman from whose chest — they have great bridal chests full of obsolete embroideries and costumes — he fished it out. She had had it for fifty years at least, he said.[3]

He mentions buying 'a complete gown from Nisyros from the Rhodian' in another letter of 3 April 1908.[4] Ellen Bosanquet provides a vivid account of pedlars in Athens:

> The pedlars are another numerous body in Athens. Turkish tradition assumes that women do not leave their houses to make purchases and that wares must be brought to their doors. The Turk has disappeared, but the tradition of seclusion lingers, and the pedlar remains. Tired little donkeys climb up and down the steep outlying streets of Athens carrying upright cupboards with glass

---

1. For example: Gill 1992; Gill 2000; Sherratt 2000. Beneficiaries include the Fitzwilliam Museum and the Museum of Archaeology and Anthropology, Cambridge, the Ashmolean Museum and the Pitt Rivers Museum, Oxford, the Victoria and Albert Museum, Liverpool Museums, the Whitworth Art Gallery, Manchester, Tyne & Wear Museums and the Marischal Museum, Aberdeen.

2. Belger Krody 2006; Johnstone 1961; Johnstone 1972; Taylor 1998; Trilling 1983.

3. Bosanquet 1938, 91.

4. Bosanquet 1938, 168.

Fig.8.1: Captioned by Wace (on reverse): 'Left to right / E.W. Webster. A.J.B. Wace. R.M. Dawkins / Sitting on top of ruined tower at entrance to fort Phylai. / Dawkins holds the bread, I the newspapers, & Webster the olives wrapped in paper.' This photograph dates from 1902–3 to Dawkins and Wace's first session in Greece. They are both wearing Norfolk jackets, the pockets of which would take their travel notebooks.

fronts like miniature shops, and in these cupboards is shown a depressing assortment of tapes, buttons, and artificial jewellery. Pedlars without donkeys are also known. One of these may be seen carrying a dozen dress lengths from door to door. Eleven are laid over the right shoulder, the twelfth is draped in sweeping folds over the extended left arm and his voice calls as he goes, 'foremata, oraia foremata, peninda lepta o pichys' (dresses, beautiful dresses, fifty lepta the piece). Counterpanes and rugs are hawked about the town in the same fashion and the small householder finds the temptation irresistible.[5]

In an unpublished extended catalogue of his embroideries,[6] Dawkins corroborates when describing some 'Turkish' towels:

> This series, mostly towels embroidered at each end… The embroidery is alike both sides and sometimes with a little tinsel. The towels are the first things I bought in 1903, 1904, and a Rhodian used to bring them to the school at Athens. Later we despised this work, of which I have no very fine examples, for which see Newberry's collection.[7] Some figured in the 1921 extra number of the Studio.[8]

The 'Rhodian' is cited throughout Dawkins and Wace's embroidery catalogues. Approximately forty-five pieces are provenanced to him.

---

5. Bosanquet 1914, 263. Pichys is a length of cloth of about a forearm or nearly half a metre.

6. Now in Liverpool Museums' Archives, undated but references suggest it was written in the mid-1920s.

7. This collection is now in the Whitworth Art Gallery.

8. Dawkins is referring to Kendrick et al 1921, in which several of Wace's pieces are illustrated and both Wace and Dawkins are cited.

They used other dealers in Athens, Smyrna, Constantinople and Cairo. The ones most frequently cited are Old Orient, Papademos, Dracopoulos[9], Stephanion, Christodoulou, Benquiat (possibly based in Constantinople) and Pezzer (possibly based in Smyrna). The Baedeker (German Edition) for Greece of 1904[10] lists Drakopoulos at Hermesstr 17, Minerva at Hermesstr 30, Old Orient at Hermesstr 30, all for *Antiquitaten* or *Stickerrein*. Dawkins often refers to Papademos as 'a notable liar' and another dealer, Stephanion, and his son as the 'Old Fool' and the 'Young Fool' expressing great scepticism of their provenancing.

By 1906, Dawkins and Wace seem to have acquired sufficient embroideries to decide to carry out research *in situ*. The BSA *Annual* for 1906–7 reports:

> In July and August [Wace] travelled with Mr Dawkins through a number of the less-known Turkish islands, studying the conditions of modern life as well as the ancient remains, and collecting information about local styles of embroidery.[11]

In 1907 they were to make another trip, unrecorded in the BSA *Annual*. These travels left impressions on both men. Dawkins remembers them in both versions of his un-published autobiography.

> With Wace I had two notable island journeys. In 1906 we visited the Dodecanese, and in 1907 the Cyclades; we were mainly in search of embroideries but did a lot of dialect collecting.... at Anaphi ...we bought so many embroideries that we ran out of money and had to go back to Athens to load up again. One morning I received a telegram that my Cousin was dead and I was needed at home .... I had to let Wace do the rest of the islands himself.[12]

Both trips involved leaving the steamer routes and hiring caiques to reach the more remote islands. Wace was to recall later 'a night spent on a rocky desert islet with nothing but sea-urchins for supper.'[13]

In 1906, for example, they took a steamer to Amorgos and then went onto to Astypalea. 'Left Amorgos at 10.00am but found difficulty in getting round the south end of the island which we did at 2 hours. Reached Astypalea harbour 12.20am on Wednesday (4/9/06) morning and slept on the caique. Fare 60 francs gold — caique with 3 men.'[14] They continued onto Telos and Nisyros by caique, but picked up a steamer from Nisyros to Cos, before continuing to Kalymnos and Leros by caique again, leaving Leros by steamer for Samos, passing by Patmos which 'we had not put on the list of the islands to be visited on our passport so we had to content ourselves with what could be seen from the harbour of the castled monastery.'[15] The 1907 trip used a similar combination of steamer and hired caique to reach areas where they felt they could see embroideries *in situ* and buy them with a direct provenance.

Why the women were prepared to sell their inheritances needs exploring further. One possibility, recognised by Dawkins and Wace, is social change or 'modern life and European imports'.[16] Dawkins noted with regard to bed-tents: 'Actual bed tents are rare and except the Paton tent with door in SK[17] I have never seen one. They had two fates: in the island they were cut up to make square curtains to fit the modern frame for a mosquito net and in trade they were un-sewn and re-sewn head and tails to make a square curtain'.[18] This implies that embroideries were being altered to suit changes in furniture styles and surplus pieces sold off, or they were simply being sold to raise some money.

9. Dawkins and Wace were inconsistent in their Greek transliterations, and used Dracopoulos, Drakopoulos or Δρακοπουλος in their catalogues. Papademos also is often written in Greek and Old Orient was shortened to O.O.

10. Baedeker 1904, 11. Wace's rather battered copy is still extant and was number 304 of his library.

11. *BSA* XII, 484.

12. R.M. Dawkins Autobiography (1950), Taylor Institution Library, Oxford F.ARCH.DAWK. 6(6) p62–4.

13. Stubbings 1958, 266.

14. Dawkins 1906 Notebook, Taylor Institution, Library, Oxford ARCH.Z.DAWK.2(2) p13.

15. R.M. Dawkins Autobiography (1950), Taylor Institution Library, Oxford F.ARCH.DAWK. 6(6) p63.

16. Wace and Dawkins 1914*a*, 49.

17. V&A T.67–1902 bought for £40.00 from W.R. Paton who had bought it in Cos from the family of Platanistas. V&A Nominal file MA/1/P540.

18. Dawkins unpublished embroidery catalogue p48, Liverpool Museum Archives.

As their collections grew, embroideries were also bought wherever Dawkins and Wace travelled in the Mediterranean and in the UK at Liberty's, Debenham & Freebody's and, most surprising, the Army and Navy Stores. Collecting clearly became obsessive and addictive (see PLATE I).

The BSA Committee Report of 1908–09 states that 'in the spring, [Dawkins] with Mr Thompson, visited Cyprus and drew up a report on the condition of the antiquities of the island, returning to Athens through Asia Minor.'[19] In contrast, M.S. Thompson recalls:

> One autumn Dawkins had to go to Cyprus to report on the museum at Nikosia, and he was good enough to ask me to come too. To get to Cyprus from Athens meant going first to Alexandria, and Alexandria of course meant two or three days in Cairo. There Dawkins spent nearly all his time researching the bazaars for Greek island embroideries, while I got my first glance at the customary tourist sights.[20]

Dawkins himself admits to the lengths he would go in order to acquire a piece:

> These I bought in the summer of 1911 from Halandrakis the schoolmaster of Patmos from his house in the Chora. They were all on a sofa ... I saw them when I was in Patmos I think with Halliday the winter before and bargained one hundred pounds Turkish. This money I took with me in 1911 to the Melos dig and then from Melos went to Athens and so to Ikaria by steamer then by caique to Patmos bought these curtains and returned to Athens I forget how.[21]

Dawkins bought more embroideries than Wace, which has led recent writers to accuse him of 'collecting textiles in quantities that might, unkindly, be called whole sale.'[22] However, Dawkins had considerably more available funds having inherited a house and ample income

from a maternal cousin, John Doyle, in 1907.[23] Wace was to lament later to G.H. Myers, 'while in Greece I saved little or nothing because I collected embroideries instead.'[24]

The main period of acquiring embroideries was 1902–14, when both Dawkins and Wace were largely based in Greece, but Wace kept buying, with discrimination, throughout the war. Writing to A.F. Kendrick, Keeper of Textiles at the Victoria and Albert Museum, Wace commented:

> There is some embroidery in the shops here but they ask such prices that one cannot buy and so I reserve myself for things that are really interesting. The other day for instance I was offered the disjecta membra of a Karpathos frock but remembering your three splendid specimens I thought it was superfluous besides being in bad condition. A man showed me the other day with pride some Rhodian strips from a bed tent and asked for the lot three thousand. It was ordinary Rhodian and not in its original state so I passed and turned my nose at it which rather surprised the dealer. He also wants 550 francs or so for a piece of so-called Yannina (really Ionian Island) work much inferior to a bit of mine you have in the loan court across the top of the tall case and which cost me 250 francs.[25]

MOTIVES FOR COLLECTING

Why Dawkins and Wace bought and collected embroideries in such quantities is not explicitly stated anywhere (yet found) by either of them.[26] However, they were both influenced by senior academics including Sir William Ridgeway, Disney Professor of Archaeology at Cambridge 1892–1926, and J.L. Myres, Wykeham Professor of Ancient History at Oxford 1910–39, both

19. *BSA* XV 1908–9, 367.
20. Unpublished autobiography of 1969, p.13.
21. Extended unpublished catalogue, p.45.
22. Taylor 1998, 177.

23. Jenkins 1955, 382.
24. Textile Museum Washington Archives: Wace to Myers 7/4/1925. G.H. Myers founded The Textile Museum Washington D.C.
25. Wace to A. F. Kendrick, 22/10/1917 V&A Archives Nominal File MA1/W2.
26. Unfortunately the letters from Wace to Dawkins for 1910–12 left to Emmanuel College Library have gone missing.

of whom were active in promoting anthropology as an academic discipline.[27]

William Ridgeway's influence on and support of F.W. Hasluck, an early anthropologist and a contemporary of Dawkins and Wace at Cambridge and at the BSA, has been researched,[28] but Ridgeway was equally influential for Dawkins and Wace. He encouraged observation of contemporary life in Greece and collecting of quirky objects. His article on the origins of the Turkish Crescent is peppered with references to his students, as is his book *Origins of Tragedy*.[29] Bosanquet, Dawkins, Hasluck and Wace are among those who provided observations and objects for Ridgeway to use.[30] *Origins of Tragedy* utilises, in particular, the accounts later to be published by Dawkins and Wace of masquerades at carnivals.[31]

Dawkins maintained a long correspondence with Ridgeway until the latter's death in 1926. Ridgeway's letters cover many subjects and testify that he also corresponded with Hasluck and Wace.[32] Ridgeway kept his ex-pupils up to date with university gossip, asked for contributions to the annual meeting of the British Association for the Advancement of Science, and constantly cajoled for publications: 'will your embroidery publication make a book that would do for our Archaeological and Ethnographical Series? Consider this point, unless you can get a publisher to pay you something for it'.[33] Further letters repeat this point and Ridgeway is more supportive of Dawkins and Wace's work on embroideries than he is of Wace's work on classical sculpture.[34] 'I am also writing to Wace by this

post. I do not think that he ought to take the Assistant Directorship at Rome. He will waste his time in journeyman business over the Capitol catalogue'.[35]

Although Ridgeway supported and encouraged his pupils in non-archaeological and more 'ethnographical work', J.L. Myres seems to have initiated the particular interest in embroidery. References can be found in letters to Myres from Wace.[36] In a letter dated 15 June 1935, Wace writes: 'Have you had the Embroidery Book to review from the Illustrated London News or Observer? If you have not had it, I must see about trying to secure you a copy, because it all started with some remarks you made to me in the spring of 1903'.[37] In another letter of 22 November 1950, he reminisces:

> I was much interested by your remembrance of your going to Palaikastro in 1903 with Ernest Gardner's cruising party. I remember sitting on the deck of the 'Pelops' in the sun as the ship rounded the N.E. point of Crete and listening to you discussing the islands and Ptolemaic naval stations in Thera and elsewhere. I also remember how you talked to Dawkins and me about island embroideries.[38]

A series of sporadic letters from Wace to Myres from 1905 to 1914 give more details. On 29 January 1905, from the British School at Rome, Wace wrote to Myres with a few queries on Mycenaean pots and continued:

> What I can tell you a little about is embroidery. I have notes of one or two pieces in the museums at Brunswick and Modena and in Fürtwangler's possession. Also Mackenzie here has shown me several pieces: and from them I discovered that the origin of one of my bits that puzzled even you is Naxos. He has also some nice Cretan — one bit with ladies carrying pomegranate flowers quite

---

27. For example see: Duckworth et al. 1906; Myres and Freire-Marreco 1912; Ridgeway 1909.

28. Salmeri 2004; Shankland 2004.

29. Ridgeway 1908; Ridgeway 1910.

30. The objects sent back to Ridgeway are all now in the Cambridge Museum of Archaeology and Anthropology and can be found at http://museum.archanth.cam.ac.uk/home/catalogue/objects.

31. Dawkins 1906; Wace 1910; Wace 1913.

32. Now in the library of Emmanuel College, Cambridge.

33. Ridgeway to Dawkins 31/10/1906 Emmanuel College Library MSS 297.

34. Wace was intermittently at the British School at Rome from 1903–8 working on a project instigated by Henry Stuart Jones of cataloguing the sculpture collections of the Commune of Rome. See Wiseman 1990, 6–7.

35. Ridgeway to Dawkins 16/6/1906 Emmanuel College Library MSS 297.

36. Myres Papers are in the Bodleian Library and are listed in Clapinson and Rodgers 1991.

37. *Myres Archive* MS Myres 50 F27. The embroidery book referred to is Wace 1935.

38. *Myres Archive* Bodleian Library MS Myres 40 F155.

'Ionic' in character, and also with birds on grape vines quite Byzantine in style. I think you ought to write a small handbook on these embroideries. In a few years time the supply will be scarcer — and unless something is done all records will be lost of them, since the vast majority of pieces fall into private hands where they are used as curtains, or cut up to decorate dresses or the like. I wish you would write something about them — everyone is interested in them. When you come to Athens in the spring, I will try and arrange that you meet Miss Pesel, who directs Lady Egerton's School. She has a nice collection of embroidery.[39]

This extract reveals that Myres was also acquiring embroideries, that a strong sense of 'salvage ethnography' prevailed and the key presence in Athens of Louisa Pesel.

In their embroidery catalogues (to be discussed below), Dawkins and Wace left a number series for Myres to complete. A minute dated 13 February 1906 in the V&A Archives from Eric Maclagan to A. F. Kendrick describes visiting Myres in Oxford where he saw 'the fine collection of Greek embroideries belonging to Mr Myres of Christchurch. This contains many finer pieces than those exhibited at the Fitzwilliam, though the localities represented is not so large'.[40]

The presence of Louisa Pesel in Athens was hugely helpful to Dawkins and Wace. She has been described as:

Designer and embroideress who trained under Lewis F. Day. She assisted W. G. Paulson Townsend with his book *Embroidery or the Craft of the Needle (1899)*, in which two of her embroideries are illustrated. She left Day's studio in 1900 but by that time had begun to exhibit her own work. A screen in the First International *Studio* Exhibition received special attention. In 1902 she was appointed designer to the Royal Hellenic Schools of Needlework and Lace in Athens and it was while she was there that she studied historic and modern embroideries from the area. She became director of the school but left Greece in 1907 to return to England. In about 1910 she was commissioned by the V&A to produce a set of stitch samplers based on English embroideries of the seventeen and eighteenth centuries. These were published in 1911. In 1913 a second series based on embroideries of the Mediterranean and the Near East were also published. Both sets of samplers are on permanent display at the V&A, which also owns a panel adapted from one of her published designs. A keen technician and teacher of embroidery, she became an Inspector of Art Needlework for the Board of Education and the first President of the Embroiderers' Guild in 1920. Her mature work was based on the revival of historical designs and techniques, and embroideries copied from her stitch sampler books are often thought to be Greek or Near Eastern.[41]

She appears in the BSA Annals as a long-term subscriber, and in the 1903–4 committee report: 'Among the un-official workers at the School may be mentioned Miss Louisa Pesel, Associate of the School and Directress of the Royal Hellenic School of Needlework, who had made use of the School library for Hellenic and Byzantine designs'.[42] She left two books on embroidery to the BSA Library with the dedicatory inscription 'in grateful recognition of the privileges of associate membership'.[43] Her entry into the BSA in an era of few women students probably came through her friendship with Bosanquet's wife, Ellen, who herself struggled with life in Athens and briefly refers to Pesel in her memoir: 'During this second session I began to make real friends. There was Louisa Pesel (known

---

39. *Myres Archive* Bodleian Library MS Myres 40 F61 & 62.

40. *V&A Archives* Nominal File MA/1/W2. The fate of this 'fine' collection is unknown. A collection of embroideries was left to the Ashmolean Museum in 1960 by Lady Myres but probably would no longer merit the description 'fine' and may have suffered the fate described by Wace above.

41. Parry 1988, 141. The stitch samplers referred to were still on display in the Textile Study Rooms of the V&A in August 2006.

42. *BSA* X 1903–4, 245.

43. The books left to the BSA were Day 1900; Paulson Townsend 1907.

to us as Peter) who helped Lady Egerton to run her embroidery school.'[44]

The circumstances and foundation of this school are described in a contemporary magazine article. It seems to have been founded out of attempts to find work for refugee women from the 'Turco-Greek war of 1897 when thousands of Thessalian women started on mules and donkeys to find in the south a refuge from the dreaded horrors of an invading Turkish army'.[45] Lady Egerton apparently further developed the school, finding a suitable home for it, acquiring Royal patronage and developing the designs and stitches used. Lady Egerton was also responsible for the employment of Louisa Pesel as Directress from 1903 to 1907. Louisa Pesel also collected embroideries (as mentioned by Wace to Myres). These are now in the collections of Leeds University[46] and their purpose was clearly to inform her teaching and publications. The latter are often highly technical and in one she thanks Lady Egerton and Mrs A.M. Daniel 'for their assistance in puzzling out some of the more intricate stitches'.[47] As a teacher of embroidery, Louisa Pesel was almost certainly responsible for explaining stitch craft to Dawkins and Wace. Their early textile notebooks are full of stitch diagrams, which they must have drawn to assist them to recognise stitches. Dawkins's diagrams are much better and more useful than those of Wace, who 'was virtually incapable of making even a rough sketch of any object, but he had an astonishing visual memory for all he studied'.[48]

The preface of Wace's first publication on Greek embroideries states:

These few words on the development of the patterns of Greek Embroideries are the result of a study of them carried on for some time

past by Mr J.L. Myres, student of Christchurch, Oxford, Mr R.M. Dawkins, Fellow of Emmanuel College, Miss Louisa Pesel, Directress of the Royal Hellenic School of Needlework, Athens, and myself.[49]

Louisa Pesel is also mentioned by Ridgeway in a letter of October 1906 to Dawkins:

I was delighted to get your letter appended to Wace's and to learn from it that you and he had altogether such a very successful voyage archaelogique. It is full time for you and he to publish your embroidery results, for Miss Peser had a say at the British Association in section H..... Your working up of the re-populating of Skyros from the mainland as confirmed by dialect and embroidery pleases me very much. Miss Peser, if that is [the] way to spell her name, pointed out the difficulty of finding a pattern of the Janina type in Scyros.[50]

Pesel's lecture entitled 'Greek Embroideries British Association York'[51] is almost certainly the lecture referred to by Ridgeway. She mentions studying the embroideries for the last four years; why they need to be recorded properly; the difficulty of dating them, few other forms of craft having survived in Greece; and that 'already the members of the British School of Archaeology are much interested in the subject, and I personally owe them individually and collectively a debt of gratitude for their help in trying to piece evidence together for the unravelling of many knotty problems.'

By 10 February 1907, Wace was pretty scathing[52] in a letter to Myres:

44. Bosanquet 1938, 61. Lady Egerton was the wife of the Head of the British Legation, Sir Edwin Egerton, a long time supporter of the BSA. The School referred to is the 'Royal Hellenic School of Needlework'.

45. Bowman Dodd 1906, 123.

46. Hann, Senturk and Thomsen 1995.

47. Pesel 1921. Mrs A.M. Daniel (née Welsh) was a BSA student in 1903–04, who married Augustus Daniel, later Director of The National Gallery. They left a number of embroideries, including Greek pieces, to the Fitzwilliam in 1949.

48. Stubbings 1958, 267.

49. Wace 1905.

50. Ridgeway to Dawkins 31/10/1906 Emmanuel College Library MSS 297. The 'voyage archaelogique' probably refers to Dawkins and Wace's travels to the Cyclades specifically to research embroideries *in situ*, reported in *BSA* XII 1905–06, 484

51. The text of this lecture is now in Leeds University Textile Collection archives.

52. This scathing tone is not explained in surviving contemporary correspondence. However, a footnote in Wace 1935 (p15) states that the articles published in the Burlington in 1906–7 (by Louisa Pesel and her sister Laura, although Wace does not cite them by name) 'are based on incomplete or inaccurate information'.

Have you seen Miss Pesel's wonderful article in the Burlington?[53] It's marvellously bad. I did think she knew better. Dawkins and I have begun the book and have been collecting more specimens. The result is that we have made one or two discoveries. We can talk over them when you come out here.[54]

Given the encouragement, interest and assistance of Ridgeway and Myres, the expertise of Louisa Pesel and an abundance of embroideries to buy, it is not perhaps surprising that Dawkins and Wace took to acquiring them. However, it is their collecting methodology which took simple acquisition a stage further into more disciplined research.

RESEARCH AND INTERPRETATION

Dawkins and Wace kept records of their collecting, which sets them apart from their fellow acquirers of Greek embroideries.[55] These records took two forms. The first was not exclusive to embroideries, being a habit they might have inherited from Bosanquet, and consisted of the travel notebooks they all kept (see PLATE IIa and b).[56]

The notebooks contain notes and observations on walking distances and times, inscriptions, architecture, fortifications, folk songs, ethnology, embroidery notes and purchases and pages of local dialects. (Dawkins tended to keep better itineraries than Wace.) All three had near unreadable handwriting, especially when using pencil. Dawkins's brother, an Arabic scholar,

described Dawkins's handwriting as '"classical" to be solved as a problem of epigraphy'[57] a description that can be applied to all three. An example of a typical embroidery reference (with diagram) from Wace's Island Notebook of 1906 is: 'Saw σπερβερι from Telos in house of doctor at Παλοι, Nisyros. Cross stitch? Door only embroidered. Colours red, blue, yellow — few leaves amongst pattern'.[58]

Dawkins and Wace catalogued and photographed their embroidery collections, borrowing pieces from others for comparison. The same small brown notebooks were used. The first entry reads:

> 1.Siphnos.
> Loaned by Old Orient for a photograph.
> March 1905.
> Photo no. 2
> Bed Curtain 4 widths .56m wide, 1.9 m long
> Coffee coloured linen - colours green,
> blue & red.
> Stitch - Patmian & in the linear pieces
> satin stitch
> Pattern arranged - *Diagram Given*
> cf 121 a&b[59]

The early entries are all similar. They record provenance, measurements, loom widths, colours, pattern and stitch, together with a photograph number. The first one hundred entries include any embroidery of interest, including loans from Old Orient, Dickins, Daniel, Louisa Pesel, and Bosanquet. Thereafter the embroideries are those belonging to Dawkins and Wace, except for the numbers 200–400 which were reserved for Myres.[60] The similarity with an archaeological finds notebook is obvious, for example those being kept at this time by Dawkins and Wace while excavating at the Sanctuary of Artemis Orthia, Sparta.[61] Wace spent much of his early years in Greece and Italy cataloguing works, culminating in various publi-

---

53. Wace is referring to Pesel 1907.

54. *Myres Archive* Bodleian Library MS Myres 40 F63 & 64.

55. I may be doing the others such as Bosanquet an injustice, but my enquiries of the relevant museum collections have not produced similar documentation.

56. The travel notebooks are unmistakable. They are small (to enable them to fit into the pocket of a Norfolk jacket) filled with checked pages, covered with brown cloth, and contained a pencil holder and pocket for cards and slips of paper. Bosanquet's notebooks are in the Archives of the BSA, Wace's in Liverpool Museum Archives, Pembroke College Special Collections or the Wace Family Archive, and Dawkins's in the Taylorian Institute (Bodleian Library Oxford). Wace's were often given an extravagant (and enigmatic) title page: 'Tramps on the Roads of Rhodes (not by B-t K-y) with various notes on the Antiquities, and Manners and Customs of that beautiful and interesting Island August, July 1908' Wace Rhodes Notebook 1908: Wace Family Archives No 076.

---

57. Mackridge 1990, 202.

58. Wace Island Notebook 1906 Liverpool Museum Archives p43 reverse.

59. Wace Embroidery Catalogue Liverpool Museum Archives.

60. This could imply that Myres had a collection of several hundred in the 1900s.

61. These books are now in the BSA Archives and the same small brown fabric covered books were used.

cations[62] and applied this experience to recording his embroidery collections.

Confusion arose later regarding Dawkins and Wace's catalogues because, at some point, possibly in the 1930s,[63] they cut up and divided the entries. The pages from the brown fabric covered notebooks were torn out and pasted into two identical red leather bound books, one for Wace and one for Dawkins, whose book is now covered with brown paper.[64] If the entries were too complicated to do this, they were re-written into the new books but keeping the numbers. The entries for others' embroideries were abandoned in the original notebooks but Wace kept these and left them to Liverpool Museums. Both Dawkins and Wace gave their catalogues to the V&A and Liverpool, but neither institution realized that they were sharing original documentation. Dawkins confused matters by re-numbering much of his collection in an extended catalogue,[65] preserved in a copy in Liverpool. It is also possible that the V&A further confused matters by removing Dawkins's labels on accessioning. At Liverpool original numbers are cross-referenced to museum accession numbers and the museum has also retained most of Wace's original labels on the embroideries themselves.[66] The photographs were entered into albums.[67] These acted as references to recognise pattern and type, and were also used to exchange photographs with the V&A,[68] suggesting that Dawkins and Wace built up a photographic reference collection to use until they felt more certain of their knowledge.

Fig.8.2: Case F at the Burlington Exhibition 1914: 'The Cyclades'. Some of the several fragments catalogued as 819 Melos can be seen in the centre. BSA Photographic Archive: Greek Embroideries Photographs Album, p.29.

62. Tod and Wace 1906; Stuart Jones 1912.

63. This date is speculative, but amongst the Wace catalogues in Liverpool Museum Archives are various notes in a very childish hand in blue pencil, and E.B. French, Wace's daughter, recalls cataloguing work being carried out on the collections at that time.

64. In a lecture given at Cambridge on 24/4/04, Richard Firth described a similar (and near contemporary) cutting up by Evans and Myres of the running 'handlists' of the Knossos tablets and mounting them in an album.

65. One has not been found at the V&A to date.

66. The author's research involves re-uniting catalogues and numbers.

67. One album is in Liverpool Museum Archives and one with Wace's family.

68. Wace's nominal file at the V&A MA/1/W2 is full of letters recording exchanges of photographs.

Dawkins had many of his embroideries mended and repaired at the Royal School of Embroidery in Athens run by Louisa Pesel, and annotated entries in his second extended catalogue. Wace does not record any repairs, but may not have indulged in this as he had considerably fewer funds. They did divide up fragmentary pieces between themselves. Catalogue entries record multiple parts, with Dawkins and Wace taking some each. This has resulted in some embroideries being scattered across museum collections. An example is 819 in the original catalogue which reads:

819 a, b etc Melos RMD & AJBW
Pieces of red & gold satin stitch border

Bought made up as Παπλωματακι
Wave pattern filled up with Cycladic & other
beasts — sirens, eagles, peacocks etc

Five fragments are now in the V&A,[69] two in the Textile Museum Washington,[70] one in Liverpool Museums[71] and one with Wace's family (see PLATE III).

As their collections became established and their knowledge grew, Dawkins and Wace published their findings and created or contributed to exhibitions. The first of these was at the Fitzwilliam Museum in 1905–6 for which a small pamphlet was produced covering classifications of patterns, stitches and dyes.[72] The preface states, 'This classification system does not aim at being perfect or final, but is to be regarded merely as a step towards further study'. The copy in Liverpool Museum Archives is heavily annotated, suggesting that Wace revised his opinions quite considerably from this early publication.

This exhibition and publication led to a long collaboration with A.F. Kendrick, Keeper of Textiles at the V&A. A minute from Kendrick to the Director reads:

Mr Wace has been for some time studying the embroideries found in Greece with the object of classifying them, and of tracing the various influences under which the typical patterns have developed. I saw him when he was in London some time ago, and we looked through the very excellent collection of these embroideries in the museum. The collection has never been satisfactorily classified, as the literature on the subject is very scanty, and the work could only be done by a person of experience in the localities where the embroideries are found. The task has been undertaken by Mr Wace and his colleagues at Athens, and small collections have been formed by several gentlemen. Mr Wace was greatly interested in some of our fine pieces in the museum, and before leaving he suggested an exchange of photographs for

mutual assistance in the work of classification. The small catalogue of the collection at Cambridge (attached) represents a step in advance of anything before contributed to the subject, and Mr Maclagen's visit to Cambridge has already been of considerable service in rendering possible a preliminary classification of the Greek and Turkish embroideries in the Museum.[73]

The correspondence that followed between Wace and Kendrick continued until the latter's retirement in 1925, when Wace took over his post. The V&A was an enormous source of information and support to Wace,[74] while the V&A used Wace's knowledge to help 'classify' and 'provenance' their holdings. The Wace nominal file records photograph exchanges, and embroideries lent by Wace to the V&A and displayed in the Loan Court in 1913.

The V&A also arranged for photography of Wace and Dawkins's exhibition of Greek and Turkish Embroideries at the Burlington Fine Arts Club in November 1914. Of the one hundred and ninety-two embroideries displayed, Dawkins lent sixty-nine pieces and Wace thirty-one. There were also loans from Bosanquet, Daniel, Dickins and Lady Egerton.[75]

The introductory essay to the exhibition catalogue, nominally by Wace, 'is the result of some years' personal study and travel in the Levant'.[76] The material covered follows the format of the leaflet published for the Fitzwilliam Museum nine years earlier introducing the subject, summarising the geographical areas, the dates of the embroideries, the materials and dyes,

---

69. T.447–1950 a–g, see Johnstone 1961, 64.

70. 81.18 and 81.19, see Trilling 1983, 114, 24.

71. 56.210.141, Taylor 1998, 54.

72. Wace 1905.

73. V & A Archives Wace Nominal File MA/1/W2: MinuteT5597/06 30/3/1906.

74. Dawkins's collection is frequently mentioned, but none of the correspondence originates from him. His nominal archive file in the V&A archives has been heavily pruned. Wace's is complete.

75. A. F. Kendrick, Keeper of Textiles at the V&A, arranged for photographs to be taken of the entire exhibition. These remain an invaluable reference and copies can be found in the V&A and in the BSA Library.

76. Wace 1914, viii. In addition 36 pieces of Turkish pottery and some 'Miscellaneous Objects' were exhibited which included two icons lent by Hasluck.

the patterns and a brief note on costumes.[77] The two articles Dawkins and Wace wrote for the *Burlington Magazine* in November and December 1914,[78] in which they describe their approach and how the embroideries were used within the context of Greek island architecture, are referenced. These writings are the only joint publications by Dawkins and Wace. There are numerous references through much correspondence about a joint book, and two draft typescripts produced for correction, annotation and editing exist. Both Dawkins and Wace's handwriting can be seen with additional comments and corrections.[79] While incomplete, it follows the same format already used twice but includes much material not previously used.[80]

Wace did publish the embroidery collection of Mrs F.H. Cook, cited by some as his definitive work.[81] However, its lavish production values — two volumes, gilt engraved binding, colour plates, black and white diagrams, belie the fact that Wace is describing a single, much smaller collection than his own and Dawkins's and that he left out or summarised detail covered by himself and Dawkins in their joint book (see PLATE IV).

DISPOSAL AND DISPERSAL

By the late 1920s, both Dawkins and Wace largely stopped buying embroideries. Neither was based in Greece. Dawkins was Bywater and Sotheby Professor of Byzantine and Modern Greek Language and Literature at Oxford from 1919, and although he used the vacations for travelling, he seems to have visited Greece only in 1928 (Athens), 1931 and 1935 (both times to

Fig.8.3: Case G at the Burlington Exhibition 1914: 'North Greek Islands'. 495 'Jannina from Paros' can be seen on the upper right. BSA Photographic Archive: Album Greek Embroideries Photographs, p.33.

Mount Athos).[82] On completing his term as Director of the BSA in 1923, Wace did not return to Greece until 1939. There are references to some acquisitions from Liberty's and other London shops, but the main period of collecting was clearly over. Other circumstances were to determine the disposal of the collections.

Much of Wace's collection was loaned to the V&A during the First World War and displayed in the 'Loan Court'. Wace corresponded with Kendrick throughout

77. Wace dismisses the subject of costume as 'a complicated subject and needs extensive illustration, so that it cannot be adequately dealt with here.' Ibid, xxxii.

78. Wace and Dawkins 1914*a*; Wace and Dawkins 1914*b*.

79. This was an approach also used by Blegen and Wace in another unpublished work: 'Helladica', French 1989, 3.

80. A copy of this joint book is in Liverpool. Wace thought it a worthwhile work as he mentions it to J.H. Iliffe, Director of Liverpool Museums in a letter of 13/2/1957 when discussing the photographs, books and papers included with the sale of his collection.

81. Wace 1935. This book was nicknamed 'The Cookery Book' by Wace. For example Johnstone 1961; Trilling 1983.

82. Dawkins 1938 Autobiographical Notes F.ARCH.Z. DAWK.6(2) Taylor Institution Library, Oxford.

the war,[83] and in a letter of December 1917 mentions: 'I hope when I get home, if one ever gets home, to be able to settle something about handing over to the museum some of my pieces as a beginning, if I did so I should especially choose pieces which would fill up gaps in the museum collection.' In January 1919 Wace wrote:

> I have long thought of trying to send you one or two of the things I have here & so today I am sending a list with numbers & short descriptions of what I have with one or two stray notes. As opportunity offers I am going to send them to you by what I hope will be a safe means. So from time to time I shall just write you two words & say numbers so and so sent off & shall be very grateful if you will let me know you have them safely or not. All that I send you thus I propose to give at once to the museum as an earnest of the bulk to follow and as a sort of thank you offering for the end of the war, but please do not let anyone know of this except Sir Cecil.[84] I do not want anyone to know yet that I have begun to give you my things.

Kendrick kept his word and all the embroideries arriving at the V&A, via Slade of the Foreign Office, were listed as entering the museum for inspection until they were formally acquired in August 1919. Eighty-four pieces were gifted, but Wace asked 'I would rather my name was not mentioned too much' and that 'The gift should be considered as a thank you offering for the victorious peace especially, in view of the fact that during the war the usual grants from the state to the V&A for purchases have been mostly suspended.'

Wace was to join the staff of the V&A in 1925 on Kendrick's retirement, but not before family circumstances determined that he sell some of his embroideries to G.H. Myers, founder of the Textile Museum Washington D.C.[85] In 1924, Wace's brother-in-law had died leaving Wace responsible for his sister, her children and their finances. He also wanted to get married but being un-employed:

> I can hardly do more unless I part with my embroideries. You know how much attached I am to my collection and will realise that only sheer necessity of this kind makes me even dream of parting with them. I had intended to give or leave them all to the South Kensington Museum as you know and I naturally would have preferred to see them go to a museum. But failing that I would rather they went to a collector like yourself who is devoted to such things and who proposes to give them to a museum himself.[86]

Long negotiations later, Myers bought for £1000 forty-five embroideries[87] that still form the nucleus of the Textile Museum's Greek embroidery collection.

In 1949, Dawkins contacted the V&A asking for assistance in sorting out the embroideries that he intended to bequeath to the museum.[88] Donald King spent four days with Dawkins and reported back to George Wingfield Digby, Keeper of Textiles, that the collection comprised about 750 pieces of which about 600 were Greek, twice the size of the V&A's existing collection and less rich in pieces of 'the first quality' but

> On the other hand, having been formed with the express purpose of including every available type, it is much more representative of the various patterns and their evolution. Combined with our own pieces, it will form a reference collection in this field which

---

83. These letters are all in the V&A Archives Wace Nominal file MA/1/W2.

84. The Director of the V&A from 1909–24 was Sir Cecil Harcourt Smith, Director of the BSA 1895–97.

85. The letters between Wace and G.H. Myers are in the archives of the Textile Museum Washington.

86. Wace to Myers 18/3/1925.

87. Wace sent Myers 90 embroideries that he considered to be worth £1000. Myers, however, did not accept all those selected and asked for a further selection. Those not bought by Myers were offered to other institutions in the United States including Cleveland Museum of Art and the Metropolitan Museum of Art as Wace did not want to pay the import duty on the silk if they were returned to the U.K..

88. The correspondence regarding Dawkins's bequest to the V&A is contained in the Dawkins nominal file MA/1/D513 which is labelled as 'weeded up to 31/12/1935'. One suspects that much correspondence between Dawkins and Wace while the latter was Keeper of Textiles has therefore been lost.

could hardly be equalled.… The museum is in no way committed to the acceptance of this collection, though Dawkins' intention to bequeath it was known and sketched out twenty five years ago.

Wingfield Digby then reported to the Director:

I discussed the question of our accepting the gift of this collection with you and I think you agree we should certainly accept it. It will make our already good collection of Mediterranean embroideries of unique importance, and although enthusiasm for this type of peasant work is likely to decline in the future we should undoubtedly have it adequately represented here and such collections can probably not be made again.

This slight hesitancy in taking on Dawkins's collection was replicated and complicated when Wace tried to sell his collection in the mid-1950s.[89] An offer to the Fitzwilliam Museum was turned down on the grounds that textiles 'are not very easy things to exhibit and, although they do not take up great space in storage, are none the less difficult to keep and make available to students.' The Ashmolean appears not to have replied and negotiations were held with the Cooper Hewitt, New York, and the Museum of Decorative Art, Copenhagen, but approaches to the (then) City of Liverpool Public Museums were more productive. Its Director, J.H. Iliffe, and its Keeper of Archaeology, Elaine Tankard, had both been BSA students in the 1920s.[90] They arranged an exhibition[91] of Wace's collection in Liverpool in December 1956 and the collection was finally bought by Liverpool Museums in 1957 for £3000 using their War Damage Fund.

CONCLUSION

Museums in the United Kingdom have some of the largest and most comprehensive collections of Greek embroideries outside Greece, almost all of which were acquired through a small group of men and (a few) women who studied at or were associated with the British School at Athens before 1914, especially R.M. Dawkins and A.J.B. Wace. The latter are generally remembered as a philologist (Dawkins) or as an archaeologist (Wace), but their contribution to the preservation and study of Greek embroideries should not be overlooked as it can be said to exemplify the founding aim of the school 'to promote the study of Greek archaeology in all its departments … of every period'. This article hopes to have begun a re-evaluation of another facet of the BSA's work in Greece by connecting archival research with the embroideries collected by Dawkins, Wace and others.

ACKNOWLEDGEMENTS

Thanks are due to all the archivists, librarians and museum curators who have assisted me, including: Penny Wilson and Amalia Kakissis, British School at Athens; Pauline Rushton, Liverpool Museums; Colin Harris, Bodleian Library, Oxford; Richard Ramage, Taylor Institution Library, Oxford; Dr H.C. Carron, Emmanuel College, Cambridge; Particia Aske, Pembroke College Cambridge; The Textiles and Dress Department, Victoria and Albert Museum; The Archives, Victoria and Albert Museum; P.W.G. Lawson and M.A. Scargall, Leeds University Textile Collection; Jennifer Harris and Frances Pritchard, Whitworth Art Gallery, the University of Manchester; Caroline Whitehead, Tyne and Wear Museums; Susan Stanton, Ashmolean Museum, Oxford.

REFERENCES

Baedeker, K. (ed.), 1904. *Griechenland: Handbuch fur Reisende.* Leipzig.

Belger Krody, S., 2006. *Embroidery of the Greek Islands and Epirus Region: Harpies, Mermaids and Tulips.* London

Bosanquet, E.S., 1938. *Late Harvest: Memories, Letters and Poems.* London.

Bosanquet, Mrs R.C., 1914. *Days in Attica.* London

Bowman Dodd, A., 1906. 'The Royal School of Embroideries in Athens', *The Century Illustrated Monthly Magazine* LXXII (1: May): 120–6.

---

89. Copies of the correspondence regarding the sale of Wace's collection are with the Wace family.

90. Hood 1998, 87–9, 105–6.

91. Tankard 1956.

Clapinson, M. and Rodgers, T.D., 1991. *Summary catalogue of post-medieval western manuscripts in the Bodleian Library: acquisitions, 1916–1975, (SC 37300–55936).* Oxford.

Dawkins, R.M., 1906. 'The Modern Carnival in Thrace and the Cult of Dionysius', *The Journal of Hellenic Studies* 26: 191–206.

Day, Lewis F., 1900. *Art in Needlework.* London.

Duckworth, W.L.H. *et al.*, 1906. 'Anthropology at the Universities', *Man* 6: 85–6.

French, E.B., 1989. 'Wace and Blegen: Some introductory thoughts and a case study', in Carol Zerner, Peter Zerner and John Winder (eds), *Wace and Blegen: Pottery as evidence for trade in the Aegean Bronze Age.* Amsterdam.

Gill, D., 1992. *Donors and Former Owners of Greek and Roman Antiquities in the Fitzwilliam Museum, Cambridge.* Cambridge.

—, 2000. 'Collecting for Cambridge: John Hubert Marshall on Crete', *BSA* 95: 517–26.

Hann, M., Senturk, C.A. and Thomsen, G.M., 1995. *The Pesel Embroideries.* Exhibition Catalogue Ars Textrina International Textile Conference. Leeds.

Hood, R., 1998. *Faces of Archaeology in Greece: Caricatures by Piet de Jong.* Oxford.

Jenkins, R.J.H., 1955. 'Richard Macgillivray Dawkins 1871–1955', *Proceedings of the British Academy* 41: 373–88.

Johnstone, P., 1961. *Greek Island Embroidery.* London.

—, 1972. *Guide to Greek Island Embroidery.* London.

Kendrick, A. F., Pesel, L. and Newberry, E.W., 1921. *A Book of Old Embroidery.* London, Paris, New York.

Mackridge, P., 1990. '"Some Pamphlets on Dead Greek Dialects": R.M. Dawkins and Modern Greek Dialectology', *BSA* 85: 201–12.

Myres, J.L. and Freire-Marreco, B. (eds), 1912. *Notes and Queries on Anthropology.* London.

Parry, L., 1988. *Textiles of the Arts and Crafts Movement.* London.

Paulson Townsend, W.G., 1907. *Embroidery or Craft of the Needle.* London.

Pesel, L., 1907. 'The Embroideries of the Aegean', *The Burlington Magazine* X (XLVI).

—, 1921. *Stitches from Eastern Embroideries Portfolio II.* London.

Ridgeway, W., 1908. 'The Origin of the Turkish Crescent', *The Journal of the Royal Anthropological Institute of Great Britain and Ireland* 38 (July - Dec.): 241–58.

—, 1909. 'Presidential Address: The Relation of Anthropology to Classical Studies', *The Journal of the Royal Anthropological Institute of Great Britain and Ireland* 39 (Jan. - June): 10–25.

—, 1910. *The Origin of Tragedy with Special Reference to the Greek Tragedians.* Cambridge.

Salmeri, G., 2004. 'Frederick William Hasluck From Cambridge to Smyrna', in D. Shankland (ed.), *Archaeology, Anthropology and Heritage in the Balkans and Anatolia: The Life and Times of F. W. Hasluck 1878–1920.* I: 71–104. Istanbul.

Shankland, D., 2004. 'The Life and Times of F. W. Hasluck 1878–1920', in D. Shankland (ed.), *Archaeology, Anthropology and Heritage in the Balkans and Anatolia: The Life and Times of F. W. Hasluck.* I: 15–70. Istanbul.

Sherratt, S., 2000. *The Captive Spirit: Catalogue of Cycladic Antiquities in the Ashmolean Museum.* Oxford.

Stuart Jones, H. (ed.), 1912. *A Catalogue of the Ancient Sculptures preserved in the Municipal Collections of Rome by members of the British School at Rome.* Oxford.

Stubbings, F.H., 1958. 'Alan John Bayard Wace 1879–1957', *Proceedings of the British Academy* XLIV: 263–80.

Tankard, E., 1956. *Mediterranean Embroideries lent by Professor A.J.B. Wace.* Liverpool.

Taylor, R., 1998. *Embroidery of the Greek Islands and Epirus.* New York.

Tod, M.N. and Wace, A.J.B., 1906. *A Catalogue of the Sparta Museum.* Oxford.

Trilling, J., 1983. *Aegean Cross Roads: Greek Island Embroideries in the Textile Museum.* Baltimore.

Wace, A.J.B., 1905. *Catalogue of a Collection of Modern Greek Embroideries exhibited at the Fitzwilliam Museum Cambridge.* Cambridge.

—, 1910. 'North Greek Festivals and the Worship of Dionysos', *BSA* 16: 232–53.

—, 1913. 'Mumming Plays in the Southern Balkans', *BSA* 19: 248–65.

—, 1914. *Catalogue of a Collection of Old Embroideries of the Greek Islands and Turkey.* London.

—, 1935. *Mediterranean and Near Eastern Embroideries from the collection of Mrs F.H. Cook.* London.

— and Dawkins, R.M., 1914a. 'Greek Embroideries - I: Ethnography', *The Burlington Magazine* 26 (140): 49–50.

— and Dawkins, R.M., 1914b. 'Greek Embroideries - II: The Towns and Houses of the Archipelago', *The Burlington Magazine* 26 (141): 4–7, 99–101.

Wiseman, T.P., 1990. *A Short History of the British School at Rome.* London.

9

Scenes pleasant and unpleasant:
the life of F.W. Hasluck (1878–1920)
at the British School at Athens

David Shankland

As for most schoolboys, the plays of Bernard Shaw held for me a certain fascination. In their clarity, forcefulness and neatness, produced in sandy-coloured cloth and large type, they lent themselves to being read and reread. *Arms and the Man, You Never Can Tell, Mrs Warren's Profession*: thinking of the titles brings back fond memories. However, I couldn't work out why Shaw had called one group 'Plays Pleasant', and another 'Plays Unpleasant'. The issues that they dealt appeared not that awful, and I found reading them equally enjoyable. I could only conclude that subjects that were once perhaps not discussed in public, or shied away from, no longer held their force: in sum, it was now perfectly all right openly to read these works of Shaw, even if they once had been received or offered with some trepidation.

The events that I shall describe in this paper may seem to verge upon the unpleasant. It is, to get these over with immediately, unfortunate (at least from his point of view) that in 1915 the School should have sacked Hasluck, by far the greatest scholar it has had, just as he was falling ill with consumption. It is equally unfortunate that this sacking should have been engineered by his erstwhile companion Wace. It is regrettable that these events should have been incorrectly presented in the history of the School by Helen Waterhouse (1986). It is a source of great regret that the archives of the London office where these events are recorded, should have been moved to Athens in 2003, away from their home for so many years, thus removing them from the convenient perusal of the scholarly community.[1]

Yet, I would urge a sense of distance, a readiness to look back at these events now, nearly a century later, without embarrassment or concealment. There can be no institution that has not dismissed its staff at one time or another, for it is inevitable that human competition will lead to some gaining, and others losing. Indeed, the School itself having disposed of Hasluck, decided equally to dismiss Wace a few years later, forcing upon him a departure that was from his point of view certainly not desired. Yet again, compared to the nightmare of the Great War, with which they overlap, all these events are as tiny struggles in the face of an overwhelming cataclysm.

Nevertheless, from the point of view of the history of the School, such events are of great interest to us now. They may help us understand a series of events and textures in the School's continuing intellectual life. I have wondered, for instance, whether the later seemingly inexplicable hostility of Evans toward Wace, discussed by MacGillivray[2], may be explained in part in that Evans appears to have been fond of Hasluck, and at once aware of and opposed to Wace's manoeuvrings that led up to Hasluck's dismissal. Perhaps Evans's papers may one day shed light upon this.

I have been struck too by the way that we can look back, a hundred years later, and see a sequence of events almost Hardyesque in the way that they unfold, each gradually gaining in significance, and leading step by step to the waning of Hasluck's star, his disgrace, and early death. Thus, it is clear that Jane Harrison's political conviction that the time was ripe for a woman candidate to the BSA's Oxbridge studentship (events well described in Waterhouse's book) led her to nomi-

1. The documentary evidence for these events is derived from the School's London archive (now held in Athens), and laid out in Shankland 2004. I am exceedingly grateful to a number of friends and colleagues for discussions during the course of this work, and I would thank in particular the late Keith Hopwood, Michael Llewellyn-Smith, Peter Mackridge, and Giovanni Salmeri. I am also grateful to Lord Renfrew, and Metropolitan Kallistos for comments made on the first version of this paper when it was given at Athens. I remain responsible for any assertions here made.

2. MacGillivray 2000.

1911 onwards, Dawkins appears to have been absent for domestic reasons, during which time Hasluck was Acting Director. Upon Dawkins's return, he was happy to share the Upper House with Hasluck and his spouse. However, when Wace became the new Director in 1913, it was necessary for Hasluck to move out. He hoped to install a small apartment in the student hostel, something along the lines of that which exists today, but was unable to persuade the Committee that this would be an appropriate arrangement.

Hasluck, having enjoyed the support of the London Management Committee for many years, was perhaps unconscious of the way that his position had been eroded. Penoyre, the London secretary, was extremely fond of Hasluck, referring to him affectionately as 'Tophet'. However, he took leave in 1912. Penoyre was replaced by the Assistant Secretary, a man called Wise who was a supporter of Wace and not, as is clear from his acerbic comments, of Hasluck and his wife.

Wace himself, having in 1912 returned to Britain, joined the Management Committee that was later to appoint him Director, and appears to have used that period to cast doubts on Hasluck's readiness to remain in post. Indeed, Wace appears to have been instrumental in persuading the Committee to recast Hasluck's terms of employment so that they were altered from continuous to a rolling contract with six months notice to be given on either side. This served to create a rising sense of uncertainty, something that committees hate when they are trying to make decisions.

Further, even Hasluck's erstwhile supporters were not at all sure about the best way to incorporate women within the school. Dawkins, for instance, appears to have been upset at the outcome of an attempt to mix men and women at an archaeological excavation. Now retired in Wales, he did not support Hasluck strongly in his predicament. Even Penoyre, now back, was lukewarm in his support, having been acutely embarrassed by Harrison in her forceful assault on the Cambridge Vice-Chancellor. Throughout this discussion too, there appear to have been questions as to whether Mrs Hasluck was not too forceful or dominant a character to wish to have at such close quarters at the School. Thus stationed away in Athens, Hasluck was caught up unwittingly in a fierce debate on the role of women and beset equally with rumours concerning his position.

Fig.9.1: F.W. Hasluck, ca.1911–12; BSA Photographic Archive: BSAA7–57.

nate a person through her Vice-Chancellor who was brave, stubborn and forceful but not bright. The other members of the London Committee, extremely irritated already by Harrison's actions, were goaded still further when that candidate, née Margaret Hardie, married Hasluck in 1912. All the indications are that the marriage was extremely successful, but it forced the first major rupture between the School and Hasluck, when in spite of his repeated pleas from a distant Athens, the London Committee refused permission for the couple to live together in the School hostel.

The immediate dispute hinged over appropriate accommodation. Dawkins was then Director. From

He had no one at court willing or able to reframe his request in terms of its importance to him personally, or otherwise defuse the situation for him.

The outcome, for Hasluck at least, was disastrous. The couple moved out of the School, but were unable to find clean lodgings in Athens, a problem that was greatly exacerbated by overcrowding caused by the Great War. From then on, his health appears to have worsened markedly. Wace complained to London of his lack of assiduity in his duties. Hasluck himself was invariably courteous in his communications, and carried on going to the School. Mrs Hasluck was less restrained, and there emerged a bitter enmity between her and Wace that culminated in his demanding the return of Mrs Hasluck's key.

Eventually, in 1915, Wace asked Macmillan, the Chairman of the School, to dismiss Hasluck. On 22 June of that year, rather reluctantly, Macmillan acquiesced, carefully thanking Hasluck for the service he had rendered the School. Hasluck remained in Athens working on counter-intelligence files. His health now extremely poor, the couple left in 1916 for France, then Switzerland. There, still accompanied by Mrs Hasluck, he lived in a sanatorium until he died in 1920, at the age of forty-two. Mrs Hasluck appears never to have forgiven the School, but continued to work in the Balkans until her own death, from cancer, during the next war.[3]

HASLUCK'S LIFE AT THE SCHOOL

So ended quietly an association with the School that had begun in 1901, when Hasluck arrived as a young scholar in receipt of that year's Oxbridge studentship. He had just graduated from King's College Cambridge with a first in the Classics Tripos. Bosanquet, the then Director, who appears to have been very helpful to the students at the School, encouraged Hasluck to work at Cyzicus, the large classical site in the Dardanelles, where the School was hoping in due course to conduct an excavation. Though a large-scale excavation never took place, Hasluck was able to join in with the School's survey, led by Henderson. He completed a dissertation on the site admirably quickly, which led to him being elected a Fellow of King's College in 1904.

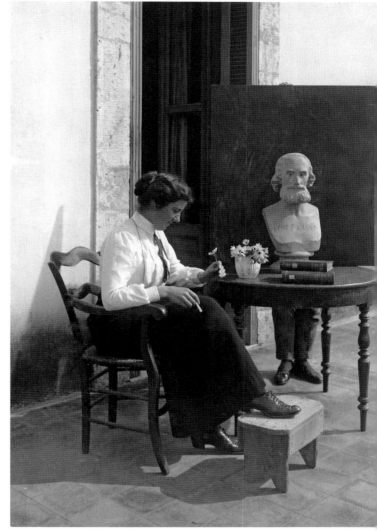

Fig.9.2: Margaret Hasluck, ca.1911–12; BSA Photographic Archive: BSAA7–58.

Despite this early sign of success, he appears to have spent little time at Cambridge, but rather strengthened links with the School, which he found pleasant and congenial. In return, he was favoured by the Committee, becoming Librarian for the session 1905–6 onwards, and Assistant Director from 1906–7. Being made Acting Director in 1911 marked the zenith of his fortunes. Indeed, it was whilst Hasluck held this position that he proposed to Margaret Hardie.

Hasluck appears to have worked efficiently and conscientiously, and run both the hostel and the library with care and attention. He bought well for the library at a time when books were not expensive. As well as

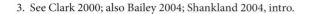

3. See Clark 2000; also Bailey 2004; Shankland 2004, intro.

having a reading knowledge of several European languages, he spoke fluent Greek, and built up a specialist collection of Greek material that is today an important part of the collections. He also bought widely in the fields of travel literature and folklore, delighting in the wide-ranging and sometimes quirky comments of the literally hundreds of accounts of the lands of the Balkans, Greece, and Anatolia that exist in the western canon. He himself travelled equally widely, not just in mainland Greece, but also to the islands. He journeyed often to Asia Minor, and latterly to Albania.

Hasluck possessed the knack of publishing his findings neatly and promptly in journal articles. This means that his work appeared regularly in the School's *Annual* as well as in the *Journal of Hellenic Studies*, occasionally too in publications such as *The Year's Work in Classical Studies*, or the *Illustrated London News*. Monographs followed a little more slowly. His fellowship dissertation for King's sadly appears to be lost. However, a reworked version was published in 1912 by the University Press, with a title as admirably brief as its sub-title is long; *Cyzicus: being some account of the history and antiquities of that city, and of the district adjacent to it, with the towns of Apollonia ad Rhyndacum, Miletupolis, Hadrianutherae, Piapus, Zeleia, etc*. After his death, his wife arranged for *Athos and its Monasteries*, a work that had been substantially completed before the war, to be published. She then edited his letters to Dawkins, many of them written when he was ill in Switzerland, which were published by Luzacs in 1926. Finally, she gathered his articles and other remains in two volumes as *Christianity and Islam under the Sultans*, the work for which Hasluck is today best known. This completes his major works.

HASLUCK'S INTELLECTUAL APPROACH

It is always tempting, looking back at a scholar's achievements, to attribute a unity of thought that perhaps, at the time of writing, did not exist. This caution would appear to hold true in the case of Hasluck, in part because of his habit of writing so succinctly, and in part because premature death deprived him of the possibility of presenting full-length statements of his theoretical position. Even *Christianity and Islam* is not free of this problem because it is an amalgam of published and unpublished material that, had Hasluck lived, would have been produced in two, or even three books.

In addition, his habit of drawing in apparently disparate topics can be misleading. This problem is most acute in his extra-ordinary letters to Dawkins, where writing purely for a friend, he covers an immense range of material, drawn from the sundry reading that was available to him in local continental libraries. This results in scintillating, dense comment that can sometimes appear obscure, even indigestible. It is perhaps a consequence of this that *Letters on Folklore* appears to exist in two printings: standard publisher's cloth, and that more frequently found (that nightmare of all authors) a remainder issue.

Nevertheless, in his years at the School, Hasluck developed gradually a position of the utmost originality, one that was both far ahead of his time and possessed a great measure of coherence. Hasluck's genius lies in the fact that he was interested in the interstices between cultures. This took him into a number of diverse but linked explorations such as the complex relationship between the present and the remains of the past, the workings (and fate) of unorthodox religious movements in times of orthodox pressure, the relationship between folklore and grand religious narratives, and the interconnections between Islam and Christianity. This underlying consistency enables his work to stand up to repeated rereading, and along with its obvious relevance to today's pluralist world, helps to explain why it should increasingly be turned to by contemporary scholars.

SCEPTICISM AND GRAND NARRATIVE

One way in which this approach is manifest in his work is that he appears to conceive of the world in terms of a multiplicity of religions and cultural traditions rather than give priority to any one in particular. Hasluck was trained in Classics, and based his scholarly achievements partly at least on his great fluency in classical languages. He wrote several articles purely on his epigraphic findings soon after his research began. Nevertheless, in contrast to many classicists, he made no attempt in his work to view the ancient civilisations as the epitome of human society. There is in general little desire to make value judgements in his work, and he distanced himself from any sense of grand narrative, looking instead at the way different traditions may come into contact, share experiences or differ from one another.

This may be seen, for instance, is in his comparative historical study of Athos and its monasteries. In spite of the cool tone of the work, he is aware of the importance of the Holy Mountain as a centre of spirituality, and this explains why he was anxious to include his own watercolours as illustrations. These, unlike his written account, are rather abstract, without figures or any extraneous intrusion or indication of daily life, and accentuate the calm monumentality of the setting. In contrast, in his text he is fascinated by the way that individual monasteries gradually become the focus of attention from two conflicting ecclesiastical movements: the one Greek Orthodox, and the other Russian. In outlining this dispute, he traces the way that the monasteries are subject to pressures driven by nationalist movements that, in their desire to exert influence, take a radically different view of the past. Rather than provide clear answers, he explores to remarkable effect the shifting relationship between history, institutions and their respective contemporary cultures. Unlike the more private *Letters*, his monograph on *Athos* is written in limpid prose, and holds a quiet but persistent place in the literature on the region.

CYZICUS

We see a similar approach in Cyzicus, where Hasluck immediately qualifies the apparent focus on one settlement by drawing in the neighbouring region: hence I think the elaborate sub-title. His emphasis is from the outset both comparative and historical, for he divides his monograph into a number of sections ('topography', 'history', 'religion', 'government') so devised as to be capable of including whatever material may emerge from his survey work, whatever its period. This means that we learn much of the longitudinal history of the region, of the transitions between different periods, and far more information than was usual on the contemporary, Ottoman settlement. From the outset his description appears expressed through the present, with detailed description of the multitude of ruins as they appeared to him at the time.

This readiness to consider present-day society alongside the place of latter-day ruins is redolent of early travellers' accounts, which Hasluck refers to throughout the work. Perhaps influenced by the best of these, such as Shaw's *Travels* (1738), Hasluck is fascinated by

the oral history, often folkloric, that they can contribute to the enquiry, which he combines with his extensive research to produce a sustained narrative. Thus:

> Klazaki is said by Gedeon to be a miserable place owing to the curse laid on it by a bishop: the cause was probably the apostasy of the inhabitants who hoped by this means to avoid paying kharatch [dues]: "the Porte," Dallaway continues, "unwilling to encourage them at the expense of the revenue, and fearing the prevalence of example, imposed a double tax on them in future." The Turkish remedy explains the efficacy of the episcopal curse.[4]

Hasluck also attempts to interweave the bare remains of the past with a living culture in a survey publication that was published only after his death, *The Church of our Lady of the Hundred Gates (Panagia Hekatontapyliani) in Paros* where the main text is provided by Jewell, an architect, but Hasluck adds a preliminary chapter and occasional notes on its history and folklore. This form of dense contextualisation is difficult to do well, because it requires a detailed mastery of a wide range of source material, but here he shows to brilliant effect how an otherwise bland survey can be brought to life. As an approach, it also contrasts sharply with the more modern, rather abstract excavation report that was beginning to become fashionable.

THE FORMATION OF MODERN DISCIPLINES

This brings us to a further reason, other than simple human interest, to revisit these two decades before and during the First World War at the School. This period shaped the disciplinary trajectories that came to dominate throughout the twentieth century. Simplifying a more intricate picture, it was a period of gradual expansion, so that it became a reasonable expectation that those students who passed through the School would find a scholarly billet, whether in one of the older or the newer universities, such as Liverpool where Bosanquet accepted a chair upon his departure from Athens. Simultaneously, there emerged a unification of thought within disciplinary practices. This led in turn to the sub-

---

4. Hasluck 1910, 34.

stantial separation of anthropology and archaeology, a separation that even today, in the first decade of the following century, has not been entirely overcome.

We are not here concerned with the world of British academia writ large. I would argue, however, that Hasluck's work and his experience at the School is relevant to these wider, complex changes. Though it goes without saying that there existed variation between archaeologists, professionalisation marked what might be termed the triumph of chronology. All excavations have as their aim some exploration of the past (and very many the idea that it is possible to label human societies according to their age and dominant cultural characteristics); but the emergence of stratigraphy as the dominant practical methodology accentuated this trend, so that the delicate sequencing of the archaeological remains within the excavation often became its central aim.

Once this was done, it became feasible to bring order to the material remains of the past in unprecedented fashion. Nevertheless, even if vital to the development of archaeology, this approach had intellectual consequences. It led to an emphasis on separation, the viewing of any one period of a site as distinct. In academic terms, this means that publications tend to specialise in one period; in practical terms it may mean that the remains of the past that are not of the immediate period of interest are treated with less respect, excavated and published with less attention to detail, or even, in the worst-case scenario, speedily removed.

This shift had the further consequence of removing the emphasis from the individuals who may have inhabited that society to the material culture of their environment. This is not to deny for one moment the extraordinary importance of painstakingly sifting for archaeological material. On the contrary, this is of the utmost worth. What I mean by this remark is that the cultural soup, as it were, within which we all live becomes overlooked. Human beings do not experience life as one period. Our conceptions and perceptions of the every-day world consist of an ever-shifting flickering between past and present, in which visions of the future also play a part, all mixed up together. This is something that psycho-analysis, which emerged equally at that time, and analytical psychology as developed by Jung, was well aware of, so that even if Jung's

conception of ancient archetypes in human behaviour sounds a little clumsy, it come closer to catching the 'now' of human consciousness than any highly dissected approach to the past.

The same is true even if we concentrate more specifically on the way that we interact with material culture. When individuals move through their habitation, whether elaborate or simple, they are at the same time interacting with previous periods: a negotiation with the past that selectively impinges and impacts on their sense of being alive in all sorts of different ways. To take a simple example, the modern day village near Çatalhöyük, the famous early site in Konya in Turkey, has dotted throughout its territory a number of mounds.[5] From the point of view of the professional archaeologist, these belong dominantly to a number of different periods, the Neolithic, Chalcolithic, Iron Age, Roman, even the Seljuk or Ottoman. However, the villagers who inhabit the area possess a relationship with the mounds even today that is much flatter but still significant: they may excavate them for mud for roofs, play on them, use them as guide marks when tending their sheep, explore them for treasure, respect them as the resting places of holy men or, conversely, regard them as malevolent. This intermingling of the past and present is as much part of the daily history of these mounds and the history of human settlement in the area as their respective place in the chronological record. This social interaction is so often left out of the archaeological record when sites are presented sequentially by their age. There are, even today, few detailed histories of mounds and their interplay with their surroundings.

The professionalisation of archaeology had further consequences. It has had the indirect result of creating specialists who, now drawing their intellectual identity from one specific period, felt no necessity to develop a really strong knowledge of the cultures where ruins may be found. This is striking when looking at those who studied the lands of the Ottoman Empire, or today's Turkey. It might be argued that even studies of Italy and Greece are subject to the same underestimation of the difficulty of appreciating the living societies

---

5. Shankland 1999.

of the region. Again, one must take into account individual variation between researchers, but it is worrying how few modern archaeologists have possessed a grammatically correct knowledge of these countries' languages. This lack of attention has now become so ingrained that even today when the more theoretically sophisticated proponents of social archaeology begin to think seriously of the wider context of the archaeological endeavour (such as, for instance, the relationship between archaeology and nationalism in the Mediterranean) they sometimes begin to publish such wider comment before even beginning to study the modern history and cultures of the peoples they are writing about.

Hasluck, however, did speak the local languages, with a standard of Greek that few outsiders could match. During his field trips, rather than excavate, he preferred to deal with living societies. He preferred to create a synthesis, a comparative analysis that draws on a huge range of source material, and as we have seen, he avoided concentrating on one particular period. Throughout his work, material culture of any age is simply a part of human experience, and is treated almost invariably as an adjunct to it.

In fact, through his long residence in the region, his extensive fieldtrips, a disinclination to excavate, and his sensitivity to social institutions, he sometimes appears close to the social anthropology that was also beginning to emerge at that time. This may be seen in his extensive studies of the Bektashis in the Balkans, reprinted in *Christianity and Islam,* which are still an impressive, albeit incomplete, contribution to the ethnographic record.[6] There is too, in the various essays that describe the fruit of his numerous excursions through the Balkans, a strong sense of the localised fieldwork that the twentieth-century social anthropologists were to claim as their own.

HASLUCK AND ANTHROPOLOGY

Does this, then, make Hasluck an anthropologist? No, or at least, not in any straightforward way, not least because the label 'anthropologist' in the sense that Hasluck was working had hardly been developed then, and

Hasluck himself was far too wary of labels to welcome such a posthumous sobriquet. His works remain distinct from that later social anthropological tradition in several ways: in his willingness to work with many periods at the same time; his unfailing readiness to look at the interaction between groups; his geographical breadth, and his willingness to combine written source material of many different kinds with what he had learned during his trips.

Nevertheless, he did anticipate a crucial characteristic of the later social anthropological movement as it was codified after his death, when Malinowski became a defining figure within the field. Malinowski insisted, as is well known, on language competence, on long-term fieldwork, and on direct contact with the peoples in question.[7] He also emphasised the present, and the endless recreation of cultural and historical traditions that takes place within human societies. In simple terms, this meant that the individual desires and assertions of any person became the focal point of the enquiry, and the past the reflection of present desires. History, then, becomes liable to be rewritten endlessly according to who is telling the tale. More than this, any form of cultural continuity becomes regarded as possible only in as much as it is capable of being taken up and pressed into service in the present or, to put the same proposition the other way round, there is no reason why any social institution or any other aspect of cultural life should survive into the present simply through inertia: it must be incorporated, maintained actively, or wither away.

It is possible to see immediate drawbacks in this position. As Gellner (1973) pointed out, is serendipity really always impossible in the diffusion of cultural characteristics over time? Later too, it became easy for this approach to be misinterpreted as implying that there is no such thing as history, which is not the case (such a claim confuses the distinction between the indisputable fact that there is only one past, and the equally evident fact that there are many different versions of that one past). It also led, ultimately, to an astonishingly solipsistic interpretation of human behaviour that on occasion seems to lead social anthropologists to con-

6. See Mélikoff 1998.

7. For an account of his career, see Goody 1995.

centrate almost exclusively on social relations and the self-conceptionalisation of any society. This means that though modern archaeologists may be accused of too often presenting a picture of a human society that is too fragmented, equally modern anthropologists can sometimes be regarded as having ignored material culture altogether. However, Malinowski's insights remain exceptionally useful. The idea that history may be rewritten by the present is today accepted throughout the social sciences.

Here lies Hasluck's extraordinary prescience. This idea infuses his writing, and forms the detailed subject of one of his most sustained essays, the first, long piece in his *Christianity and Islam under the Sultans*, entitled 'Transferences from Christianity, and vice versa'. As Hasluck carried on polishing and shaping this essay, almost up until the day he could work no more, we may assume that it is his final theoretical statement.

RAMSAY AND 'TRANSFERENCES'

'Transferences' is cast in the form of a debate with Sir William Ramsay, a substantial figure at that time. Ramsay was a prolific writer, possessed of great energy, stamina and vigour and, incidentally, the teacher of Mrs Hasluck for her first degree at Aberdeen, where he held the Chair in Classics. He was a founder member of the British Academy, and an active member of the School. He was also a pioneer in survey research in Anatolia, producing while he was still a fellow at Cambridge a work that is still useful today, *The Historical Geography of Asia Minor* (1890). This was based on exhaustive excursions through Anatolia, some of which he shared with David Hogarth.[8] He also wrote with Gertrude Bell an important account, *1001 Churches*, on the group of buildings of that name near Konya, in central Anatolia (1909).

Ramsay was also a committed biblical archaeologist, in that he felt that the material record reflects the history of the Church, and could be used as a literal guide to the scriptures. This meant that his survey work fed directly into his extensive writings on religion, and he wrote substantial volumes on St Paul and the later Roman Empire (1906). In his day Ramsay appears to have been popular,

both as a speaker and a writer, for this work on the history of religion. Today, he tends to be remembered for his historical geography, and, by those in the field, for the great accuracy with which he transcribed his many epigraphic discoveries. However, the two sides of his academic work are linked, in that the underlying impetus for his great exertions was at least in part provided by a conviction of the importance of the Church, and the place that Christianity holds in the world.

In his work, he tended to deplore the Ottoman Empire, and asserted a particular disdain for the Turkish inhabitants of Asia Minor. This disregard reflected itself also in his political convictions, which were firmly Gladstonian, and there can be little doubt that he heartily welcomed the collapse of the Ottomans. This orientation appears also to have helped him to reach an emphatic interpretation of cultural continuities. Ramsay's potential dilemma was that, though he wished to investigate a particular period of Anatolian history, that is, the Later Roman and Byzantine, the territory that he surveyed contained a mix of many cultures, particularly Greek Orthodox and Muslim.

His response was simple: he decided that the only part of contemporary religious Anatolian life that was truly Islamic was the mosque. All other manifestations of religious village culture, such as shrines, tombs, or other sacred locations and related customs, could not be Muslim. These must, therefore, be relics of the past, relics that have survived through the years until the present. This static interpretation of human cultures implies a complete lack of creativity on the part of the living societies of the region. It also meant that he was able to regard the area ethnographically, as well as archaeologically, as the representation of the living past, and it facilitated greatly his drawing on examples of life in Anatolia for his historical writings.

Ramsay regarded this approach as a great deal more than a practical sleight of hand or initial presumption that could be excused on the grounds that it yielded useful results. He published in several papers an explicit working out of this theory, and presented it to international conferences as a way of achieving an accurate historical assessment (a list is given on the first page of *Christianity and Islam*).

In his piece, Hasluck, whose intellectual position was almost the antithesis of Ramsay's, briefly sketches Ram-

8. Ramsay 1897, Hogarth 1896.

say's thesis. He then systematically considers the different ways that Christianity and Islam may be said to have overlapped, and the degree to which they may have said to have influenced each other, hence the expression 'transference'. This takes him into a consideration of the conversion of mosques to churches, and churches to mosques, in illustration of which he offers his usual many detailed examples. As opposed to Ramsay's asseveration of cultural continuities, Hasluck claims to have demonstrated convincingly that the contemporary social conditions are the dominant factor in deciding whether a particular point remains the focal point of worship, or whether a new location becomes regarded as sacred.

> … inherited sanctity seems due less to any vague awe attaching to particular localities than to the desire to continue the practical benefits, especially healing, derived from the cult of the dead.

> … The continuance of their vogue as religious centres depends directly on the continuance of their population…An isolated sanctuary, if on a frequented route, especially the great pilgrim road to Mecca, stands a greater chance of wide popularity than one remote from it: if the road becomes less populous, then sanctuary suffers with it.…it is apparent that many sites of extraordinary sanctity both in ancient and in Christian times have at the present day lost all tradition of that sanctity.

> The inference is that changes in political and social conditions, especially changes of population, of which Asia Minor has seen so many, can and do obliterate the most ancient local religious traditions, and consequently, that our pretensions to accuracy in delineating local religious history largely depend on our knowledge of these changes. Without this knowledge, which we seldom or never have, the assumption too often made, on the grounds of some accidental similarity, that one half-known cult has supplanted another, is picturesque but unprofitable guess-work.[9]

Hasluck was aided in having an opponent who adopted such an extreme position, curiously enough just as Malinowski was in his equivalent argument with Elliot-Smith on cultural diffusion. Nevertheless, the intellectual leap that Hasluck made was as profound as Malinowski's: in order to reach this conclusion, he puts the social place of events at the forefront of any analysis of the material past.

THE ROOTS OF HASLUCK'S THOUGHT

Hasluck, on the cusp of the modern conceptions of the disciplines of archaeology and anthropology, adopted a fluid position that led him to anticipate the insights of both while it fully resembled neither. He would appear to fall into exactly that predicament that Kuhn (1996) outlines so lyrically when he discusses the emergence of scientific revolutions: without a cohort of like-minded colleagues to create a distinct ethos, Hasluck remains a solitary figure, waiting forlornly for the intellectual ideas of the world at that time to coalesce, but unless they do so, forced to work alone, and neglected.

Malinowski may have developed his scepticism toward cultural continuities through his early work on the philosophical theories of Mach (notably Mach's assertions as to the difference between appearance and reality in the course of scientific research). We may then regard Malinowski's theories as a combination of continental philosophy with a practical readiness to explore the variety of human societies that was then being stimulated by Frazer, and other early modern anthropologists.[10] In parallel fashion, Salmeri in an immensely suggestive essay (2004), proposes that it may be possible to seek Hasluck's intellectual vigour in the atmosphere of King's at that time, and in particular in the way that the Cambridge Tripos was reconfigured under Ridgeway. This train of thought is helpful to our wider understanding of intellectual history, for it implies that we may fruitfully revisit the existing dynamism of that English pre-war epoch on the eve of modernisation, and find there a greater sophistication than is often realised.

Looking further into the past, it is also potentially relevant that Hasluck attended the Leys School, Cam-

---

9. Hasluck 1929, 113–8.

10. Gellner 1995.

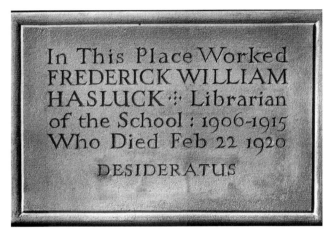

Fig.9.3: Marble commemorative plaque in the BSA Library; BSA Corporate Records—Athens: Athens Property, Hasluck memorial .

bridge. The Leys School is an interesting establishment: a non-conformist religious school for the children of those of Methodist background who have attained a degree of affluence and a position in life.[11] This appears to have imbued Hasluck with the confidence that may accompany a public school education, but with a greater degree of quietism than might be normal. It may also help to explain why, though trained to the highest level, he nevertheless retained some sense of detachment, almost as if always looking from the outside in.

That Hasluck may have avoided exposure may help to explain why his work was never fully recognised in his own School. It could be argued that the emerging professionalism that I have discussed arose from the earlier and large intellectual movement which emphasised research on Greece as the epitome of the classical past. There was an underlying assumption that such concentrated research into history, regarded as the unveiling of a pure culture, would be one of the most important activities of the School. This meant that the complexities of Hasluck's position, as exemplified in his debate with Ramsay, could never be seen as central to its activities.

THE LONDON COMMITTEE

In looking back at these early events, it may be useful to clarify that I do not wish to imply that the Committee

in London was ill intentioned. That Hasluck should have flourished at all, caught between the forcefulness of the old and the equal forcefulness of the new, is a great tribute to the relaxed and creative way in which the British School at Athens was founded. Indeed, the advantage of the Foreign Schools in general is that they permit the free exploration of a multitude of fascinating academic problems without that weight that sometimes impedes university life.

There is hardly space to discuss the way that the bureaucracy of the School as it was originally founded first facilitated, then somehow served to snuff out the pioneering spirit that produced Hasluck. However, one might point again to the emergence of professionalism as a possible reason. The great strength of so many British academic (and other) societies is that they are run by a group of trustees who gain no remuneration from their activities. This means that a relaxed, but knowledgeable, group of dedicated members can often sustain a high standard.

Yet at the same time, the ease with which such small committees can be disrupted means that they are vulnerable to external influences. Without unceasing vigour, they may also easily develop a tendency toward incompetence or scholasticism. It may be no coincidence, then, that first Dawkins, and then Hasluck appeared to have fitted in easily, and had no great need or desire to fight to assure their standing in life through the School. Their work, as Dawkins himself wrote in his reminiscences, proceeded comfortably.[12] In contrast, Wace appears far more forceful, and his path was far from smooth. The introduction of his far from selfless combativeness could be one reason that, in spite of the often important work that was later to be conducted at the School, its early genius could never quite be reproduced.

It may also be helpful to note too that I do not visualise the Committee as being chauvinist in any straightforward way. There were those amongst its members who simply deplored the suffragette movement, but in practical terms it appears that Macmillan was hoping to preside over a gradual integration of women into the School's activities. Both in dismissing Hasluck at

11. See Houghton 2000.

12. Olsen 2004.

Wace's request, and in refusing the abrupt introduction of women to the hostel, there appears to be a sense of duty, of maintaining the status quo, that is not personal in intent. Hasluck himself refrained from expressing any recrimination at all. In all the correspondence, other than with reference to his desperate attempts to live with his wife at the School, there is no harsh or bitter word. Even after his untimely dismissal he continued to offer his work unfailingly for the *Annual*.

As a final thought as to how we may understand these events from Hasluck's point of view, I have been struck by the pertinence of comments that Clive Bell made in his work *Civilization*. Bell, famous for his pacifism, for his aesthetic ethic, for his early leadership in founding the 'Bloomsbury' set, for his creation of a reading group at Cambridge, seems to be nearer somehow to our day than was Hasluck. In fact they were both born in 1881, and were exact contemporaries at Cambridge. Bell was at Trinity, and Hasluck at King's, but there is seemingly at least a parallel in the way Bell lays out his respective characteristics of the 'civilised' individual, and the quiet, restless, detached intellectualism that marked Hasluck's life and work. The following quotations are drawn from Chapter VI, 'Civilization and its disseminators'[13]

> The thoroughly civilised person will be willing at any moment to follow intellect into the oddest holes and corners…he will try to put himself above rage and prejudice, which have the same inhibitory effect.

> A civilized man will be tolerant and liberal…just as he discovered that by putting the padlock of prejudice on any door of the mind inevitably he turned away some of its most charming visitors, so he will learn that there are very very few cases of anger which will not yield to intelligent treatment.

> A thoroughly civilized person, though deeply concerned about politics, will neither appeal to those grand old principles which are nothing to the purpose, nor deem his natural desire to hold what he has more meritorious than the desire of his opponent

to get it for himself. He will not deceive himself with words and phrases…

> To enjoy life to the full is his end, to enjoy it as a whole, and in its subtlest and most recondite details; and to this end his chief means are the power of thinking and feeling, intensely cultivated. He is a man of taste in all things. His intellectual curiosity is boundless, fearless, and disinterested. He is tolerant, liberal and unshockable…never truculent, suspicious or overbearing.

REFERENCES

Bailey, R., 2004. 'Margaret Hasluck and the Special Operations Executive (SOE), 1942–1944', in D. Shankland (ed.), *Archaeology, Heritage and Anthropology in the Balkans and Anatolia, the life and works of FW Hasluck, 1878–1920*, 1: 151–81. Istanbul.

Bell, C., 1928. *Civilization, an essay*. London.

Clark, M., 2000. 'Margaret Masson Hardie' in J. Allcock and A. Young (eds), *Black Lambs & Grey Falcons: Women Travellers in the Balkans*: 128–48. Oxford.

Gellner, E., 1973. *Cause and Meaning in the Social Sciences*. London.

—, 1985. *Relativism and the Social Sciences*. Cambridge.

—, 1995. *Anthropology and Politics: Revolutions in the Sacred Grove*. Oxford.

Goody, J., 1995. *The expansive moment: the rise of social anthropology in Britain and Africa, 1918–1970*. Cambridge.

Hasluck, F., 1902. 'Sculptures from Cyzicus', *BSA* 8: 190–6. London.

—, 1910. *Cyzicus: being some account of the history and antiquities of that city, and of the district adjacent to it, with the towns of Apollonia and Rhyndacum, Miletupolis, Hadrianutherae, Piapus, Zeleia, etc.*, Cambridge.

—, 1913. 'Christianity and Islam under the Sultans of Konia', *BSA* 19: 191–7. London.

—, 1924. *Athos and its Monasteries*. London.

—, 1926. *Letters on Religion and Folklore*, annotated by Margaret M. Hasluck. London.

—, 1929. *Christianity and Islam under the Sultans*, edited by M. Hasluck. Oxford.

Hogarth, D., 1896. *A Wandering Scholar in the Levant*. London.

Houghton, G. and Houghton, P., 2000. *Well-Regulated Minds and Improper Moments: A History of the Leys School*. Cambridge.

---

13. Bell 1928, 162–94.

Huxley, D. (ed.), 2000. *Cretan Quests: British Explorers, Excavators and Historians*. London.

Jewell, H. and Hasluck, F., 1920. *The Church of Our Lady of the Hundred Gates (Panagia Hekatontapyliani) in Paros*. London.

Kuhn, T., 1996. *The Structure of Scientific Revolutions*. Chicago.

MacGillivray, J., 2000. *Minotaur: Sir Arthur Evans and the archaeology of the Minoan Myth*. London.

Mélikoff, I., 1998. *Hadji Bektach: un mythe et ses avatars: genèse et évolution du soufisme populaire en Turquie*. Leiden.

Ramsay, W., 1890. *Historical Geography of Asia Minor*. London.

—, 1897. *Impressions of Turkey during twelve years' wanderings*. London.

—, 1906. *Pauline and other Studies*. London.

—, 1909. *The Revolution in Constantinople and Turkey*. London.

— and Bell, G., 1909. *The Thousand and One Churches*. London.

Salmeri, G., 2004. 'Frederick William Hasluck from Cambridge to Smyrna', in D. Shankland (ed.) *Archaeology, Heritage and Anthropology in the Balkans and Anatolia, the life and works of FW Hasluck, 1878–1920*: 71–104. Istanbul.

Shankland, D., 1999. 'Integrating the past: folklore, mounds and people at Çatalhöyük' in A. Gazin-Schwartz and C. Holtorf (eds), *Archaeology and Folklore*: 139–57. London.

— (ed.), 2004. *Archaeology, Heritage and Anthropology in the Balkans and Anatolia, the life and works of FW Hasluck, 1878–1920*. Istanbul.

Shaw, B., 1898. *Plays Pleasant and Unpleasant*. London.

Waterhouse, H., 1986. *The British School at Athens: the first hundred years*. London.

10

F.W. Hasluck and *Christianity and Islam under the Sultans*

Paschalis M. Kitromilides

It is no exaggeration to suggest that for the history of scholarship on the post-Byzantine world, the death of Frederic W. Hasluck at the age of forty two in 1920 was a great tragedy. This is a haunting impression that strikes anyone who looks at the list of his writings and even more so at the record of his unfinished projects. The impression becomes stronger when one reads his work. It is not just the sheer volume of original material he collected and the breath-taking range of the subjects that attracted his interest over a period of just two decades. I think it is mostly the capacity of his writing to provoke reflection upon the experience of past societies, a stimulus to rethink and to reconceptualise. There is something different about his work, which presupposes what is best in European scholarship without ever becoming merely conventional. I have often wondered why that might be so and, in preparing for the Conference 'Scholars, Travels, Archives', I think I came up with an answer: what makes Hasluck's work different as historiography, especially a work like *Christianity and Islam under the Sultans*, is that it tries to capture and record images of pre-modern and especially pre-national society. It therefore runs against the current of conventional historiography, which thinks about the past in national terms, and follows an agenda which is primarily set by the aspiration to recover the national past of modern societies which have been connected to nation-states. Hasluck's work leads precisely in the opposite direction: it tries to rescue pre-national pluralism which is directly threatened by the agenda of nationalism and appears doomed to extinction on account of the policies of the nation-state.

Christianity and Islam precisely records and documents two facts of life of pre-modern society that are totally intolerable to nationalism. One is the pervasive cultural and social syncretism which defines life in pre-modern society. Hasluck chose to focus on the most symbolically evocative expression of syncretism in pre-modern society, its religious aspect, which has left

Fig.10.1: F.W. Hasluck; BSA Photographic Archive: SPHS–6266.

the most tangible traces in monuments of faith and in places of worship. Religious syncretism, however, does not operate in a social vacuum. It encapsulates much broader phenomena of symbiosis and social pluralism which make the historical ontology of pre-modern or traditional society very different from the homogeneous and culturally levelled society constructed by the modern state.

Fig.10.2: *The Kilise Mosque, Church of St Theodor; Istanbul.*

The second fact of life in pre-modern society that seems to emerge from Hasluck's account is the fluidity and plasticity of religious and ethnic identities, which seem at any given point along the trajectory of pre-modern society — that is in society before its attachment to the modern state — to be capable of a number of alternative forms of subsequent development. This is precisely what negates the historical teleology presupposed by nationalism, which understands forms of pre-modern ethnic consciousness as just preparatory stages in a foreordained course of development leading up to national plenitude. It is this teleological logic that is negated by the documentation of syncretism, and by the way it makes imaginable the potential of multiple alternative future collective destinies for particular population groups.

All these are conjectures and scenarios that arise from a reflective reading of Hasluck's work. This is what makes it so valuable and so challenging. There is one further thought I should like to record, however, in

order to complicate the picture a little further and especially in order to warn against a misleading impression that may emerge from the argument about pluralism and symbiosis in pre-modern society. This thought has to do with the role of violence and its impact not only in effacing traditional syncretism and pluralism but also in bringing it about. Conventional wisdom usually regards the role of violence as connected to the levelling of social pluralism, but things work the other way around as well: violence can initiate dislocations and relocations that result in the emergence of pluralism. Hasluck's work is replete with evidence for this second causal chain of social and cultural change.

After these broader considerations let me turn to the work itself and to the multiple possible readings to which it lends itself. As is well known, *Christianity and Islam* is a posthumous book. It was first published in 1929, nine years after the author's death, thanks to the loving care and dedication of his widow, Marga-

Fig.10.3: St James the Persian, Nicosia; Lacarrière 2003, 34–5.

ret Hardie Hasluck.[1] It was composed of the notes and partial manuscripts of the author, originally intended for two different projects. The one was provisionally planned as 'Transferences from Christianity to Islam and Vice Versa', which eventually made up Part I of the published version, occupying most of volume I. This part focuses mostly on sanctuaries and places of worship and their transfer from one religion to the other or their use by both religions. It constitutes a most valuable record of the author's field research primarily in Asia Minor and to a lesser extent elsewhere. The other project was entitled 'Studies in Turkish Popular History and Religion' and was published as Part II of volume I. This is primarily a study of heterodoxy in the Islamic society of Asia Minor, including the very important examination of the origins of Bektashism. This is pio-

neering work indeed and a very important specimen of religious history.[2]

Miscellaneous notes from each project which could not fit into the more or less unitary texts of Parts I and II were placed in Part III which makes up the second volume. This is indeed a Miscellany which records valuable primary evidence gathered on the author's field trips. Its most important part is certainly the extensive sections on the expansion of Bektashism which transpose the focus of attention from Asia Minor to the Balkans.[3]

Margaret Hasluck states in her editorial note that the title of the work was coined by herself. I dare suggest that a slightly revised version of the title might capture and convey more precisely the spirit of the content and also the impact of the material recorded in Hasluck's

1. Hasluck 1929, I–II. A new two-volume edition was published in Istanbul: The Isis Press, 2000.

2. See also Shankland 2004, 26–8.

3. Cf. the appraisal by Irène Mélikoff (2004, 297–307).

Fig.10.4: Holy Spring of the Dormition of the Virgin Vefa, Istanbul, 1 July 2006; author's photograph.

work: *Encounters between Christianity and Islam under the Sultans*. It should be clarified also that the chronological breadth of the material evidence — primarily archaeological — recorded in the work is such that the term Sultans should be taken as referring not only to those of the House of Osman but also to the Seljuk Sultans of Konya who preceded them.

A work so complex and so rich in its contents invites multiple readings. Its unfinished character and therefore open-endedness proves, not a weakness but a main strength, in that it functions as a temptation to the reader's imagination to explore further possibilities of research along the lines suggested by Hasluck. In this direction I could suggest from my own experience some instances of additional evidence for the phenomena of religious encounters described by Hasluck, thus adding more detail to the vast map of cultural syncretism he has drawn in his work. We can follow his lead on an imaginary journey in the Orthodox East, predictably setting off from Cyprus, crossing over the Cilician Sea to Asia Minor and ending up in Constantinople.

The evidence on Cyprus in Hasluck's work is rather sparse. To what he writes on the Church of St James the Persian[4] (FIG.10.5) in my native Nicosia and on Kirklar Tekke[5] and on the cult of St Therapon in Larnaca a lot could be added,[6] including a visit to the sanctuary of St Sozomenos near the obviously converted village of Potamia.[7] Examples of common worship of Christian and Muslim Cypriots in the outlying regions of the island are multiple and can be gleaned from the interior of Paphos and from the Karpass peninsula, areas of endless fascination first explored by David Hogarth in the late nineteenth century.[8]

Let me just recall the example of the Cypriot church chanter Emmanuel Christodoulou Hadjiphilippou from Choulou village in Paphos, who at a moment of religious enthusiasm climbed up the minaret of the

---

4. St James the Persian in Nicosia is mentioned by Kyprianos 1788, 395 as a Capuchin sanctuary. It could perhaps be identified with the 'chapelle de Saint Jacques' belonging to sire Simon de Montolif, mentioned in a 1468 document of payments from the royal household of the kingdom of Cyprus. See Richard and Papadopoullos 1983, 111. As a Latin sanctuary it passed into the hands of the Turks after the Ottoman conquest of Nicosia in 1570 and that is probably why it had to be purchased from a janissary in 1627–28 by a French missionary, Pacifique de Provins. From then on and throughout the seventeenth century San Giacomo features frequently in the correspondence of the Latin clergy of Cyprus with the Vatican. See Tsirpanlis 1973, 66, 67, 116, 118, 166, 167, 172. Of special relevance is a report by the missionary Giuseppe Maria da Bourges, dated 12 August 1662, which records the veneration of an old wall painting of St James the Persian in the Capuchin church of Nicosia by Greeks and Turks alike, who came to the church every day to pray for relief from pain. See *ibid.*, 178. This then is the captive church of St James which today can be seen surrounded by ruins in the buffer zone in Nicosia. I am indebted to my friend Rita Severis for guiding my research on St James.

5. See Jefferey 1918, 183 but especially Gunnis 1936, 453, who expressly notes that 'the shrine is equally holy to Moslem and Christian'.

6. Jefferey 1918, 19 and esp. 364 noting 'St Arabo' in the village Ay. Therapon in the highlands of Limassol, recording also a holy spring and Gunnis 1936, 165–166, 425 on other shrines of St Therapon. A fascinating account on the translation of the cult of St Therapon from Cyprus to Bulgaria is provided by Galia Valtchinova, 'Christian-Muslim religious symbiosis according to Hasluck, comparing two local cults of Saint Therapon', in Shankland 2004, II, 159–81.

7. Jefferey 1918, 206 and Gunnis1936, 205.

8. Hogarth 1889. Hogarth is keenly aware of the ethnic pluralism of Cypriot society, but remains uninterested in forms of modern religious syncretism. Hasluck was quite aware of the significance of Hogarth's work. See Hasluck 1926, 57.

village mosque and chanted the Koran with the local Hodja's approval. My mother Magda Kitromilides, who records this incident from the early twentieth century, also states that Emmanuel was dissuaded from repeating this practice of partaking in the rituals of both religions because the village priest as a penalty for his action forbade him to chant in church for several days, thus depriving him of an important source of his livelihood.[9]

Let us cross over to Asia Minor. In this case readers of Hasluck have at their disposal an inexhaustible treasure on the basis of which to extrapolate, annotate and enrich his own account. This treasure is the oral history archive of the Centre for Asia Minor Studies in Athens. If one looks at the contents of Hasluck's first volume, especially its Part I, one gets a strong impression of the affinities between his own survey of religious syncretism in Asia Minor and the groundwork upon which the research of the Centre developed later on. Although his work does not seem to have influenced the Centre's intellectual universe —in contrast for instance to the work of R.M. Dawkins— the Centre's projects touched on many subjects he first brought into focus in Asia Minor research. I remember Aglaia Ayioutanti, Madame Merlier's closest associate, referring to him with admiration and respect.

The Centre's archive is replete with testimonies adding detail and depth to the phenomena of religious syncretism recorded by Hasluck, enriching especially knowledge of such phenomena for the region of Cappadocia.[10] Besides St George, two other Christian saints whose cult attracted faithful from both religions throughout Asia Minor were St Charalambos, protector against the plague, and St Mamas, protector of shepherds and their herds and animals. Extensive evidence of religious syncretism and shared places of worship is also recorded for the region of Pontos along the Northern coast of Asia Minor and into the highlands of the Pontic Alps, with its epicentre in the

Fig.10.5: Holy Spring of the Dormition of the Virgin Vefa, Istanbul, 1 July 2006; author's photograph.

great shrine of the Dormition of the Virgin at Sumela Monastery.[11]

Our final stopover will be in contemporary Constantinople, not the imperial Istanbul of the Sultans but the megapolis under the Turkish Republic in the opening decade of the twenty first century (see PLATE V). One very important part of Istanbul's Christian heritage are its innumerable holy springs, αγιάσματα ('ayazma' in modern Turkish), still tenderly cared for by the Orthodox communities in the broader Istanbul region on both sides of the Bosporus. Some of them have been common places of worship of Christian and Muslim faithful throughout the centuries. Hasluck unfortunately did not record the holy spring of St Therapon in the walls of Top Kapi, still in Orthodox hands but

---

9. Kitromilidou 2001, 20.

10. Some of the testimonies, focusing on common worship of Christian Saints, have appeared in publications of the Centre over the years. See for instance Marava Hadjinicolaou 1995, 37–44, 46–7, 53–5, 60–1; Loukopoulos and Petropoulos 1949, 30–2, 61, 96 and Petropoulos and Andreadis 1971, 68, 76, 88, 92–4.

---

11. An authoritative source is Bryer 2002, III, 277.

Fig.10.6: *Foundation inscription, St Therapon holy spring, Istanbul; author's photograph.*

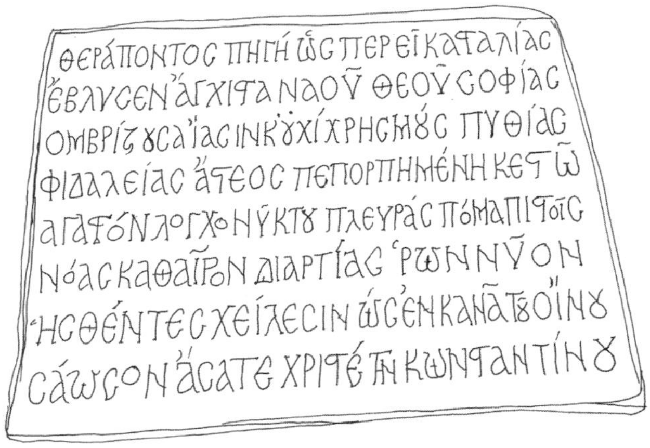

Fig.10.7: *Transcript of foundation inscription of St Therapon holy spring, Istanbul.*

often visited by Muslims.[12] (FIG.10.6) The same is true of the αγιάσματα of St Dimitrios at Kurucesme on the Bosporus[13] and of St Catherine at Modi on the Asiatic side[14]. The most famous and popular, however, is the holy spring of the Dormition of the Virgin at Vefa in the heart of Istanbul.[15] (FIG.10.3) On the first of each month when the priests come to bless the holy water, throngs of Muslim Istanbullular crowd into the grounds of the sanctuary and into the underground chapel to receive the blessing of the holy water and to pray. A visual record of July 1, 2006 (FIGS.10.4, 10.5) illustrates a phenomenon which would have greatly fascinated Hasluck. It would have been very interesting from an anthropological point of view to study these worshipers and to try to trace their geographical origins and religious backgrounds. Such an investigation could perhaps supply evidence of the survival of forms

of religious life first recorded by Hasluck in Ottoman Anatolia and still lingering in Istanbul as Turkey stumbles on the way to the European Union.

REFERENCES

Anonymous, 1936. *Αναμνηστικόν λεύκωμα επί τη πανηγύρει του αρχαίου Βυζαντινού ιερού αγιάσματος του Αγίου ιερομάρτυρος Θεράποντος.* Constantinople.

Atzemoglou, N., 1990. *Τ' αγιάσματα της Πόλης.* Athens.

Bryer, A.A.M., 2002. *The Post-Byzantine Monuments of the Pontos. A Source Book.* Aldershot.

Gedeon, M., 1904. *Εορτολόγιον Κωνσταντινουπολίτου προσκυνητού.* Constantinople.

Gunnis, R., 1936. *Historic Cyprus.* London.

Hasluck, F.W., 1926. *Letters on Religion and Folklore*, annotated by M. Hasluck. London.

—, 1929. *Christianity and Islam under the Sultans*, ed. by Margaret M. Hasluck. Oxford.

Hogarth, D., 1989. *Devia Cypria. Notes of an archaeological journey in Cyprus in 1888.* London.

Jefferey, G., 1918. *A description of the historic monuments of Cyprus.* Nicosia. Reprinted London 1983.

Kitromilidou, Magda M., 2001, *Κυπριακά δημοτικά θρησκευτικά ποιήματα από το ανέκδοτο χειρόγραφο του Εμμανουήλ Χριστοδούλου Χατζηφιλίππου, Χουλιώτη.* Nicosia.

Kyprianos, Archimandrite, 1788. *Ιστορία χρονολογική της νήσου Κύπρου.* Venice.

Lacarrière, J., 2003. *Λευκωσία. Η νεκρή ζώνη.* Athens.

Loukopoulos D. and Petropoulos, D., 1949. *Η λαϊκή λατρεία των Φαράσων.* Athens.

---

12. Atzemoglou 1990, 17–9. For details see Anonymous 1936. On the wall facing the entrance the holy spring of Hagios Therapon preserves an ancient inscription, stressing its location close to the great church of Hagia Sophia. The inscription is rather poorly published by Atzemoglou (1990, 17). It is republished here (Fig.10.6) and transcribed (Fig.10.7). I am grateful to my colleague at the National Research Foundation Ioannis Meimaris for his help.

13. See Gedeon 1904, 271 and Atzemoglou 1990, 104–5.

14. Papas 2001, 375–84, esp. p.380 noting that among the pilgrims who visit the holy spring frequently 'there are many Turks, Armenians, Syrians and others'.

15. Vapheiadis 1918. See also Atzemoglou 1990, 21–3.

Marava – Hadjinicolaou, A., 1995. *Ο Άγιος Μάμας*, second edition, ed. by P. M. Kitromilides, Athens.

Mélikoff, I., 2004. 'Hasluck's study of the Bektashis and its contemporary significance', in D. Shankland (ed.), *Archaeology, anthropology and heritage in the Balkans and Anatolia: The life and times of F. W. Hasluck 1878–1920*, I: 297–307. Istanbul.

Papas, Athanasios, Metropolitan of Ilioupolis and Theira, 2001. 'Το ιερόν αγίασμα Αγίας Αικατερίνης Μοδίου', *Ανθηφόρος Μητροπολίτου Δέρκων Κωνσταντίνου*: 375–84. Athens.

Petropoulos, D. and Andreadis, E., 1971. *Η θρησκευτική ζωή στην περιφέρεια του Ακσεράϊ-Γκέλβερι*. Athens.

Richard, J. and Papadopoullos, Th. (eds), 1983. *Le livre des remembrances de la secrète du royaume de Chypre (1468–1469)*. Nicosia.

Shankland, D., 2004. 'The life and times of F.W. Hasluck (1878–1920)', in D. Shankland (ed.), *Archaeology, anthropology and heritage in the Balkans and Anatolia: The life and times of F. W. Hasluck 1878–1920*, I: 26–8. Istanbul.

Tsirpanlis, Z.N., 1973. *Ανέκδοτα έγγραφα εκ των αρχείων του Βατικανού (1625–1667)*. Nicosia.

Valtchinova, Galia, 2004. 'Christian-Muslim religious symbiosis according to Hasluck: comparing two local cults of Saint Therapon', in D. Shankland (ed.) *Archaeology, anthropology and heritage in the Balkans and Anatolia: The life and times of F.W. Hasluck 1878–1920*, I: 159–81. Istanbul.

Vapheiadis, C., 1918. *Ιστορία του εν Βέφα μεϊδάν βυζαντινού ιερού αγιάσματος της Κοιμήσεως της Θεοτόκου*. Constantinople.

11

Three different views of the Holy Mountain: Athos through the eyes of F.W. Hasluck, R.M. Dawkins and Ph. Sherrard

Kallistos Ware

On my earliest visit to Greece, fifty-two years ago, I stayed initially — as so many other English travellers have done — in the British School at Athens. At dinner on my first evening, a Saturday in March 1954, I asked the others when the Sunday Liturgy began in the local Orthodox churches. Nobody knew the answer. Although several of those present had been resident in Greece for many months, none of them had ever attended an Orthodox service. 'There's a place down the road that keeps ringing bells,' said one of my fellow-diners, referring to the nearby Moni Petraki, 'but I've no idea what goes on inside.'

I was momentarily disconcerted by what I saw as a singular lack of curiosity about the life of contemporary Greece. But then I reflected to myself: 'This is after all an institute for classical studies, a School of Archaeology' — as the inscription on its gateposts indicates — 'and therefore I should not expect its inmates to take an interest in Christian Hellas.' Yet, in thinking this, I was seriously incorrect. For, during its history over the past 120 years, the British School at Athens has in fact numbered among its members a series of eminent specialists in Byzantine and modern Greek studies. In this paper I shall look at three of them, F.W. Hasluck, R.M. Dawkins and Philip Sherrard, all of whom wrote books about the Holy Mountain of Athos. What have the three of them to say about this peninsula in northern Greece, which since the tenth century has been the chief centre of Orthodox monasticism?

Incidentally, from my later experience of Orthodoxy I have come to realize that, on that first evening at the British School, I posed the wrong question. My Greek Cypriot parishioners in Oxford do not ask, 'When will tomorrow's service *begin*?' They enquire: 'When will it *end*?'

F.W. HASLUCK

Frederick William Hasluck (1878–1920)[1] did not live to see the publication of his book on the Holy Mountain, *Athos and its Monasteries*, for it only appeared in 1924, four years after his early death. His widow Margaret (née Hardie), who prepared the work for the press, states that it 'was practically complete by 1912'.[2] Thus it was presumably written during his second period (1911–14) as Assistant Director and Librarian at the British School. In the book he did no specify when he had actually visited Athos, how often and for how long; but it was evidently before the Balkan Wars of 1912–13, that is to say, at a time when the monastic republic was still within the Ottoman Empire. He delayed publication of the book because, according to his widow, he wished to add a chapter on the changes brought to the Holy Mountain as a result of the Balkan Wars; and with characteristic thoroughness he felt that he must first make a further visit and examine the situation on the spot. This regrettably he was never able to do, initially because of the outbreak of hostilities in 1914 and his own heavy involvement in war work, and subsequently because of the collapse of his health from 1916 onwards.

In his Preface, Hasluck pointed out that there had been no book in English dealing with the subject of Athos in general since Athelstan Riley's *Mountain of the Monks*, published in 1887.[3] He went on to explain that he had two specific goals: 'The present volume is intended to serve, first, as an introduction to Athos for the general reader, for whose benefit I have endeav-

---

1. On his life, see Lock 2004, 715-6.
2. Hasluck 1924, vii.
3. Hasluck 1924, v; cf. Riley 1887.

Fig.11.1: Athos, Iveron, general view, photograph by F.W. Hasluck; BSA Photographic Archive: SPHS–8534.

oured, as far as possible, to keep Greek words out of the text, and, secondly, as a guide to visitors on the spot'.[4] It will be noted at once that Hasluck was writing not for the specialist but for a wider public, and so his approach and manner of presentation were somewhat different from that adopted in his master-work *Christianity and Islam under the Sultans*, which was intended for a much more 'academic' audience.[5] At the same time, however, in *Athos and its Monasteries* he provided footnote references to his sources, as well as a five-page bibliography.[6]

Hasluck's book falls into two parts: first, an historical account of Athos, ending with a chapter on its

administration and another on its architecture; second, a detailed description of the twenty sovereign monasteries, dealing with their foundation, subsequent development and present-day buildings. There are numerous illustrations, most of them from Hasluck's own drawings. The style is clear, succinct and precise, albeit somewhat dry. The author concentrates on the external facts of Athonite history, supplying an abundance of statistics and dates. There is very little about the inner life of the monks, about their hopes and fears, their prayer and spirituality. Hasluck never refers, for example, to St Gregory Palamas and the Hesychast controversy in the fourteenth century, to St Nikodimos of the Holy Mountain, the Kollyvades and the publication of the *Philokalia* in the eighteenth century, or to the dispute in the Russian houses concerning the 'Glorifiers of the Name' (*Imyaslavtsy*) during 1912–14. Probably Hasluck felt that such matters lay outside his competence.

There is, however, one important theme to which

---

4. Hasluck 1924, v.

5. See Hasluck 1929.

6. Hasluck 1924, 197-202. For an exhaustive Athonite bibliography up to the early 1960s, see Doens 1964, 351-483 (1860 items); for the chief publications since then, see the select bibliographies in Golitzin 1996, 294-302, and in Speake 2002, 278-82.

Hasluck gave special consideration in the historical section of his book; and that is the question of continuity and change in Athonite governance. He was closely interested in the way whereby the monastic constitution of Athos has remained basically unchanged from the tenth to the twentieth century, while yet being regularly modified in response to altered circumstances. He was interested also in the interaction between different national groups on the Mountain, Greeks, Slavs, Georgians and Romanians. These issues of survival and adaptation, and likewise of cultural exchange, were central to his major study *Christianity and Islam*, and they also recur throughout his *Letters on Religion and Folklore*.[7] In this way Hasluck's work on Athos fits into the main agenda of his scholarly work.

Unlike Riley before him and Robert Byron shortly afterwards,[8] Hasluck did not seek to write a travel book, such as would provide a day-to-day narrative of what he saw and did on Athos; nor do we find any personal reminiscences about the Holy Mountain in his *Letters on Religion and Folklore*, where there are in fact only a few passing allusions to Athos. It would have been fascinating to learn his impressions of the monastic republic as it was at the very end of the Ottoman period, with the monks numbering (in 1912) no less than 7,754 (more than half of them non-Greeks),[9] and with the communities still enjoying high material prosperity. What was the daily programme of the monks, what kind of work did they undertake, what was their social background, their education (or lack of it), and their attitude to the outside world? What conversations did he have with leading Athonite figures? Did he meet any notable *gerontes* ('elders')? Here, however, we are disappointed, for all this lies outside the plan of Hasluck's book.

Nevertheless, there are occasional comments of a more personal nature that catch our attention. He laments that, with the coming of steamships, 'not a little of the romance of a pilgrimage to Athos has vanished'.[10] What would he have said today, with the ferry boats growing ever vaster and more crowded, and with buses and taxis plying along the motor-roads that now disfigure the Athonite landscape! Predictably he comments on the ubiquity of Russian pilgrims and, somewhat less predictably, on the almost equal ubiquity of Greek insurance agents.[11] The 'rank and file' of the Russian monks, he notes, 'are probably the simplest and most medieval on the Mountain'; but in their souvenir shop, or 'bazaar' as he calls it, they combine this simplicity with 'businesslike management' on 'the soundest commercial lines'.[12] I was intrigued but at first surprised by his remark about 'the striking similarity of Athos administration to that of our own older Universities'.[13] On reflection, however, I suppose that there may be some resemblance between the Holy Community at Karyes and the erstwhile Hebdomadal Council at Oxford.

Most striking among his personal observations is his admission that he went to Athos with a 'strong prejudice' that was largely dispelled by his actual experiences on the Mountain:

> I came to Athos first with a strong prejudice against monasteries in general and Greek monasteries, as contemplative and non-productive, even parasitic, in particular; this prejudice, based both on natural bias and on impressions formed in other parts of the Levant, was considerably modified before I left the Mountain. My quarrel with the individual monk was disarmed by the extreme simplicity and obvious honesty of the Athonite point of view. This of necessity toned down my repugnance to the system, since it evidently suited a number of individuals and is only beginning to become an anachronism.[14]

All in all, Hasluck seems to have left the Mountain with positive impressions, and he emphasized in par-

7. See Hasluck 1926.

8. See Byron 1928.

9. For Athonite statistics in the twentieth century, see Gothóni 1993, 31. By 1943 the number of monks had fallen to 2,878, and by 1971 to 1,145. Since then there has been a steady increase, and by the year 2000 the number had risen to 1610: see Speake 2002, 174.

10. Hasluck 1924, 3.

11. Hasluck 1924, 4.

12. Hasluck 1924, 124-5.

13. Hasluck 1924, 79.

14. Hasluck 1924, 80-1.

ticular 'the kindness I received almost everywhere on Athos'.[15]

Professor René Gothóni, the Finnish specialist on pilgrimage to the Holy Mountain, has warm praise for Hasluck in his work *Tales and Truth*.[16] In his discussion of descriptions of the Holy Mountain from the fifteenth to the twentieth century, he calls Hasluck's work 'a cornerstone of Athos literature'. In Gothóni's estimation, Hasluck was 'a busy librarian bee', who checked his facts with scholarly accuracy and was thoroughly familiar with the previous bibliography on the subject. (It should be added that, in his book on Athos as in his other works, Hasluck did not simply rely on research in libraries, but almost always had actually visited the places of which he speaks, and had worked diligently on the site.) Gothóni sees Hasluck as 'the first English writer to exhaust multilingually the sources on Mount Athos'. Hasluck's book is in fact far too short to be considered exhaustive — he was, after all, writing for the 'common reader' — but otherwise I accept Gothóni's assessment. Within his self-imposed limitations, Hasluck was certainly successful, and his book is still worth consulting.

R.M. DAWKINS

When planning my first visit to the Holy Mountain, I approached the Russian priest in Oxford, Hieromonk (later Archbishop) Vasilii Krivocheine, who had himself lived on Athos for over twenty years, and I asked him for advice about preparatory reading. He replied by recommending just one book: 'Read Dawkins!' It was good advice.[17]

Richard MacGillivray Dawkins (1871–1955), author of *The Monks of Athos*,[18] was Director of the British School at Athens during 1906–14, at much the same time as Hasluck was Assistant Director.[19] When, however, he came to write his book about Athos, published

in 1936, Dawkins was no longer at Athens, having been elected in 1920 to the Bywater and Sotheby Chair of Modern and Byzantine Greek in the University of Oxford, a post that he held until his retirement in 1939. Dawkins's book, which is about four times longer than Hasluck's, embodied material that he had collected during the course of four visits to Athos, in 1905, 1931, 1933 and 1935, amounting altogether to a total of about eleven weeks.[20] Thus, while Hasluck's work reflected the position on Athos before the First World War, Dawkins — although familiar with the pre-war conditions — was describing mainly the inter-war situation.

Hasluck and Dawkins had often travelled together, and they shared a common interest in the religious folklore of Christian Greece (and other regions). Hasluck's *Letters on Religion and Folklore*, published posthumously, were in fact written to Dawkins, although Dawkins's side of the correspondence has not so far appeared in print. Yet, despite this common interest, the two have written very different books about the Holy Mountain. Whereas Hasluck concentrated on the exterior facts of Athonite history and on the dating of the monastic buildings, Dawkins's theme is the inner life of the monks, their legends, corporate memory and self-perception: how they interpreted their past history, how they understood their relationship with God and the communion of saints, what the miracle-working icons of the Mother of God meant to them, and so on.

The work of Dawkins is also much more personal than that of Hasluck. Although Dawkins insisted that his book is not meant to be a travel journal,[21] he often referred to his meetings with particular monks, and described the long walks that he took through the more remote areas of the Holy Mountain.[22] He was clearly sensitive to the natural beauty of Athos, and took an interest in its flora and fauna. While much of the book is based on oral information that he had himself collected, he also made use of written sources, although he did not undertake any independent research into manuscripts.[23]

---

15. Hasluck 1924, 81.

16. Gothóni 1994, 115-22 (especially 115, 117).

17. For myself, if asked today I would give the same reply; but I would add, 'Also read Speake!' (see Speake 2002).

18. See Dawkins 1936a. Shortly afterwards he issued a 14-page brochure with additions and corrections to his book (Dawkins 1936b). He included further material on Athos in an article published seventeen years later (Dawkins 1953).

19. On the life of Dawkins, see Halliday and Gill 2004, 538-40.

---

20. Dawkins 1936a, 23.

21. Dawkins 1936a, 26.

22. See, for example, Dawkins 1936a, 35-9, 93-6.

23. Dawkins 1936a, 24.

Dawkins had originally come to Greece to undertake archaeological work, but he quickly became attracted to the study of Greek dialects. This led to the publication of, among other books, his major monograph on *Modern Greek in Asia Minor* (1916). Initially, when recording folktales in the course of his travels, he was concerned with them not for their own sake but as philological evidence. Gradually, however, he came to give attention also to their content, and this led to a series of publications at the end of his life, in particular *Forty-Five Stories from the Dodekanese* (1950), *Modern Greek Folktales* (1953), and *More Greek Folktales* (1955). His book on Athos anticipated these later studies. He called it 'a collection of the legends of Athos'.[24] Although Dawkins used here the word 'legend', which might perhaps be taken in a pejorative sense, and although he occasionally displayed a gentle irony, his attitude towards the monastic stories that he assembled was on the whole courteous and respectful, albeit somewhat detached. He wrote of the monks in friendly terms, and he did not sneer.

Dawkins did not exclude the possibility that the 'legends' which he recorded might contain a basis of fact. But he wisely added, 'No purpose is served by trying to induce the narrators of a legend to tell a consistent and logical story.' While there is indeed truth in legends, it is not truth of a strictly historical kind. Their value lies in the light they shed on 'what people think and believe'.[25] They provide 'a picture of a way of thinking, or rather a way of feeling'.[26] It is, Dawkins continued, a manner of thinking and feeling very remote from our own in the twentieth-century West. The legends 'present to us a way of looking at the world which has come down to us straight from the Byzantine age'.[27] Of the three strands that constitute contemporary Greek culture — the classical, the Byzantine and the modern — the first and the third are largely absent from Athos; only the second remains. The monks, Dawkins added, have 'hardly an idea of historical evidence'; 'rationalism has made no marks on Athos'. At the same time, he detected no 'fraud' or even 'conscious invention'.[28]

Fig.11.2: Athos, Vatopedi, campanile, photograph by F.W. Hasluck; BSA Photographic Archive: SPHS–9666.

The 'legends', then, were important to Dawkins, not as historical evidence concerning the distant past, but as a living testimony to the mentality of the present-day monks. And what was his considered opinion concerning the moral character of these monks and their way of life? On the whole it was affirmative, although by no means uncritical. In common with Hasluck, Dawkins commented on the 'simplicity' of the Athonite monks, 'a simplicity which goes with unquestioning faith, and a constant feeling of the presence of the unseen world'.[29] Dawkins has here put his finger upon what is surely a fundamental element in Athonite spirituality: its

24. Dawkins 1936*a*, 9.

25. Dawkins 1936*a*, 257-8.

26. Dawkins 1936*a*, 377.

27. Dawkins 1936*a*, 379.

28. Dawkins 1936*a*, 42-3.

29. Dawkins 1936*a*, 42.

sense of the unbroken interweaving of the visible with the invisible, of time with eternity, of the present age with the Age to come. Athos is indeed a 'thin' place, in which the wall of partition between earth and heaven, for those with eyes to see, often grows so attenuated as to become all but transparent.[30]

This sense of the immediacy of the Divine means that, for the monk, all things are seen in symbolic terms, with the outer acting always as a sacramental sign of the inner: as Dawkins put it, 'Everything in the monastic life has its *noema*, νόημα, its symbolic meaning.'[31] But, while all visible things are treated as signs and sacraments of the invisible, at the same time Greek monastic spirituality is not only other-worldly but this-worldly. In the words of Dawkins, 'Sanctity in Greece is supernatural, not in any sense non-natural…. The Greek ascetic… is not to be alienated from the world, for whose rebirth he constantly looks.'[32] In this connection Dawkins remarked how the monks, alongside their quest for the kingdom of heaven, continue to retain a lively interest in their *patrida* or native place, about which they are always pleased to hear news.

Dawkins was favourably impressed, as Hasluck had been, by the openness of the monks towards visitors, whatever their background, and by their generous hospitality: 'kindness towards all is the rule'.[33] Unlike other travellers on Athos in the 1930s, such as Robert Byron, he did not complain about bed-bugs. He even defended Athonite *cuisine*: 'the diet is monotonous and for our habits rather too sparse: nothing worse'.[34] On the whole I agree here with Dawkins. Like him, I have found that the only really nasty thing that has ever been set before me is the dried stockfish. Cold bean soup and wizened olives — the staple fare at most monasteries during my early visits — may be monotonous and spare, but they are eatable. Today, it should be added, the food in many places has greatly improved, with abundant salads and fresh fruit. But sadly, due to the vast number of visitors, the monastic hospitality has grown less cordial

and more impersonal than it was in the days of Hasluck and Dawkins.

For Dawkins, the place where the Athonite spirit could be experienced in its purest and most undiluted form was in the 'Desert' at the southern tip of the peninsula, beneath the immediate shadow of the mountain peak, in the *kellia* and hermitages of St Anne, Kerasia, Katounakia and Kapsokalyvia. Hasluck had little to say about the eremitic and semi-eremitic life in this part of Athos, and it is not clear how much time he had actually spent there. Dawkins, on the other hand, was thoroughly familiar with the more remote settlements outside the twenty sovereign monasteries. 'In these cottages and hermitages of the Desert', he wrote, 'are the most genuinely devoted of all the monks of Athos. Everywhere I found hard work, great simplicity and austerity of life, and the kindest hospitality.' This secluded and precipitous region, he continued, is 'the industrial centre of Athos', where the monks earn their keep through such crafts as icon-painting, wood-carving and incense-making.[35] He noted the practicality of the monks: 'In general the monks are like sailors and do everything themselves.'[36] Other twentieth-century pilgrims, such as Gerald Palmer (1904–84), have shared Dawkins's predilection for the southern tip of Athos.[37] Here, even today, there are fortunately no motor roads, and the stillness of the Holy Mountain remains undefiled. May it always be so!

In a book published in 1935, a year before that of Dawkins, and ominously entitled *Black Angels of Athos*, the Greek American sociologist Michael Choukas concluded by painting a deeply depressing picture of the future of the Holy Mountain:

> The monastic community of Athos is facing today the danger of outside intervention and probable extinction…. The phantom of dissolution is already casting its widening shadow over those sacred hills and mountain tops…. The next generation of monks may be predestined by human providence to put the final stamp of failure upon the mate-

---

30. Cf. the quotation from Evelyn Underhill, in Ware 2008, 143.
31. Dawkins 1953, 218.
32. Dawkins 1936*a*, 51, 269.
33. Dawkins 1936*a*, 268.
34. Dawkins 1936*a*, 319.

35. Dawkins 1936*a*, 130.
36. Dawkins 1936*a*, 327.
37. See Ware 1994.

rial remnants of this greatest of all human experiments of our millennium — to close up shop and return to their homes and their worldly occupations. To predict that this will happen within the next generation is hazardous — not because it may not happen; but because it may occur sooner.[38]

Dawkins for his part displayed no such pessimism. In *The Monks of Athos* he depicted a community that was certainly in his view archaic, but he did not suggest that it was in a state of terminal decline. In this regard he has been proved right, whereas the sociologist Choukas has been proved resoundingly wrong. Seventy years after Choukas penned his sombre obituary, Athonite monasticism, so far from disappearing, has undergone a notable revival. Under the leadership of outstanding abbots and *gerontes*, many of the twenty monasteries are today filled with young monks marked by a spirit of dedication and hope. Where, on my early visits forty-five years ago, I saw scarcely a single black beard, now it is often difficult to find beards that are white or grey. Where previously the monastic services were all too often performed wearily and with resignation, out of a sense of duty, now they are carried out with eagerness and joy. My third Athonite author from the British School, Philip Sherrard, noted the beginnings of this renewal. But he also felt that all was not well.

Before leaving Dawkins, however, we need to ask a final question, even though we do not have a ready answer. As we have noted, he found that the monks of Athos were virtually untouched by 'rationalism' or the spirit of critical inquiry. In fact, when he was there in the 1930s, as also when I was first there in the early 1960s, the number of monks in the entire Holy Mountain who had received a university education could probably have been numbered on the fingers of two hands. Today, as a result of the recent renewal, the situation is greatly changed. Alike in the twenty sovereign monasteries and in the Desert, there are now many who have undertaken higher studies, not only in theology but in history, philosophy, medicine or science, often in western universities, sometimes to a doctoral or post-

doctoral level. They have been exposed, in a way that was not the case with earlier Athonite generations, to the 'mindset' of the Enlightenment and even of Post-Modernism. How, then, do they view what Dawkins termed the 'legends' of Athos, and what the monks themselves might prefer to call its 'traditions'? How far are there contemporary Athonites who are willing to assess these 'traditions' by the criteria of modern secular scholarship?

This is something on which Sherrard, familiar as he was with the renewed Athos, must sometimes have pondered. In fact he does not actually address this question in his writings. But he has much else to tell us about the Holy Mountain that is of the highest interest.

PHILIP SHERRARD

Philip Owen Arnould Sherrard (1922–95) first visited Greece as an army officer at the end of the Second World War.[39] He quickly acquired a keen interest both in modern Greek poetry and in the Greek Orthodox Church, which he joined in 1956. His links with Greece were strengthened by his marriage in 1946 with a Greek whom he had met in Athens, Anna Mirodia.[40] He was first registered at the British School at Athens for the academic year 1950–51, and during 1958–61 he served as Assistant Director of the School; he was Librarian during 1961–62, and during 1963–69 he continued to be registered as a Student, while holding a Guggenheim Senior Fellowship. After a period at London University (1970–77), as Lecturer in the History of the Orthodox Church at King's College and at the School of Slavonic and Eastern European Studies, he spent his later years mainly on his estate at Katounia, near Limni (Euboea), which he had bought in 1959. He welcomed the freedom from university routine, the spiritual space for thinking and writing, that life at Katounia provided. More fundamentally, he strongly preferred rural Greece to urban London.

---

38. Choukas 1935, 295-6.

39. On Sherrard's life and writings, see Ware 1998, ix-xlv.
40. This marriage was eventually dissolved, after which Sherrard married the publisher Denise Harvey, who has reissued most of his books and is editing some of his unpublished writings.

Fig.11.3: Philip Sherrard; BSA Photographic Archive: BSA A6–129.

Brought up in what he termed the 'liberal scientific humanism' characteristic of the 'Bloomsbury World',[41] Sherrard found this secular outlook radically challenged by what he encountered on his arrival in Greece at the end of the war. Both in the modern Greek poets from Dionysios Solomos onwards and in the living tradition of the Orthodox Church, he discovered an understanding of human life altogether deeper and richer than that in which he had grown up: an approach that was more traditional, more imaginative, open to a sense of the sacred, sensitive to the value of symbols, conscious of the links that bind human beings to the world of nature. It is interesting to note how his interest in poetry and his attraction to Orthodoxy overlapped: for it was a Byzantine poet who first drew him to the Orthodox Church, the mystical writer St Symeon the New Theologian (959–1022). He chose Symeon as the subject of a lecture that he delivered at the British School during his first period there: 'a bit of a shock for the mostly archaeological audience', he wrote to his friend George Seferis.[42]

Sherrard's studies in modern Greek poetry led to the publication of his first major work, *The Marble Threshing Floor* (1956). Here he examined Solomos, Costis Palamas, Cavafis, Sikelianos and Seferis, not only from a philological and literary standpoint, but also as witnesses to a transcendent and eternal realm, to what he called 'the world of spiritual reality, or archetypes', that is to say, to the 'Great Realities' or 'primordial truths' that cannot be known through sense-perception or discursive reasoning but only through 'contemplation'.

Sherrard's parallel concern with the Orthodox Church led to his second major publication, *The Greek East and the Latin West: A Study in the Christian Tradition* (1959). In some circles this was criticized for neglecting political and economic factors. Sherrard did not in fact deny the importance of such factors, but he believed that history and culture can in the end be understood only from a spiritual perspective. Despite a certain one-sidedness, *The Greek East and the Latin West* has proved deeply influential on a younger generation of Orthodox thinkers, both in the English-speaking world and in Greece. Sherrard's later writings were largely a working-out and fuller application of the ideas in these two seminal works, with particular reference to the growing ecological crisis.

Sherrard's earliest journey to Mount Athos seems to have been in April 1951. Writing to Seferis after he returned, he described it as 'the most extraordinary of the many extraordinary places in this land of yours'.[43]

---

41. These phrases occur in a talk by Sherrard, as yet unpublished, 'The Other Mind of Europe', that is to be included in a forthcoming edition of his correspondence with George Seferis, prepared by Denise Sherrard (née Harvey). I am grateful to Mrs Sherrard for making this talk available to me, along with extracts from the correspondence.

42. Letter dated 1 May 1951.
43. Letter dated 1 May 1951.

This was the first of many such visits, on two of which I had the great pleasure of being his companion. I can recall vividly the long walks that we made together, most notably from the Serbian monastery of Chilandar to Chromitsa, close to the northern frontier of Athos, and from Karyes southwards along the ridgeway, before descending to Simonopetra. Each walk lasted some four hours, and on neither occasion did we meet a single other person. As a walker Sherrard maintained a brisk pace, and though his junior by twelve years I had difficulty in keeping up with him.

Sherrard's close familiarity with the Holy Mountain led to the writing of a substantial book, *Athos the Mountain of Silence*. This has had a somewhat curious bibliographical history. It first appeared in 1959 in a German translation by Titus Burckhardt, issued by the Swiss publishing house Urs Graf-Verlag (Olten). The original English appeared in the following year, published by the Oxford University Press. Both the German and the English editions contained fine colour photographs, mostly by Paul du Marchie. Then in 1982 there appeared a work with a slightly different title, *Athos the Holy Mountain*, issued under Philip Sherrard's name and published by Sidgwick and Jackson. This was illustrated with an entirely new set of photographs by Takos Zervoulakis. Those in colour are for the most part excellent, but others in black-and-white are excessively dark and often blurred.

Somewhat disingenuously, Sidgwick and Jackson sought to give the impression that the 1982 publication *Athos the Holy Mountain* was a new work. Nowhere in the book itself was there any reference to the work that had appeared in 1960, *Athos the Mountain of Silence*. On the dust cover, however, there was a cryptic note, saying of Sherrard: 'He has written a previous book on Mount Athos in 1960 which was published in Germany.' I doubt whether Sherrard himself was responsible for this misleading and inaccurate sentence. In reality, the 1982 book is substantially identical with that published in 1960. The only significant difference in the text, apart from abbreviations and minor stylistic alterations, is that the 1982 revision incorporated large extracts from an article written by Sherrard in 1977 on 'The paths of Athos'.

Sherrard's work, like those of Hasluck and Dawkins, was not a travel book or narrative description of his various visits, but a general account of the history and life of the Holy Mountain. The first half, on the evolution and external organization of Athonite monasticism, was not particularly original. While composed with elegance and charm, for the most part it reproduced what had already been said by earlier authors, as Sherrard himself acknowledged in his Foreword. In the later chapters, on the other hand, dealing with the inner motivation of the monastic vocation and the contemplative prayer of the monks, he broke new ground. Here, in a way that had not been attempted by previous writers, he sought to answer in depth the basic question: 'Why should anyone actually choose to become an Athonite monk?' Compared with Hasluck and Dawkins, and with his other predecessors in the field of Athonite studies — Athelstan Riley, Robert Byron, Amand de Mendieta and Sidney Loch — Philip Sherrard had the major advantage of being himself a member of the Orthodox Church, and so he was able to offer a picture from the inside, in a manner that the others could not.

Why become an Athonite monk? The answer that Sherrard gave can best be summed up in three words: repentance, freedom, silence. Repentance is to be understood in this context not merely in negative terms but, much more profoundly, in a positive fashion. While it does indeed presuppose a sense of guilt, of heartfelt sorrow over sin, it signifies primarily — as the literal meaning of the Greek term *metanoia* indicates — a 'change of mind', a radically new way of looking at ourselves, at our neighbour, and at God. It is not to look back to the past with discouragement, but to look forward to the future with hope. It is to look up, not down. Sherrard made this clear in his treatment of the gift of tears. The monk weeps, either outwardly or inwardly. But these are tears, he insisted, not simply of mourning over sin but also of joy at sin forgiven. To illustrate this affirmative meaning of repentant weeping, he aptly quoted the monastic poet who had so greatly influenced him, St Symeon the New Theologian: 'Give me tears of repentance, love's tears, tears of liberty, tears cleansing my mind's darkness and filling me with heavenly radiance!'[44]

---

44. Sherrard 1960, 83.

Fig.11.4: Athos, Pantokratoros, view from the sea, photograph by F.W. Hasluck; BSA Photographic Archive: SPHS–8537.

'… tears of liberty…': this leads us to the second theme, freedom. Here, as with repentance and tears, Sherrard stressed the affirmative aspect of the monastic vocation. The ascetic self-restraint practised by the monk may appear at first sight to involve loss and deprivation. It is tempting to define monasticism negatively as renunciation of marriage and material goods, repudiation of one's own preferences and desires, lack of sleep, abstinence from food, and so on. The underlying purpose of all this self-denial, however, is not negative at all but supremely positive. In Sherrard's words, its aim is 'to secure more ample freedom to "follow Christ"'.[45] Such exactly is the point of asceticism: it is the doorway to freedom. Discipline, whether physical or spiritual, if practised aright does not oppress but liberates. The monk observes self-denial, not out of hatred for material things, but so as to draw closer to God. Having ceased to lust, he is able to love. As the Athonite monks told a nineteenth-century visitor, Jakob Fallmerayer, in words quoted by Sherrard: 'Here you will find soft breezes, and the greatest of all blessings — freedom and inward peace. For he alone is free, who has overcome the world, and has his dwelling in the laboratory of all virtues on Mount Athos.'[46]

'…freedom and inward peace', said the monks to their German guest. 'Peace', however, means much more than just the absence of exterior tumult and distraction. It denotes a sense of direction, a state of wholeness and integration; and this wholeness can be attained only through silence. Here we come to our third key concept: silence, stillness of heart, *hesychia*. Like repentance and renunciation, this too is to be

---

45. Sherrard 1960, 30.

46. Sherrard 1960, 2.

understood in affirmative terms. It is not emptiness but fullness, not an absence but a sense of presence, not just cessation of speech or a pause between words, but an attitude of listening, of waiting upon God. Understanding stillness or *hesychia* in this way as an entry into unitive contemplation, Sherrard cited the words of Abba Philemon in *The Philokalia*: the purpose of the 'way of silence' is to 'cleanse the mind', to be 'stripped of the passions and purified', and so to be 'united with God'.[47] Having attained, through God's grace, this experience of purification and union, the hesychast — whether on Athos or anywhere else — discovers the meaning of St Paul's words, 'Pray without ceasing' (1 Thess. 5:17). He becomes, that is to say, not simply a person who *says* prayers from time to time, but a person who *is* prayer all the time. The monk finds that everything he does acquires 'symbolic significance', states Sherrard,[48] agreeing here with Dawkins. Every act in his daily life, however seemingly trivial, points beyond itself to the realm of the Eternal.

While silence or stillness is primarily an inner quality, a standing before God in the depths of the heart, yet exterior quiet is also crucially important; for the outer influences the inner. Precisely in this regard Sherrard became more and more troubled by something that struck him painfully on his successive visits to the Holy Mountain: and that was the loss of silence. In his article on 'The paths of Athos', written thirty years ago, he deplored the way in which silence was being 'murdered' by 'the groans and clankings of lorries'.[49] Today the situation is incomparably worse. Motor vehicles are everywhere. The forest echoes with the whine of chain saws; mobile phones twitter and twangle in the pockets of the monks.

Sherrard began his article by acknowledging the positive features in the monastic renewal on the Holy Mountain. But he expressed his disquiet at the neglect of the ancient cobbled paths by which in earlier generations pilgrims and monks had journeyed laboriously from monastery to monastery, either on foot or by mule. Today, by contrast, they are conveyed swiftly

and effortlessly by minibus or jeep. Sherrard saw in this abandonment of the paths the symptom of a far deeper spiritual *malaise*. The incursion of motorized transport and other forms of modern technology, in his view, was impairing the rhythm and ethos of traditional Athonite life. With the monks supervising building works, looking after crowds of visitors, hurrying by land-rover from place to place, communicating with each other and the outside world by e-mail, what has happened to the silence and peace that marked the old Athos? What has happened to the simplicity that so deeply impressed Hasluck and Dawkins?

There is, however, an obvious rejoinder that can be made to Sherrard and to those who share his concerns, as I myself do.[50] 'Your view of the monastic life is too romantic,' many of the monks say to us. 'We who actually live here have to be more practical.' If the monks of an earlier era used mules, oil lamps and wood stoves, so it can be argued, that was not because these things are specifically monastic or intrinsically sacred, but because such was the way people lived at that time also in the secular world outside Athos. Now that technology has changed in society at large, there is no reason why the monks should not likewise avail themselves of the labour-saving devices employed by their non-monastic contemporaries. This will leave them with more time for distinctively monastic pursuits such as keeping vigil, reciting the Jesus Prayer, or reading the *Philokalia*.

I can illustrate this from my own experience in 1965–66 as a deacon at the Monastery of St John the Theologian on Patmos. We deacons were expected each Saturday, in preparation for the Divine Liturgy on the following day, to wash ourselves thoroughly, including our hair. For the others, with hair almost down their waist, this was a formidable task (my own hair was shorter). In my cell — actually a series of four rooms — I had electric light but no central heating or running water, apart from a single cold water tap. I had to boil water in a saucepan on a primus stove, and to wash by degrees, so as to avoid catching a chill in the midwinter cold. By the standards of that era, there was of course nothing unusual about this. But it took

---

47. Sherrard 1960, 92; cf. 99-102.

48. Sherrard 1960, 80.

49. Sherrard 1977, 100. His views on the Athonite paths are discussed by Ware 2008, 154-7; see also Gothóni 1994, 165-70.

---

50. See Ware 1993, 29-32.

Fig.11.5: Athos, Costamonitou, entrance, photograph by F.W. Hasluck; BSA Photographic Archive: SPHS–8548.

a considerable time, about an hour, whereas a shower would have taken five or ten minutes. Arguing with a malevolent primus stove may help some to acquire sanctity, but such was not my own experience.

Today Patmian and Athonite monks frequently enjoy the use of hot water and central heating. In the twenty-first century, it may be claimed, these things are not a luxury but a normal convenience. With hot water the monk can quickly wash himself and his clothes. Central heating precludes the need to cut and store firewood, and reduces the risk of fires. The monk can pray undistracted without having regularly to replenish his wood stove. Electricity enables him to read at night in a good light, without having to break off and trim an oil lamp. Moreover, oil lamps have to be kept clean, and this is time-consuming. The cleaning used

to be done by lay servants, but where can such servants be found today? In any case, as a matter of principle should monasteries rely on servants?

Such are the arguments of the pro-technology lobby. I am partly convinced, yet not wholly so. Those who, like myself, share Sherrard's memories of the 'pre-industrial' Athos that existed until the 1960s, are bound to regret the erosion of silence in the major part of the Holy Mountain. We cannot but be alarmed at the accumulation of mechanized *debris*, of discarded tar barrels and rusting tractors, that now defiles the Garden of the Theotokos. Technology diminishes what was once a precious characteristic of the Holy Mountain: the sense of closeness to the realm of nature, of trust in God, of dependence upon the unseen world. How far, we need to ask, can there be a positive use of mechanization that enhances rather than undermines the spiritual purpose that is the Mountain's *raison d'être*? Let us hope that in years to come a fourth member of the British School at Athens, a worthy successor to Hasluck, Dawkins and Sherrard, will write another book about Mount Athos which answers that question.

REFERENCES

Amand de Mendieta, E., 1955. *La presqu'île des caloyers: Le Mont-Athos*. Bruges.

—, 1972. *Mount Athos: The Garden of the Panagia*. Berlin/Amsterdam.

Byron, R., 1928. *The Station. Athos: Treasures and Men*. London.

Choukas, M., 1935. *Black Angels of Athos*. London.

Dawkins, R.M., 1936a. *The Monks of Athos*. London.

—, 1936b. *Additions and Corrections to the Monks of Athos*. Oxford.

—, 1953. 'Notes on life in the monasteries of Mount Athos', *The Harvard Theological Review* 46: 217–31.

Doens, I., 1964. 'Bibliographie de la Sainte Montagne de l'Athos', in *Le Millénaire du Mont Athos 963–1963. Etudes et Mélanges* 2. Actes du "Convegno internazionale di Studio" à la "Fondazione Giorgio Cini" (3–6 septembre 1963) à Vénise: 337–495. Chevetogne.

Golitzin, A., 1996. *The Living Witness of the Holy Mountain: contemporary voices from Mount Athos*. South Canaan, PA.

Gothóni, R., 1993. *Paradise within Reach. Monasticism and Pilgrimage on Mt Athos*. Helsinki.

—, 1994. *Tales and Truth. Pilgrimage on Mount Athos Past and Present*. Helsinki.

Halliday, W.R. and Gill, D., 2004. 'Richard MacGillivray Dawkins', *Oxford Dictionary of National Biography* 15: 538–40. Oxford.

Hasluck, F.W., 1924. *Athos and its Monasteries*. London/New York.

—, 1926. *Letters on Religion and Folklore*. London.

—, 1929. *Christianity and Islam under the Sultans* 1–2. Oxford.

Loch, S., 1957. *Athos: The Holy Mountain*. London.

Lock, P.W., 2004. 'Frederick William Hasluck', *Oxford Dictionary of National Biography* 25: 715–6. Oxford.

Riley, A., 1887. *Athos or The Mountain of the Monks*. London.

Sherrard, P., 1960. *Athos the Mountain of Silence*. London/New York/Toronto.

—, 1977. 'The paths of Athos', *Eastern Churches Review* 9: 100–7.

—, 1982. *Athos the Holy Mountain*. London.

Speake, G., 2002. *Mount Athos: Renewal in Paradise*. New Haven/London.

Ware, K., 1983. 'Wolves and monks: life on the Holy Mountain today', *Sobornost incorporating Eastern Churches Review* 5.2 : 56–68.

—, 1993. 'Athos after ten years: the good news and the bad', *Sobornost incorporating Eastern Churches Review* 15.1: 27–37.

—, 1994. 'Gerald Palmer, the *Philokalia*, and the Holy Mountain', *Friends of Mount Athos: Annual Report 1994*: 23–8.

—, 1998. Foreword to Philip Sherrard, *Christianity: Lineaments of a Sacred Tradition*: ix–xlv. Edinburgh/Brookline, MA.

—, 2008. 'Two British pilgrims to the Holy Mountain: Gerald Palmer and Philip Sherrard', in R. Gothóni and G. Speake (eds), *The Monastic Magnet: Roads to and from Mount Athos*: 143–57. Oxford/Berne.

12

The Byzantine Research Fund Archive: encounters of Arts and Crafts architects in Byzantium

Amalia G. Kakissis

Early in 1888, Robert Weir Schultz and Sidney H. Barnsley, two young students of the Royal Academy of Arts visited Greece for the first time with the purpose of engaging in the study of Byzantine Architecture. Two years and three trips later, they had produced hundreds of documents recording, in detail, Byzantine monuments in the Mediterranean — several for the first time (FIG. 12.1). The exceptional success of this endeavour fuelled interest in the UK in Byzantine studies, which in turn brought more architects out into the field, and contributed to the creation of one of the most valuable archival resources on Byzantine monuments. This unique collection, known today as the Byzantine Research Fund (BRF) Archive[1], is housed in the Archive of the British School at Athens and consists of approximately 1,500 drawings and 1,000 photographs created between 1888 and 1949 by a small group of British architects who undertook the systematic investigation, recording and publication of the art and architecture of the monuments in the Byzantine world. Also included in the Archive are numerous notebooks[2] and the BRF Corporate Records, which provide valuable insight into the activities of the architects and other members of the Fund. Additionally in the Corporate

Fig.12.1: Hagioi Theodoroi (Vrondochion Monastery), Mystra, Laconia; interior looking west. Robert Weir Schultz is photographed here by Sidney Barnsley while investigating the remnants of the floor of the church, ca. 1889–90; BSA BRF–02 .01.14.027

*. I would like to thank the Managing Council of the British School at Athens for permission to publish this material. Also, for helpful suggestions and guidance, I am very grateful to the following people: Dr Eleni Calligas, Prof. Robin Cormack, Sir Michael Llewellyn-Smith, Mary Greensted, Dr Julian W.S. Litten, Gavin Stamp, Penny Zarganis-Wilson and Prof. Giovanni Salmeri.

1. The archival collection retains a slightly shortened form of the name of the organization which originated it: *The Byzantine Research and Publication Fund*.

2. The BRF Archive contains notebooks of the following architects: Robert Weir Schultz, Sidney H. Barnsley, William Harvey, Walter S. George, G.U.S. Corbett, Swanson, and A.H.S. (Peter) Megaw.

Fig.12.2: Robert Weir Schultz (middle) and Sidney Barnsley (right), photographed here with an unidentified member of the American School of Classical Studies, during one of their trips to Greece, 1888–90; BSA Photographic Archive: BSAA7–30.

Records there is information about the formation and subsequent history of the collection itself, dating from 1888 to 1990.[3]

The BRF Archive is the result of the close and rewarding relationship of British scholars — in particular architects — of the Arts and Crafts movement and the British School at Athens. The Arts and Crafts movement, which played such a significant role in the Gothic and neo-Byzantine revivals of the late 1880s, greatly influenced the education and training of the architects who were sent to Italy, Greece, Turkey and the Near East to study, at firsthand, the origins of the Gothic styles and Byzantine architecture. They spent much of their time painstakingly recording these medieval remains,

which made a lasting impression on them and provided inspiration for their later building projects back in England. Today, these documents in the BRF Archive constitute an invaluable resource for the study of Byzantine art and architecture as well as shedding new light on an important chapter of the history of architecture.

The bulk of the records of the BRF Archive was created by a handful of architects, with assistance from their fellow students at the BSA. Apart from Schultz and Barnsley, chief among the contributors of the architectural records were Ramsay Traquair, Walter S. George, William Harvey, Harry H. Jewell and A.H.S (Peter) Megaw (FIG.12.2). Several prominent BSA members provided additional photographs or updated information on monuments; they included Ernest Gardner, R.M. Dawkins, R.C. Bosanquet and Alan Wace — all of whom had been Director of the School at various times; Walter Leaf, one-time School Treasurer; Frederick Hasluck, Assistant Director and Librarian, and John Penoyre, Secretary.

The British School at Athens, founded only two years before the first architects came to Greece, greatly facilitated their work. It provided them with a dependable base in Athens, which supplied them not only with accommodation and access to a growing library, but also with one of their most valuable resources: the other BSA members and their network. The environment of the School served as a ground for exchanging ideas and members thrived on each others' company and interests. In the early days of the School many students arrived with particular agendas, such as Ancient History and Archaeology but, in addition to their main subjects, most also had a wide range of interests including folklore, modern literature and linguistics, anthropology, and religion. The BSA members were supportive of each others' work and exchanged information whenever possible.

For instance, Leaf and Bosanquet, who were School Officers during Schultz and Barnsley's stay, contributed photographs and sent updated information on Daphni monastery in Attica and churches in Athens. Later, Wace and Hasluck, in addition to frequently acting as guides and translators, also submitted photographs and later contributions to the BRF publications, since they too were interested in Byzantine studies. This small group of BSA scholars helped Schultz and Barnsley

---

3. The enormous task of organizing the BRF Archive was first attempted in 1990 by Guy Sanders and Eric Ivison, shortly after the collection was transferred from London to Athens. Currently, the collection is the object of an extensive, multi-phase project which consists of: Conservation, Cataloguing, Digitisation and Publication/Presentation to upgrade the state of the catalogue and make it accessible to a wider public. The first phase of this project, concerning photographs and drawings of monuments in Attica, was recently completed and is now fully available online at http://www.bsa.ac.uk/archive.

enormously; however, the support and interest of the BSA members was not restricted to the architects' stay in Athens. Back in London, several BSA members continued to contribute financially to Byzantine Studies and several of them, such as former BSA Directors Gardner and Dawkins, later became part of the Byzantine Research and Publication Fund Committee.

The other major influence on the work of the BRF architects came from their connection to the Arts and Crafts movement. Initially, Schultz and Barnsley were exposed to the ideas and aspirations of the movement both in their scholarly education at the Royal Academy and in their professional training at the architectural Office of Richard Norman Shaw. A further strong source of influence on their development was the Art Workers' Guild,[4] founded by a group of five young architects, all members or former members of Shaw's Office.

Schultz,[5] who became Master of the Art Guild himself in 1934, became interested in architecture in his mid-teenage years. While attending classes at the Watt Institution and School of Arts, he was apprenticed to R. Rowland Anderson (1834–1921), the leading architect in Edinburgh at the time. David Ottewill, in his essay 'Robert Weir Schultz (1860–1951): An Arts and Crafts Architect', suggests that Anderson's work in both Gothic and Classical styles and his study of medieval architecture must have been very significant in forming Schultz's ideas. Additionally, Anderson's connections to the Marquess of Bute, his patron, would be important for Schultz's career, since the Marquess later became Schultz's most important patron.[6] After completing his apprenticeship with Anderson, which lasted from 1878 to 1884, Schultz was taken on by the office of Richard Norman Shaw[7] in London in January 1884. The following year he was admitted to the Royal Academy, where he spent his evenings studying.[8]

Fig.12.3: *Detail of the interior of the Panagia (Theotokos) Church, looking east; Hosios Loukas monastery, ca. 1888–90, taken by R. Weir Schultz and S. Barnsley. Sculptural decoration was very appealing to Arts and Crafts artisans as it represented the marriage of designer and craftsmen which they strived for in their work. BSA BRF–02.01.04.053.*

4. Crawford 2004, 34.

5. He changed his name to Robert W. Schultz Weir in 1914; Ottewill 1979, 109, fn 1. He was born in Port Glasgow, Scotland in 1860 and died in Hartley-Wintney, England in 1951; Stamp 1981, 4, 70.

6. Ottewill 1979, 89, 92; Stamp 1981, 9, 14–15; Bullen 2003, 164.

7. Todd 2004, 78.

8. Royal Academy of Art: Admission Records: Robert Weir Schultz; Schultz exhibited several of his drawings —in particular his Byzantine work— at the Academy. Royal Academy of Arts: List of Exhibitors: 1769–1904 and 1905–1970.

Fig.12.4: A student member sitting on the balcony of the Upper House of the British School at Athens with the Acropolis in the distance. Schultz and Barnsley used the BSA as their home base when they were not travelling around Greece. It was here that they spent much of the winter, researching and inking their drawings. Photograph by R. Weir Schultz and S. Barnsley, ca. 1888–90; BSA BRF Schultz and Barnsley photo collection: WI.A–50.

The Royal Academy was brimming with change at the time, with battles being fought over old and new ideologies on the practice of architecture. Barnsley, the other BRF pioneer (1865–1926), was a contemporary of Schultz at the Academy and, although they did not meet then, both were taught by R. Phéne Spiers (1838–1916). Spiers was an authority on Byzantine Architecture, Master of the Royal Academy and an active member of the Art Workers' Guild.[9] He attended first the Birmingham School of Art, then run by Edward R. Taylor, a personal friend of William Morris[10] whose socialist ideology constituted much of the Arts and Crafts movement, and then, in 1885, followed

his brother Ernest to the School of Architecture at the Royal Academy.[11] In 1886, Barnsley went to work in the office of Norman Shaw in London where he met Schultz and William Richard Lethaby (1857–1931),[12] Shaw's chief assistant and one of the founding members of the Art Workers Guild. Lethaby introduced the young men to new philosophies in architectural theory and had a profound effect on Schultz's career, becoming his mentor.[13] It was in fact on the advice of Lethaby that Schultz first went to Greece and the Near East for a first hand view of Byzantine architecture.[14]

Lethaby had travelled around the Near East himself, studying several Byzantine Monuments. Born in Devon, Lethaby had quickly worked his way from an apprenticeship with a local architect to being Chief Clerk to Shaw in 1879. As a talented designer he contributed to buildings such as Scotland Yard in London, but also worked on other materials including books, furniture and stained glass. His interest in architectural history led to his involvement in the Society for the Protection of Ancient Buildings which led the way in the preservation and authentication of older buildings against the Victorian practice of almost completely rebuilding and redesigning them. Through this group Lethaby befriended William Morris (1834–96)[15] and Philip Webb (1831–1915)[16], both pioneers of the Arts and Crafts movement, eventually becoming an influential member of the movement in his own right as well as co-founder of the Art Workers' Guild in 1884.

The Guild was formed by two separate groups, the St George's Art Society, made up mostly of architects who were or had been members of the Shaw Offices, including Lethaby, Edward Schroeder Prior, Ernest Newton, and Mervyn McCartney; and The Fifteen,

9. Ottewill 1979, 90.
10. McGrath 2003, 45.

11. Barnsley entered the School of Architecture on 31 December 1885, and his brother Arthur Ernst Barnsley on 23 July 1885. Both were recommended by Richard Norman Shaw; Royal Academy of Arts: Admission Records. Barnsley also exhibited one of his Byzantine drawings at the Academy in 1891; Royal Academy of Arts: Royal Academy Exhibitors 1769–1904: 122.
12. Todd 2004, 59, 100, 154.
13. Ottewill, 1979, 88.
14. Ottewill, 1979, 90; Royal Academy of Arts: Annual Report, 1887 prizes. Bullen 2003,168–9.
15. Todd 2004, 68; Crawford, 2004, 23–6.
16. Todd 2004, 86–7; Stamp 1981, 6–7.

Fig. 12.5: View of the Propylaea from the top of the Parthenon taken by R. Weir Schultz and S. Barnsley when they worked on the Acropolis, ca. 1888–90; BSA BRF Schultz and Barnsley photo collection: WI.A–36.

a group of designers, including writers and illustrators, founded by Lewis Day. The philosophy of the Arts and Crafts Movement developed out of the Gothic Revival as a reaction to the industrialization and commercialization of Victorian Britain. The architect Augustus Welby Northmore Pugin (1812–52)[17] 'provided the foundation from which the moral aesthetics of Arts and Crafts evolved'[18] and believed that there should be a reunification of the 'spiritual and the everyday'[19], in other words the re-uniting of designer and craftsman. He felt that the revival of medieval Gothic combined these ideas best and so his 'vision of Christian architecture came to underpin the Arts and Crafts style.'[20] John Ruskin (1819–1900)[21] and Morris, considered the

founders of the Arts and Crafts Movement, developed these concepts further. Ruskin promoted hand-carved ornamentation and felt that it reflected the 'the sense of human labour and the care spent upon it.'[22] (FIG.12.3) In reaction to the industrialization at the time, Ruskin's ideas of individuality in design gave momentum to the improvement of design standards across Britain, including the founding of several schools of art specifically to teach these arts and crafts.

Morris, who was both a craftsman and designer, in addition to being an active socialist (an important ideology for the Arts and Crafts movement), wanted to apply the unity of craftsmanship and design and to simplify design in order to raise standards and keep costs down. His views were aligned with those of the architect G.E. Street (1824–81),[23] his mentor in Oxford, who believed in an interdisciplinary approach to archi-

---

17. Todd 2004, 74–5.

18. Cumming and Kaplan 1995, 11.

19. Cumming and Kaplan 1995, 12.

20. Todd 2004, 96.

21. Todd 2004, 77; Crawford 2004, 22.

---

22. Cumming and Kaplan 1995, 12.

23. Todd 2004, 80.

Fig.12.6: View of interior of the katholikon looking north-east, Hosios Loukas monastery, Phocis; photographed by R. Weir Schultz and S. Barnsley, ca. 1888–90; BSA BRF–02 .01.04.059.

tecture and that 'an architect should not only be a builder but also a painter, a blacksmith, and a designer of stained glass' (see PLATES VI and VII).[24]

Interest in Byzantium at the turn of the century was at a peak. Byzantine art and architecture very much melded with the philosophies of the Arts and Crafts Movement and many scholars saw Byzantium as the closest remnant of the continuity between Classical and Modern Greece. These intellectuals moved in the

same circles and as a result numerous institutions like the British Museum, the British Academy, the Society of Antiquaries, the Society of the Dilettanti, the Society for the Promotion of Hellenic Studies, the Royal Institute of British Architects (RIBA), the Royal Academy and various Universities including Oxford, Cambridge and the University of London all had members involved in the study of Byzantium. These institutions were the very ones that rallied behind the founding of a base in Greece for British scholars.

The British School at Athens was founded by a small group of learned men who saw the value of establishing a base in Greece for travelling scholars from Britain. George Macmillan and Professor (later Sir) Richard Jebb were two of the pioneers in this endeavour. Macmillan, a scholar of Classics when he first visited Greece in the spring of 1877, was destined to work in the family publishing business instead of pursuing an academic career. As an alternative to academia, he channelled his enthusiasm for Classics into forming a group known as 'The Society for the Promotion of Hellenic Studies' in 1879.[25] Jebb, a distinguished scholar of classical languages and literature, first taught at the University of Glasgow in 1875 and then in 1889 became Regius Professor of Greek at Cambridge University. He actively supported various institutions and societies that promoted classical studies, including the Society for the Promotion of Hellenic Studies and the British Museum. He was also one of the original fifty members of the British Academy.[26]

In 1883, a Committee was formed to develop plans for a British School at Athens. Francis C. Penrose (1817–1903), who had been Surveyor of the Fabric of St. Paul's Cathedral since 1852 and a member of RIBA was enthusiastic and immediately became an active member of the BSA Committee. Penrose had previously come to Greece in 1845, during his appointment as Travelling Bachelor of the University of Cambridge. Impressed with Penrose's work on the buildings of the Athenian Acropolis, the Society of the Dilettanti later commissioned him to continue his examination of the

---

24. Cumming and Kaplan 1995, 15.

25. Macmillan 1929, i–iii; Waterhouse 1986, 6.

26. BSA Corporate Records—Athens: Correspondence: R. Jebb 1882–86, 1935; Waterhouse: 1986, 6–7; Beard and Stray 2005.

Fig.12.7: Robert Weir Schultz (left) and traveling companion in inner courtyard of Metropolis in Mystra. Although Schultz and Barnsley, and later Walter S. George, recorded several of the monuments in Mystra, none were published. Photographed by S. Barnsley, 1888–90; BSA BRF Schultz and Barnsley photo collection: WI.F–5.

Parthenon, which he did in the autumn of 1846. The results of his research were eventually published by the Society in 1851, under the title *An Investigation of the Principles of Athenian Architecture*.[27]

Penrose not only drew up the plans for the first building of the School without charging a fee, but also visited Athens twice to check on the progress of its construction (FIG.12.4). He accepted the offer by the

BSA Committee to undertake the Directorship for the School's first session 1886–87, and thus moved into the building he had himself designed.[28] Macmillan, who agreed to serve as the first Secretary of the BSA, negotiated with the RIBA a commitment to an annual contribution of £50 — a standard stipulation for all who wanted to remain part of the Committee of the

---

27. It was also during his years in Greece that he painted several watercolours of places around the country — now held in the Archive of the British School.

28. This building, named the Upper House, is currently the residence of the BSA Director. The drawings of the building are held in the Archive of the Royal Institute of British Architects. *BSA AR* 1886–87, 4; Waterhouse 1986, 7–9, Beard and Stray 2005, 379.

Fig.12.8: The narthex, Hagios Ioannis Stoudiou, Istanbul. According to J.B. Bullen in Byzantium Rediscovered, *two capitals from this monument were incorporated in the Church of the Wisdom of God in Lower Kingswood, Surrey along with two capitals from the Vlachernae Palace — saved from target practice by Dr Edwin Freshfield. BSA BRF–02.02.01.01.*

BSA.[29] It was this very important connection with the Royal Institute of British Architects and other institutes like it — such as the Royal Academy of Arts — that opened the door to a continuous stream of architectural students to Greece from Britain at the turn of the century.

In its second active session, 1887–88, the BSA welcomed three new students who were training to be architects. The first was Ravencroft Elsey Smith (1859–1931), winner of a RIBA Studentship, who joined the excavations at the temple of Aphrodite in Paphos, Cyprus.[30] The other two were Schultz and Barnsley, who both held Studentships from the Royal Academy of Arts. Schultz was awarded the Academy's Gold Medal and Travelling Studentship, worth £200, in December 1887.[31] In the company of Barnsley, he arrived in Athens in early 1888, travelling via France and Italy. On this first trip to Greece, Schultz and Barnsley's main objective was to study Byzantine monuments — which

they did mostly in and around Athens, along with a brief survey trip to the Peloponnese — but they also studied classical material. While Schultz worked on various forms of Ionic capitals and a project to draw the moulding of the Propylaea in full scale, Barnsley made several drawings of antiquities (FIG.12.5).[32]

Schultz returned to Greece in January of 1889 — alone this time — to continue work on the Byzantine monuments, taking part in the BSA excavations of the theatre in Megalopolis and a project on the mouldings of the Propylaea funded by the Society for the Promotion of Hellenic Studies.[33] After their initial research trips to Greece, Schultz and Barnsley realized that there was a great dearth of detailed information on Byzantine monuments. Dissatisfied with the work of predecessors like Charles Felix Marie Texier and R. Popplewell Pullan, French explorers and archaeologists who published one of the earliest monographs on Byzantine Art in 1864, they proposed a project for the detailed recording of the monuments. Through a special appeal and a contribution from the BSA Committee, £250 was raised allowing them to return to Greece in November 1889.[34] Although they were barely able to cover their expenses with this money, they dedicated the next 12 months to surveying as many Byzantine sites on the mainland as possible. Their agenda was to make 'measured architectural studies of the different subjects', 'enlarged detail drawings of all the ornamental parts', and write as complete as possible a 'descriptive and detailed account of the scheme of the Iconography and of the architectural structural peculiarities of the buildings as well as noting any point of historical interest'. Although they got many tips pointing them to Byzantine structures tucked away in various parts of the country, they scouted out much on their own with the assistance of local guides.[35]

29. Macmillan 1911, 20.

30. *BSA AR* 1887–88, 4.

31. Royal Academy of Art: Annual Report 1887; *BSA AR* 1887–88, 5; Ottewill 1979, 90; Stamp 1981, 8.

32. *BSA AR* 1887–88, 9–10.

33. *BSA AR* 1888–89, 4–5, 8; BSA BRF Archive: Notebooks: SCH 10 (Mouldings); SCH 17, 18 (Megalopolis).

34. Sir Edwin Freshfield, one of the biggest benefactors of this trip, also became a trustee of the BSA Committee at this time. *BSA AR* 1889–90, 4.

35. *BSA AR* 1890–91, 23. Schultz and Barnsley also credit two Greek scholars, Dr George Lambakis and Professor Lambros of Athens for their assistance; *ibid*, 29.

Schultz and Barnsley spent most of their 1890 research trip drawing extensive plans and taking numerous photographs — with the newly acquired School camera — of such places as St Luke's monastery in Phocis (Hosios Loukas) (FIG.12.6), and Daphni monastery in Attica. (PLATE VIII) In the winter they spent their time mostly in Athens, documenting most of the Byzantine churches there along with Byzantine ornamental pieces then at the National Archaeological Museum. When not out in the field, their time was spent back at the British School inking up some of their drawings. It was during this period that they had the most time to interact with the other students at the BSA and take part in the general work of the School.[36]

During several tours of the Peloponnese they stopped by Monemvasia, amongst other places, and spent time at Mystra (FIG.12.7). Towards the end of their research trip they headed to the north of Greece and, finding impressive structures in Arta, stayed to record them. Crossing into what was then Ottoman territory, they moved on to Thessaloniki, and although fascinated by the monuments, they were also overwhelmed by the length of time required to properly document them. They succeeded in partly documenting the church of Hagia Sophia (in Thessaloniki), and their parting suggestion in their report to the BSA in 1890 was for the next project to concentrate on the monuments of Thessaloniki.[37] Throughout all their trips they kept detailed notebooks and, although both contributed to the architectural records, it appears that Schultz concentrated more on the detailed architectural measurements and Barnsley more on the ornamental design. Barnsley also appears to be the one who was usually behind the lens and perhaps developed the photographs, as he jotted down the ratios for developing solution in one of his notebooks.[38] During their twelve month trip, Schultz kept a meticulous log book documenting all the places they travelled to, along with a detailed list of their spending from boat tickets to accommodation, guides, coal for heating, drawing equipment and food.[39]

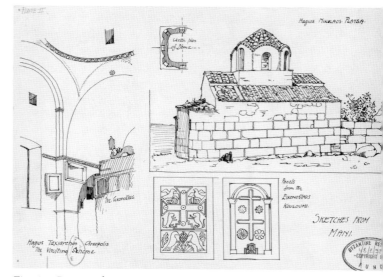

Fig.12.9: Drawing by Ramsey Traquair showing decorative details from various churches in Mani; BSA BRF–01.01.14.139.

In addition to their drawings and photographs, Schultz and Barnsley contributed to the collection of Byzantine literature in the BSA Library. When they first arrived in Athens, the BSA had hardly any books on the subject, so they bought books themselves to use for their research which they then donated to the BSA. Later they gave copies of their own articles and monographs to the School Library as well.

In November 1890, both Schultz and Barnsley returned to England intending to finish their drawings and ink their plans in preparation for publication. However, immediately upon their return, Barnsley was commissioned to design the Church of the Wisdom of God in Lower Kingswood, Surrey by Dr Edwin Freshfield, an antiquarian and Arts and Crafts devotee, who had contributed towards their research trips to Greece (FIG.12.8).[40] Barnsley did this and later went on to design furniture along with his brother Ernest and the famed Arts and Crafts furniture designer, Ernest Gimson.[41]

Schultz, meanwhile, continued inking plans and compiling information for the publication of the Byz-

---

36. *BSA AR* 1890–91, 25.

37. *BSA AR* 1890–91, 29.

38. BSA BRF Archive: Notebooks: BAR 3.

39. BSA BRF Corporate Records: 1890 Logbook by Schultz and Barnsley. The BRF Corporate Records are as yet uncatalogued.

40. McGrath 2003, 46; Brandon 2003; Bullen 2003, 166–7.

41. Todd 2004, 36–9, 155–8; Crawford 2004, 65; McGrath 2003; Ottewill 1979, 91–2. The Barnsley Brothers and Gimson are credited with what is known as the Cotswold furniture designs in the Arts and Crafts Movement.

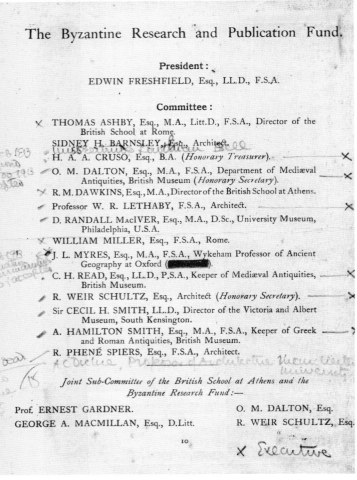

Fig.12.10: List of BRF committee members with later annotations by R. Weir Schultz who was its Honorary Secretary until the Fund was absorbed by the BSA in 1937; BSA BRF Corporate Records: Minute book.

antine monuments upon his return. Yet he too, within a year, had set up his own practice at 14 Gray's Inn in Bloomsbury. His patron, the 3rd Marquess of Bute, occupied Schultz for the next ten years on various building projects including St John's Lodge in Regent's Park, London. After this, Schultz expanded his practice to country houses, hospitals, gardens and churches, his major work being St Andrew's Chapel in Westminster and Khartoum Cathedral in the Sudan plans of which he drew from his knowledge of Byzantine buildings.[42]

Schultz and Barnsley remained friends and collaborated together on various projects throughout their

careers. Both of them, in fact, contributed greatly to the Arts and Craft Movement. Even though Schultz was now involved with numerous other projects in England, he remained dedicated to publishing the Byzantine monuments to which he and Barnsley had devoted so much time. Constraints on the architects' time, however, and the lack of proper funding for publications, resulted in the Byzantine Monuments project being put on hold for nearly a decade. In 1901, the first publication, *The Monastery of Saint Luke of Stiris, in Phocis, and the Dependent Monastery of Saint Nicolas in the Fields, near Skripou, in Boeotia,* was finally printed. An impressive book with many colour plates and highly detailed drawings, it was the first to show Hosios Loukas in such detail. (PLATES IX and X) The publication would not have been possible without the aid of Freshfield, who fully funded the monograph.[43]

Shortly after Schultz and Barnsley's publication on Hosios Loukas came out in 1901, another architect nurtured in the Arts and Crafts tradition started to explore Greece. Ramsay Traquair (1874–1952), born and educated in Edinburgh, was the son of a Scottish scientist and Phoebe Anna (née Moss),[44] a leading artist of the Arts and Crafts movement known for her embroideries, enamelwork, illustrated manuscripts and mural decorations. Traquair studied at the Edinburgh Academy, then went on to the Edinburgh College of Art to study art and architecture. In 1900, he was accepted as a member of RIBA[45] and spent a few months studying architecture in Italy. He joined the British School at Athens in the academic session 1905–6, and concentrated on Byzantine and Medieval remains in Greece, mostly in the Peloponnese, and in Constantinople, where he assisted Prof. A. van Millingen, a leading figure in Byzantine architecture, in measuring and describing twenty churches. During his travels, Traquair became acquainted with William Miller, historian and journalist, who also had an interest in 'Frankish' history. He returned again to Greece in 1909, with support from the Byzantine Research Fund

---

42. Ottewill 1979, 93, 104–7; Stamp 1981, 60–3.

43. Schultz and Barnsley 1901, v–vi; Weir 1936, 90.

44. Todd 2004, 82–3.

45. Nobbs 1939, 147. He eventually was nominated and voted in as fellow of the RIBA in 1921; RIBA: Biographical Files: Traquair, Ramsay.

to continue his study of the 'Frankish' castles in Mani (FIG.12.9).[46]

The Byzantine Research and Publication Fund was created almost two decades after Schultz and Barnsley had first come to Greece to study Byzantine architecture. The result of growing interest in Britain in Byzantine Studies, the Fund's objective was to sponsor and publish the work of British architects studying Byzantine and 'Frankish' monuments throughout the Byzantine world. Officially created in 1908, the Fund worked on a basis of subscriptions and private donations which funded various research trips, Traquair's researches in Mani being one of the first, and subsequent works conducted by several architects in Thessaloniki, the Middle East, Constantinople and an excavation in Egypt.[47]

Freshfield, who as we have seen was already a generous sponsor of Byzantine studies, initially presided over the Fund, and Schultz was Honorary Secretary. An impressive line up of scholars were committee members. (FIG.12.10) They included Ormonde M. Dalton,[48] Keeper of Medieval Antiquities at the British Museum; Miller, who was at the time based in Rome;[49] Thomas Ashby, Director of the British School at Rome; Dawkins, then Director of the BSA; J.L. Myres, Professor of Ancient History at Oxford and former member of the BSA; Cecil H. Smith, Director of the newly founded Victoria and Albert Museum and former director of the BSA; and Spiers, the architect and Royal Academy professor.[50] The connection with the British Museum played an especially important role later in the safe keeping of the BRF material during the Second World War.

Traquair's relationship with the BRF was short-lived because, after a brief period of teaching and practising architecture in Edinburgh, he accepted the Macdonald Professorship of Architecture at McGill University

Fig.12.11: W. George, known for his meticulousness and dedication, in addition to documenting several of the monuments in Thessaloniki, was also asked to supervise the restoration of many of them during his time there. Here he is being honoured by Queen Elizabeth II for his accomplishments in his later years as one of the architects to build New Delhi, India. BSA BRF Corporate Records: BRF Committee Records.

in Montreal, Quebec in 1913. He published his studies on the Churches of Mani in an article in the BSA Annual in 1909. His studies on Frankish architecture in Greece appeared in the BSA Annual (1906 and 1907) and the Journal of the Royal Institute of British Architects (1924). In his new position at McGill, he was thereafter occupied with teaching architecture and the history of architecture and turned his sights to the history of French-Canadian building styles.[51] He became an authority on this subject and published several articles before his retirement in 1939, after which he was able to produce more elaborate publications such as his book-length studies The Old Silver of Quebec (1940) and The Old Architecture of Quebec (1947).

While Traquair was out exploring the monuments in Greece for the first time, Walter Sykes George (1882–1962) was just completing his training under A. Beresford Pite and Lethaby at the Royal College of Art in London (FIG.12.11). Born in a family of Quaker architects and raised in East Anglia and Manchester, George began his studies in architecture at the School of Art in Ashton-under-Lyne in 1894, and continued at the School of Art in Manchester in 1899. After completing

46. Traquair 1908–9, 177; Nobbs 1939, 147; BSA BRF Corporate Records: Correspondence: R. Traquair to R. W. Schultz, 1909–10.

47. BSA BRF Corporate Records: Minute Book.

48. Dalton was also a contributor to the BRF funded publication, The Church of the Nativity at Bethlehem (1910) along with W. Harvey, W.R. Lethaby, H.A. Cruso and A.C. Headlam.

49. Miller wrote an article in the Journal of Hellenic Studies in 1907 about the Frankish remains in Monemvasia using photographs taken by himself and by Alan Wace, some of which were deposited in the BRF Archive.

50. BSA BRF Corporate Records: Minute Book: front page.

51. Nobbs 1930, 147; RIBA: Biographical files: Traquair, R.: obituaries 1952.

Fig.12.12: View of Thessaloniki from Hagia Sophia, with Hagios Georgios (Rotunda) visible on the far right, taken by R. Weir Schultz and S. Barnsley who visited the city towards the end of their 1889–90 research trip. They evaluated the monuments so as to report on the damage caused by the fire of 1890. They were able to take several photographs and do some drawings but, since their finances were coming to an end, in their final report they suggest another campaign to properly record the monuments of Thessaloniki. In 1906, Walter George was finally sent to undertake this work. BSA BRF–02.01.07.286.

his studies in 1901, he spent the next six years training in London. By the time he won the Soane Medallion from the Royal Institute of British Architects in 1906, George had already travelled to Italy, hence he then set out to Greece, Egypt and Turkey. He became a member of the BSA and remained associated with the School until 1915. His time in Greece was spent in various places including the School's excavations in Sparta, where he drew the architectural remains unearthed during four seasons, but most of his travels and time were spent pursuing research on Byzantine monuments in Macedonia and Constantinople.[52]

In Macedonia he concentrated his efforts on the various churches in Thessaloniki, picking up work previously begun by Schultz and Barnsley (FIG.12.12). With the support of the Byzantine Research and Publication

Fund George returned to Thessaloniki between 1908 and 1910, specifically to record the church of Hagios Demetrios. He was fortunate to be present during the removal of the plaster that had been applied to the inside walls of the building when it had been turned into a mosque. Upon the plaster's removal, incredible mosaics were revealed. The extensive drawings George made of Hagios Demetrios at this time soon became invaluable; as they are the only extant drawings to record the monument shortly before the great fire of 1917 destroyed most of it. (PLATES XI and XII) During this period George also travelled to Constantinople and there documented the church of Hagia Eirene, which was eventually published in 1912 by the Fund.[53]

---

52. *BSA XII, BSA AR* 1907–8, 449. George's work for the Sparta Excavations can be found in: BSA Excavation Records: Sparta.

---

53. BSA BRF Corporate Records: Correspondence: W.S. George to R.W. Schultz: 1907–10. BRF Archive: Notebooks: GEO 1–2. Some of George's work in Macedonia and Constantinople was exhibited at the Royal Academy from 1908 to 1915; Royal Academy of Arts: Corporate Records.

During his trips back and forth to Greece between 1906 and 1912, George also found time to work for two seasons with the University of Liverpool at their excavations in Egypt and the Sudan. Additionally, he undertook small projects in England, such as designing or restoring small homes, while working at The Temple in London and, for a time, with Schultz at his office at Gray's Inn. Although World War I prevented George and many others from continuing most of their work abroad, George remained involved with the BSA until 1915, when he accepted a job as Resident Architect in charge of Sir Herbert Bakers (1862–1946) site preparations of the building of the city of New Delhi, India.[54] There, in the service of two great Arts and Crafts architects, Baker and Edwin Lutyens (1869–1944),[55] George spent the remainder of his career and life, tirelessly working on various projects in the public and private sector, in addition to being a founding member of the Institute of Town Planners in India.[56]

George's work on the monuments of Thessaloniki was shared by William Harvey (1883–1962) who, as Gold Medalist of the Royal Academy in 1907, travelled to Greece, Egypt and Palestine. Born in Tottenham, Middlesex in November 1883, he was educated at Regent Street Polytechnic and entered the Royal Academy in July 1903 (FIG.12.13).[57] It was during his second trip to Greece in 1908, sponsored by the Fund, that he worked intensely on various monuments in Thessaloniki, including Hagios Demetrios, Hagia Sophia and Eski Djouma (Panagia Acheiropoiitos), as well as travelling to the Middle East to record the Dome of the Rock in Jerusalem and the Church of the Nativity in Bethlehem.[58] It was on Lethaby and Freshfield's instigation that Harvey went to Jerusalem and Bethlehem, as they themselves had studied Byzantine monuments in the Middle East and felt that they were in need of

Fig.12.13: While in Greece, William Harvey, seen pictured here, spent most of his time documenting Byzantine monuments but, as all architects who came to the British School, he applied his skills towards helping the excavation teams as well. In Sparta he drew architectural members for the 1908 season. BSA 1936 Exhibition, 147a, Sparta Team 1908, detail.

proper documentation (FIG.12.14).[59] Harvey went on to produce a monograph on the Church of the Nativity in Bethlehem published by the Byzantine Research and Publication Fund in 1910, and continued to write on architectural subjects, including Byzantine, in journals such as *The Builder*, *The Architectural Review*, and the *Architect's Journal*. Starting his professional career back in Britain, he worked with, amongst others, Sir Herbert Baker for a period of time and became very involved with the rescue of historic buildings.

---

54. RIBA: Biographical Files: application for Fellow submitted 7 February 1929.

55. Todd 2004, 61.

56. RIBA: Biographical Files: candidate sheets (1929), obituary (1962).

57. Surrey History Centre, Woking: Finding Aid; Royal Academy of Art: Admission papers.

58. BSA BRF Corporate Records: Correspondence: W. Harvey to R.W. Schultz: 1908–08; BRF Archive: Notebooks: HAR 1–2.

59. Today Harvey's work in Bethlehem is represented in the BRF Archive mostly by his photographs, taken while he was working on the Church of the Nativity in Bethlehem. Harvey was paid by the Fund for most of his work in Bethlehem but he kept most of the drawings after their publication. Some of them are located in the Victoria and Albert Museum and others in his private collection in Surrey History Centre — collection ref. 623. His biographical information, largely given by his son, John H. Harvey, is included in the Finding Aid of his collection in Surrey.

PROPORTIONS OF PRESENT, CRUSADING + ORIGINAL OPENINGS TO CHURCH. ANCIENT LINTOL ARCH + TRUSS OF CORNICE AT TOP OF PICTURE.

Fig.12.14: Church of the Nativity in Bethlehem. View of wall showing present, crusading and original opening to the building photographed in 1908 by Harvey, who annotated a good number of the negatives with notes. He was sent to document the Church of the Nativity in Bethlehem and the Dome of the Rock in Jerusalem on the suggestion of William Lethaby and Robert Weir Schultz. BSA BRF–02.03.01.014.

The last monograph to be published by the Fund was the work done by Harry H. Jewell on the Church of Our Lady of the Hundred Gates (Ekatontapyliani) in Paros (FIG.12.15). Little information is available on Jewell other than that he was admitted as a student of the Royal Academy in 1906 and left in 1911. A recipient of the Academy's Gold Medal in 1909, Jewell followed usual practice and set off travelling around Europe, studying architecture in France, Italy, Greece and Turkey. He first arrived in Athens in March 1910, and spent two months studying architecture and sculpture both in Athens and Constantinople. His other plan while in Greece was to make detailed drawings of the Church of Our Lady of the Hundred Gates in Paros

in 1910 on behalf of the Byzantine Research Fund.[60] After many difficulties between Jewell and the BRF Committee, involving various delays on Jewell's part in delivering the drawings and continuous requests for further funds, the publication of the Paros church was finally completed in 1920, with a historical chapter on the monument contributed by Hasluck, who had previously collaborated in an article about Daou Pendeli monastery with Heaton Comyn, BSA architectural student in 1902,[61] and had been asked by the BRF Committee to write the history section of the book in order to expedite the publication process.[62]

With the promotion of Byzantine studies always in mind, the Fund sponsored the research of several architects and scholars involved in the field throughout its existence. As mentioned above, through its subscriptions and donations it was able to publish *The Church of the Nativity at Bethlehem* in 1910 by William Harvey and *The Church of St Eirene at Constantinople* in 1912 by Walter George. Political instability in the Balkans and Turkey greatly curtailed researches in those areas and with the beginning of World War I, all the Fund's activities were suspended. The Fund briefly resumed action in 1919 with the publication of *Our Lady of the Hundred Gates* the following year, but increased costs and the difficulties of post-war conditions did not allow for further publications or sponsored researches. In 1922 the Fund ceased accepting further subscriptions.[63]

Nearly two decades were to pass before another kindred spirit came along to study the BRF material. The last entry made in the Fund's Minute Book is dated 7 May 1931, and was made by Schultz, then Honorary Secretary. In a typewritten letter which was sent to all who had been listed as subscribers when the Fund ceased accepting subscriptions in 1921, Schultz raised the prospect of reviving the activities of the Fund in the near future.[64] The renewed hope came in the form of a

60. *BSA* XVI, BSA Annual Report 1909–10, 294.

61. BSA BRF Corporate Records: Correspondence re: Jewell: 1910–20; Comyn uses Daou Mendeli, the mediaeval name for Daou Pendeli, in his drawings. For H. Comyn see Comyn 1902–03, 388–90.

62. BSA BRF Corporate Records: Minute Book: 28 November 1911.

63. BSA BRF Corporate Records: Minute Book: 25 May 1922.

64. BSA BRF Corporate Records: Minute Book: 7 May 1931.

student named Arthur Herbert Stanley (Peter) Megaw (1910–2006), from the School of Architecture, University of Cambridge (FIG.12.16).[65] During Megaw's time, the Director of the School of Architecture at Cambridge was Theodore Fyfe (1875–1945), a long-time architectural student of the BSA and well-known for his work with Sir Arthur Evans in Knossos.[66]

Fyfe, whose architectural education was steeped in the Arts and Crafts tradition, had been apprenticed to A. Beresford Pite, Walter George's former teacher, and Sir Ashton Webb, before being awarded a travelling studentship from the Architectural Association in 1899. With this studentship he travelled to Greece and became Architectural Student of the British School at Athens. The following year, on the advice of Hogarth, then BSA Director, Sir Arthur Evans appointed Fyfe site architect at his excavations at Knossos, Crete. Fyfe, along with Evans and Hogarth, went to Knossos in March 1900, to start what would become a ground-breaking excavation. Fyfe worked with Evans in Knossos until 1905, and during that time managed to investigate other interesting buildings including the church of Hagios Titos in Gortyna, which he published in 1907 in *The Architectural Review*.

Fyfe's experience in Greece and his contact with Schultz and Lethaby[67] must have been just the right combination for Megaw, then a student under his directorship, to be enticed into Byzantine archaeology. After completing his studies at Cambridge, Megaw tried his hand as a practising architect but, with few prospects in London during the Depression, he turned to archaeology to apply his knowledge of architecture. After being awarded a travelling studentship from Cambridge, he was admitted to the BSA in the 1930–31 session. A letter dated 24 November 1931, requesting admission to the BSA, shows that Megaw's choice to study Byzantine architecture had already been made: 'I

Fig.12.15: Postcard of Ekatontapyliani sent to R. Weir Schultz by Harry H. Jewell as an update of his work there. The final publication of this Church proved to be a long drawn out affair because of disputes with Jewell. He started the work in March 1910 and the publication finally came out in 1920. BSA BRF Corporate Records: Correspondence.

have been elected to the Walston Studentship and will go out to Greece in January next to study Byzantine architecture'.[68] It is very likely that by then Schultz and Megaw had already met and discussed the possibility of reviving the researches of the Fund.

During his first year at the BSA Megaw decided, in consultation with Schultz, to work on the church in Skripou, Boeotia, on the monastery of Sagmata, and to make detailed studies of the churches in Salamis and the Church of the Holy Apostles in Athens.[69] This last resulted in an article for the *Annual* of the BSA. Additionally he visited Thessaloniki in order to meet with George Soteriou, then Ephor of Byzantine Monuments, and report to Schultz on the progress of the restorations work there. As a departure from the Byzantine monuments and like so many architects before him, Megaw spent some time on BSA digs, in his case at the trial excavations in Isthmia.[70]

Megaw returned to the BSA the following year, with the Craven Fellowship from Cambridge and funds from the

<hr />

65. The new School of Architecture at Cambridge was developed by Edwin Schroder Prior (1852–1932), a distinguished Arts and Crafts architect and scholar, after he was made Slade Professor in 1912. Prior had been a pupil of Shaw's from 1874 until 1880 when he started his own practice. One of Prior's best known works is the church of St Andrew, Roker, Sunderland and, of his extensive writings, his book *The Cathedral Builders*.

66. *BSA* VI, BSA Annual Report 1899–1900, 130.

67. Fyfe 1907, 60, fn 2.

68. BSA Corporate Records—London: Correspondence 1931–32: Index M.

69. BSA BRF Corporate Records: Correspondence: Report by Megaw in 1932.

70. *BSA* XXXII 1931–32, BSA Annual Report 1931–32, 257.

Fig.12.16: When Peter Megaw first came to the BSA as a student in the early 1933–34 session, Schultz had a good portion of the original drawings copied and sent out to him. These, along with Megaw's annotations and additional notes and photographs, were given to the BSA by the Megaw Estate after his death in 2006. The Megaw Papers are as yet uncatalogued. Here Megaw is shown at an Easter lunch in 1966, when he was Director of the BSA. BSA Photographic Archive: Members, O. Dickinson Album–10.

BRF, to continue the study of Byzantine monuments. Now he spent most of his time in the Peloponnese, in particular Mani, and some time in Chios.[71] Another student, Mr. H. Casson, also came out to study Byzantine architecture that year, and accompanied Megaw to the Peloponnese and around Athens[72] before travelling up to Thessaloniki and then Constantinople.[73] (PLATE XIII) In the 1933–34 session Megaw was appointed Macmillan Student at the BSA and he, along with the BSA Director, Humfry Payne, engaged in negotiations with Soteriou for a collaborative publication of Hagios Demetrios in Thessaloniki with the Greek Archaeological Society (FIG.12.17). The plan submit-

ted to the Greek Archaeological Service for a joint British School-Archaeological Service publication had been drawn up by Megaw in consultation with Schultz and George. Although discussions about this project continued for the next 15 years, various political and bureaucratic problems involving the Service dissolved the relationship between the two sides and the publication never materialized as it was initially conceived.[74] Soteriou eventually brought out the publication of the church of Hagios Demetrios in 1952.

It was also during the 1933–34 session that Schultz made copies of all his drawings, and formally donated them to the School for students to study.[75] With this gesture, it appears that Schultz not only wanted to facilitate Megaw's work on the Byzantine monuments but he probably also saw the School as the logical place for these documents to be best utilized.

As Senior Student, Librarian and Macmillan Student in the 1934–35 session, Megaw continued to work on the church of Hagios Demetrios, making his own notes, plans and photographs. He also visited Mt Athos in the company of Dawkins, who having served both as BSA Director and on the Committee of the BRF, had done his own research there previously with Hasluck and Wace. Many changes transpired at the BSA the following year. Megaw became Assistant Director and then, shortly afterward, Acting Director — when Payne unexpectedly died towards the end of the session. And, at the end of that tumultuous year at the BSA, Megaw was appointed Director of Antiquities in Cyprus where he remained until 1960.[76]

Schultz was very supportive of Megaw's decision to take up the appointment in Cyprus, even though he must have seen him as the person who would carry on the work of the BRF. By now 67 years old and no longer able to undertake the work himself, Schultz thought seriously about how to keep the BRF alive. His answer was obvious, that

71. *BSA* XXXIII 1932–33, BSA Annual Report 1932–33, 211.
72. BSA BRF Archive: Drawings: Attica: Omorphi Ekklesia—Galatsi by Megaw and Casson.
73. *BSA* XXXIII 1932–33, BSA Annual Report 1932–33, 210.

74. The BRF's last assignment was given to G.U.S. Corbett who worked from Nov. 1948–June 1949 on drawings for the joint Anglo-Greek publication of the Basilica of Hagios Demetrios in Thessaloniki; *BSA AR*, 1948–49, 3. Corbett's drawings and accompanying text survive in the BRF Archive as do copies of photographs of Hagios Demetrios by Soteriou and copies of drawings by his architect Zachos. BSA BRF Corporate Records: Correspondence/Memoranda: 'Proposed Anglo-Greek publication on St Demetrios, Salonika: 1932–60'. For further discussion on the publication of Hagios Demetrios see also Cormack 1985, 48–51.
75. *BSA AR* 1933–34, 8.
76. *BSA AR* 1935–36, 1.

Fig.12.17: Hagios Demetrios, interior view of the nave looking west during restoration work; 1932. Megaw was very involved in the work and in the negotiations for the Anglo-Hellenic publication of Hagios Demetrios. BSA BRF–02.01.07.249.

the BRF could live through the British School at Athens. In 1937 Schultz, in his capacity as Honorary Secretary of the Fund, proposed to the BSA Committee that the property and management of the Fund be handed over to the School with a sub-Committee in place to make decisions on its activities and use of its funds. The BSA Committee accepted and has since managed the BRF.[77]

Even though Megaw was in Cyprus, his intimate knowledge and devotion to the BRF throughout his life and his close friendship with Schultz played a major role

in keeping the collection intact in the following decades. Megaw assisted Schultz in reorganizing much of the BRF material in Schultz's possession and even helped him to create, in 1948, the first extensive list of the material then mostly housed at the British Museum. This list and an added memorandum regarding ownership was deposited with the BSA by Schultz in 1949 and was used by his executors to transfer complete ownership of the material to the BSA on Schultz's death in 1951.[78]

77. BSA BRF Corporate Records: Correspondence: Schultz to BSA: 1937–38.

78. BSA BRF Corporate Records: Minute Book: 26th June 1918; Correspondence/Memos: Schultz 1948; Deed of Transfer from Schultz Estate: 1952; Cormack 1969, 19; Cormack 1985, 57.

the Second World War.[79] In 1960, when the British Museum outgrew its space, the storage of the collection was offered to the Warburg Institute, where it was transferred and kept in the Photographic Library. The collection of drawings and photographs was finally transferred to Athens in 1988, and stored in the newly-created Archive Room, which had been built as part of the 1986 Library extension (FIG. 12.18).[80]

The intertwining of various intellectual circles in Britain from the late 1880s to the mid 1930s, among them the Arts and Crafts architects, classicists, artists, historians, and archaeologists produced great new developments in the area of Byzantine studies. The Byzantine Research Fund Archive is an exemplary product of the creativity of these scholars which today provides us with a unique resource on Byzantine architecture and adds another facet to the history of architecture and intellectual development of the time. It was the keen interest of the Arts and Crafts scholars to explore Byzantine lands that so greatly enhanced this aspect of Byzantine studies. But it is due to its relationship with the British School at Athens that the BRF was able to flourish; and this relationship is the reason the collection survives mostly intact today.

As a new institution in Greece, the existence of the British School was essential in creating this groundbreaking work. As the architects themselves benefited greatly by being a part of the School, so did the School benefit from them. The Byzantine section of the Library expanded vastly through contributions of publications and later original materials, such as photographs and drawings, from the BRF architects and other interested scholars.

The BRF had many supporters, but it was Schultz's lifelong devotion to the work he had started with Barnsley that proved the first crucial factor sustaining the Fund over many decades. From his own personal experiences at the BSA, Schultz saw the benefit of having the School involved in the Fund from the beginning; not only as

Fig.12.18: Hosios Loukas monastery from afar, taken by Barnsley, ca. 1889–90. This image, along with about 200 others, make up the Schultz and Barnsley photographic collection which was transferred to the British School at Athens with the kind assistance of the Photographic Department of the Warburg Institute, to be reunited with the remainder of the photographs in the BRF Collection. BSA BRF Schultz and Barnsley photo collection: WI.H–1.

Sometime after Schultz handed over the management of the Fund to the BSA, he made arrangements for the material in his possession — both drawings and photographs — to be moved to the British Museum which was very near his office. As a result of the generous offer by Sir John Forsdyke, Director of the British Museum and a good friend of Schultz, the material was stored at the British Museum for the duration of

79. BSA BRF Corporate Records: Correspondence: Clay to Gombrich July 28, 1960. Letter from Edith Clay, Secretary of the BSA to Prof. Gombrich, Director of the Warburg requesting the relocation of the BRF drawings from the British Museum to the Warburg Institute. See also Cormack 1969, 19; Cormack 1985, 50–1.

80. BSA BRF Corporate Records: Correspondence: Waywell to Hill: 20. September 1988.

a base for the architects who were sent out to Greece by the Fund, but more so for the intellectual discourse with its members. The other crucial factor in keeping the BRF together was the relationship between Schultz and Megaw. When Megaw came on board with the Fund, Schultz thought the BRF had a renewed lease on life but unfortunately this was to last just a few years before Megaw left for Cyprus. Although Megaw never had the opportunity to publish much more of the BRF material, he remained its guardian until his death in 2006.

In the obituary he wrote for Schultz in the BSA Annual Report of 1950–51, Megaw lamented that even though Schultz and Barnsley's drawings in the BRF were far more precise and detailed than others created during the same period, they unfortunately were never used to their full capacity (FIG. 12.19).[81] This was also the case with most of the material in the BRF collection; in fact, of the hundreds of monuments represented in the BRF Archive only four were published extensively before 1920. Other monuments have been published only in part as short articles in the *Annual of the British School at Athens* and other small publications; most recently, select items from Walter George's material from the church of Hagios Demetrios in Thessaloniki were published in 1985 by Robin Cormack in the exhibition catalogue, *The Church of Saint Demetrios: The Watercolours and Drawings of W.S. George.*

The aspirations of the BRF Archive Project today are to make these very valuable materials accessible to a wide spectrum of researchers and finally to continue Schultz's vision of publishing the Byzantine Research Fund Archive in its entirety.

REFERENCES

MANUSCRIPTS

British School at Athens, Corporate Records; Byzantine Research Fund

Royal Academy of Arts. Archives: Admission Files, List of Exhibitors

Royal Institute of British Architects. Archive Collections: Biographical Files

Surrey History Centre, Woking. Collection Reference 623 Finding Aid: William Harvey

Fig.12.19: Robert Weir Schultz drawing Byzantine decorative sculptural artifacts in the National Museum while W.J. Woodhouse, a fellow BSA student studying terracottas, looks on, ca 1888–90; BSA BRF Schultz and Barnsley photo collection WI.E–50.

PUBLICATIONS

Ainalov, D.V., 1961. *The Hellenistic origins of Byzantine art,* trans. from the Russian by Elizabeth Sobolevitch and Serge Sobolevitch, edited by Cyril Mango. New Brunswick, NJ.

Beard, M. and Stray, C., 2005. 'The Academy Abroad: The Nineteenth-Century Origin of the British School at Athens' in M. Daunton (ed.), *The Organization of Knowledge in Victoria Britain.* Oxford: 372–387.

Blakesley, R., 2006. *The Arts and Crafts Movement.* London.

Brandon, M. J., 2001. 'The lost jewel in the Arts and Crafts crown: The Church of the Wisdom of God', unpublished BA (Honours) Thesis, Fine Arts Valuation, Southampton Institute.

Bullen, J. B., 2003. *Byzantium Rediscovered: The Byzantine Revival in Europe and America.* London; New York.

Carruthers, A., 1984. *Gimson and Barnsley: a catalogue of drawings by Ernst Gimson, Sidney Barnsley and other designers of the Arts and Crafts Movement.* Cheltenham.

---

81. *BSA AR* 1950–51, 16–7.

Cormack, R., 1969. 'The Mosaic Decoration of Saint Demetrios in Thessaloniki: a re-examination in the light of
the drawings of W.S. George', *BSA* 64: 17–52.

—, 1985. *The Church of Saint Demetrios in Thessaloniki: The
Watercolours and Drawings of W.S. George*. Thessaloniki.

Comyn, H., 1902–3. 'Church of the Ruined Monastery at
Daou Mendeli, Attica', *BSA* IX: 388–90.

Crawford, A., 2004. 'United Kingdom: Origins and First
Flowering', in W. Kaplan (ed.), *The Arts and Crafts
Movement in Europe and America: Design for the Mod-
ern World 1880–1920*: 20–67. London.

Crinson, M., 1996. *Empire Building: Orientalism and Victorian Architecture*. London, New York.

Cumming, E. and Kaplan, W., 1995. *The Arts and Crafts
Movement*: 9–65. London.

Elwall, R., 1987. 'Robert Weir Schultz', *Architect (RIBA)* 94/5
(May): 10.

Fyfe, T., 1907. 'The Church of St. Titus in Gortyna', *Architectural Review* XXII, 129: 60–7.

Gardner, E.A., 1892. *Excavations at Megalopolis, 1890–1891*.
London.

George, W.S., 1912. *The Church of St. Eirene in Constantinople*. London

McGrath, M., 2003. 'Sidney Barnsley: a quintessential Arts
and Crafts architect and craftsman', in M. Greensted and
S. Wilson (eds), *Originality and Initiative: The Arts and
Crafts archives at Cheltenham*: 46–60. Cheltenham.

Greensted, M., 2005. *Anthology of the Arts and Crafts Movement: Writings by Ashbee, Lethaby, Gimson and their
Contemporaries*. Aldershot.

Harvey, W. *et al*, 1910. *The Church of the Nativity at Bethlehem*. London.

—, 1935. *Structural survey of the Church of the nativity, Bethlehem*. London.

Jewell, H.H. and Hasluck, F.W., 1920. *The Church of Our
Lady of the Hundred Gates in Paros*. London.

Kalligas, H., 2006. 'Twin reflections of a Byzantine city:
Monemvasia as seen by Robert Weir Schultz and Sidney H. Barnsley in 1890', in R. Cormack and E. Jeffreys
(eds), *Through the Looking Glass. Byzantium Through
British Eyes*: 23–44. Aldershot.

Livingston, K., and Parry, L. (eds), 2005. *International Arts
and Crafts*. V&A Publications. London.

Macmillan, G.A., 1929. *A History of the Hellenic Society,
1879–1929*. London.

—, 1911. *A Short History of the British School at Athens*. London.

Megaw, A.H.S, 1931–32. 'The chronology of some middle
Byzantine churches', *BSA* 32: 90–130.

—, 1932–33*a*. 'Byzantine architecture in Mani', *BSA* 33:
137–62.

—, 1932–33*b*. 'The date of H. Theodoroi at Athens', *BSA* 33:
163–9.

Miller, W., 1907. 'Monemvasia', *Journal of Hellenic Studies*
XXVII: 229–41, 300–1.

Nobbs, Percy E., 1939. 'Ramsay Traquair, Hon. M.A. (McGill)
F.R.I.B.A in his retirement from the Macdonald Chair
in Architecture at McGill University', *Royal Architectural Institute of Canada Journal*, June: 147–8.

Ottewill, D., 1979. 'Robert Weir Schultz, 1860–1951. An Arts
and Crafts architect', *Architectural History* 22: 88–115.

Schultz, R.W. and Barnsley, S., 1901. *The Monastery of Saint
Luke of Stiris in Phokis, and the Dependent Monastery
of Saint Nicolas in the Field*. London.

Schultz, R.W., 1897. 'Byzantine Art', *Architectural Review*, I:
192–9, 248–55.

Weir Schultz, R., 1936. 'Exhibition Illustrating Byzantine
Studies with special relation to the Byzantine Research
and Publication Fund' in *British Archaeological Discoveries in Greece and Crete 1886–1936 — Catalogue of
the exhibition arranged to commemorate the 50th anniversary of the British School of Archaeology in Athens*:
90–106. London.

Stamp, G., 1981. *Robert Weir Schultz, Architect and his work
for the Marquees of Bute*. Mount Stuart.

Todd, P., 2004. *The Arts and Crafts Companion*. London.

—, 2005. *William Morris and the Arts and Crafts home*. London.

Traquair, R., 1905–6. 'Laconia: The Mediaeval Fortresses',
BSA XXII: 258–76.

—, 1906–7. 'Topography: Mediaeval Fortresses of the North-
Western Peloponnesus', *BSA* XIII: 268–84.

—, 1908–09. 'Mediaeval Churches: The Churches of Western
Mani', *BSA* XV: 177–213.

—, 1924. 'Frankish Architecture in Greece'. *Journal of the Royal
Institute of British Architects* XXXI-Third Series: 33–86.

Van Millingen, A., 1912. *Byzantine churches in Constantinople: their history and architecture*. London.

13
British School at Athens research on Byzantine Attica

Eugenia Drakopoulou

In 1890, W. Leaf, a member of the British School at Athens, created a photograph of the apse of the church of Hagios Andreas, in Hagia Philothei Street, near the Metropolis of Athens (FIG.13.1). The church was demolished in the same year together with the monastic complex, a drawing of which was made by R. Weir Schultz, another member of the British School (FIG.13.2). In the late 19th and early 20th centuries, British architects, during their training at the Royal Institute of Architecture and the Royal Academy's School of Architecture, undertook an investigation of the art and architecture of Byzantine monuments.

In 1908, a Byzantine Research and Publication Fund was established in association with the British School at Athens, a step which was all the more welcome to the Committee of the School because they had long regretted their inability, on financial grounds, to publish much of the admirable research carried out in this field by their former distinguished students, Schultz and S.H. Barnsley. The drawings had been created from 1890 to 1903 by Schultz, Barnsley, F.W. Hasluck and H. Comyn, and the photographs were taken between 1890 and 1900 by Schultz, W. Leaf, R. Bosanquet and R.E. Smith.[1]

Both the drawing and photograph bear witness to the architectural complex that had existed in that location before the building of a new church and before the erection of the buildings of the Athens Archdiocese on the site of the monastic complex. The same monument is closely related to the history of Athens during the Ottoman period, a period whose features are hardly visible in modern Athens. This piece of evidence becomes even more valuable, if we take into consideration that the monastery was founded in 1550 by one of the most significant families of Athens, the

Fig.13.1: East apse with fresco decoration, Hagios Andreas church, Hagia Filothei monastery, Athens; W. Leaf, 1888–90; BSA BRF–02.01.01.001.

---

1. Macmillan 1911. See also the website: www.bsa.ac.uk

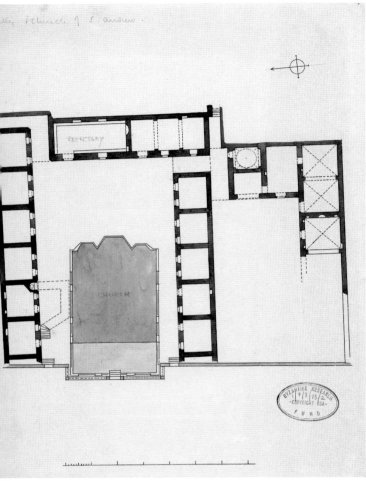

Fig.13.2: Plan of monastic complex, Hagia Philothei monastery, Athens; R. Weir Schultz & S. Barnsley, 1888–90; ink, pencil, watercolour; BSA BRF–01.01.01.002.

Benizeloi.[2] The monastic complex, which was built on earlier Byzantine ruins, functioned as a nursing home, a poorhouse and an educational centre for the young ladies of Athens. All these were organized by Rigoula Benizelou, the later Saint Filothei, who bequeathed her property to these institutions and who was martyred in 1589. Also of great importance are the unpublished drawings of the Archive, made with ink and watercolour which include descriptions of the same demolished monastic church from the north, west and east, as well as a long section, where one can see sculptures above the gate at the east side.

Leaf's photograph of the same church, decorated with wall paintings from the 17th century that have obviously been damaged after the Greek Revolution, is also significant in that it shows the decoration of the monument. So far, we have been aware of some fragments of wall paintings only, which are now in the Byzantine Museum in Athens.[3] This example, namely the information about the monastery of Hagia Philothei in the centre of Athens, whose existence is nowadays indicated only by the name of the street behind the Metropolis, aptly illustrates the significance of this archive for the Byzantine and post-Byzantine monuments of Attica and especially Athens.

The archive includes altogether 268 drawings of 23 monuments in Attica,[4] from 1890 to 1903, 100 photographs of the 1890s, and the notebooks of the research groups. This rich and unpublished material of the British School, which I came across while carrying out research in the summer of 2006 for the requirements of the present conference,[5] adds valuable pieces to a puzzle which is difficult to reconstruct, that of the buildings of Athens in the Byzantine era and during the Ottoman occupation.[6]

The reasons for this difficulty are more or less known. The present image of Athens is mainly the result of buildings from two historical periods: antiquity, Greek and Roman, and the modern period, that is, the last two centuries. The long intermediary Byzantine and Ottoman periods are indicated by just a few monuments, mainly churches. It is known that not only before, but also after the liberation from the Turks and the creation of the independent Greek Kingdom, both the state and individuals were extremely interested in

---

2. See Sicelianos 1960.

3. See Soteriou et al 1927, A, 56–7; B, 107–9. Chatzidaki 2000, 258. Byzantino kai Christiniko Mouseio 2004, 103.

4. Hagios Andreas, Hagioi Apostoloi, Hagioi Asomatoi, Hagios Dionysios Areopagitis, Panagia Gorgoepikoos, Hagios Ioannis Theologos, Kapnikarea, Soteira Lykodimou, Panagia Pantanassa, Metamorphosis, Hagioi Theodoroi, Hagia Zoni kai Hagios Spyridon, Hypapanti, monastery of Daou Pendeli, Daphni monastery, Kaisariani monastery, Omorfoklissia, Phaneromeni (Salamis).

5. I would like to express my gratitude to Dr Eleni Calligas and the Archivist Ms Amalia Kakissis for their cooperation and support during my research.

6. For the medieval history of Athens, see Kazanaki 2006*b*, 385–95, which also contains useful bibliographical information.

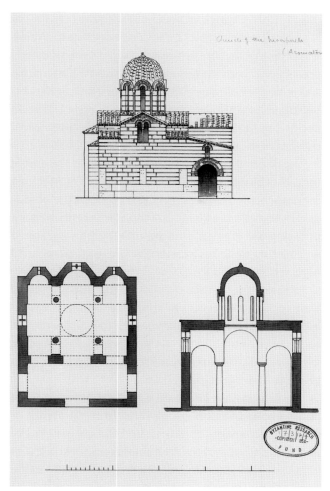

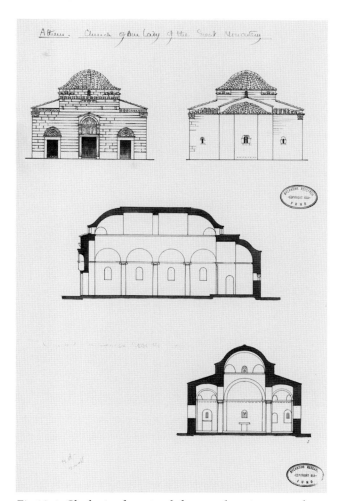

Fig.13.3: Clockwise from top: north elevation, transverse section, ground plan, Hagioi Asomatoi church, Athens; R. Weir Schultz & S. Barnsley, 1888–90; pencil, ink, watercolour; BSA BRF–01.01.01.023.

Fig.13.4: Clockwise from top left: west elevation, east elevation, longitudal section, transverse section, Megalo Monastiri, Athens; R. Weir Schultz & S. Barnsley, 1888–90; pencil, ink, watercolour; BSA BRF–01.01.01.090.

promoting and, consequently, conserving the ancient monuments, whereas modern buildings, fortifications, residences and many Christian churches were demolished for town planning and residential reasons, but also because their building materials were required for the construction of private buildings.[7]

Foreign travellers also were much more interested in ancient monuments than in medieval ones.[8] It seemed as though everybody was looking for the city's illustrious past, like Michael Choniates, Metropolitan of Athens from 1192 to 1204 and a man of letters, who wrote:

'Although I live in Athens, I do not see Athens anywhere... All the glory of the city is lost... So forgive me for having constructed a fictitious graphic image of her since I am unable to see the celebrated city of the Athenians'.[9] It appears that Choniates overlooked the Byzantine aspect of the city as much as foreign visitors and, unfortunately, Greek architects and archaeologists did centuries later. During Choniates's period, at the end of the 12th century, many churches had already been built in Athens by capable Byzantine architects. The

---

7. See Mallouchou-Tufano 2000, 311–43.
8. See Tsigakou 2000, 280–307.

---

9. Οικών Αθήνας ουκ Αθήνας που βλέπω ... όλωλε σύμπαν των Αθηνών το κλέος... συγγνωστός ουκούν, είπερ ουκ έχων βλέπειν των Αθηναίων την αοίδιμον πόλιν, ίνδαλμα ταύτης γραφικόν εστησάμην, Lampros 1879–80, 397–8.

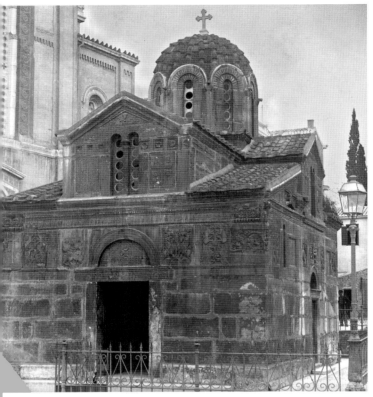

Fig.13.5: *View from west, Panagia Gorgoepikoos church, Athens; R. Weir Schultz & S. Barnsley, 1888–90; BSA BRF–02 .01.01.007.*

members of the British School studied and depicted these same churches at the end of the 19th century.

Information about monuments that underwent modifications in later periods is especially valuable as the following examples illustrate: the church of Hagioi Asomatoi of the 11th century before its restoration in 1960 (FIG.13.3), the 11th century Panagia Pantanassa in Monastiraki before the alterations that took place in 1907 when the square was rebuilt and before the significant changes it underwent in 1911 (FIG.13.4), as well as the Metamorfosis tou Sotiros of the same century, one of the earliest churches in Athens, whose appearance was altered following extensive repair work between 1908 and 1917 (PLATE XIV).[10]

What is also significant is the aesthetic value of these drawings. Examples such as the Kapnikarea church, the Church at Omorphi Ekklisia, the Panagia Gorgoepikoos and the small Metropolis alongside the modern Metrop-

olis of Athens, which is associated with the activities of Michael Choniates (PLATE XV),[11] demonstrate this value. It appears that the British research teams were particularly preoccupied with the last church. It was built of marble and incorporated in its outside walls, in a unique decorative manner, 90 ancient Greek, Roman, early Christian and Byzantine reliefs, of which the archive has 14 excellent drawings and 27 photographs (FIG.13.5; FIG.13.6).

The photographs of the archive, taken at the end of the 19th century, constitute rare documents of Athenian monuments.[12] This is especially true when the photographs depict lost moments of the monuments' history, as is the case with Daphni monastery, photographed when it functioned as a church before the final removal of its iconostasis (FIG.13.7).

In these photographs it is clear that the architects were trying to represent not only the monument itself but also its surrounding area, as is the case with the Kapnikarea church or the dome of Soteira Lykodimou, which now is the Russian church, with the Lycabettus hill in the background.

The material is completed with 12 drawings and 14 photographs of marble sculptures from surviving or ruined monuments of Athens and the greater area of Attica and from ancient monuments transformed into Christian ones (Erechtheion, Parthenon). Finally, in the notebooks one can find a lot of detailed information about the condition of the monuments and their decoration.

The majority of the drawings and photographs of the Attica Byzantine Archive — 86 drawings and 45 photos — relate to the Daphni monastery, the history of which is connected with the great French Byzantinist Gabriel Millet, who was responsible in 1888 for the restoration of this important 11th century monument. The drawings of the Daphni monastery offer valuable information about a monument that has undergone substantial alterations since 1899,[13] especially after a series of earthquakes in the 19th and 20th centuries.

The work of Gabriel Millet at Daphni and Mount Athos, amd the work of other foreign scholars such as

---

10. For the Byzantine churches of Athens see Soteriou et al 1927–33; Megaw 1931–32; Chatzidakis 1958.

11. Chatzidakis 1958.
12. Kaisariani monastery, Hagioi Theodoroi, Hagios Andreas, Hagioi Apostoloi, Kapnikarea, Soteira Lykodimou, Papagia Gorgoepikoos, Daphni monastery.
13. Millet 1899.

the Frenchmen Gailhabaud and Couchaud, published in the mid 19th century, and the drawings of Danish architects and of the French doctor Paul Durant published much more recently,[14] should be seen as part of the 19th century western Romantic movement with its powerful leaning towards medieval thought and art. This movement brought to light the individual characteristics of each people, in contrast to the imposition of a classicist uniformity. The result of this tendency was the systematic study and recording of the Byzantine monuments of Greece — in which the Romantic scholars recognized the structural elements of their contemporary monuments — in a way that sometimes was amateur and sometimes scientific.

The material of the BSA for Attica is distinguished by the professionalism, precision and authority of its specialized scholars.

The creator of most of the drawings of Attica was the architect Robert Weir Schultz,[15] who began working in Greece in 1887 on the advice of Lethaby, having won a Royal Academy Gold Medal and Travelling Studentship. He continued working in Greece as a member of the British School at Athens.

It appears that the intervention of Lethaby was decisive owing to his own relation to medieval art in general and especially to the Byzantine monuments. Lethaby was founder and first principal of the London Country Central School of Arts and Crafts. He was a personal friend of the Arts and Crafts Movement[16] pioneers William Morris[17] and Philip Webb and became a significant member of their circle. He was also an influential writer on architectural subjects with a specific interest in medieval and especially Byzantine art, as his books *The church of Sancta Sophia Constantinople: a study of Byzantine building* (1894) and *Medieval Art* (1904) indicate.

Lethaby's encouragement of Schultz and of the other travelling student of the Royal Academy, Sidney Barnsley, another British architect and member of the Arts and Crafts Exhibition Society, bore excellent fruit in the form of their admirable monograph, which includes abundant

Fig.13.6: East façade (central apse), Panagia Gorgoepikoos church, Athens; R. Weir Schultz & S. Barnsley, 1888–90; BSA BRF–02.01.01.026.

illustrations, in colour as well as in black and white, of the monastery of Hosios Loukas in Phocis.[18] Unfortunately, as Macmillan notes in the short history of the School, the publication of more valuable material on the Byzantine churches of Greece and Salonica, and also of a series of full size drawings of Greek moldings made by Schultz, was prevented at the time by lack of funds.[19]

Some samples of Schultz's unpublished works in the BRF Archive reveal a technical perfection and an aesthetic approach that verge on artistic creation. In the Daphni monument, in 1900, Schultz recorded with patience and skill not only the architectural features but also the marble decorations, the wall paintings and the mosaics. He copied the decorative subjects of the mosaics (PLATE XVI) and many representations such as the Baptism, the Nativity, or the Transfiguration, with great care. He even copied the whole iconographic

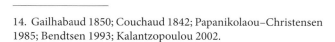

14. Gailhabaud 1850; Couchaud 1842; Papanikolaou–Christensen 1985; Bendtsen 1993; Kalantzopoulou 2002.

15. See Robert 1979; Stamp 1981.

16. Kaplan 2004; Cumming 2006.

17. Thompson 1993.

18. Schultz and Barnlsey 1901. See also Kalligas 2006.

19. Macmillan 1911, 2.

Fig.13.7: View of the interior of the katholikon looking north-east, Daphni monastery, Attica; R. Weir Schultz & S. Barnsley, 1888–90; BSA BRF–02.01.01.089.

programme for example of the Kaisariani monastery.

In his attempt to reconstruct the Byzantine mosaics and the wall paintings in the painter's manner, he demonstrates not only his academic interest in scientific recording, but also his deeper interest in the way in which the Byzantine craftsman worked.

Indeed, the medieval past and the working conditions of medieval craftsmen were at the centre of interest for the architects of the Arts and Crafts Movement, where Schultz belonged, as well as for the Pre-Raphaelite painters — especially Dante Gabriel Rossetti,[20]

who collaborated closely with William Morris in creating works of medieval inspiration. The architects and painters of these movements in England endorsed the same socialist ideology and preferred the working conditions of the medieval craftsman to the inhumane working pace imposed by industrialization.

By drawing and painting with patience, precision, and high aesthetic sensibility, Schultz tried to penetrate the way in which the Byzantine and post-Byzantine painters decorated churches. In the same spirit, with immense patience and precision, he followed the course of the work of the craftsman of the past, taking meticulous notes about the colours and the detailed creation of the faces (PLATE XVII), taking photographs, and then producing pictorial copies of high aesthetic quality of the 11th century mosaics in Daphni (PLATE XVIII).

His work on Byzantine techniques influenced his course as an architect and decorator and is obvious in his later works in England and Scotland, especially in church decoration and the conservation of monuments: e.g. his work in 1910 in the Chapel of St Andrew in Westminster Cathedral. He published this work as *Designs for the mosaic decoration of St Andrew's chapel, Westminster Cathedral* ten years after the study of the Daphni mosaics.

The study and publication of this very rich Byzantine Archive of the British School at Athens will throw light, when completed, on the history of the ruined and reconstructed Byzantine monuments of Attica, thanks to the high quality and accuracy of the drawings and especially of the photographs. At the same time, it will reveal the influences of Byzantine architecture and decorative art on British architects of the 19th and early 20th century. Once more we are in front of the phenomenon of interaction among the European cultures.

REFERENCES

Bendtsen, M., 1993. *Sketches and Measurings.* Copenhagen.

Blomfield, R. T., 1940. *Richard Norman Shaw.* London.

Byzantino kai Christiniko Mouseio (Athens), 2004. *Ο κόσμος του Βυζαντινού Μουσείου.* Athens.

Chatzidaki, N., 2000. 'Ψηφιδωτά και τοιχογραφίες στις βυζαντινές και μεταβυζαντινές εκκλησίες της Αθήνας', in *Αθήναι από την Κλασική Εποχή έως Σήμερα (5ος αι. π.Χ — 2000 μ.Χ.).* Athens.

Chatzidakis, M., 1958. *Βυζαντινή Αθήνα.* Athens.

Couchaud, A., 1842. *Choix d' églises byzantines en Grèce.* Paris.

---

20. Prettejohn 2000.

Cumming, E., 2006. *Hand, Heart and Soul: The Arts and Crafts Movement in Scotland*. Birlinn.

Gailhabaud, J., 1850. *Monuments anciens et modernes*, v. II. Paris.

Hitchcock, H-R, 1958. *Architecture: Nineteenth and Twentieth Centuries*. London.

Kalantzopoulou, T., 2002. *Μεσαιωνικοί ναοί της Αθήνας από σωζόμενα σχέδια του Paul Durant*. Athens.

Kalligas, H., 2006. 'Twin reflections of a Byzantine city: Monemvasia as seen by Robert Weir Schultz and Sidney H. Barnsley in 1890', in R. Cormack and E. Jeffreys (eds) *Through the Looking Glass. Byzantium Through British Eyes*: 23–44. Aldershot.

Kaplan, W., 2004. *The Arts and Crafts Movement in Europe and America*. London.

Kazanaki, M., 2006. 'Μεσαιωνική Αθήνα', in A. Laiou (ed.), *Οικονομική Ιστορία του Βυζαντίου από τον 7ο έως τον 15ο αιώνα*, Β΄: 385–95. Athens.

Lampros, S. (ed.), 1879–80. *Μιχαήλ Ακομινάτος. Τα Σωζόμενα*: 397–8. Athens.

Macmillan, G.A., 1911. *A Short History of the British School at Athens*. London.

Mallouchou-Tufano, F., 2000. 'Από τον 19ο στον 21ο αιώνα: μεταμορφώσεις του αρχαιολογικού τοπίου στην Αθήνα', in *Αθήναι από την Κλασική Εποχή έως Σήμερα (5ος αι. π.Χ — 2000 μ.Χ.)*: 311–43. Athens.

Megaw, A.H.S., 1931–32. 'The chronology of some middle Byzantine churches', *BSA* 32: 90–130.

Millet, G., 1899. *Le monastère de Daphni. Histoire, architecture, mosaïques*. Paris.

Ottewill, D., 1979. 'Robert Weir Schultz, 1860–1951. An Arts and Crafts architect', *Architectural History* 22: 88–115.

Papanikolaou–Christensen, A., 1985. *Αθήνα 1818–1853, Έργα Δανών καλλιτεχνών*. Athens.

Pevsner, N., 1963. *Victorian Architecture*. London.

Prettejohn, E., 2000. *The Art of the Pre-Raphaelites*. Princeton.

Rubens, G., 1986. *William Richard Lethaby, His Life and Work 1857–1931*. London.

Saxby, D., 1995. *William Morris at Merton*. London.

Schultz, R. and S. Barnsley, 1901. *The Monastery of Saint Luke of Stiris in Phokis, and the dependent Monastery of Saint Nicolas in the Field*. London.

Sicelianos, D., 1960. *Old and New Athens*, trans. Robert Liddell. London.

Soteriou, G.A., A. Xyggopoulos and A. Orlandos, 1927–1929–1933. *Ευρετήριο των μεσαιωνικών μνημείων της Ελλάδος*, 1–3. Athens.

Stamp, G., 1981. *Robert Weir Schultz, Architect and his work for the Marquees of Bute*. Mount Stuart.

Thompson, P., 1993. *The Work of William Morris*. Oxford.

Tsingakou, F.M., 2000. 'Η επανανακάλυψη της Αθήνας από τους ζωγράφους περιηγητές', in *Αθήναι από την Κλασική Εποχή έως Σήμερα (5ος αι. π.Χ — 2000 μ.Χ.)*: 280–307. Athens.

14
William Miller: Medieval historian and modern journalist

Paul Hetherington

The year 2006 was an appropriate time to consider the work of William Miller and his association with the British School at Athens, as it was just eighty years earlier, in 1926, that he had been elected an Honorary Student of the School. From then his name appears in each issue on the relevant page in the journal of the School until the general practice was ended.[1] This offers a good starting-point not only for assessing his past achievement and present standing as a historian of the medieval Levant, but also for relating these to his lifelong practice of journalism.

William Miller's life was mildly unconventional. He was born in 1864 into the family of an enterprising Cumberland mine owner, his mother dying when he was quite young.[2] After attending Rugby school he went up to Oxford, and so was the first member of his family — and as it turned out, the last — to attend a university. After gaining a double first at Oxford[3] he read for the Bar, to which he was called in 1889; but he never practised the law. From early on in his life he was the recipient of a modest private income, and so he never had to take a full-time salaried position. Instead he first embarked on what was to be one of his lifelong interests by starting to travel quite extensively in the Balkans and Greece. Also at this time he began one of his careers that would persist throughout his life — that of political journalist and (later) newspaper correspondent.

Miller married in 1895, and his wife (Ada Mary Wright) would accompany him on his travels. At his death they had been married for 50 years. In 1903, just before he was 40, the pair left London and settled in Rome,[4] where perhaps surprisingly in view of his now well established interest in the Balkans and Greece, he remained until 1923. Even then, it seems that we have to thank the new Fascist regime, and probably Mussolini's march on Rome in October 1922, for creating an atmosphere that he disliked sufficiently for him to decide to move to Athens. He would refer to this move as 'retirement' but his continued level of activity there makes it difficult to accept this description. Even this was not to be his final home. The German invasion of Greece in April 1941 meant that, by then aged 77, he and his wife had hurriedly to pack everything required for their immediate needs. Leaving behind personal belongings and his fine library, they went down to Piraeus and embarked on a ship bound for Durban in South Africa. He was to pass the last four years of his life there, in the Ocean View Hotel. He died in 1945 at the age of 80, just after the war had ended. His widow remained in Durban, surviving him by five years. They had no children.

Owing to the circumstances of his later life, very few of Miller's personal papers or letters have survived. He and his wife had no need to write to each other, they had neither siblings nor children, and their abrupt departure from Athens meant that they had to abandon all but their essential possessions. The city archivists in Durban assure me that they have nothing of his, or of his wife, in their records.[5] He may have passed all that was possible on to the British School in Athens,[6] but clearly most has disappeared. His published writing, which is very extensive, is our only source for his intellectual approach.

---

1. *BSA* 28 (1925–26), 290 to 33 (1932–33), 235, after which the practise was discontinued.

2. I would like to thank Mrs C. Craghill for her help on the Miller family background.

3. First class Classical moderations 1884, First class *literae humaniores* 1887; he was a student at Hertford College.

4. Miller's address was in central Rome at 36 via Palestro.

5. I would like to thank Mrs Phyllis Connerty of the Don Africana Library in Durban for her help.

6. The archive of the BSA holds six of these boxes.

Fig.14.1: Tripolis Railway Station, March 1904; BSA Photographic Archive: BSAA3–80.

In Athens he lived first at 11 Odos Loukianou, but later moved to 8 Odos Vissarionos [Bessarion]. I like to think that he chose this street because of its name: a street named after a late medieval Greek metropolitan who went to Rome and became a cardinal might have seemed an auspicious address for someone who came from Rome to live in Greece. The address of the apartment where he and his wife lived now presents a post-war construction. It was reported in *The Times* after his death that 'his library was stolen or destroyed by the Germans.'[7]

Until he sadly died in June 2006 aged 95, one person was still living who knew William Miller in Athens. This was Peter Megaw, whom I visited while preparing this paper, to ask if he could give me any first-hand impressions or recollections.[8] Megaw told me that as a raw young student at the British School in the nineteen

thirties he was rather overawed by this distinguished old man fifty years his senior. Miller and his wife were well-known socially in Athens life, and many students or visitors to the city enjoyed their hospitality. Megaw remembers him spending much time in the garden of the British School, to the upkeep of which he contributed, and where he walked his dog. He was apparently an almost daily presence in the School and its garden, and the contribution that he made particularly to Greek Studies is closely linked to the environment of the School. The dog will be mentioned again later.

Of the two documents of a personal nature that English people can originate in their life, the more public, where they reveal their achievements and express something of how they wish the world to perceive them, is their entry in *Who's Who*. In his entry Miller announced himself as 'Author and newspaper correspondent'.[9] His omission of the word 'historian'

7. *The Times*, 10 Nov. 1945, 7.

8. For an obituary of Megaw, who was Director of the British School 1962–68, see *BSA AR* 2005–6, 60–2.

9. *Who's Who*, Vol. 96, London 1944.

gives us a hint of not only how he saw himself and wished himself to be known, but also how he viewed the function of the historian. He gave the titles of most of the books that he had written, but could not give comparable titles to his work as a correspondent, which he refers to elsewhere as 'the grass of the field'. It is because of this, and because his journalistic work is so closely interwoven with his academic writing, particularly on medieval and later Greek history, that it is worth assessing this side of his work in association with his historical studies. I hope that this will convey a more complete and rounded view of William Miller than can be gleaned only from his full-length academic writings.

I should mention his most prominent books, although they can be found in any good academic library. He is still denoted on the title page of one of his first, *The Balkans*, (1896) as a member of the Inner Temple and barrister at law. The book had three editions, the latest in 1922, each one with an extra chapter to bring it up to date. Likewise his *The Ottoman Empire and its Successors* (1913) was updated in later editions, the fourth in 1936, each time with extra sections bringing it up to the year of issue. Spyridon Lambros[10] felt that it was sufficiently important to make a Greek translation of the first edition, and its continuing value led to a re-printing of the fourth edition in 1966, giving it a life of 53 years. This practice of updating suggests that Miller viewed the past as a positive and unbroken continuum linked to the present, and which could be assessed in a comparable way.

Another early book, *Travel and Politics in the Near East* (1898), is the first which points towards his specialised knowledge of Greece. Although it is in the tradition of much 19th century travel writing, it is written with greater insight into political life than most such studies.

Miller published two further books of a general nature on Greece and Greek culture, politics and society. *Greek Life in Town and Country* (1905) conveys a huge amount of material, displaying his wide experience, empathy and deep knowledge of the country and its people. It has been described as 'one of the most informative, perceptive and sympathetic books ever to have been written about modern Greece'.[11] *Greece* (1928) gives more space to political questions. Its chapters on 'The Greek Republic 1924–27', 'Education', 'The Greek Press and Literature' and 'The Greek Constitution of 1927' can still be read with interest and profit.

In both volumes Miller commented on the role of the 'foreign archaeological schools', and in particular the British School at Athens. He draws attention to how much better funded than the British are the French and German schools. He also pointed out how the Gennadios Library was first offered to the British, but the finance to make the purchase could not be raised from either private or public sources. Chapters of both these books were translated into Greek and published in Athens - a considerable compliment to an English writer.[12]

Among his other publications on Hellenic themes in the 1920s were a short *History of the Greek People (1821–1921)* (1922),[13] a volume titled *Trebizond the last Greek empire* (1926), and a brief and knowledgeable publication on the English in Athens.[14]

It is pre-eminently *The Latins in the Levant* (1908),[15] and *Essays on the Latin Orient* (1921) that reveal Miller's capacity for reducing complex and detailed issues to a clear and coherent narrative unity. These masterly studies are his most lasting gifts to medieval scholarship, and of enduring value. When listing his works, he always put them before any others. They are books of their period; but it is still impossible to study these centuries of Levantine history without having digested them.

As a historian he was essentially self-taught, never having formally studied medieval history. He published in Greek, German, French and Italian, besides English.

---

10. Spyridon Lambros (1851–1919), a prolific author, was Professor of History at Athens University. He was briefly Prime Minister of Greece in 1916.

11. Clogg 2000, 32.

12. Parts of the earlier book were translated into Greek in the newspaper *Νέον Ἄστυ*, and of the latter (which formed one of the series 'The Modern World') in the journals *Πρωΐα* and *Ἑστία*.

13. A Greek translation by K. Kairophylas was published in Athens 1924.

14. Miller 1926*b*.

15. It will thus have had a life of 100 years when this publication appears. A Greek translation was published by Lambros in 2 vols (Athens 1909–10).

He must have written with great ease. As a man of his age, he seems never to have learnt to use a typewriter, which was seen as a device for secretaries, at least in his youth; everything that I have seen was written by hand.

These books are still with us; it is his output as a journalist, of which he could only give a hint in his *Who's Who* entry, and which is so much less accessible, which deserves further exploration. He was the foreign correspondent of the *Morning Post*, first in Rome and then in Athens, for 34 years from 1903 until 1937. This paper, with *The Times*, was the most influential of the English newspapers of the period, and was well-known in the 19th century for having among its contributors literary figures of the standing of Wordsworth and Coleridge. It was eventually bought by the *Daily Telegraph* in 1937. Miller's journalism alone occupies several volumes of newspaper clippings in the BSA archive. In addition he was a regular contributor to the *English Historical Review* from 1892 for nearly 50 years.

I am able to write in these terms because in his last months in Athens — up to January 1941 — he was finalising a comprehensive list of all his publications, which he must have deposited in the BSA Library before leaving for South Africa. The Index to the five boxes that contain his papers runs to over 50 hand-written pages, in which he enumerates the publishing history of his 25 books, 219 academic articles, and almost 800 reviews in journals. Even so, it does not mention his hundreds of contributions to the *Morning Post* which were printed anonymously as 'From our own correspondent'.[16]

Political journalism must have appealed to Miller from an early age. His later achievements as a historian suggest that for him history and journalism were comparable, journalism being a treatment of modern history. His early writings for the *Westminster Review*, dating from the early 1890s, when he was just qualified as a lawyer, seem to confirm this.[17] These early articles were the beginning of a continuous output of high-grade factual commentary that was to continue for over 40 years.

A remarkable analytical paper, 'The Payment of Members,' published in 1898 strikes another note. Here he carefully analysed evidence for Belgium, Germany, Italy, Spain, Portugal, Denmark, New South Wales, Queensland, Victoria, New Zealand, Natal, Newfoundland, Bulgaria, and others as to whether the members of parliaments were paid, and if so how much, whether they got free travel, etc.[18] It must have taken a great deal of correspondence and application, not just in pre-Google, but pre-Air Mail days, to arrive at these details for countries such as the Australian states and Bulgaria, let alone for western Europe. The subject must have seemed important to him, and the idea presents itself: might he not, during the years of his early thirties, have been considering embarking on a career in politics or public service? He would not yet have thought of himself as a medieval historian: contemporary political life was still absorbing much of his interest.

In his later thirties one can trace a growing interest in earlier periods. In 1900 he published an article on 'The Story of Monaco'.[19] It may be that this was a hint that he was beginning to chronicle, for his later book *The Latins in the Levant* of 1908, the complex history of the Grimaldi family; they had appeared as Aegean 'dukes' in Naxos and Thasos, before they settled down in their tiny principality on the Côte d'Azur. From 1900, starting with 'Napoleon in the near East',[20] some of his articles appeared also in Greek translation.

Greece begins increasingly to dominate Miller's output in the early years of the century, when he was in his forties. He started to combine writing for journals with more permanent forms, revising his articles for inclusion in later volumes. For example 'The Ionian Islands under Venetian Rule' which first appeared in the *English Historical Review* of 1906, later formed a section of *The Latins in the Levant*, and in 1921 was brought up to date in *Essays in the Latin Orient*. Other articles

---

16. I would have been unable to assemble this information without the kind assistance of the Librarian, Penny Wilson.

17. E.g. Miller 1890*b*, which was followed by articles on the Balkans, Turkey and Greece: Miller 1890*a*; Miller 1891.

18. Miller 1898*a*. Payment to members of the British parliament ceased in 1894. This was also the case for German, Italian, Spanish and Portuguese members, who were deemed to be giving 'voluntary service'. Members in Bulgaria and Belgium were paid a daily rate, in Greece a sessional rate and in Denmark received free theatre tickets, free travel and a daily payment.

19. Miller 1900*b*.

20. Miller 1900*a*; a translation was published in the Greek press shortly after.

in *The Quarterly Review, Byzantinische Zeitschrift, The Westminster Review, Journal of Hellenic Studies, Journal of the British and American Archaeological Society in Rome* and other journals were treated in the same way. He clearly had no difficulty in dealing with both modern and medieval subject-matter simultaneously.[21] Nearer to home, Miller wrote articles about George Finlay (with whom his own life overlapped by eleven years)[22] at roughly the same time as he was writing 'The Historians Doukas and Phrantzes'.[23] He contributed also to the *Cambridge Medieval History*, and wrote many entries for the *Encyclopedia Britannica*, as well as more than thirty reviews in Greek for *Hellenika*, and numerous other minor articles and reviews.

After establishing himself in Rome, Miller was able to report first-hand in many scores of despatches on events in Italy, including the rise of the Fascists to power.[24] Continuing his journalism in Athens, he commented with unrivalled authority on the turmoil of Greek politics in the 1920s and mid-1930s.[25]

During the period 1915–16, when Miller was still living in Rome, a proposal was made for the foundation at King's College London of a Chair of Modern Greek and Byzantine History, Language and Literature. (The current holder of this chair, Professor Roderick Beaton, is a contributor to this volume.) The chair was to be named after Adamantios Koraes (1748–1833), the great classical scholar of the enlightenment and supporter of Greek independence. The varied and disastrously passionate history of the early years of the Chair has been recorded in an excellent slim book by Richard Clogg.[26]

Fig.14.2: Greek life, ca.1910: a village mule; BSA Photographic Archive: SPHS–7885.

The moving figure in the initiative was the Principal of King's College, the classicist and philhellene Professor Ronald Burrows, who was a prominent supporter and friend of Eleftherios Venizelos, and a leading light in the Anglo-Hellenic League. Correspondence held in King's College Library shows that from an early date Miller was a prime candidate for the new post. Burrows, who had been making his own enquiries, wrote to Miller in the summer of 1916, confident that he would take up the offer; this despite the appointment being technically a committee decision, the source of the funds being still undecided, and there being a war on. Miller must have realised that the funding question was critical. In his reply in September 1916 with typical acumen he immediately homed in on the potential problems, and asked: 'From what sources are the funds for the proposed chair to be derived? If they are to be provided directly or indirectly by a foreign government then I may at once decline all further consideration of

21. For example see Miller 1923*a*, Miller 1923*b*, and Miller 1923*c*.
22. Miller 1924*c* and Miller 1924*b*. Joan Hussey disagreed with the latter.
23. Miller 1926*a*.
24. *Morning Post*, 30 Oct. 1922, 'The Fascisti in Power', where Miller ('From our own correspondent') reports that 'Mussolini will probably form a government'.
25. For example, again 'From our own correspondent', *Morning Post*, 28 May 1935, 'A Monarchy for Greece', in which he addressed the possible restoration of the monarchy that was abolished in 1924: 'In a long experience of Greek affairs I have never known so complicated a situation'.
26. Clogg 1986, particularly 1–24.

Fig.14.3: West face of the chancel arch of Hagia Sofia, Andravida, Elis, in 1906–09. Photograph by R. Traquair, BSA BRF–02.01.13.044.

the matter.'[27] It was left to Miller, writing from Rome in 1916, to suggest that all discussion should wait until the war was over.

Not to be deterred, Burrows wrote again next month, and Miller had to point out that 'At present even such details as the moving of one's books and furniture to England cannot be executed, I am afraid … … But I must leave you with a perfectly free hand in the matter.'

Having established to his own satisfaction that the chair would be free of any governmental control, Burrows returned to the attack. He wrote in May 1918, still seven months before the Armistice, to repeat his offer, stating 'I very earnestly wish you to stand.' Miller's courteous response would be a candidate for an anthology of letters of refusal. He replied that 'After mature consideration of the post, however, I cannot [stand for the election]. If an offer of this kind had been made to me 15 years ago, when I left London I would have accepted it … … But I am now 53 and no-one should begin an entirely new profession at that age. No man makes a career after 50; no man who is ambitious becomes a

journalist in England. …. I well know that even the best journalistic work (which mine is not) is like the "grass of the field"'. And then comes a truly memorable line: 'Also both my wife and I dislike the London climate, and were never well there.' How many scholars, offered the opportunity of being a foundation professor in a major London institution, would turn it down on grounds of the local weather? He may have thought that his response was rather extreme as he concluded, in his finely legible hand: 'Were I to accept your offer, and were I elected, it would only be a delusion for me (because I would not be up to the work), and an almost certain delusion to you and your friends.'

Most people would regard that as a final refusal, but not Burrows. In June 1918 (still well before the end of the War) he wrote again to Miller, whom he still had not met, with the surprising opening line: 'I am sure you're thinking me a pertinacious beggar', and asked, with I feel a note of desperation, if he would take the job for three, or even two years. He ended 'Hasluck is the only other person considered, and he has TB.'

Miller must have looked out from where he lived in Rome in the via Palestro, and felt that it was still the best place to be. How everyone in London must have wished, as controversy erupted around the Chair in the early 1920s, that Burrows in his three earnest requests could have prevailed. As it was, Arnold Toynbee, himself a former student of the British School at Athens, was appointed to the Chair, but soon fell foul of the Greek subscribers as a result of his reports for the Manchester Guardian on the Greek-Turkish war in Asia Minor, which were taken by the subscribers to be anti-Hellenic propaganda. Toynbee resigned from the Koraes Chair in 1923. King's College's loss was very much the gain of the British School in Athens, to which Miller moved in the same year. Later in the 1920s he made a donation to King's College of some rare books from his library in Rome; I suspect it was to show that there were no hard feelings over his turning down Burrows's repeated pleadings.

The second of Miller's personal documents, to which I referred earlier, is his Will. He wrote this in 1934 conscientiously marking his seventieth year. It contains just one unexpected feature. Among the bequests is £500 to the British Archaeological School, Athens, 'partly to be devoted to maintaining and improving

---

27. All the correspondence quoted here is held in the Archive of King's College London, Burrows Papers, ref: KAP/BUR/333. I would like to thank the staff there, particularly Caroline Lam, for their help.

the Finlay Library by the purchase of books relating to the history of Greece from 1204 to the present time,' to which Miller adds: 'and partly to the maintenance and improvement of the garden, in which my dear little dog lies buried, and to the upkeep of her grave.' The record of the first part of this expenditure is still maintained in the School accounts.[28] There are also bequests to the English Church in Athens, the RSPCA in London and its Greek equivalent. As for his 'dear little dog', Penny Wilson, the School's Librarian, told me of a one-day project that was undertaken by all the archaeology post-graduate students to locate the grave. I believe it was successful. There is also a record of William and Ada Miller's devotion to their elderly cat, which they must have taken with them to Durban; they risked missing their emergency passage as they were incensed that it could not have a berth to itself.[29]

Miller's devotion to his pets was given a wider public by a sequence of brief columns he contributed to a journal called *The Animal's Friend*, published in London. They outnumber any other category of his writings during the 1930s, continuing until July 1940. They deal with such subjects as the treatment of animals by the ancient Greeks, contemporary animal welfare in Patras and Volos, and the opening of the first Dogs' Refuge in Athens in the National Gardens.[30] Another article records the installation of the first public drinking fountain and water trough for animals in Athens, on June 6th 1931,[31] at the junction where the road from Piraeus meets Odos Ermou. The Metropolitan Animals Drinking Fountain Association, a British charity,[32] was involved. For the installation of the fountain (essentially a stone trough with a water inlet) not only the mayor of Athens, but none less than the prime minister, Mr Venizelos, and his wife, Mrs Venizelos, were present, with other city officials. The British School

Fig.14.4: View from the SW of the church of Vlachernae, near Killini, Elis. Photograph by R. Traquair, 1906–09; BSA BRF–02.01.13.002.

of Archaeology was represented by Walter A. Heurtley, the then Assistant Director, who left his studies to attend. Miller, ever interested in the world of politics, must have sponsored the event, and would have been much in evidence at it. The drinking fountain is no longer to be seen, but then neither are the animals to drink from it.

These are two of the episodes to which Miller was devoting his time in his later sixties and seventies.[33] They are interspersed with articles such as 'Recent Bibliography on Trebizond',[34] and interesting brief notices on 'The Centenary of the University of Athens' and 'The Centenary of the Archaeological Society of Athens' which took place in consecutive years and which he attended.[35] His Will specified that if his wife should predecease him, all the remainder of his estate, after the

---

28. *BSA AR* 2005–6, 22.

29. I am grateful to Shelagh Meade for passing on this information to me.

30. *The Animal's Friend* 35 (July 1929), 172.

31. *The Animal's Friend* 37 (July 1931), 165.

32. The aim of the Metropolitan Drinking Fountain and Cattle Trough Association, which is still an active charity, is to 'promote the provision of drinking water for people and animals in the United Kingdom and overseas'.

33. Another is given in the same journal (40, July 1934, 76), when Miller reports on bird-tables in Athens, three of which had been donated by the University of London Animal Welfare Society.

34. Miller 1937*a*, where details of 29 items are given.

35. Miller 1937*b* and Miller 1938. Miller reported that he had also been present at the celebration of the 75th anniversary of the University, organised by Sp. Lambros, and he revealed that the first meeting of the Archaeological Society had been held in 1837 on the Acropolis, actually inside the Parthenon. In 1937, ten Britons were given diplomas and *King Lear* was performed in modern Greek at the Royal Theatre.

minor bequests mentioned, should be divided between four named British animal welfare charities.

Miller was a lifelong swimmer, and recorded the details of this activity in a personal notebook (retained in the archive of the British School) which exemplifies his extreme devotion to accuracy. It amounted to an obsession, which took the form of counting, and then recording, the number of strokes that he had swum on any one day, and multiplying it by the number of days' swimming in any one year. So in this notebook, which must have been for his personal use only, we can read that in 1927, for example, he calculated that he swam 47,301 strokes; even in 1940, aged 76, he noted swimming 19,365 strokes. Fitness apart, this does seem to be carrying his pursuit of factual accuracy to extremes. Numerical precision was given public expression when he reported in his column in *The Animal's Friend* that in four months after the inauguration of the first drinking trough in Athens 40,981 animals had drunk from its waters.[36]

If we try to summarise the progression of William Miller's interests as they are revealed through his extensive and varied writing over almost fifty years, we see that his most consistent object of enquiry and analysis was contemporary events which he experienced at first hand, sometimes only a day or two before analysing them. He must have been writing as many of the events were still unfolding. It was not until his later thirties that he embarked on the area of study which was to provide his most lasting monument: the period of the penetration of the western powers into Greece following the fourth crusade.

In *The Latins in the Levant* Miller provided a masterly synthesis of the complex and varied narrative of events in mainland Greece and the Archipelago, based throughout on original sources. While the starting-point of his study — the arrival of the western powers in Greece in 1204 — had long been acknowledged as a moment of fundamental change in Levantine and European history, Miller was able to approach the subject from a fresh point of view, indicated by the time-frame of his sub-title, *A History of Frank-*

ish Greece (1204–1566). This allowed him to pursue the long tale of invasions and incursions that the area experienced. No country was more open to the influx of other peoples. During these centuries Franks, Provençales, Florentines, Venetians, Angevins, Catalans and of course Turks all at some time, either peacefully or (more often) by force, penetrated Greek territory and settled some part of it.

This work remains Miller's most substantial achievement. *Essays in the Latin Orient* lacks the coherence of *The Latins in the Levant,* but the essay form enabled him to range widely, including studies of Roman and Byzantine Greece, as well as analysis of 'Turkish Greece (1460–1684)', 'The Venetian Revival in Greece (1684–1718)', and six essays which he called 'Miscellanea from the Near East', all with their roots in medieval Balkan and crusading history.

To juxtapose for the first time the two fields of Miller's writing — journalism and history — underlines how his contribution to Byzantine and Modern Greek studies, through the British School, was broader and more inclusive than has been recognised. His development as an historian can be seen to have grown out of his lifelong work as a journalist, in recording events of the present and recent past. His work as an historian — or 'author' as he called himself — was inextricably linked with this, so that he can be seen throughout his life working simultaneously, and perhaps uniquely, on both modern and medieval themes.

I wondered at one point whether, if Miller had been born a century later, he might not have become one of the high-powered television historians who appear on British screens from time to time, but no: his independence and the socially agreeable and tranquil pace of life that he clearly enjoyed, would have been too disrupted by the demands of the editors and producers. They would have got the same answer as did Ronald Burrows when he tried to attract Miller to King's College London to be the first holder of the Koraes Chair.

Would it have been possible for him to follow in the later 20th century the same very varied diet of interests that he had in the first half of the century? I suspect not. I think he must have felt that he had established the way of life that suited him best, and helped him to produce his best work. The British School was able to provide an

36. *The Animal's Friend* 38 (Jan. 1932), 9; it is not recorded how this figure was reached.

appropriate and sympathetic environment for him, to the lasting benefit of Greek studies. One thing is clear: William Miller's description of himself as 'author and newspaper correspondent', even allowing for the conventions of the context in which it appeared, greatly understated his gifts; his achievements far exceeded such a limited formula.

REFERENCES

Clogg, R., 1986. *Politics and the Academy; Arnold Toynbee and the Koraes Chair*. London.

—, 2000. *Anglo-Greek Attitudes: Studies in History*. London.

Miller, W., 1890a. 'Prince Bismarck's position', *Westminster Review* 133: 333–44.

—, 1890b. 'The Making of Modern Germany', *Westminster Review* 133: 125–43.

—, 1891. 'The Politician as Historian', *Westminster Review* 136: 286–94.

—, 1896. *The Balkans*. London.

—, 1898a. 'The Payment of Members', *Westminster Review* 149: 25–39.

—, 1898b. *Travel and Politics in the Near East*. London.

—, 1900a. 'Napoleon in the near East', *Westminster Review* 151: 172–84

—, 1900b. 'The Story of Monaco', *Gentleman's Magazine* 288: 22–34

—, 1905. *Greek Life in Town and Country*. London.

—, 1908. *The Latins in the Levant. A History of Frankish Greece (1204–1566)*. London.

—, 1909–10. *Ιστορία της Φραγκοκρατίας εν Ελλάδι (1204–1566)*, transl. Sp. Lambros: vols. 1–2. Athens. [Title changed to …. *στην Ελλάδα (1204–1566)* in 1964 reprint.]

—, 1913. *The Ottoman Empire and its Successors*. London.

—, 1914. *Η Τουρκία καταρρέουσα*, transl. Sp. Lambros. Athens.

—, 1921. *Essays on the Latin Orient*. Cambridge.

—, 1922a. 'Giolitti and Italian Politics', *Contemporary Review* 122: 576–84.

—, 1922b. *A History of the Greek People (1821–1921)*. London.

—, 1923a. 'Nine months of Fascismo', *Contemporary Review* 123: 372–81.

—, 1923b. 'The Chronology of Trebizond', *English Historical Review* 38: 408–10.

—, 1923c. 'The Greek Dilemma: Monarchy or Republic', *Contemporary Review* 123: 286–92.

Fig.14.5: The Megara Easter dances; BSA Photographic Archive: SPHS–4514.

—, 1924a. *Ιστορία του Ελληνικού Λαού (1821–1921)*, transl. K. Kairophylas. Athens.

—, 1924b. 'George Finlay as a Journalist', *English Historical Review* 39: 552–87.

—, 1924c. 'The Finlay Papers', *English Historical Review* 39: 386–98.

—, 1926a. 'The Historians Doukas and Phrantzes' *Journal of Hellenic Studies* 46: 63–71.

—, 1926b. *The English in Athens before 1821*, Anglo-Hellenic League, London.

—, 1926c. *Trebizond the last Greek Empire*. London.

—, 1928. *Greece*. London.

—, 1937a. 'Recent Bibliography on Trebizond', *English Historical Review* 52: 109–10.

—, 1937b. 'The Centenary of the University of Athens', *Journal of Hellenic Studies*, 57: 80–1.

—, 1938. 'The Centenary of the Archaeological Society of Athens', *Journal of Hellenic Studies* 58: 254.

Who's Who, 96, London 1944

The Animal's Friend

Morning Post

The Times

15

Academics at War: The British School at Athens during the First World War

Richard Clogg

Less has been written about the activities of the foreign archaeological Schools[1] in Greece during the two World Wars than about other periods in their history. In part, this is due to the fact that archaeological activity was largely in abeyance for the duration of the conflicts. In part, it is due to the fact that the larger Schools were often harnessed directly or indirectly to the war effort of the countries involved, a role which, for self-evident reasons, they have not been anxious to stress. Many alumni of the Schools in both World Wars were engaged in military, sabotage or intelligence activities in Greece and elsewhere, for the obvious reason that they were familiar with the country's terrain, history, culture and, above all, language, at a time when knowledge of Greek was not widespread.[2] There is abundant evidence that most of the foreign Schools of the combatant countries in both World Wars demonstrated scant regard for Greek sovereignty. It is not altogether surprising, therefore, to find that the activities of the foreign Schools during critical periods in the history of Greece, when they had priorities other than the pursuit of scholarship, are something of a closed book.

The most egregious example of nefarious activity on the part of an archaeological School in Greece is that afforded by the German Archaeological Institute. After the Nazis came to power in Germany the distinguished Georg Karo was dismissed as director in 1936 because of his Jewish origins. He was succeeded in 1937 by Walther Wrede, a committed Nazi bent on politicising the work of the Institute at the expense of archaeology. He combined the role of director with the functions of *Landesgruppenleiter*, the Nazi party official with responsibility for German expatriates in Greece of whom there were a not negligible number in the late 1930s.[3] When the German Archaeological Institute was amalgamated with the Austrian Archaeological Institute following the *Anschluss*, Wrede directed the unified institution. It should be noted that Wrede's activities on behalf of the Nazi party began long before Greece, or Germany for that matter, was caught up in the Second World War. By contrast, the activities of the BSA during the First World War which I describe in this paper resulted exclusively from the exigencies of war: I have come across no indication that the School was seen as a source of political intelligence during peace time.[4]

During the First World War, for much of which Greece was neutral, the resources of the French School were deployed to further the diplomatic (and intelligence) interests of France. A recent study of the French School at this time makes this unabashedly clear in the title alone, *L'Ecole Française d'Athènes pendant la Grande Guerre: une institution universitaire au service*

---

1. I have used 'foreign archaeological schools' as a convenient shorthand since archaeology was their main field of activity; but the scholarly remit of (at least) the British and French Schools was much wider, embracing all aspects of Greek history and culture.

2. Some indication is given of the involvement during the Second World War of alumni of the British School at Athens and of the American School of Classical Studies in Greek affairs, and of the sometimes fraught relations that existed between them, in Clogg 2000. Within the US Office of Strategic Services, the cohort of peacetime archaeologists was actually known, not altogether flatteringly, as the 'archaeological captains'.

3. On German archaeological interest and activity in Greece during the Second World War, see Vasileios Petrakos's valuable study (1994), 105–8, 115, 117–28, 131–4, 137–42.

4. In the introduction to the Greek translation (Thessaloniki 1989) of A.J.B. Wace (the director of the British School throughout the First World War) and M.S. Thompson's *The Nomads of the Balkans* (1914) it is suggested that 'in all probability' their work on the Vlachs had been carried out on higher orders. This, in my view, is unlikely. It is not possible to prove a negative but I would think that their fascinating researches were inspired more by intellectual curiosity than political calculation. I owe this reference to Dr Paul Halstead.

Fig.15.1: A.J.B. Wace ca. 1911-12; BSA Photographic Archive: BSAA7–62.

de l'Entente.[5] In other words, the School's priorities at the time were not the promotion of scholarship, or the advancement of the interests of Greece, the host country, however these might be perceived, but rather those of the Entente Powers. After the School's premises had, presumably unilaterally, been declared to be extra-territorial, French intelligence had plans to install a wireless transmitter, an 'elaborate' photographic studio and

a chemical laboratory.[6] The German Archaeological Institute was likewise harnessed to the German war effort during the First World War. Compton Mackenzie, the head of British intelligence in wartime Athens, depicted one of his rivals, Baron Schenck, as a 'kind of gigantic spider living at the German Archaeological School in Charilaos Tricoupis Street and spinning webs of marvellous intricacy'.[7]

A strange anomaly is that, during the Second World War, three members of the American School of Classical Studies were permitted to stay on in Athens and Corinth under German/Italian occupation after the United States had entered the war in December 1941, two of them for the duration. Lucy Shoe Meritt in her history of the American School of Classical Studies says that, of the three archaeologists concerned, two elected to stay in Greece, while the third did not consider leaving.[8] But in Greece under occupation the decision of 'enemy aliens' to remain would scarcely have been theirs alone.

What could be said of the French School, namely that during the First World War it was an institution in the service of the Entente could, as we shall see, equally well be said of the British School. As for Greece, so for the British School, a decade of intermittent conflict, which included the First War, began with the Balkan Wars of 1912–13. On the outbreak of hostilities, the School secured the good will of the Greek authorities by offering beds for the wounded together with accommodation for nurses. The offer to house the wounded was made by the School's Director at the time, R.M. Dawkins, but, in the event, was not taken up. As Dawkins wrote to the London Secretary, J. ff. Baker Penoyre, he did not propose asking that the School should make any (presumably material) contribution to the war effort but hoped that the Managing Committee in London would agree with him 'as to the advantage of playing up to the Greeks just now: also humanity'. British nurses were, however, housed in the School's hostel: by February 1913, some six or seven nurses were staying in the School which, as a

---

5. Valenti 2001, 5–14.

6. Note this reference is to the expurgated edition of Mackenzie 1932/1987, 8–9.

7. Mackenzie 1931, 259.

8. Meritt 1984, 11, 15–9.

consequence, was 'winning great applause'. This was convenient, as the Marasleion School next door was being used as a temporary military hospital.[9]

Greece's neutrality in the period until it entered the war on the side of the Entente in June 1917 necessarily posed the problem of how the British School should conduct itself vis-à-vis the German Archaeological Institute, with which the School had long maintained good relations. In December 1914, A.J.B. Wace, who had by this time succeeded Dawkins as director, wrote to George Macmillan (the chairman of the Committee between 1903 and 1933) in London, to express his satisfaction that the Managing Committee had decided to keep the School open despite the outbreak of hostilities. It had, he believed, made a good impression in Greece: 'Greece generally is so friendly to the Allies especially since the Turks have joined the other side that any little thing which helps British prestige in the Near East helps British influence in the political situation'. Gustave Fougères, the Director of the French School, was in Athens and the German Foreign Office had sent Georg Karo back to Greece 'so that if the School had not been opened it would have been rather a shock to the friends of England in Greece for they believe so strongly in the power of the British Empire'. Since the Germans had thought it worthwhile to attempt to win the sympathy of the Greeks 'so we should certainly endeavour to keep it when we have it'. Wace also wrote to Penoyre that it was necessary to keep a dig going because the German Archaeological Institute was said to be doing something at Mycenae.[10]

Wace went on to recount some of the difficulties consequent on the presence of German archaeologists in Athens now that hostilities between Britain and Germany had broken out. He had contacted Karo indirectly through Professor Georgios Sotiriadis. He had passed on the message that he was very sorry that the war had intervened to interrupt their friendship and that he did not want political differences to separate him from his friends 'but at the present time I did not see how we could meet'. Karo had replied indirectly in similar terms to both Wace and F.W. Hasluck, the Assistant Director and Librarian of the British School. Wace had previously consulted the Legation as how best to proceed. It was made clear that the official line was that contacts be suspended, a policy that was being followed in relation to diplomats of the Central Powers in the Greek capital.

On Christmas Day 1914, on his way back from Church, Wace had bumped into Karo in the street (not a difficult thing to do even in the vastly larger present-day Athens) when they had shaken hands and exchanged 'suitable greetings' in a distant echo of the famous Christmas truce on the Western front. Wace had found his and Karo's points of view to be much the same. Karo did not 'want the war to end personal friendships as he has always been fond of England and Englishmen, but he feels that if he met English friends just now a casual tactless word might embitter relations and that there would be days when in view of his strong patriotic feeling he would not want to see any Englishman'. It is not a little ironic that, despite the strength of his patriotism, Karo should have been dismissed from the directorship of the German Archaeological Institute when the Nazis came to power. Karo made it clear that the German Institute was not going to expel any Britons who were honorary members and that, moreover, he would continue with his subscription to the British School. The *Athenische Mitteilungen* would continue to be exchanged for the School's *Annual*. In fact the exchange resumed only in November 1920. Wace wrote that 'friendship between the Schools and between us personally is suspended till the war is over, in abeyance was Karo's phrase'. 'Good sense and good taste', Wace believed, should be the watchword.[11]

It was during the three years of Greece's neutrality, between August 1914 and June 1917, that the question of the role of the foreign Schools arose in the most pronounced form. The question is whether at this period they may be regarded, if not as institutions for

9. Dawkins, BSA, to Penoyre, 26 November 1912; 3 December 1912; 5 February 1913, BSA Corporate Records—London: Correspondence. The papers kept in London were transferred to the central archive in Athens in 2003.

10. Wace to Macmillan, 29 December 1914; Wace to Penoyre, 1 December 1914, BSA Corporate Records—London: Correspondence.

11. Wace to Macmillan, 29 December 1914, BSA Corporate Records—London: Correspondence.

the training of spies, as has sometimes been alleged, then as harbouring intelligence activities. After June 1917, when Greece under the leadership of Eleftherios Venizelos entered the First World War as an ally of the Entente, that question lost much of its sting so far as Britain and France were concerned, since they were operating in Greece on allied territory.

Volume twenty-three of the *Annual of the British School at Athens*, covering the 1918–19 session, gives a very comprehensive listing of the war service of former Students of the School. This contains almost ninety names, including those of seven who lost their lives. As might be expected, many of those on active service served with the so-called 'Gardeners of Salonica', the British forces serving on the Macedonian front, or in the Aegean. This was a logical deployment, making use of their linguistic skills and knowledge of the terrain and of Greek waters. At least two of them, J.C. Lawson and Stanley Casson, published accounts of their experiences. Lawson, a member of the Royal Navy Volunteer Reserve serving with the British Naval Mission to Greece, wrote about his experiences in *Tales of Aegean Intrigue,* published in London in 1920.[12] Compton Mackenzie was scathing about the value of this book. Acknowledging that it gave a good account of the Venizelist movement in Crete, he claimed that Lawson's 'complete ignorance of all that was happening anywhere else coupled with an exaggerated notion of his own influence makes his narrative valueless as anything more than a guide to local events'.[13] Lawson, in civilian life a Fellow of Pembroke College, Cambridge, had been a Student in 1898–99. He was awarded the Greek Orders of the Redeemer and of Military Merit.

Casson's *Steady Drummer*, mainly about his service on the Macedonian front, was published in London in 1935. He had been a Student of the School in 1912–13. After service in France and Belgium, he was a member of the Salonica Field Force between 1916 and 1918. In 1917 he was attached to the Allied Control Commis-

sion in Thessaly. In 1918–19, he was on the General Staff at General Headquarters in Salonica and Constantinople. For his wartime services he was awarded the Greek Order of the Redeemer. During his time on the Salonica front antiquities came to light in the course of the construction of trenches, gun emplacements and dug-outs. It seems that the British were rather less scrupulous in adhering to Greek law in relation to antiquities than were their French colleagues, a number of whom were likewise deployed on the Salonica front. The finds of the British were significant.

There seems to have been a curious kind of freemasonry among archaeologists on both sides of the Salonica front, for J.L. Myres, in his obituary of Casson, who died in 1944 while on service with the Special Operations Executive, records that the officer detailed to escort the Bulgar flag of truce had been made an Honorary Member of the Bulgarian Archaeological Institute. According to Myres, Casson, on being commissioned into the East Lancashire Regiment, 'handled his platoon as he had learned to treat Greek peasant-excavators'. On the Salonica front, he found 'an Intelligence mess like a College Common Room, with learned colleagues, too, among the French and the Serbs'.[14] At the request of General Sir George Milne, the Commander-in-Chief of the British Salonica Army, a request that in the circumstances the Greek authorities could scarcely have refused, the finds uncovered by the British were moved from their temporary museum in the White Tower in Salonica and deposited in the British Museum.[15] This move proved so unpopular that a member of the Greek Archaeological Service (seemingly Evstratios Pelekidis, Ephor of Antiquities in Macedonia and Director of the Salonica Archaeological Museum) physically sat on the crates in an unsuccessful attempt to prevent their being shipped to London.

At least four former Students of the School served in naval intelligence in Greek waters during the First World War. J.L. Myres, for instance, cut a dashing figure in command of a motorized caique, a tug and a former royal yacht. In these, he launched cattle-raids on the Anatolian coast to prevent the livestock being

12. A.M. Woodward, Wace's successor as Director of the School, was amused to note that in a bibliography in the *Revue des Études Grecques* Lawson's book had been entered in the section Crète Minoenne, Woodward to C.A. Hutton, joint London Secretary, 23 June 1923, BSA Corporate Records—London: Correspondence.
13. Mackenzie 1932/1987, 344.

14. *BSA* XL–XLI (1939–1945) 1.
15. Gardner, Casson and Pryce 1919, 43.

shipped to Germany. In one of these raids some two thousand head of cattle were taken. The British Minister in Athens, Sir Francis Elliot, took a dim view of this marauding. Vice-Admiral John de Robeck records that he received from Elliot 'a devil of a letter' of complaint. This de Robeck thought 'extremely silly', describing it as one which might have been written by the (neutral) Greek Foreign Minister. Accordingly, he had sent Elliot a 'corker' by way of reply.[16]

As Compton Mackenzie recorded, 'the Assyrian Myres came down like a wolf on the Turkish fold'. Mackenzie observed that the exploits of 'the Blackbeard of the Aegean', as Myres was known, while they may have delighted the ward-rooms of the British Mediterranean fleet and may on occasion have inconvenienced the enemy, were nonetheless eventually discontinued 'as doing more harm to the Greek population on the [Anatolian] mainland than to their Turkish masters'. Myres's own agents, however, maintained that his exploits tied down as many as 6000 Ottoman troops that might have been deployed elsewhere.[17] As Mackenzie put it, there was indeed 'something irreconcilable between Myres the Assyrian pirate and Myres the purveyor of information to the Commercial Department [of the British Legation], between Myres the Blackbeard of the Aegean and Myres the Gladstone Professor of Greek at the University of Liverpool'.[18] For his wartime services, in which he reached the rank of acting commander in the Royal Naval Volunteer Reserve, Myres received the OBE and the Greek order of George I.

Whereas Wace resolved in gentlemanly fashion to look the other way when in danger of encountering colleagues from the German Archaeological Institute, Myres was altogether more robust in his attitude. In August 1916, he wrote that he had just seen a copy of a letter from Dr Theodor Wiegand of the Royal Muse-

Fig.15.2: J.L. Myres; BSA Photographic Archive: BSAA7–12.

ums in Berlin to a member of the American Embassy in London (the USA at this time, like Greece, being neutral). In this, Wiegand had complained of the damage done to his store house at Yeronda, the site of the Temple of Apollo at Didyma in Asia Minor. Myres believed that Wiegand was seeking to make propaganda out of the incident. The facts, so Myres claimed, were these. Myres had heard that the 'German house' at Yeronda was 'being used as an armoury under the direction of a German artificer, for sorting and refitting the smuggled rifles which were coming from Samos and from Greece at that time'. He had therefore agreed with a proposal that a British squadron should destroy the house. As it lay close to the Temple, the 'most careful precautions' were taken to avoid damage. Two aeroplanes were observing for the British destroyer and Myres himself went up in one of them 'with free leave to signal "cease fire" if I saw any risk of damage to the

---

16. Halpern 1987, 146.

17. See Myres 1980, 22. This account by Myres's son of his father's Aegean exploits is informative and entertaining.

18. Mackenzie 1931, 253. Mackenzie wrote that the Royal Navy accepted what he termed Myres's 'feats of brigandage and terrorism' as 'the sort of thing any professor might do to whom a temporary commission had been recommended by their Lordships of the Admiralty', *ibid.* 250. By the time of the First World War, Myres had moved from Liverpool to become Wykeham Professor of Ancient History at Oxford.

ancient monuments of the place'. The 'German house' was duly destroyed and this had led to Wiegand's complaints of 'sacrilege' and the 'bombardment of a Christian village'.[19]

At least three current members of the School were not only involved in intelligence work but were based there. These were Wace himself, the Director, who had been a Student in 1902–3; F.W. Hasluck, the Assistant Director and Librarian who had been a Student in 1901–2; and his wife Margaret Hardie, a Student in 1911–12. (Their recent marriage had scandalised the School's old guard.) Wace in both World Wars worked for British intelligence; during the Second World War being attached to the Inter-Services Liaison Department, the Middle Eastern manifestation of MI6. The report of the British School for 1916–17, diplomatically records that Wace's services had again been lent, with the 'cordial approval' of the School, to the British Legation. He was stated to be 'principally employed' as Director of Relief for British Refugees from Turkey (a group that included Cypriots and Maltese), a worthy-sounding cause and one which provided useful cover for his intelligence activities. Wace admitted as much, when he wrote to J. ff. Baker Penoyre, the London Secretary, à propos the latter's obituary of Hasluck in the *Times* (24 February 1920) following his death in 1920 from tuberculosis after a protracted illness. In this, Penoyre had made reference to Hasluck's 'unselfish labour among refugees' but Wace wrote that 'the British Refugee Commission for which he [Hasluck] worked was merely camouflage for Intelligence - & though it looked after some refugees Hasluck had practically nothing to do with them … His great achievement was the card index for the Intelligence — which was a wonderful piece of work - & is I believe still in use … He cared nothing for the work but merely for his beloved card index as a sort of mechanical contrivance'.[20]

Wace himself devised a scheme to prevent purported spies of the Central Powers from moving between Egypt and Greece, and was responsible for the evolution during the course of the First World War of what

Mackenzie described as 'the whole of that great system of passport control round the world which made life hideous for travellers during the war …'.[21] Wace did not, however, wholly abandon his archaeological concerns for the duration. He enjoyed showing the sights of Athens to officers on leave from the Salonica front, who had introductions from peacetime colleagues such as Casson, A.M. Woodward, Marcus Tod or M.S. Thompson. There was also talk of his being asked to talk about archaeology to the military 'to prevent the destruction of remains etc'.[22]

Wace offered accommodation in the School's hostel to those who were described as 'British subjects at present employed on Government work in Athens'. In September 1915, he wrote to Macmillan that he had been giving hospitality to 'King's Messengers, Foreign Office people and similar men engaged in government service …[William] Erskine [the Counsellor] of the Legation who is staying with me in this house [i.e. the Upper House where the Director resided] thinks I am doing quite right and I should not offer hospitality to anyone he did not approve of … seeing that we have a government grant and are a British Institution I think we should under the circumstances offer hospitality to men engaged on government service'.[23]

When the Buxton brothers, Noel and Charles, champions of the Bulgarian cause, passed through Athens, Wace had invited them to lunch to meet one or two Greeks and see 'the Greek point of view about Macedonia and so on'. He also wanted Greeks to see that the Buxtons were 'perfectly reasonable and fair-minded men'. Wace impressed on the Buxtons that the School did not concern itself only with Greek antiquity but with 'anything from Neolithic times to the day before yesterday that had anything to do with Greece, *except in so far as current political questions were concerned* [my italics]'. R.W. Seton-Watson, the indefatigable champion of the oppressed nations of Eastern Europe, whose oppressors, conveniently, were the Central Powers, met with Wace on his way to Nish in Serbia on behalf of the

19. Myres to A.T. Waugh, 3 August 1916, BSA Corporate Records—London: Correspondence.

20. Wace to Penoyre, 28 March 1920, BSA Corporate Records—London: Correspondence.

21. Mackenzie 1931, 208.

22. Wace to Penoyre, 18 May 1918, BSA Corporate Records—London: Correspondence.

23. Wace to Macmillan, 3 September 1915, BSA Corporate Records—London: Correspondence.

Serbian Relief Fund in the company of the historian G.M. Trevelyan. Wace wrote of the encounter that 'the trouble for such people is that travelling as they do they meet only officials and hear only the official point of view'. He believed that the School could help by 'introducing them to ordinary Greeks and so they can get in touch with ordinary Greek public opinion'. In telling Macmillan, in London, of these contacts Wace wrote that he might be 'exceeding the proper limit of the School's activities', although nowadays no-one wanted archaeology so it was necessary to think what could be done to help in other ways. He was concerned that people in Britain should realise that the School is 'alive and not a narrow-minded institution'.[24]

That Wace's wartime services to the British government extended far beyond relief for British refugees from Turkey is confirmed by a letter sent to him at the behest of Lord Curzon, the Foreign Secretary, in which thanks were expressed for his 'invaluable services' in placing his 'unique knowledge of certain aspects of the political and racial problems in the Balkans' at the disposal of the Legation.[25] Wace saw the duty of the British School during his directorship as extending much beyond the field of archaeology. As he wrote, in December 1919, to Lord Granville, the British Minister in Athens, throughout the war the School had sought to do 'its elementary duty as a British Institution to the full extent of its means … that such services as we were able to render have been so much valued by His Majesty's Government is a source of great gratification to us and we can only regret that we could not do more for our country'.[26]

The intelligence activities being conducted at the British School by the director and other members at a time when, it must be emphasised, Greece was still

neutral, seem to have been pretty much an open secret in Athens, where most clandestine matters tend to be open secrets. This makes all the more surprising the bullying tone which Wace adopted when he wrote, as director of the School, in February 1916 to Konstantinos Kourouniotis, head of the Archaeological Section of the Ministry of Education and Ecclesiastics, as the British School translated Θρησκεύματα.

Wace noted that he had recently visited Kourouniotis to complain of the 'false and libellous' statements that had appeared in the pro-government, anti-Venizelist newspapers *Embros* and *Nea Imera* to the effect that the School was a centre of espionage and an office of the 'reputed "English Secret Police"', a claim that was not wholly divorced from the truth. Wace had invited Kourouniotis to visit the School to confirm that the statements in the newspapers were 'absolutely baseless', to publish an official *démenti* denying the allegations and to stop the further circulation of such falsehoods. A few days later *Embros* had declared the Greek police to have been the source of the allegations in *Embros* and *Nea Imera* and hence, so Wace was forced to conclude, the 'scandalous libels about the British School' were made with the authority of the Greek government itself, which presumably desired that the School should be 'officially insulted'. Wace, however, professed himself reluctant to accept this, preferring instead to believe that the source of the libels was not the Greek government itself, but 'some [unspecified] malevolent and secret hostile influence jealous of the friendship which has invariably existed between the Greek nation and this School'. He concluded by requesting the publication of an official statement by the Greek government in all Athenian newspapers that it was 'utterly untrue' that the School was a centre of espionage and that steps be taken to prevent the publication of similar false statements. He repeated his previous assurances that the British School had never been used 'for any such purpose, is not at present so used and never will be' as long as he had the honour to be director.

Somewhat surprisingly, the Minister of Education, with the approval of the Prime Minister, the octogenarian Stephanos Skouloudis, did publish the requested *démenti* in *Embros*. A few days later, Wace complained to Kourouniotis that the two newspapers had once again, at the instigation of the police, returned to the

---

24. Wace to Macmillan, 29 December 1914, BSA Corporate Records—London: Correspondence.

25. *BSA* XXIII, 1918–19, 223 An example of Wace's political reporting may be found in a memorandum of 15 January 1917, written aboard H.M.T. Abbasieh in Salamis Strait, to which the Legation and School had temporarily withdrawn following the crisis of December 1916. Wace asked that if any use were to be made of the memorandum then his name should be suppressed, FO 371/2865, R27448. I owe this reference to Dr Dimitris Portolos.

26. Wace, Athens, to Earl Granville, 26 December 1919, BSA Corporate Records—London: Correspondence.

charge, stating that a 'certain person' had been dining at the School. Wace complained about what he termed the 'outrageous impertinence' of publishing the names of persons who had dined with him.[27] Once again he called for measures to be taken to prevent further insults.

The British School, Wace maintained, was the 'official representative' in Greece of all those in Great Britain who devoted themselves to the study of 'Hellenic literature and art'. The School enjoyed the support of the British government, the universities of Oxford and Cambridge, the Society for the Promotion of Hellenic Studies and many other institutions of learning. In allowing the police to publish libellous statements about the British School in the press, the Greek government was officially insulting not only the School but its supporters in England. He concluded his intemperate outburst with a curious threat. If the government was not prepared to afford the School the protection he asked for, he would send his two letters to George Macmillan, the chairman of the School's Managing Committee, for publication in *The Times*, so that the School's supporters might know that the Greek government was 'hostile to the promotion of Hellenic studies'. Wace subsequently noted that his second letter had the desired effect, for Kourouniotis had called and said that Skouloudis had given the necessary instructions.[28] To add insult to injury, Wace's correspondence with Kourouniotis appears to have been conducted in English.

The 'certain person' observed by the Greek police dining with Wace was likely to have been Compton Mackenzie, the head of British intelligence in Athens and in civilian life a man of letters. Mackenzie was the author of a number of highly entertaining books about his flamboyant exploits during the First World War. These are *Gallipoli Memories* (London 1929); *Aegean Memories* (London 1940); *First Athenian Memories*

(London 1931) and *Greek Memories* (London 1932, reprinted in expurgated form in 1939). All are full of arresting, amusing and occasionally scarcely credible detail and are written with the skill of a master storyteller. *Greek Memories* led to his prosecution in 1931 under the draconian Official Secrets Act for revealing forbidden details of his service in Greece. He was found guilty and fined £100 but his reputation (and finances) benefited greatly as a result of the ensuing publicity. As a consequence of the trial, *Greek Memories* was withdrawn for amendment. Copies of the withdrawn first edition are extremely rare.[29] Hasluck and Wace figure in passages in the book expurgated at official behest as well as in the unexpurgated version of the book.

In his books, Mackenzie makes no secret of the fact that he looked upon the British School as a home from home. He seems to have been invited by Wace to lunch in the Director's House, together with Erskine, on a daily basis, for he recalled that there were few things from this period that he remembered 'with such pleasure as that Mess, which provided every day an opportunity to slip back out of the war into a civilized existence'. Wace was a source of 'great scholarship and humour, a worldly humour too and not in the least pedagogic'.[30] In October 1915, Mackenzie was apparently the only outsider staying in the hostel and had the one spare key to the gate.[31] At about this time, D.G. Hogarth, who had been director of the School between 1897 and 1900, came to discuss the possibilities of intelligence work with Mackenzie in his room at the British School. But instead of working in Athens, as Mackenzie had originally suggested, Hogarth became closely associated with the Arab Bureau in Cairo, which, *inter*

---

27. Compton Mackenzie (1931, 301) records that *Embros* and *Nea Imera* regularly noted his purported movements of the previous day. An instance of this practice is given in the unexpurgated edition of *Greek Memories* (1932, 37): 'thence he [Mackenzie] drove in a carriage to the English School [i.e. the BSA] where he remained several hours working with other agents who came to interview him there'.

28. Wace to Kourouniotis, 9 February 1916; 21 February 1916, BSA Corporate Records—London: Correspondence.

---

29. The original text with the excised passages helpfully highlighted has, however, been published by University Publications of America, np 1987.

30. Mackenzie 1931, 194.

31. Wace to Penoyre, 5 October 1915, BSA Corporate Records—London: Correspondence. The issue of keys to the School was clearly a subject of some contention. Margaret Hasluck in Athens returned her key to the library to Penoyre in London, explaining that Wace's first letter requesting its return was 'rude and bullying, his second was a threat. You will therefore understand that it is impossible for me to hand the key to him', Margaret Hasluck to Penoyre, 13 October 1915, BSA Corporate Records—London: Correspondence. Wace's letters were, in fact, not that offensive.

alia, oversaw the derring-do among the Arabs of T.E. Lawrence, who had been Hogarth's archaeological protégé.[32] While staying in the School when laid up with a 'game' leg, Mackenzie was visited on clandestine business by a British naval officer. This visitor, Captain Potts of the Royal Naval Volunteer Reserve, a man of immense physical strength, nonetheless came off worst in an encounter with the Roman portrait bust that graced — and continues to grace — the entrance hall of the School. This, in the gloom, he had mistaken for a would-be assassin bent on attacking the ailing Mackenzie. In the confusion the bust was knocked to the ground, making a 'pretty mess' of Potts's hand.[33] There is a slight chip in its beard. Could it be that this was inflicted by Captain Potts's knuckles?

Mackenzie appears to have lodged for extended periods at the School, where he worked alongside Hasluck. The illness, tuberculosis, that was soon to take his life was already apparent. In paying fulsome tribute to Hasluck's 'patient, accurate, and exquisite mind', he wrote that the fact that he had had to abandon his research interests 'in order to devote what he could not but have felt was probably the rest of his life to war work remains in my memory as an act of heroism'. Mackenzie looked on his colleague Hasluck as his 'chief mental consolation' in the chaotic circumstances of the Greek capital in 1916.[34] Hasluck and Mackenzie devised the card index that was initially based on coloured cards: crimson for 'proved spies'; yellow for purveyors of false information; green for those who had helped the British; mauve for 'ladies of easy virtue'; and white for 'the great indeterminate majority'. The colour scheme was soon abandoned for the proven spy, characteristically, often turned out to be perfectly innocent, while the supposed 'green friend a yellow traitor'. Under Hasluck's aegis the index grew by the end of 1916 to over twelve thousand cards. Macken-

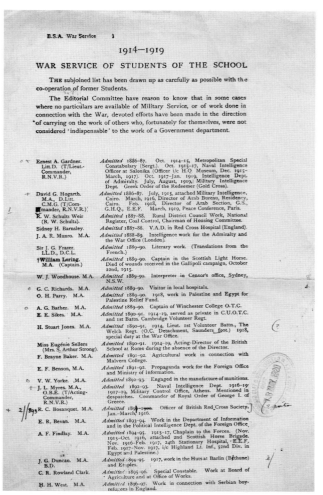

Fig.15.3: First page of 1914–19 War Service List; BSA Corporate Records—Athens: Athens Property.

zie continued to oversee the work and, by September 1917, there were some twenty-three thousand cards.[35] These various activities indicate that Wace, in denying to Kourouniotis in such an offensive manner that the School was a centre of intelligence work, was, to put it mildly, being economical with the truth.

During his time in Greece and Greek waters, Myres developed ambitious plans for institutionalising on a permanent basis the School's wartime intelligence activities. In November 1917, he wrote to Macmillan that he had been trying to devise some means whereby the British School could be made 'more useful from the national point of view'. Lord Granville, Elliot's suc-

32. Another scholar involved with intelligence matters and the Arab Bureau and who had been a Student at the British School in 1907–8 was Harry Pirie-Gordon. See Gill 2006, passim.

33. Mackenzie 1931, 200–1.

34. Wace did not share Mackenzie's high opinion of Hasluck. In May 1915, he complained that Hasluck, as Assistant Director, had given him no help. Instead he had adopted an 'attitude of passive obstruction', Wace to Macmillan, 31 May 1915, BSA Corporate Records—London: Correspondence.

35. Mackenzie 1931, 197–9.

cessor as British minister in Athens, would shortly be forwarding to the Foreign Office Myres's suggestions for the use of the School as a centre for 'organized study [Myres's emphasis] by selected British officers (disabled or convalescent: university or public school men, and former teachers preferred) of modern Greek social and economic conditions, in conjunction with friendly Greeks desirous of rehabilitating [*sic*] Greece on lines adapted from British traditional notions of sportsmanship and fairplay'. He had not discussed the project with Wace, who was away, but intended to talk it over with him fully on his return. 'The main thing', he wrote, 'is to let the B.S.A. become a "British School" in the best sense, while the Greeks are in a mood to learn at it, while co-operating to make some of our people understand Greece'.[36]

In addition to this proposal, which was in effect an attempt to formalise the British School's role as an intelligence centre, Myres had a bee in his bonnet about remaking the Greek character. He wished to make the Greeks more like the English, or at least the English upper middle class, and envisaged the School as playing a pivotal role in this bizarre undertaking. In a confidential memorandum of 18 November 1917, headed 'British General-Intelligence Centre for Greece and Near East', he wrote of the question frequently raised by 'educated Greeks' of 'providing instruction in British institutions, and training for young Greeks in British ways'. Until some better solution were to be found, the British School might serve as 'the nucleus of a "British School" in this other sense'. It could begin on an informal basis by housing 'as convalescents[37] a small number of former public school masters, disabled from active service, but capable of organising classes, games and other elements of British public school and univer-

sity life'.[38] These would come for a short period and a more permanent staff would be selected from among the most suitable: 'in many cases the same man would be at the same time studying and teaching; the most effective combination of all, at any time'. This would be particularly important 'in the existing state of Greek feeling'. Quite what he meant by this is not clear.

The Greek people, he continued, were 'naturally high spirited and self-conscious' but they had been 'demoralised by various influences' and could only be 'rehabilitated' by the restoration of self-respect. The Greeks had much to learn 'as to administration and the development of the resources of their country'. 'They are capable of learning easily, if they have confidence in their teacher; and their confidence is easily earned if they feel that they are parties to a fair bargain'. So much had been achieved in the past 'by explorers and excavators' because these had come 'expressly to learn about Greece and the Greeks, not to teach European notions'. He invoked the example of the British presence in Cyprus where 'our best work' had been done on these lines and had been 'commended by Greeks to Greeks on this very ground, that our best people take the trouble to understand before they *insist* [my italics] on changes'.[39] Myres proved reluctant to abandon the strange educational bees in his bonnet. In an address to the annual general meeting of the Anglo-Hellenic League in June 1919, for instance, he referred to the 'educational experiments foreshadowed under the catchword of a "Greek Eton"'. If the latter were to succeed, he declared in all apparent seriousness, 'in being either "Eton" or "Greek", I suspect that its curriculum must be that of ancient Persia — to ride and to shoot, and to tell the truth'.[40]

The Foreign Office seemed initially to see some merit in Myres's scheme. An official, Leonard Whibley, a classical scholar, sometime Student at the School

36. Myres, British Legation, Athens, to Macmillan, 19 November 1917, copied to Sir Arthur Evans and Professor E.A. Gardner, BSA Corporate Records—London: Correspondence.

37. Myres was always careful to stress that those to be involved in his schemes would be chosen from those unfit for military service and not shirkers or the dreaded 'conchies', conscientious objectors to conscription.

38. In a memorandum on his educational proposals preserved among his papers, Myres stressed that, in the case of schools, it was 'essential that there should be an adequate playground, and provision for the customary recreations of English school life', Ms Myres 93, Bodleian Library, Oxford.

39. Myres, Confidential Memorandum, 18 November 1917, BSA Corporate Records—London: Correspondence.

40. Myres 1919.

and a 'good clubman', wrote there were questions of organisation and finance that would have to be considered by the Foreign Office, but officials would like to know whether the Managing Committee would allow the School's buildings to be used, and whether the School would participate in other ways if the scheme came to maturity.[41] Not surprisingly, however, Myres's proposals met with a cool reception on the part of the Committee. Macmillan complained in early January 1918 to Penoyre that Myres's memorandum contained statements about the School's original objects and the conditions under which the Treasury grant had been renewed since the outbreak of the war which were 'gravely open to question , and which come with an ill-grace from an ex-student & Committee man'. He said that he had had a very helpful talk with Sir Francis Elliot, Granville's predecessor as British minister, who was now a member of the Managing Committee. 'Generally speaking', Elliot was of the view that the School might promise 'friendly co-operation' so far as its constitution allowed but was dubious about many of Myres's proposals. Macmillan's basic impression was that the School should consider the scheme as 'in effect the emanation of our friend J.L.M.'s fertile brain, and that the FO has no desire to press the Committee to do anything inconvenient'.[42]

The whole matter was considered at a meeting of the Managing Committee specially convened for the purpose. Various points were 'freely and extensively discussed' and a resolution opposing the scheme was passed unanimously. This acknowledged that the Foreign Office had already recognised the readiness of the School Committee to do everything in its power to help His Majesty's Government during the war. However, the Committee was of the view that Myres's scheme was 'quite outside the scope of the School'. Moreover, the director, Wace, had not been consulted. It appeared to the Committee that 'the objects contemplated by Commander Myres's scheme may well be regarded as desirable in themselves, but would seem to belong for their execution rather to the Foreign Office and the British Legation than to a School founded in the main for the promotion of the study of Ancient Art, Archaeology and History'.[43]

Some days later, Elliot wrote to a colleague that he had taken it upon himself to read the opening paragraphs of the Myres memorandum which had not previously been communicated to Macmillan. These had contained serious mis-statements. It was not, for instance, the case that the Treasury's grant to the School had been renewed 'on the express understanding that the School is available for national purposes'. Moreover, to say that 'the Director, Mr Wace, has been working in the Legation and Consulate' was to give a 'very bald and insufficient account of the value of his services'. Furthermore, no account had been taken of the contribution in 'intelligence and staff work in the Levant of a considerable number of past and present members of the School, including Mr Myres himself, whose qualifications for the work upon which they are employed are the direct consequences of their connection with the School'. The School, Elliot continued, had its 'own proper objects', the pursuit of which would be resumed when the war was over: 'the acquisition of military or commercial information is not among them, and is incompatible with them. The machinery for this purpose must be set up by H.M. Government and must be controlled by them'.[44]

Thus we can see that neither the British School nor the Foreign Office had any enthusiasm for Myres's schemes to institutionalise on a permanent basis the School's temporary wartime role as a centre for intelligence activities. The pugnacious Myres did not take the Committee's rejection of his proposed scheme lying down. In a letter of 28 January 1918 to Macmillan, he apologised if his memorandum had given rise to resentment and repeated the criticisms that he had made of Wace. These principally related to Wace's apparent refusal to make the School available to officers on duty. Wace had argued that he needed to keep rooms available for any ex-Students of the School who might find

---

41. Whibley, however, was later to describe Myers's scheme as 'a wild cat affair', Whibley to Macmillan, 18 December 1917, 10 January 1918, BSA Corporate Records—London: Correspondence.

42. Macmillan to Penoyre, 3 January 1918, BSA Corporate Records—London: Correspondence.

---

43. Macmillan to Whibley, 9 January 1918, BSA Corporate Records—London: Correspondence.

44. Elliot to Montgomery, 15 January 1918, BSA Corporate Records—London: Correspondence.

themselves in Athens. He had declined Myres's offer to vacate the rooms if they were to be needed for ex-Students. Another of Wace's arguments had been that the School's water supply was inadequate. According to Myres, Wace had said that it was more important to water the garden than to provide enough bath water for the Hostel.[45]

A few days earlier, on 22 January, Macmillan had written to Myres a reproachful letter in which he stated that he found it difficult to understand 'on what ground of superior knowledge' he had sought to 'lay down the law either to the F.O. or the B.S.A. Committee'. He protested yet again about Myres's claim that the School had 'not played its part in the war': 'as coming from an old Student and a member of our Committee, we must further regard it as disloyal'.[46] Myres, giving his address as the Interallied Passport Bureau, British Section, Athens, responded by repeating his view that he 'had long felt that the School was not doing its duty'. Greeks had compared the School's recent conduct 'most unfavourably' with its services during the Balkan Wars.[47] Macmillan clearly relished writing to Myres in February to report that the Foreign Office had written to express its recognition of the 'great services' rendered by the School during the war. This assurance meant that the Committee was 'comparatively indifferent to the views expressed by subordinates in Athens'.[48] Macmillan took further comfort from Professor Ernest Gardner's report in June 1918 that Sir Reginald ('Blinker') Hall, the Director of Naval Intelligence, thought that the School had been 'perfectly right' in refusing to have anything to do with Myres's scheme: 'so you see that the Admiralty Intelligence Division, under which of course Myres is working, does not give any official support to his suggestions'.[49]

Myres was not one to give up easily. In May 1918, he again wrote to Macmillan, to complain that the latter had not sought the views of others familiar with conditions at the School in connection with his complaints about the way in which Wace was running it. He accused Macmillan in failing in his duty as 'a Trustee responsible to a body of subscribers'. This was a letter which Macmillan deemed to be 'very impertinent' and which led to a formal reprimand from the Managing Committee, which unanimously resolved at its meeting on 16 July that 'the Committee have received through the Chairman, with extreme surprise and regret, Professor Myres' letter dated May 1st, 1918. In their opinion the tone of the letter is wholly unjustifiable and entitles both the Chairman and the Committee to a suitable apology'. Whether Macmillan and the Committee ever received such an apology is not clear[50] but manifestly the quarrel was at some stage patched up, for Myres succeeded Macmillan as chairman of the Managing Committee of the School in 1933.

Further trouble was brewing when R.M. Dawkins wrote, in February 1918, to Macmillan, claiming that the School under the directorship of his successor, Wace, had been unwelcoming to those engaged in 'various kinds of work for the war'. Dawkins did not want to comment on Myres's scheme but complained that a great opportunity was being missed of both 'service to the country and of acquiring friends for the future'. He regarded it as discreditable that the hostel at present housed only five or six men, when there was more than enough room for ten or twelve: 'Men are not encouraged to go to the Hostel, it is in fact so unpopular that they do not care to go'. A mess and the tennis court should have been made available, while the Finlay Library should have been opened as a common room. He felt very strongly that Wace was demonstrating 'a lack of a sense of duty to the country and a failure to do the best for the interests of the School'. Dawkins asked that his letter be circulated to all members of the Managing Committee.[51]

---

45. Myres to Macmillan, 28 January 1918, BSA Corporate Records—London: Correspondence.

46. Macmillan to Myres, 22 January 1918, BSA Corporate Records—London: Correspondence.

47. Myres to Macmillan, 16 February 1918, BSA Corporate Records—London: Correspondence.

48. Macmillan to Myres, 19 February 1918; Whibley, Foreign Office, to Macmillan, 13 February 1918, BSA Corporate Records—London: Correspondence.

49. Ernest Gardner, Admiralty, to Macmillan, 9 June 1918, BSA Corporate Records—London: Correspondence.

50. Myers, London, to Macmillan, 1 May 1918; Macmillan to C.A. Hutton, Acting Secretary, 3 May 1918; C.A. Hutton to Myres, 18 July 1918, BSA Corporate Records—London: Correspondence.

51. Dawkins, Athens, to Macmillan, 16 February 1918, BSA Corporate Records—London: Correspondence.

Not surprisingly, Wace reacted angrily to Dawkins's letter. In a précis of his letter to Macmillan in response, Wace expressed surprise that Dawkins, who had been director on the outbreak of the war, had not discussed these matters while he was recently in Athens for twelve days. Only on the last day had Dawkins showed Wace a copy of his letter to Macmillan. A mess had been organised at intervals despite the difficulties involved, while the Finlay Library had been opened as a common room until the autumn of 1916, when it had been closed as a consequence of thefts of its valuable books, many of which had belonged to the great historian George Finlay himself. It had been re-opened in the summer of 1917 when Casson had been in residence and had volunteered to be in charge. War workers were treated as associates of the School, with all privileges save use of the library. Not only had Wace encouraged those engaged in war work to stay at the School, despite serious problems with the water supply, but he had advocated the admission of women war-workers, for whom a Ladies Common Room had been established. As he clearly did not have the confidence of two members of the Managing Committee, Myres and Dawkins, Wace continued that he would be prepared to resign if the Committee saw fit, although his 'relations with the Foreign Office would have to be considered'.[52]

On 18 February 1918, Wace wrote to Dawkins himself seeking to answer his strictures. One of the problems at present in the Hostel was that, as A.W. Gomme, a former Student of the School on war service in Greece, had told him, the men [*sic*] were so 'unsociable to one another'. If Myres was ever at the School then he might have persuaded the residents to be more sociable. Wace had hoped that Gomme would run the Hostel, but he did not have the time and, in any case, he was unpopular with the other men there. 'If you think seriously', Wace wrote, 'that the School is going to the devil and you think you can prevent it please help all you can and I for one as I told you as soon as you made your complaints to me when you came to say goodbye, will resign at once if the C[ommi]ttee think my being

Fig.15.4: R.M. Dawkins; BSA Photographic Archive: BSAA7–68.

director is helping the School to go to the devil or likely to cause a serious split on the C[ommi]ttee'.[53]

Macmillan, towards the end of March, replied on behalf of the Committee to Dawkins's letter of complaint. He expressed himself surprised by Dawkins's 'rather severe indictment' of Wace and by the fact that he had raised the issues with Wace so late in the day and had not mentioned his concerns when he was staying in the Hostel between November 1915 and April 1916. On the same day, Macmillan wrote to Wace in Athens to assure him that the Committee shared Wace's surprise that Dawkins should have 'suddenly fired off this series of charges just on the eve of his departure', and that it had no intention of accepting Wace's pro-

---

52. Undated précis of Wace to Macmillan à propos Dawkins's letter to Macmillan, BSA Corporate Records—London: Correspondence.

53. Wace to Dawkins, 18 February 1918, BSA Corporate Records—London: Correspondence.

Fig.15.5: War Memorial; BSA Corporate Records—Athens: Athens Property.

posed resignation or the changes that he had contemplated in an attempt to meet Dawkins's complaints. He concluded by saying that the Committee felt strongly that 'everything in reason should be done to create a friendly atmosphere in the Hostel, and that the normal attitude should be one of conciliation'.[54]

That the British School was harnessed during the First War to the British war effort, and more particularly in furtherance of the government's intelligence activities, is clear beyond peradventure. As was only to be expected, many former students of the School were deployed in the Aegean or with the so-called 'Gardeners of Salonica' on the Macedonian front, where their knowledge of the languages and topography of the Eastern Mediterranean was put to good use. Moreover, the premises of the School housed the all-important card index of individuals of interest to the British authorities. The use of the School premises at a time when Greece was neutral, between the outbreak of hostilities and Greece's entry into the war in June 1917 on the side of the Entente, was but one more instance of the numerous ways in which Greek sovereignty was compromised by the belligerent powers

during the course of the war. The unanimity with which the School, and indeed the Foreign Office, rejected J.L. Myres's proposal to institutionalize wartime intelligence activity on a permanent basis is an indication that these activities were deemed appropriate only for the duration of hostilities. Once peace had been restored the School's priorities reverted to the furtherance of scholarship.

It is clear that the School under Wace's directorship was not a happy ship. But in his defence one might adduce the fact that, in addition to the difficulties associated with running a rather inward looking institution in time of war, he had to deal with larger-than-life and somewhat obstreperous characters such as J.L. Myres. In conclusion, it should always be borne in mind that the British were by no means alone in deploying the School in furtherance of their war aims during the First World War. Other schools, on both sides of the conflict, likewise made use of their resources and premises for war purposes.

REFERENCES

Casson, S., 1935. *Steady Drummer*. London.

Clogg, R., 2000. 'Distant Cousins: SOE and OSS at Odds over Greece', in R. Clogg, *Anglo-Greek Attitudes: Studies in History*. Basingstoke.

Gardner, E.A., Casson S. and Pryce, F.N., 1920. 'Antiquities found in the British Zone 1915–1919', *BSA* XXIII (Session 1918–1919): 10–43.

---

54. Macmillan to Dawkins, c/o British Legation, Athens, 22 March 1918; Macmillan to Wace, 22 March 1918, BSA Corporate Records—London: Correspondence.

Gill, D.W.J., 2006. 'Harry Pirie-Gordon: Historical Research, Journalism and Intelligence Gathering in the Eastern Mediterranean (1908–19)', *Intelligence and National Security* XXI: 1045–59.

Halpern, P., 1987. *The Royal Navy in the Mediterranean 1915–1918*. Aldershot.

Lawson, J. C., 1920. *Tales of Aegean Intrigue*, London.

Mackenzie, C., 1931. *First Athenian Memories*. London.

—, 1932/1987, *Greek Memories*. (University Publications of America). Reprint of original, unexpurgated edition. London.

—, 1939. *Greek Memories*. Expurgated edition. London.

Meritt, Lucy Shoe, 1984. *History of the American School of Classical Studies at Athens 1939–1980*. Princeton.

Myres, J.N.L., 1980. *Commander J.L. Myres, R.N.V.R.: the Blackbeard of the Aegean: a lecture delivered at New College, Oxford on 29th May, 1975 by his son J.N.L. Myres*. London.

Myres, J.L., 1919. *Address to the Annual General Meeting of the Anglo-Hellenic League on Friday 20 June 1919*. London.

Petrakos, V., 1994. *Τα Αρχεία της Ελλάδος κατά τον Πόλεμο 1940–1944*. Βιβλιοθήκη της εν Αθήναις Αρχαιολογικής Εταιρείας 144. Athens.

Valenti, C., 2001. 'L'École Française d'Athènes pendant la Grande Guerre: une institution universitaire au service de l'Entente', *Guerres Mondiales et Conflits Contemporains* 204: 5–14.

Wace A.J.B. and Thompson, M.S., 1914. *The Nomads of the Balkans: an Account of Life and Customs among the Vlachs of Northern Pindus*. London.

Waterhouse, Helen, 1986. *The British School at Athens: the First Hundred Years*. London.

16

The Archaeology of Greek Ethnography

Roger Just

At its inception the social anthropology of Greece and the Greek-speaking world,[1] more generally of the Mediterranean area, was a child of the late 1950s and early 1960s — and dates are going to be of some importance to my argument. A series of major international conferences organized between 1959 and 1963 by John Peristiany and Julian Pitt-Rivers marked the birth of what remained (for some time at least) the recognized sub-discipline of Mediterranean anthropology,[2] while the anthropology of Greece was firmly established by the publication in 1962 of Ernestine Friedl's *Vassilika: A Village in Modern Greece,* shortly followed in 1964 by what remains the foundation stone of Greek ethnography, John Campbell's *Honour, Family, and Patronage: A Study of Institutions and Moral Values in a Greek Mountain Community.* Two further important ethnographies then appeared in the 1970s: Juliet du Boulay's renowned *Portrait of a Greek Mountain Village* (1974) and, for Cyprus, Peter Loizos's *The Greek Gift* (1975). Together with the contributions on Greece that appeared in a number of edited volumes of the 1960s and 1970s (Pitt-Rivers 1963; Peristiany 1965, 1968 and 1976; Dimen and Friedl 1976) these four ethnographies now constitute what could be thought of as the 'classics' of the anthropology of Greece. The following decade then saw the publication of another eight ethnographies, four by British and American scholars (Loizos 1981, Danforth 1982, Herzfeld 1985,[3] Hirschon 1989) but now joined by three anthropologists writing in French (Handmann 1983, Couroucli 1985, Xanthakou 1988, 1989).[4] Between 1990 and the turn of the century there was an explosion of publication with at least eighteen ethnographies appearing in English or French (Cowan 1990, Herzfeld 1991 & 1997a, 1997b, Stewart 1991, Seremetakis 1991, Hart 1992, Sant Cassia and Bada 1992, Faubion 1993, Dubisch 1995, Panourgia 1995, Argyrou 1996, Karakasidou 1997, Sutton 1998, Just 2000, Kenna 2001a and 2001b; Xanthakou, 1993) — and apologies to anyone whom I may inadvertently have omitted. To these must again be added a number of edited volumes on Greece or on the Mediterranean including Greece in both English and French: e.g. Piault (ed.) 1985; Peristiany and Handman (eds) 1989; Loizos and Papataxiarchis (eds) 1991. Now, at the start of the twenty-first century, Greek ethnography is safely in the hands of a new generation of younger scholars in Britain, the USA and France, many of whom have already produced monographs, and many of whom (as they have been for the last 20 years) are by origin Greek or Cypriot. I think, for example, of Yalouri (2001), Kirtzoglou (2004), Papadakis (2005) and Theodossopoulos (2003) — to whom, by the way, I am indebted for providing me with a convenient bibliographical checklist in the introduction to his own ethnography.

Given that the production of this corpus involved some direct lines of pedagogic descent (Campbell, for example, taught du Boulay, Hirschon, Herzfeld, Just and Stewart; Herzfeld taught Cowan and Sutton; Loizos taught Papataxiarchis, Sant Cassia and Theodossopoulos; both Herzfeld and Loizos taught Argyrou etc) and certainly of cumulative inspiration and acknowledgement (Loizos, for example, examined Hirschon's and Just's dissertations), it would be tempting to talk in genealogical terms of a first, second and

---

1. I include Cyprus throughout in discussion of 'the anthropology of Greece'.

2. The first conference was held at Burg Wartenstein in 1959 at the European headquarters of the Wenner-Gren Foundation: subsequent conferences were held in 1961 and 1963 in Athens sponsored by the Greek Ministry to the Prime Minister's Office (Peristiany 1965, 9).

3. I am using a somewhat restricted definition of ethnography. Herzfeld also made a major contribution to the study of modern Greece with his historical volume published in 1982.

---

4. There were also important French collected volumes published in the 1980s: Piault (ed.) 1985; Peristiany and Handmann (eds) 1989.

third generation of anthropological scholars working in Greece (and Cyprus) from the 1960s through to the end of the century. It is, however, a little difficult to sort people out into distinct generations since dates of research and dates of publication do not necessarily coincide. Both Margaret Kenna and I, for example, were unconscionably late publishers. But suffice to say that the anthropology of Greece, even if measured solely by the publication of full-length single-authored ethnographies, steadily grew and ramified over the second half of the twentieth century and into the twenty-first. Add to the above monographs the many journal articles and volumes of collected essays that have also appeared and, very importantly, the burgeoning contribution of Greek anthropologists now working in Greek institutions and often publishing in Greek as well as English, and there can be little doubt that since the 1960s the anthropological literature on Greece has become, in Theodossopoulos's words, a 'vibrant and expanding body'. In short, from the point of view of a regionalist, the anthropology of Greece has been a success story, and we can look back at nearly half a century of productive ethnographic work and accumulated intellectual capital and at the establishment of anthropology as a growing discipline within Greek academia itself.

And yet I must confess to a little disappointment and a little puzzlement, for despite its achievements I do not think that the anthropology of Greece has ever made the impact on the discipline as a whole that it should have, or that it has ever received due recognition within it — and what can be said of the anthropology of Greece in this context applies more generally to what was once called the anthropology of the Mediterranean. My evidence is circumstantial, but if one looks at general or introductory works on anthropology, or at histories of the discipline, or at the sort of works appearing from time to time that attempt to assess anthropology's achievements and to map out its directions, then there is plenty about Africa, plenty about India, plenty about Melanesia and South America and nowadays even plenty about 'anthropology at home' in Britain and Europe and the USA, but the anthropology of the Mediterranean and of Greece make scant

appearance.[5] Moreover, it is my impression that most anthropology undergraduate students at most universities in Britain and the USA do not read Greek or Mediterranean ethnography unless there happens to be someone on the academic staff whose speciality it is. Certainly it doesn't seem to be the sort of stuff that appears in first-year introductory courses. In short, a knowledge of the anthropology of the Mediterranean and of Greece is not 'mainstream', and according to accepted narratives of the discipline (or rather, given their omission from accepted narratives), the anthropology of the Mediterranean and of Greece would not seem to have contributed much to the shape and history of the discipline.[6] Why?

That question, based on similar but earlier observations on the status of the anthropology of Greece, was, of course, the starting point for Michael Herzfeld's *Anthropology Through the Looking-Glass* (1987) to which this short paper is indebted. But my own answer, though not incompatible with Herzfeld's, takes a somewhat different tack. Herzfeld's argument is that the marginality of anthropology to Greece and of Greece to anthropology 'suggests that prevalent ideas about the Greeks' role in the modern world may mirror, in some ironical fashion, ideas about the ways in which anthropologists — and their compatriots everywhere — go about understanding the world' (1987, 2). He thus embarks on a sophisticated project 'that is political as well as epistemological; ethnographic as well as anthropological; and descriptive as well as analytical' (ibid.1) and that is intended to highlight 'the symbolic character of anthropology as the exploration and expression, not of exotic societies, but

---

5. There are exceptions. Herzfeld (2001) — as might be expected — discusses Greece and the Mediterranean. Hendry (1999) mentions the work of Campbell and du Boulay. Delaney (2004) discusses aspects of Turkey, where she worked (but no works of other Mediterraneanists). But Greece and the Mediterranean are conspicuously absent from most text books and accounts of the discipline.

6. The influence of Pierre Bourdieu constitutes an obvious exception, but I am inclined to discount it first on the grounds that Bourdieu's early ethnographic work was in Algeria whereas my argument relates to Europe (and it was perhaps one of the oddities of 'Mediterranean anthropology' that it grouped together Southern Europe and North Africa); second, because Bourdieu subsequently shifted towards sociology, and his theoretical contributions were developed in that context as much as (if not more than) in his Mediterranean work.

on the contrary of those globally dominant societies that themselves created the discipline' (ibid.1) — in which context Greece, as simultaneously both the ideological source of European 'civilization' and (in 1987) still a 'backward' nation, was an embarrassing anomaly. My argument is less ambitious and seeks merely to suggest that the achievements of the anthropology of Greece, together with those of Mediterranean anthropology as a whole, went unnoticed because they occurred at a time when the discipline was not given to the sort of radical self-scrutiny of which Herzfeld's book is itself an interesting example.

As I remarked at the outset, dates are important. The period from roughly the 1930s through to, somewhat arbitrarily, the early 1970s is generally labelled in histories of anthropology as 'functionalist'. I'm not going to elaborate here on what was meant by 'functionalist', largely because I don't believe that most anthropologists of the time really were functionalists in any strict sense,[7] but what is I think true is that from the 1930s through to the 1970s there was a broad consensus about the business of anthropology. This, I realize, is a broad-brush statement. There were, of course, all sorts of arguments and debates (sometimes quite acrimonious) about specific issues. There were contending theories and named 'schools' of anthropological thought. There was also the perception of a general division between American 'cultural anthropology' and British 'social anthropology'. But this was all the stuff of vigorous academic exchange, and at least in retrospect it appears that however much they might have differed and argued amongst themselves, anthropologists of that period thought they knew what they were doing and got on with it. If there was a loyal (and only occasionally disloyal) opposition in the 1960s and 1970s, it came from Marxist and Marxist-inspired anthropologists (influential in Britain and France — very much less so in the USA); but there was not, I think, the feeling of any overwhelming definitional crisis in the discipline, nor was the parading of intellectual self-criticism and self-doubt and the undermining of accepted paradigms endemic to (or required by) anthropological discourse

of the period. That came later and with growing stridency from the mid-1980s onwards. Importantly, then, the establishment of the anthropology of the Mediterranean and of Greece coincided with what might be called anthropology's 'consensus period'[8] — but equally importantly, it coincided with that consensus period in its last phase.

The irony is that the early Mediterraneanists, those working and writing in the 1960s and 1970s, were not in fact working within the accepted paradigms of established anthropology. On empirical grounds, it would have been difficult for them to do so, for their chosen ethnographic contexts were too different. It is easy to say (as critics later said) that Mediterraneanists chose Greece and Spain and Portugal and Southern Italy because at the time these were the least 'developed' countries of Europe and, moreover, chose rural villages and backwaters within those countries because these seemed to supply the closest European analogues to the 'tribal' societies with which anthropologists had been traditionally concerned.[9] The fact remains that Greece, Spain, Portugal[10] and Italy were not Africa, South America, Melanesia or (native) Australia, and their differences presented new and substantially different challenges. As Davis (1977, 1–16 and *passim*) pointed out in his critical review of Mediterranean anthropology up to the mid-1970s, Mediterranean societies were societies with long traditions of literacy and extremely well-documented languages. They were societies with centralized states and complex bureaucracies. They were class societies

---

7. That is to say, in the theoretical terms set out by, somewhat variously, Radcliffe-Brown and Malinowski.

8. I borrow the phrase from Ardener (1989, 194).

9. It should be pointed out that 'Mediterranean anthropology' as initially conceived encompassed the largely Islamic societies of North Africa and the eastern Mediterranean as well as those of southern Europe. This was one of a number of grounds for claiming that 'Mediterranean anthropology' constituted a false unity, and by the 1980s anthropologists progressively shifted to talking about the anthropology of southern Europe or simply Europe. The debates, of course, were a classic example of the problems entailed in establishing any 'culture area', for there are always both continuities and discontinuities between regions. In what follows, however, my argument relates to the European societies of the Mediterranean. Anthropologists working in North Africa might be considered to have been engaged in rather more traditional pursuits if for no other reason than that as 'Europeans' they were continuing to work in non-European societies.

10. Portugal was conventionally grouped with the northern Mediterranean countries. It has, of course, no Mediterranean shore.

with long histories of class conflict and class antago-nism. On the northern littoral, they were the homelands of Christianity. Finally, in a list intended to be indica-tive, not exhaustive, they were (again on the European littoral) societies whose kinship system was family or household-centred with monogamous marriage and without the sort of explicit systems of moieties, clans, lineages and sub-lineages that so preoccupied anthro-pologists of more exotic regions. Perhaps, as Herzfeld suggests (1987, 5–16) all these differences could be summarized by saying that what Mediterraneanists of the 1960s and 1970s encountered were societies that shared most of their basic features with the societies from which they themselves had come. They were soci-eties whose fundamental values and institutions and traditions and politics were anything but alien to the world of a British or American or French anthropolo-gist. Indeed, as Herzfeld again emphasizes, the histories and trajectories of Mediterranean societies and those of the anthropologists' own were intertwined.

Nowadays, when so many anthropologists are engaged in 'anthropology at home' or 'urban anthropol-ogy' or in studying various facets and sectors of indus-trialized societies (whether western or non-western) — migration, ethnic groups, occupational groups, reli-gious groups, nationalism, sexuality, tourism, expatri-ates, cultural monuments and museums etc (the list is endless) — there seems nothing unusual about this situ-ation. Anthropology is no longer defined as the study of 'other' societies, much less as the study of 'primitive' or 'tribal' or 'small-scale' societies. But in the 1960s and 1970s it was a new situation. Anthropology had, as one commentator put it, 'come part-way home' (Cole 1977), and, as I have remarked, that presented new challenges. Arguably, Mediterraneanists responded to some of those challenges better than to others[11] — but they did, perforce, respond to them, and it is my contention that in so doing they produced a new and different sort of anthropology. What they did not do is loudly to pro-claim that fact. Indeed, if anthropologists of Greece and the Mediterranean had a besetting sin, then I think it was an excess of modesty. Perhaps they were modest people — but I refrain from speculating on individual

character. Certainly they wrote in more modest times when the requirements of academic advancement (and of academic publishers and institutions) did not demand, as they seem to today, that every book and article be presented as 'theoretically ground-breaking'. But a good part of the irony is that the early anthro-pologists of Greece and the Mediterranean effectively denied their own innovation. They continued to write *as if* what they were doing was what everyone else had done before. They got on with the job of ethnographic description and analysis. The language of the consen-sus — its categories, its concepts, its topics — held. The fact that Mediterraneanists were subtly undermining and altering those categories, concepts and topics went largely unnoticed — even, I suspect, by many Mediter-raneanists themselves. Theirs was, in short, a properly Kuhnian paradigm shift, recognizable only in retrospect, and where everything had to change in order to remain the same; a revolution so velvet that no one even noticed the government had fallen. By the late 1980s, when anthropology as a whole was in turmoil, when grizzled heads were being displayed and ambitious demands for intellectual revision proclaimed in the corridors of academe, no one remembered the Mediterraneanists — except, perhaps, to denounce them as members of the Ancien Régime. But I believe that what they achieved prefigured substantively — though not rhetorically — much of what was then being demanded.

I am aware of making large claims. Let me attempt to substantiate them by briefly looking at three related topics: 'social structure', 'kinship' and 'gender'. 'Social structure' was the watch-phrase of the consensus period (though not much heard nowadays). It was clas-sically defined by (amongst others) Evans-Pritchard in his 1940 study of the Nuer of southern Sudan:

> By social structure we mean relations between groups which have a high degree of consist-ency and constancy. The groups remain the same irrespective of their specific content of individuals at any particular moment, so that generation after generation of people pass through them (1976 [1940], 262).

In 1954, when Julian Pitt-Rivers published pretty much the first Mediterranean ethnography, *People of the Sierra* [in Andalusia, Spain], he too took time off in the introduction to a work he specifically states to be

---

11. See Davis' fairly trenchant criticisms (1977, 5–10).

otherwise non-theoretical to supply the reader with a definition of 'social structure':

> For [a social anthropologist] the word 'structure' implies something composed of interdependent parts, and the parts of a social structure are not individuals but activities or institutions. A society is not an agglomeration of persons but a system of social relations (1961, xi).

So far, so Evans-Pritchard. But then an interesting change in emphasis occurs:

> So, in this book, I have attempted to define the *values* attaching in Alcala to possessions and status, to sex and the family, to political authority and the *moral code* of the community, to the supernatural and the natural and to show how they are related to one another and to the social structure of the whole country (1961, xii, my emphases).

It's a subtle shift. 'Social structure' is still claimed to be what it's all about, but we seem to be moving from a structure of institutions — in Evans-Pritchard's account, essentially political institutions — to a structure of values.

The shift was, of course, almost inevitable. As I have said, the Mediterranean was not sub-Saharan Africa. Social structure in the sense of a clan and lineage system that was simultaneously a political system and a kinship system did not exist in societies where political organization was the domain of the state and kinship centred around family and household. As a focus of attention, moral values had to take their place. In a Greek context the shift was exemplified by Campbell's 1964 study of the Sarakatsani — *Honour, Family, and Patronage: A Study of the Institutions and* Moral Values *in a Greek Mountain Community* — although note that the term 'institutions', almost *de rigeur* for a work of that period, still appears in the title.[12] But although the shift was ethnographically and empiri-

cally driven — Pitt-Rivers and Campbell were far too perceptive observers to force Mediterranean life into an Africanist mould (cf. Herzfeld 1987, 58) — ethnographic and empirical shifts have their theoretical (and methodological) consequences. The study of 'moral values' launched anthropology into a much more subtle — and much more uncertain — field of enquiry. Political structures and political institutions can be relatively confidently delineated — but what reader was going to be happy with a digest of provincial Greek bureaucratic administrative arrangements of the sort that might have matched Evans-Pritchard's account of Nuer social structure? Admittedly Evans-Pritchard's account of the Nuer also entailed moral values: the Nuer's (now contested) commitment to an agnatic ideology. To that extent the innovation was not a radical break. But the sort of moral values that Pitt-Rivers and Campbell and other Mediterraneanists were attempting to describe, and which at the time were gathered together under the rubric of 'honour and shame', could not simply be read-off or held to inhere in the structure of enduring 'relations between groups'. They inhered in personal relationships, in daily exchanges, in mutual evaluations and judgements and criticism, in forms of self-presentation and self-display, in actions and reactions and emotions and affects. By that token they were much trickier to grasp and very much trickier to convey. The existence of an institution (let us say the organization of young men into age sets) as characteristic of a certain society or societies has a degree of objective undeniability; the existence of particular values and attitudes as equally characteristic of and shared by all the members of a particular society or societies is *a priori* much more difficult to maintain, for at the very least it requires making generalizations (however accurately) about the individuals who comprise that society that are always deniable. In the end it was the tendency to talk about moral values as if they had the same objective status within 'social structure' as institutions that opened the way for the scapegoating of 'honour and shame' by critics of Mediterranean anthropology. But that criticism of Mediterranean anthropology elides both the achievements and the innovations of its practitioners, for the very attempt to study moral values demanded a much more detailed and sensitive attention to the minutiae of inter-personal exchange,

---

12. For later Mediterranean anthropologists, many of them students of Campbell, 'moral values' decisively displaced 'social structure'. Note the subtitle of de Pina-Cabral's ethnography (a student of Campbell's): *The Peasant Worldview of the Alto Minho* (1986). *Pace* its use in American anthropology, 'Worldview' refers to values. Cf. the subtitle of Stewart's ethnography: *Moral Imagination in Modern Greek Culture*.

a much more intimate knowledge of what seemed to make individuals tick, a much more fine-grained account of actions and language and events than most anthropologists had previously essayed. It demanded precisely, for example, what is nowadays seen as one of the advantages of working within one's own society by the more radical proponents of 'anthropology at home': the ability 'to pick up on those niceties of interaction and ambivalences and ambiguities of exchange where the most intricate (and interesting) aspects of socio-cultural worlds are constructed, negotiated, contested and disseminated' (Rapport 2002, 7).[13] In turning away from the certainties of social structure — which they nevertheless continued to invoke — to the more labile field of moral values and attitudes, Campbell and his contemporaries made a decisively modern turn, except that whereas anthropologists nowadays are inclined to spend a lot of time reminding us that the world is irredeemably messy (Freidman 1997), true to the consensus period Campbell and his contemporaries did their best (and it is a best that has not been much bettered) to sort that messiness out. Unlike many later anthropologists for whom both society and culture have become something of an embarrassment (let alone social structure), and for whom the individual 'agent' has become promoted to centre stage, they could not take refuge in the assertion that everything is negotiated, contested and shifting and uncertain; nor, obviously, could they take credit for having done so.

As already suggested, in the consensus period the notion of 'social structure' and the notion of 'kinship' were closely allied. This had a curious consequence which many students of anthropology nowadays have difficulty in comprehending: namely, a distinction made between 'kinship' as a form of social and political structure and 'family' as the private and domestic realm of the individual. Unfortunately no such distinction could be made in the Mediterranean (or anywhere much in Europe) where kinship takes the form of kindreds, i.e. bilateral groupings of relatives that surround each individual. As Campbell put it:

Kindred relations are considered by the Sarakatsani to be *extensions from the family* … And although the kindred is a system of personal relations while the family is a corporate group, the systematic character of the former, and the structure of the latter, are necessarily interdependent and consistent (1963, 76).

Since such individually-oriented kindreds could not assign people to discrete non-overlapping groups, they were bad candidates for political or economic mobilization and thus for constituting the basis of 'social organization'. This is not to suggest that kinship — recognized family connections — did not (and do not) play a political role in Greece or Spain or Italy or, for that matter, in most European societies. They certainly do — but the political consequences of kinship are effected through the cultivation of individual relationships and estimations of worth or usefulness underwritten by the ideal (and idealized) moral obligations of relatedness rather than deriving from the fact that kinship groups constitute political units in and of themselves. Hence Campbell's sub-title: *Honour, family, and patronage*. If Mediterraneanists were going to study 'kinship' (and, true again to the consensus period, it would have been unthinkable not to even if their informants had not continually reminded them of its importance), then so far as 'structure' went, what they were left with was really only the domestic unit, the household, for it alone constituted a 'corporate group' in the jargon of the time. In terms of 'values', however, what they had was the centrality of household and family to everyone's moral universe and the overarching moral obligations that relatedness ideally entailed — and it was to the moral centrality and those obligations that they turned.

At the time, this was somewhat out of kilter with anthropology's fascination with (and increasing abstraction of) the varieties of kinship structures to be found around the world. And to tell the truth, matters were probably not helped by Pitt-Rivers, who, having written extensively on Mediterranean kinship, nevertheless declared that it was of little interest to kinship specialists (1977, 72). I suppose he was right. It wasn't at the time, and Mediterranean kinship did not feature in anthropology's mainstream comparative studies,

---

13. See Herzfeld's extensive writings on aspects of language use (particularly Herzfeld 1985) and 'cultural intimacy' (1997a).

even though Mediterraneanists tried to play the game. John Peristiany edited a volume in 1976 entitled *Mediterranean Family Structures* — and note again the term 'structures'. Actually it did become clear later to some people that Mediterranean kinship and Greek kinship showed quite considerable 'structural variation', evidenced, amongst other works, by Renée Hirschon's superb study of forms of matrilocality amongst the descendants of Asia Minor refugees in Piraeus (1989), Maria Couroucli's account of *lignages* in a village in Kerkyra (1985), and Michael Herzfeld's discussion of 'patrigroups' in Crete (1985). (And I again limit myself here to ethnographies; there have also been important articles by Loizos and Papataxiarchis (1991), Papataxiarchis (1998) and others, all of which reveal structural variations within Greek kinship).[14] But it was still really the moral centrality rather than the formal structure of the family and household about which anthropologists of Greece and the Mediterranean had most to say. Juliet du Boulay's *Portrait of a Greek Mountain Village* is the paradigm example.

By the 1980s, however, within mainstream anthropology everything was changing. The comparative study of kinship structures died. Perhaps it had become too abstract, too formalized, too arid — perhaps just too difficult. Certainly it was the object of a great deal of opprobrium. Admitting to being a kinship specialist was not something one did in polite company. Predictably, however, a decade later, the study of kinship was resurrected — but it was very self-consciously resurrected by theoreticians as 'the new kinship'. Gone was all the talk about social structure; gone were all the typologies of patrilineal, matrilineal, ambilineal, agnatic and bilateral; gone were clans, sub-clans, lineages and moieties; gone, indeed, was even the notion of kinship as some form of biologically based system. For 'kinship' now read 'relatedness' — the manner in which individuals forge social and personal connections between each other through work, through care, through cohabitation, through commensality, through shared emotional and moral commitments and so forth. For a Mediterraneanist, and for an anthropolo-

gist of Greece, this has a dreadful ring of *déjà vu*. Given that in the hey-day of kinship studies we were led to believe that the Mediterranean and Greece did not have much to contribute to the formal study of kinship (and given, indeed, that kinship in the Mediterranean was primarily about the moral and symbolic importance of the family and the domestic unit) it was precisely about kinship in the form of work, care, cohabitation, commensality, shared emotional and moral commitments etc that Mediterraneanists had written.

Let me take a particular instance. Within the 'new kinship', the 'household' or simply 'the house', is now a hot topic, and looks back to the 1980s when Levi-Strauss coined the phrase 'house societies' to accommodate a number of societies that seemed to him to have contradictory (or at least plural) methods of kinship recruitment. It was the house itself, he decided, that was the basic unit of such societies and that overrode such issues as patrilineal/matrilineal, filiation / residence etc. The societies he was referring to were Amerindian, and also the aristocratic houses of Japan and northern Europe. But what had almost every Mediterranean anthropologist been writing about for nearly thirty years? The household was the basic building block of Mediterranean village society (Pina-Cabral 1992). Nevertheless, Levi-Strauss' rejection, or confusion, of formal principles had an immediate appeal to the 'new kinship' theorists, and Levi-Strauss (but not Mediterranean anthropology) is frequently cited in their works. Moreover, in a relatively recent volume, *About the House, Levi-Strauss and Beyond* (Carsten and Hugh-Jones (eds) 1995) we are enjoined to consider 'houses together with the people who inhabit them as mutually implicated in the process of living' (1995, 45). I cannot help but think of Juliet du Boulay's lovely passage from her ethnography published in 1974:

> The house, therefore, in terms of village thought, is indissolubly linked with the history of the family, and with the practical observance of a high code of honour and a pattern of responsibility which bind members in a close positive relationship to each other during their lives, and which continue after death. … The house, representing the continuity of the generations as well as the years of their own toil, is involved with their lives in

---

14. For the northern Mediterranean as a whole, see Pina-Cabral (1992).

a way that is deeper than that resulting from mere affection, and invests them with the dignity of a status within the ancestral hierarchy which they are stripped of when they move … into a house which to them is nothing but a place to live (1974, 17–8).

Again, I would suggest that had anthropologists of Greece and the Mediterranean theoretically attacked kinship studies as they were conceived at the time, rather than simply trying to get on with getting Mediterranean kinship right, they might now be credited with many of the 'innovations' currently claimed by the 'new kinship' — which leads me to my third issue, gender.

A major and very explicit plank of the 'new kinship' has been its claim to marry gender studies with kinship and thereby to rescue kinship studies from their arid (and androcentric) sterility. There have been explicitly feminist ethnographic writings about Greece. Jill Dubisch's edited volume in 1986 *Gender and Power in Rural Greece* is an obvious example, and it established a fruitful tradition. However, I know that John Campbell never counted himself a feminist, and nothing that I have ever read by Juliet du Boulay makes me think that she considered herself a feminist. I don't think John Peristiany was either. And yet the fact that the anthropology of Greece and the Mediterranean was drawn to the study of 'social structure' (because it was part of the consensus period's canon) only to have to recast it as moral values, and was drawn to the study of 'kinship' (because it was the dominant form of social structure in the consensus period) only to have to recast it as household and family, meant that women were more routinely written about in Greece and Mediterranean ethnography than anywhere else in anthropology. This is grudgingly recognized by some critics, but Goddard's comment in 1994 remains that in Mediterranean anthropology 'gender difference remains assumed and untheorized' (1994, 59).[15]

I suppose I know what she means. Anthropologists of Greece and the Mediterranean wrote about women and about gender because, once engaged with the explication of moral values and once engaged with an investigation of the practical mechanics of the household and domestic unit, the activities of women and the role of women (both practically and symbolically) were an utterly inescapable part of the ethnographic reality with which they were confronted. And I think they described and analysed that reality with a great deal of sensitivity. What they did not do was to make an issue about their theoretical contribution to anthropology as a result, or about the restitution of women to ethnographic prominence — although it probably didn't help that the dominant or at least explicit gender ideologies of southern Europe were androcentric (and very much more so thirty years ago than now). But I don't think it requires a radically revisionist reading of the anthropology of Greece and the Mediterranean to claim that 'the social construction of gender' — minus, of course, that phrase itself — actually constituted a large part of what was being written about from the 1960s through to the 1980s. The early concentration on 'honour and shame' in rural Greek society ensured a thorough exploration of the ideal values and characteristics attributed to men and to women, and, importantly, of their formation and complementarity within the social and economic conditions prevalent in Greece at the time. This was basic to Campbell's work. It was equally basic to du Boulay's work, with an important emphasis on Orthodox ideology and the symbolic significance (thoroughly translated into the every-day estimations made within village life) of the opposed figures of the Panayia and Eve. And it was basic to Hirschon's work in Piraeus, where space itself becomes gendered (the house versus the street) and at the same time women's bodies become themselves living metaphors of spatial divisions (closed and open). All this was written about, however, in fundamentally ethnographic terms. Had anthropologists of Greece abstracted their findings to construct some general, more explicit (and I would suggest cruder) schema of the construction of gender roles — had they 'fully theorized it', as Goddard suggests, by talking, for example, in Foucaultian terms about an interlocking regime of economic power, domestic production and reproduction, religious authority and embodied values, then perhaps they might have stolen the march on much of what is being talked about in anthropological theory

---

15. Goddard notes 'It is significant that … the by now bulky literature on honour and shame is noticeably absent from Moore's [1986] comprehensive introduction to the anthropological study of gender' (1994, 60). But was it rejected or overlooked?

today. But they did not. True to the ethos of the consensus period, they simply produced ethnography.

And so my thesis, my explanation, for why the anthropology of Greece and the Mediterranean has not passed into accepted narratives of the development of the discipline as a whole is a simple one. It was too early. In fact what Mediterranenanists were doing was 'ground-breaking', but they were doing it at a time when the ground still seemed remarkably solid. There was not the need to make large claims or to pit their findings against an established anthropological tradition. And to an extent they continued to talk the language of that tradition, however much their own work could have subverted it. It was perhaps a case of new wine in old bottles. By the time anthropology plunged into full auto-critique, by the time others elsewhere were deriding the fixities of 'social structure', demanding a more intimate and nuanced view of social life, throwing out the arid taxonomies of kinship theory, and looking at the gendered construction of personhood, the anthropology of Greece and the Mediterranean seemed to date from the very period that was under attack.

What I have written may sound like a hard-luck story. In the end I think it is not. Those early ethnographies of Greece and the Mediterranean stand the test of time for those who continue to read them — and they do continue to be read. Moreover, as I commented at the outset, ethnographies of Greece — or rather, ethnographic accounts set in Greece — continue to be produced by a new generation of anthropologists, many of them Greek, and most of whom are appreciative (perhaps more appreciative than they were fifteen years ago) of what was earlier written. Their new ethnographies are not attempts to imitate earlier works. Greece has changed. Anthropology has changed. Arguably, the very idea of 'an anthropology of Greece' (along with regional studies as a whole) is in eclipse. Modern ethnographies are much more issue- or topic-oriented: migration, nationalism, conservation, material culture, consumption, personhood, gender, social memory, tourism etc, and younger anthropologists are pursuing those topics *within* Greece rather attempting an anthropology *of* Greece — and they are doing so with remarkable success. Perhaps one advantage of a topic-oriented anthropology is that by allowing more comparative discussion of issues across geographical boundaries, it may thereby better incorporate the anthropology of Greece and of the Mediterranean into the mainstream of the discipline than it ever was when Mediterranean anthropology attempted to constitute a regional sub-discipline of its own. Students may not study 'the anthropology of Greece' or 'the anthropology of the Mediterranean' anymore, but if they are studying gender, they may read Kirtzoglou; if they are studying material culture, they may read Yalouri; if they are studying nationalism, they may read Papadakis; and if they are studying the sociology of conservation, they may read Theodossopoulos. And who knows, as a result they may then go back and read Friedl and Campbell and du Boulay and Loizos? My plaint relates merely to the history of the discipline, not to what anthropological work in Greece still has to offer.

REFERENCES

Ardener, E., 1989. *The Voice of Prophecy and Other Essays,* ed. M. Chapman. Oxford.

Argyrou, V., 1996. *Tradition and Modernity in the Mediterranean: The Wedding as Symbolic Struggle.* Cambridge.

Campbell, J.K., 1963. 'The kindred in a Greek mountain community', in J. Pitt-Rivers (ed.), *Mediterranean Countrymen*: 73–96. Paris.

—, 1964. *Honour, Family, and Patronage: A Study of Institutions and Moral Values in a Greek Mountain Community.* Oxford.

Carsten, J. and Hugh-Jones, S. (eds), 1995. *About the House, Levi-Strauss and Beyond.* Cambridge.

Cole, J., 1977. 'Anthropology comes part-way home: Community studies in Europe'. *Annual review of Anthropology* 6: 349–78.

Couroucli, M., 1985. *Les Oliviers du Lignage.* Paris.

Cowan, J.K., 1990. *Dance and the Body Politic in Northern Greece.* Princeton.

Danforth, L.M., 1982. *The Death Rituals of Rural Greece.* Princeton.

Davis, J., 1977. *People of the Mediterranean: An Essay in Comparative Social Anthropology.* London.

Delaney, C., 2004. *Investigating Culture. An Experiential Introduction to Anthropology.* Oxford.

Dimen, M. and Friedl, E., 1976. *Regional Variation in Modern Greece and Cyprus: Towards a Perspective on the Ethnography of Greece.* Annals of the New York Academy of Sciences 268.

du Boulay, J., 1974. *Portrait of a Greek Mountain Village.* Oxford.

Dubisch, J. (ed.), 1986. *Gender and Power in Rural Greece.* Princeton.

—, 1995. *In a Different Place: Pilgrimage Gender, and Politics at a Greek Island Shrine*. Princeton.

Evans-Pritchard, E.E., 1976 [1940]. *The Nuer. A Description of the Modes of Livelihood and Political Institutions of a Nilotic People*. Oxford.

Faubion, James D., 1993. *Modern Greek Lessons. A Primer in Historical Constructivism*. Princeton.

Friedl, E., 1962. *Vassilika: A Village in Modern Greece*. New York.

Friedman, J., 1997. 'Simplifying complexity: assimilating the global in a small paradise' in K. Fog Olwig and K. Hastrup (eds), *Siting Culture*. London.

Goddard, V.A., 1994. 'From the Mediterranean to Europe: honour, kinship and gender', in V. Goddard, J.R. Llobera and C. Shore (eds), *The Anthropology of Europe. Identities and Boundaries in Conflict*: 57–92. Oxford.

Handman, M.-E., 1983. *La Violence et la Ruse. Hommes et Femmes dans un Village Grec*. La Calade, Aix-en-Provence.

Hart, L.K., 1991. *Time, Religion, and Social Experience in Rural Greece*. Lanham, Maryland.

Hendry, J., 1999. *An Introduction to Social Anthropology*. London.

Herzfeld, M., 1982. *Ours Once More: Folklore, Ideology, and the Making of Modern Greece*. Austin.

—, 1985. *The Poetics of Manhood: Contest and Identity in a Greek Mountain Village*. Princeton.

—, 1987. *Anthropology through the Looking-Glass: Critical Ethnography on the Margins of Europe*. Cambridge.

—, 1991. *A Place in History: Social and Monumental Time in a Cretan Town*. Princeton.

—, 1997a. *Cultural Intimacy. Social Poetics in the Nation-State*. London.

—, 1997b. *Portrait of Greek Imagination: An Ethnographic Biography of Andreas Nenedakis*. Chicago.

—, 2001. *Anthropology. Theoretical Practice in Culture and Society*. Oxford.

Hirschon, R., 1989. *Heirs of the Greek Catastrophe: The Social Life of Asia Minor Refugees in Piraeus*. Oxford.

Just, R., 2000. *A Greek Island Cosmos:Kinship and Community on Meganisi*. Oxford.

Karakasidou, A.N., 1997. *Fields of Wheat, Hills of Blood. Passages to Nationhood in Greek Macedonia, 1870–1990*. Chicago.

Kenna, M., 2001a. *Greek Island Life: Fieldwork on Anafi*. Amsterdam.

—, 2001b. *The Social Organisation of Exile*. Amsterdam.

Kirtzoglou, E., 2004. *For the Love of Women. Gender, Identity and Same-Sex Relations in a Greek Provincial Town*. London/New York.

Loizos, P., 1975. *The Greek Gift: Politics in a Cypriot Village*. Oxford.

—, 1981. *The Heart Grown Bitter: a Chronicle of Cypriot War Refugees*. Cambridge.

— and Papataxiarchis, E. (eds), 1991. *Contested Identities: Gender and Kinship in Modern Greece*. Princeton.

Moore, H., 1986. *Feminism and Anthropology*. Oxford.

Panourgia, N., 1995. *Fragments of Death, Fables of Identity. An Athenian Anthropology*. Madison, Wisconsin.

Papadakis, Y., 2005. *Echoes from the Dead Zone, Across the Cyprus Divide*. London.

Papataxiarchis, E., 1998. 'The devolution of property and kinship practices in late- and post-Ottoman ethnic Greek societies', *Melanges de L'École Francaise de Rome* 110(1): 217–41.

Peristiany, J.G. (ed.), 1965. *Honour and Shame. The Values of Mediterranean Society*. London.

— (ed.), 1968. *Contributions to Mediterranean Sociology: Mediterranean Rural Communities and Social Change*. Paris.

— (ed.), 1976. *Mediterranean Family Structures*. Cambridge.

— and Handman, M.-E. (eds), 1989. *Le Prix de l'Alliance en Méditerranée*. Paris.

Piault, C. (ed.), 1985. *Familles et Biens en Grèce et à Chypre*. Paris.

Pina-Cabral, J. de, 1986. *Sons of Adam, Daughters of Eve. The Peasant Worldview of the Altho Minho*. Oxford.

—, 1992. 'The primary social unit in Mediterranean and Atlantic Europe', *Journal of Mediterranean Studies* 2(1): 25–41.

Pitt-Rivers, J., 1977. 'The moral foundations of the family', in J. Pitt-Rivers (ed.), *The Fate of Shechem or the Politics of Sex*: 71–93. Cambridge.

—, 1954. *The People of the Sierra*. Chicago.

Rapport, N. (ed.), 2002. *British Subjects. An Anthropology of Britain*. Oxford.

Sant Cassia, P. and Bada, C., 1992. *The Making of the Modern Greek Family. Marriage and Exchange in 19th Century Athens*. Cambridge.

Seremetakis, N.M., 1991. *The Last Word. Women, Death, and Divination in Inner Mani*. Chicago.

Stewart, C., 1991. *Demons and the Devil: Moral Imagination in Modern Greek Culture*. Princeton.

Sutton, D. E., 1998. *Memories Cast in Stone. The Relevance of the Past in Everyday Life*. Oxford.

Theodossopoulos, D., 2003. *Troubles with Turtles. Cultural Understandings of the Environment on a Greek Island*. Oxford.

Yalouri, E., 2001. *The Acropolis. Global Fame, Local Claim*. Oxford.

Xanthakou, M., 1988. *Cendrillon et les Soeurs Cannibales*. Paris.

—, 1989. *Idiots de Village. Conversations Ethnopsychiatriques en Peloponnese*. Toulouse.

—, 1993. *Faute d'Epouses on Mange des Soeurs*. Paris.

17

'Home from home': The role of the BSA in social anthropological fieldwork

Renée Hirschon

'Anthropology is gossip writ large and
thrown upon the screen'
            attributed to Ruth Benedict,
            American anthropologist

At first sight, the title of this paper seems straight forward, but not long after researching the topic, namely to examine the role of the British School at Athens (BSA) in the development of social anthropological studies in Greece in its first decades, I became aware of some problems. It soon became clear that the title is based on a number of unexamined assumptions. The formulation — 'home from home' - derived from my notion that the BSA represents a small island in the heart of Athens, replicating a bit of the home island itself, a kind of British microcosm, proved to be too simple. This became apparent when I started collecting information from colleagues about the BSA as they recalled it. I learned that the BSA did not offer the same thing, namely a safe haven, for all fieldworkers in anthropology. Thus, my first assumption that the island hidden behind the high walls in Souedias Street would be essentially a welcoming environment for all, a refuge and a sanctuary, was mistaken.

My initial error was that I had ignored the specific and highly significant characteristics of what constitutes any 'home' and, consequently, who is likely to feel more or less 'at home' in any place. Furthermore, I discovered that the phrase 'home from home' is ambiguous in itself. To native Greek speakers it conveys nothing; for them this idiom does not communicate the sense of *familiar place in a foreign place*, which is a commonplace for native English speakers. A further complication is that the rather similar phrase, 'home away from home', used by Greek Australians in the diaspora, implies more than recreating the physical space and ambience; in addition, it requires a replication of the fabric of social life associated with the 'patrida'.[1]

Thus, I realised that a number of unexamined assumptions lay behind my title, one of which arises from the fundamental premise of the methodology of social anthropology. The established convention entails a period of fieldwork by an outsider using participant-observation techniques. This involves the anthropologist living in an unfamiliar society, where confrontation with the 'other', and the distance between the observer and the observed, raises one's awareness of cultural and social differences and their significance, and provides a stimulus for the task of interpretation.

Following this classical tradition of anthropological enquiry prevalent in the immediate post WWII period, it could be said that the early anthropologists in Greece were dealing with exotica — put crudely, they could be seen to be studying the way of life of the 'Bongo Bongo', the tribe out there with whom the anthropologist should be deeply engaged, through the method of participant-observation. The foundations of the discipline were laid down in this way in the early decades of the 20th century by founding fathers such as Radcliffe-Brown, Malinowski and Evans-Pritchard, who worked among distant and isolated tribal societies. Their valuable contribution was accompanied by the temptation to romanticise or exoticise 'other cultures'. An unforgettable moment at a Modern Greek Studies Association conference in Philadelphia in the early 1980s highlighted this point. Following presentations by a panel of non-Greek social anthropologists in which they delivered their insights into modern Greek society, an eminent Greek folklorist and senior academic, the late Professor Alkis Kyriakidou Nestoros, stood

---

1. I am grateful to Dr Vassiliki Chryssanthopoulou for a useful discussion on the need to differentiate between between these two rather similar phrases, as understood by Greek speakers.

Fig. 17.1: John Campbell, here with John Chadwick; BSA Photographic Archive: BSAA6–125.

up at question time, drawing her fur coat around her. Her response to the interpretations of younger foreign academics about her own society was trenchant: 'I feel like a Trobriand Islander in front of five Malinowskis', she expostulated.

From this perspective and in this tradition, anthropological fieldwork has usually been an exploration by the foreign observer of the unknown, uncharted world of the natives, from whom, I assumed, a desperately needed respite and escape would be required from time to time. My initial assumption had been that the BSA

would offer a haven from the rigours of isolation in the field, far from one's own kind. Certainly, it did represent a 'home from home' for some of my colleagues, though in rather different ways, but it soon became clear that reactions were by no means standard; indeed, it was not so for several others.[2]

This investigation is based on the personal recollections of practising anthropologists and thus it conforms well with the current climate of reflexivity which has overtaken much of the discipline since the mid 1980s (see below). João de Pina-Cabral has pinpointed the trend succinctly, noting that 'anyone who is an ethnographer has to confront the possibility of being an object of ethnography'.[3] The starting point of my investigation is the work of John Campbell, whose study of the Sarakatsani shepherds in Epirus in the mid–1950s was not only a pioneering step in Greek ethnography, but also one of the first studies in European anthropology. Published in 1964 as *Honour, Family and Patronage*, this classic study set the pattern for the development of future studies and confers on him the title, appropriately, of godfather of social anthropology in Greece. His words (cited as 'JKC') lie at the centre of this presentation, since he has kindly allowed me to present some of his views and recollections of the importance of the BSA during the period of his fieldwork.

THE BSA IN ANTHROPOLOGICAL PERSPECTIVE

On reflection, from the accounts of the seven anthropologists represented here, certain patterns emerge, together with sets of common and differentiating features.

What comes out of these accounts is that the experience of the BSA is an intensely personal one, a conclusion derived from the wide range of responses presented. One differentiating criterion emerges

---

2. Material for this paper comes from the first generation of anthropologists doing fieldwork in Greece in the 1960s, 70s and 80s, starting with John Campbell in 1954–55. I wish to thank my colleagues who kindly agreed to act as my informants and whose anonymity I try to maintain. With one exception, they are all non-Greeks. They have provided their views which constitutes the ethnographic detail from which the anthropologist, in this case, I myself, draw out broad patterns and generalised observations.

3. de Pina-Cabral 2006: 666.

as a critical factor, namely the place of origin of the anthropologist fieldworker. It soon became clear that the background and home culture of the anthropologist determined the degree to which he or she might feel 'at home'. Since the School was (and is) a reflection, a mirror of a particular segment of British society, its practices and customs were also based on lines of inclusion and exclusion, something equivalent to class distinctions. It provided a well organised and refined environment, where appropriate behaviour was crucial, where politeness and honourable conduct was the norm, while it was also set about with unwritten rules. Thus, the School could be, and was, a familiar environment providing a welcome respite for middle-class, privately educated British students. However, for those who were from a grammar school or a lower middle class background, it could be an intimidating environment. Similarly, for the 'colonials' — the few American, and antipodean (Australian, South African) students — the atmosphere and ethos of the BSA could feel almost as alien as the Greek countryside. To some of them, the School was so archetypically British, it could actually appear quite foreign, and not feel familiar nor even comfortable. From this perspective, oddly enough, the BSA itself could have been the site of anthropological observation and interpretation, something like the culture of another 'Bongo-Bongo' group!

This is illustrated in the experience of three colleagues who told me of separate incidents where they unwittingly infringed the rules in rather minor ways. They were reprimanded after the fact, to their intense embarrassment, and this left them with a nagging sense of injustice. One of them commented, ruefully, 'No one warned me that I shouldn't have done that — there were these unwritten rules'. In this way it was rather like being in a group whose taboos are inadvertently broken by the uninitiated fieldworker or, closer to home, like an Oxford college, where the Fellows do not explain to a newcomer what the rules are, assuming that they are part of an hereditary endowment. As JKC characterised it succinctly, 'In some respects, it's rather like a British boarding school' and those who have spent childhood years in such an institution are the most likely to find it a 'home from home'

In order to understand these varying responses, an analytical perspective is useful for what it reveals about the ethos and practices of the School. Just as social class is a major organising principle in British society, so it is reflected in the organisation of the School. There was a hierarchical division, (much as there is in an Oxford college), between what we might call the 'functionaries' —the office staff, cooks, cleaners, gardeners— and the 'luminaries' —the Director and Assistant Director, the Secretary of the School, the Librarian, senior academics and research students. As one British anthropologist noted 'The people below stairs were not seen to be the same as those above stairs'. Although social stratification is evident in Greek society, class distinctions do not operate in the same way as in British society. An obvious adaptation would have to occur as non-Greek and Greek employees of the School accommodated to the ways in which different social norms and expectations were acted out. The School is therefore, in itself a site for cross-cultural interaction.

Another feature which emerged from responses concerned the status of social anthropology at the BSA in the post World War II period. Particularly in the early days, anthropologists were seen to be rather odd. The position of anthropologists was that of a minority — if not of marginality. John Campbell stated this clearly,

> There's a big difference now. In my day anthropology was unknown but now it's a mainline subject. When I was there originally, doing my fieldwork, I was just peculiar. There were only archaeologists in the School at that time, if you except an editor of the Blue Guide and a somewhat exotic Swedish sculptress.

He illustrated the prevailing attitude with the following anecdote from the time when he and his wife Sheila were evicted from Epirus during the mid–1950s Cyprus crisis.

> We'd no sooner arrived, and were given a room with a double bed and went to sleep exhausted. During the night we were assaulted by a bloody great army of bedbugs. You could tell what they were- they disappeared when the lights went on. We reported it to Jane Rabnett, the School Secretary who took a rather censorious view of the incident. 'It's not us, it's *you* who've brought them, after all, *you've* been living with sheep', was her

Fig.17.2: Renée Hirschon with Eliso, a neighbour in Kokkinia, 1972; author's photograph.

response. They didn't seem to realise that the archaeologists too were excavating in primitive conditions on their digs, and *they* must have brought the bugs. But we were seen as curious specimens, doing something no one had done before.

THE BSA IN TROUBLED TIMES; LEGITIMATING RESEARCHWORK

The political climate and particular political events in Greece have directly affected the work of social anthropologists. In particular, the 1950s' independence struggle in Cyprus, the 1967–74 military dictatorship in Greece, the 1974 coup and Turkish army intervention in Cyprus, were events which directly affected anthropologists in the field.

John Campbell's words illustrate one of the most important functions of the BSA for fieldwork researchers in Greece:

The British School was a 'home from home' in several ways. Certainly, it was a great help that one had an institutional address. You have to remember, I was doing my fieldwork in 1954 and this was only 4 or 5 years after the civil war ended in 1949. In some areas of Greece people were highly suspicious of each other as well as of foreigners, and being a member of the BSA gave one a semblance

of respectability. In the field, I didn't say I was an archaeologist, I sometimes said I was a sociologist and I promoted myself enormously by saying I was a professor (καθηγητής), but of course in the Greek system this is also the title accorded to school masters!

Certainly, no one amongst the Greek archaeologists, apart from our friend, Sotiris Dakaris, had any idea of what one was doing because it hadn't been done before. But in any case it was an enormous help to have the BSA connection in the background if one got into difficulties. Indeed, I did eventually get into serious trouble with the brewing up of problems over Cyprus. In fact we got thrown out of the Epirus. We went down to Athens and spent two or three months in the School while I manoeuvred to get back to the field. I spent all my time trying to get back and eventually we did. The BSA had links with the Embassy, so I was able to get assistance when I ran into trouble with the authorities. That's one of the main things the BSA did for me then.

It's all rather curious, because when I was a soldier in 1944 the School was shut down, and was looked after by the Swiss. I'd gone to the BSA at that time out of curiosity and I can remember going into the library. I looked at the names in the book, and saw the last entries before the Germans arrived. So when I turned up in Athens ten years later in 1954, I knew where to go. I didn't have many other introductions apart from a letter from the Greek ambassador in London. That was the only introductory document I had to show that I wasn't a spy. Of course they were quite sure I was a spy, since the people who had been in the School before the war turned up during the Occupation as British liaison officers.

The BSA was not always very happy about my relations with the Greek authorities up in the Epirus, especially when the Cyprus situation became critical. There was fighting in Cyprus and Cypriots were being imprisoned. In Yannina there were agents trying to raise funds for EOKA operations in Cyprus. Once, I was cornered in a shop by a group of these people who remonstrated with me about how I should remember what Lord Byron had done for Greece and so please would I contribute. I said I couldn't possibly do anything against my fellow country men fighting in Cyprus. They said the money was only for blankets, and food — untrue, of course. Unfortunately, this incident was picked up by the local newspaper who portrayed me as a latter day Byron, and I was soon contacted by the Embassy.

The British School was always very sensitive about its standing with the Greek government since they relied on good relations to obtain licences for excavations, so they were not in the least amused when I got into hot water. Nevertheless, they understood our difficulties. It was a very pleasant, communal, comradely time at the British School... Rather like a boarding school, that kind of atmosphere, you know, with a lot of curious rules — not allowed to wash your underpants in the basin or hang them in the bedroom.

Nevertheless, I must emphasise again that whenever we were in political trouble over the Cyprus crisis, we received generous support from the then Director, Sinclair Hood, despite the embarrassment this might have caused him in the School's relations with the Greek Archaeological Service. And when we had a serious car accident in Epirus, Sheila, who suffered severe concussion, was flown to Athens and was cared for with great concern and kindness.

For us, the British School was important psychologically, the fact that one could always rely on it. For us, it certainly was a 'home from home'.

About two decades later when Greece was in the grips of a harsh military dictatorship I was engaged in rather different kind of fieldwork. I was not studying a rural community but was living right in the midst of the metropolis, in a densely populated, very poor part of the city, the refugee settlement of Kokkinia, now known as Nikaia. This was in 1971–72 at the height of the junta, and my foreign presence in a disreputable urban slum, well known as a left wing and Communist stronghold, inevitably provoked suspicion. I was warned by neighbours that there were informants in the area, and that I was being watched. I was visited by security police on two occasions, once after a bomb exploded in the square near my dwelling, blowing up the bust of Metaxas. The atmosphere was very tense.

As I was aware of being under surveillance I took the expedient measure of writing all my field notes in duplicate in case I was raided, using A4 double sheeted notebooks with carbon copy, and I hid the second copy. Here the School played a valuable role as sanctuary and in providing a base for friendships. I arranged to get the second copy of my notes out of the country with an archaeologist friend who had finished his research and was returning to the UK. He transported several volumes of my A4 notebooks to Manchester where they were kept safely for a few years.

I certainly appreciated the feeling of 'touching base' when I came on a visit to deliver a set of my field notes for safe keeping. It gave me a sense of security in the knowledge of a more liberal world beyond the brutal oppression of Greek life under the military regime. The garden beyond the high walls, the orderly English ambience, were reassuring and restorative. At the same time, however, its effect could easily insulate one from the harsh reality outside. This was one reason why I didn't use the School much while doing my fieldwork. Another reason was in order to blunt any inference that I might have affiliations with 'foreign powers'. Anthropology demands that one engages with the local society in an intimate way, and too much contact with the School would have prevented that. My way of integrating into the society of poor, marginalised people in a deprived refugee community was to be as powerless, unobtrusive, and embedded in the local community as possible.

PERSONAL RESPONSES TO THE BSA

The secure base offered by the BSA is appreciated in other accounts, which range from the enthusiastic to the ambivalent:

The BSA didn't really give me much. It was the library that was really helpful. I didn't stay in the School. To stay at the BSA was counterproductive. As an anthropologist, what you need is to be thrown into a Greek environment. I preferred to stay in Athens in a flat in Pangrati. Anthropologists need linguistic competence above all, you need to be out in the city, in kafeneia, reading newspapers, talking to people. Yes, I used the library, that was great, and I did meet interesting people, mainly archaeologists. I'd have tea in Finlay but frankly, I didn't enjoy sitting around making polite conversation, it was just like an Oxford common room — too confining. In fact it was more British than the UK. But yes, the BSA did act as a base. I stored my stuff there before moving back to UK, and it was certainly in safe keeping.[4]

This contrasts with the unambiguously positive view of a British female anthropologist working there a decade earlier. She said:

> It offered such a good place, those wonderful scented pines, I loved going there. It was cool, it was clean, had simple rooms with wooden floors like a good Greek hotel, and they even made your bed. It had good food, Greek things like chorta and fasolada, you could get to the doctor, you could even have a bath!

A less enthusiastic view was that of a British male student, doing fieldwork in the late 70s, reflecting the perceived peripheral position of anthropology at the School:

> As an institution it played no role in my life. It was a citadel of archaeologists and ancient historians, and most archaeologists have no interest in Greek society. They might have had some romantic ideas about peasant life but they liked to belong to a foreign School. It was a kind of colonial approach while I wanted to be part of Greek society, so I

had no interest in speaking English. There was no critical mass of anthropologists, so there was really nothing to attract me to the School. I went to other places for intellectual contact. At the School, people were friendly, but it wasn't much use for anthropologists. I did use the library, though; it was good, especially for folklore.

As a base from which to operate, the School did serve some students admirably, however, notably a female Greek student doing her D.Phil in Oxford:

> For me the BSA was an oasis. I loved going there to work in the library. It didn't have many anthropology books, but it was a quiet pleasant environment. It had a continuity with the atmosphere of England which I missed. I wrote up my material there after fieldwork. It was just like being in Oxford, it helped being in that ordered academic environment. It helped structure your time, unlike being in my chaotic Greek society. I used to go into tea and meet people, sometimes from the American School. I enjoyed the quiet atmosphere and the library and everyone was very helpful.

Another colleague was also unequivocally positive:

> What the BSA offered me more than anything else was a secure base in Greece and, up to a point, a sanctuary. I really find it difficult to know how I could have coped without it initially. I arrived in Greece with very little Greek, few contacts and no very specific idea of where I was going to go —. The School provided me with a place to catch my breath and settle in, and to talk to a lot of people who had known Greece for a long time. Just arriving in Athens with my backpack and wandering the streets would have been awful.

This recollection of a male Australian/'colonial' stands in sharp contrast with the experience of a female Australian/'colonial' who had started her work in Greece over a decade earlier. She arrived in Athens from the UK in the mid 1960s and was not an Oxbridge student. She said that she didn't even know that the

---

4. USA male student, late 70s – 80s.

School existed and later 'thought it was an archaeological place'. She was initially connected to the National Social Science Centre (EKKE), under John Peristiany at the time, and the British School 'was not even mentioned. It didn't seem to be relevant'. At a later stage in her career she did use the School and she recalled how she went to the School to enrol as a member in the mid 1980s. Her ten year old son was with her but he was not allowed to enter the buildings, not even the hallway, so she had to leave him sitting outside on a bench. Not surprisingly, she had rather mixed feelings about the School and its rules. In answer to my question, she replied:

> Yes, I did feel marginal: I was somewhat odd, not quite classifiable. I was an anthropologist, I was female, I was married with a child. There was a gender division of labour in the School, so there were women, of course, but they had lowly jobs, like cleaning, cooking, secretaries. I could get on with the cooks and the cleaners, speaking Greek. They were intrigued by my work, how I could be spending time in that God-forsaken place (an Aegean island). I didn't use the BSA much because I had to live out with my family. Actually, it was intimidating, that tray with drinks and ouzo in Finlay. It was like an English gentlemen's club. I only used to go in for notepaper, and to collect mail. So, on the other hand, the BSA was very useful as an academic base; it provided credentials, and a postal address. The phone box was in that lovely quiet garden and not out in the noisy streets.

We can here contrast two women research students (both married to UK classicists): the Greek experienced the BSA as an oasis and a haven from Greek pressures, the other, a 'colonial' felt marginal, being a married woman with a child, and an anthropologist. What emerges is the variable character of the experience of each person, and for a number of the researchers the idea of 'home from home' is well expressed.

In the words of a male fieldworker living on a small and distant island:

> Once established, I did return to the School at intervals — I can't remember how many

times, but usually after 4–5 months in the village. It was a sort of sanity break, being able to retreat 'stous dikous mou', linguistically as much as anything else. It allowed me periods of mental (and physical) debriefing. It was a way of temporarily 'going home'. I made good friends at the British School, mainly archaeologists. The point is that each time I was able to come back to the school for a couple of weeks, to lick my wounds, gather my thoughts, get some encouragement and have a shower!

THE CHANGING SCENE

It is not surprising that the School is not the same as it was in the first decades after World War II. It has not been shielded from changes in the home society where the economic pressures on educational institutions have become acute:

Recalling past times, one colleague said

> It was marvellous before, because everything was done for you. You would leave shoes and laundry outside your door, and they would appear miraculously cleaned. Now, things have changed and you have to do your own washing and cooking, and the basement has this huge set of kitchen equipment, but all you use is a microwave or kettle.

Volunteering his opinion on this topic, JKC said:

> The School has changed: the whole communal aspect has broken down. Now, if you're living in the hostel you only get breakfast. They've forgotten the importance of sharing lunch, dinner, and afternoon tea, which created a communal atmosphere of togetherness. Commensality is a significant institution. Of course I appreciate that there were funding difficulties, but sadly, that was an unfortunate change.

THE CHARACTER OF ANTHROPOLOGICAL RESEARCH

It becomes clear from these accounts that the role of the School for anthropologists is as variable as the personality and aims of the anthropologist. This arises from

Fig.17.3: Easter Sunday in the Director's garden, 1976; BSA Photographic Archive: Members, O. Dickinson Album–34.

the subject itself, which requires the anthropologist to work in a highly personal way. To some degree and to some level, it is based in a tradition requiring that you become one of the natives. So, a constant theme emerges, the peculiar nature of anthropology, a discipline which demands intense involvement in contemporary life. That clearly is not what archaeologists are expected to do. This contrast with the methodology of archaeology reveals how different is the experience offered by the BSA for scholars in different disciplines. As one anthropologist pointed out, archaeologists are mainly interested in *things*, not people. They can be very little involved with contemporary Greek life. 'Their only contact is with the dig workmen' said one colleague, while two others have remarked that, as anthropologists, they were envied for their local knowledge: 'I could be critical of some young archaeologists who never learned any modern Greek, who seemed frightened to go into the Greek world outside, and huddled together in the School', said one, who

recalled how non-anthropologists saw him as a local expert on life beyond the garden walls.

Anthropology as a discipline derives its unique insights from the particular methodology of participant observation, the aim being to become a member of 'the tribe', adopt the local customs, in order to see the world through the eyes of 'the natives'. This is why the language issue is critical and underlines the importance of language competence for non-Greek anthropologists. It is one key factor and here, the School does not nor can it provide what is needed, which explains why anthropologists sometimes see the School as peripheral to their professional interests. One colleague did try to combine its benefits with the linguistic academic demands, and spent two months living in the School while attending classes to learn modern Greek. At least two others preferred to rent a flat and come to grips with life in the city, as a foil to the life they were learning about in the countryside.

Since the BSA library did not cater much for anthropology at that time (in contrast with the Canadian Institute of Archaeology during the 1980s), the library only served those who had interests in folklore and in historical documents and travellers' accounts.

THE BSA, POST MODERNISM AND INDIGENOUS ANTHROPOLOGY

To give a fuller picture of the role of the BSA in anthropological research and the way in which the BSA might function as a 'Home from home', changes since the 1980s must be considered: they are evident in the approaches to methodology and fieldwork, and to the role of ethnography and the status of Greek anthropology itself. On the one hand, the effects of post-modernist trends were felt and on the other, anthropology was introduced as a subject in some Greek universities.

From the mid 1980s, new challenges to the then established anthropological discourse were posed by the cumulative effect of feminist anthropology and of post-modernism. A critical phase developed in the practice of social anthropology, with the launch of a post-modernist attack on classical methods of writing ethnography.[5] At this time epistemological issues were raised regarding truth and verification, subjectivity and interpretation, and the different positions of natives and foreign researchers. The writing of ethnographic texts following intensive fieldwork was no longer to be taken for granted. Ethnography was no longer seen as a matter of keeping good field notes, and consciensiously writing up results with an aspiration to objectivity Clifford's critique emphasised 'the constructed and artificial nature of cultural accounts' stating that ethnography 'is always caught up in the invention, not the representation of cultures'.[6]

This new approach questioned the nature of transparent reporting, placing subjectivity and reflexivity at the centre, and questioned the authenticity of accounts by outsiders. Overall, this post-modernist position countered any notion of objective analysis or factual representation, and constituted a definitive rejection of positivistic epistemology.[7]

At about the same time, the long-delayed introduction of social anthropology into Greek universities was taking place. As a founding member of the first full department of social anthropology in Greece, established in 1987 at the University of the Aegean, I recall the many discussions about the ways in which anthropology in Greece and the training of students should be organised. An underlying issue was the established convention of fieldwork in foreign cultures as opposed to an 'anthropology at home'[8] and thus, the difference between the ethnographic work of a foreign observer and that of the indigenous ethnographer, the native researcher. Such questions would not have arisen in Greece in the previous period since there were no indigenous anthropologists anyway (John Peristiany being one exception), for anthropology in Greece had been the preserve of foreign researchers. Interestingly, the direction taken was that Greeks educated abroad as well as those trained in Greek universities predominantly chose sites and topics close to home. A distinct feature that characterised the early period of anthropology in Greek academia was the introverted nature both of the general climate and of the reaction to its subject matter.[9] As a result, much anthropology practised by Greeks at that time was 'omphaloscopic';[10] indeed, it could be said to be more like 'navel gazing' than 'Bongo Bongo' studies. Gefou-Madianou noted also the tendency among some Greek anthropologists unwittingly to exoticise sub cultures and marginalised communities in Greece itself.[11]

The debate about the status of anthropological research by indigenous as opposed to foreign academics covers several dimensions, among them the language issue. Authority for statements about Greek society and culture have been challenged by some Greek anthropologists (as distinct from anthropologists of Greece) who are sceptical about the capacity of outsiders to understand Greeks and their cultural practices, and who typically express scepticism about foreign colleagues' ability to speak and understand the language

---

5. Clifford and Marcus 1986.

6. Clifford and Marcus 1986: 2.

7. Clifford and Marcus 1986: 11.

---

8. Jackson 1987.

9. Noted by Gefou-Madianou 1993, 2003, Bakalaki 2003, Alexakis 2004.

10. Gefou-Madianou 1993: 175.

11. Gefou-Madianou 1993: 162.

Fig.17.4: Roger Just at the BSA; BSA Photographic Archive: Members, O. Dickinson Album–133.

well. For some, this stance includes the conviction that the outsider cannot experience or interpret the situation as the insider does.[12] Relevant to the topic of this paper is that social anthropology *in* and *of* Greece is no longer confined to foreign researchers[13] and that the BSA can offer its many facilities to only a small proportion of those who are now involved in advancing the discipline, viz. to its foreign students. Although Greek anthropologists registered at British universities could obviously be members of the School, very few of them make use of this possibility. But for the non-Greek anthropologist it undoubtedly will continue to be a significant institution, offering what is required in response to the varying personal needs of students.

CONCLUSION — SUMMARY

Shared by all is the view that the BSA was a replica of a certain aspect of the home society, maybe even more so ('more British than the UK'); it was bound by rules and presuppositions of correct behaviour ('rather like a boarding School', 'an Oxford college'). Without doubt, as was emphasised in many accounts, the School provided the stamp of legitimacy, and of

serious credentials. It maintained a valuable link with Greek officialdom and facilitated dealing with some of the bureaucratic tangles of official life in Greece. Even among those who expressed a rather negative view of the School , they acknowledged its role in providing credentials. Undoubtedly the BSA had a utilitarian value, a legitimating function. But what comes through clearly is that it provided even more for some; the School provided an emotionally secure base, an oasis of calm, and a well-ordered environment. It was a place where anthropologists and archaeologists became acquainted and, mostly, became friends, and it helped to promote contacts with students from other foreign research schools.

John Campbell's words sum up well the conclusions of this investigation into the role of the BSA in anthropological studies in Greece:

> In terms of home from home, the British School was for us a place where we made friendships, some life-time ones, where we enjoyed many hilarious and some serious excursions. Its presence made us feel psychologically secure. That's what it meant to us. Ultimately, it's all very personal.

REFERENCES

Alexakis, E., 2004. ᾽Ανθρωπολογική ῎Ερευνα και Θεωρία στην Ελλάδα, η περίπτωση τριών επιστημονικών περιοδικών', in ῎Οψεις της Ανθρωπολογικής Σκέψης και ῎Ερευνας στην Ελλάδα: 203–19. Athens.

Bakalaki, A., 2003. ῾Ελληνοκεντρισμός και πολιτισμική κριτική: για τη διδασκαλία της Ανθρωπολογίας στο Πανεπιστήμιο' in Το Παρόν του Παρελθόντος. Ιστορία, Λαογραφία, Κοινωνική Ανθρωπολογία (Επιστημονικό Συμπόσιο, 19–21 Απριλίου 2002): 287–306. Athens.

Okely, J. and Callaway, H. (eds), 1992. *Anthropology and Autobiography*, London.

Campbell, J.K., 1964. *Honour, Family and Patronage*. Oxford.

Clifford, J. and Marcus, G. (eds), 1986. *Writing Culture: the poetics and politics of ethnography*. Berkleley, USA.

de Pina Cabral, J., 2006. 'Anthropology challenged: notes for a debate', *JRAI (NS)* 12: 663–73.

Gefou-Madianou, D., 1993. 'Mirroring Ourselves through Western eyes: the limits of indigenous anthropology' in Henk Driessen (ed.), *The Politics of Ethnographic Reading and Writing*, Nijmegen Studies in Development and Cultural Change 13: 160–81. Verlag Breitenbach, Saarbrucken, Fort Lauderdale.

---

12. See Gefou-Madianou 1993, 2003 for a balanced assessment of the situation.
13. See Bakalaki 2003.

—, 2003. 'Αναστοχαστική Ανθρωπολογία και ακαδημαϊκός χώρος: τροχιές, διλήμματα, προοπτικές', in *Το Παρόν του Παρελθόντος. Ιστορία, Λαογραφία, Κοινωνική Ανθρωπολογία* (Επιστημονικό Συμπόσιο, 19–21 Απριλίου 2002): 283–400. Athens.

Jackson, A. (ed.), 1987. *Anthropology at Home*. London.

18

Studying the past in the present: archaeological engagement with modern Greece

Paul Halstead

Foreign archaeologists, though normally drawn to Greece by the country's remarkable antiquities, have frequently found themselves equally captivated by modern Greece. Knowledge of modern Greek, coupled with widespread travel, has sometimes led to suspicions (not always groundless — as other contributors to this volume make clear) of spying, but most foreign archaeologists have engaged with modern Greece in ways that have nothing to do with international politics. For most of us, fieldwork in Greece has entailed extended stays away from the big cities in small villages or market towns that, even today, offer much that is of interest because it is unfamiliar. Few of us return home without some influence on our behaviour, on our tastes in music, food or drink, and perhaps on our vocabulary. Some of our distinguished predecessors combined a wealth of archaeological research with fundamental ethnographic studies of the rural communities among which they worked and travelled: for example, Wace and Thompson's account of the Vlachs of Samarina[1] or Dawkins's publications on modern Greek dialects and folk-tales.[2] Today archaeologists are increasingly specialized and it is hard to think of contemporary polymaths who could match the breadth of scholarship of Wace and Thompson or Dawkins, but academic engagement with modern Greece flourishes.

On the one hand, a series of archaeological survey projects has adopted a regional and diachronic framework in which early modern and contemporary Greece have been accorded the same importance as prehistory, classical antiquity or the medieval period. For example, British projects on Melos[3], in Boiotia[4] and on Kythera[5],

the Anglo-American and Greek survey on northern Kea[6] and American projects (with relevant British participation) in the southern Argolid[7] and Messenia[8] have explored the recent past of their chosen regions using various combinations of archival, oral and also archaeological data.[9]

On the other hand, archaeologists have used their experience of contemporary life in rural Greece as a source of insights into the distant past. Experience of the present has of course always shaped archaeologists' reconstruction and interpretation of the past: for example, Arthur Evans relied on his village workmen to identify the charred grains found at Knossos, while his interpretation of the architecture of the 'Palace of Minos' was clearly influenced by his own upbringing.[10] In recent decades, however, archaeologists have become increasingly aware of the need to be explicit and systematic in their use of present-day analogy to interpret the archaeological record.[11] Rural modern Greece has, for a variety of reasons (not least the innovative work of the University of Minnesota Messenia Expedition),[12] been a rich quarry for 'ethno-archaeological' research undertaken with the aim of using the present as an analogical key to the past. This paper is concerned with this particular form of archaeological engagement with modern Greece. Because of the remit of this volume, the paper focuses primarily on the work of British scholars and scholars based in British aca-

---

1. Wace and Thompson 1914.
2. E.g., Dawkins 1916.
3. Renfrew and Wagstaff 1982.
4. Bintliff and Snodgrass 1985.
5. Broodbank 1999.

6. Cherry et al. 1991.
7. Jameson et al. 1994.
8. Davis 1998.
9. E.g., Forbes 2000*a*; 2000*b*; Davies 2004; Slaughter and Kasimis 1985; Vroom 1998; Wagstaff and Augustson 1982; Whitelaw 1991; Zarinebaf et al. 2005.
10. E.g., MacNeal 1974.
11. E.g., Binford 1978; 1981; Hodder 1982.
12. McDonald and Rapp 1972; cf. Fotiadis 1995.

demic institutions, but it should be emphasized that the field of ethnoarchaeology is by no means monopolized by British scholars and, in the context of Greece, much important research has been conducted especially by American and Greek colleagues.

THE PRESENT PAST

Analogical research in Greece has tackled a range of topics from geoarchaeological analysis of the collapse of buildings[13] and construction of terrace walls,[14] through functional analysis of field systems and rural structures,[15] to oral and material studies of ceramic production and distribution and of the transmission of ceramic traditions[16]. This paper, however, focuses more narrowly (and in line with the author's professed expertise) on analogical investigation of farming and land use practices — a particularly active area of research, thanks to the persistence of small-scale farming and related tardy mechanization of agriculture in many parts of Greece. This focus provides ample scope both to illustrate the different types of question addressed by analogical research in Greece and to discuss the important theoretical problems that these raise. To these ends, a rough distinction may initially be drawn between analogical research designed to find out *what* people did in the past and that exploring *why* they did it. For example, a recent zooarchaeological study inferred that the Neolithic inhabitants of Knossos used female cows as draught animals, because of the occurrence of certain bone pathologies previously observed in modern draught cattle (from other parts of Europe).[17] Consideration of the recent use of draught animals in Greece and other parts of the Mediterranean suggested various reasons *why* Neolithic farmers in Knossos may have used draught animals rather than manual labour (e.g., time stress) and draught *cows* rather than draught *oxen* (e.g., cultivation on a modest scale)[18]. Both the inference of *what* Knossian farmers

did (they used draught cows) and the discussion of *why* they may have done so were based on analogical research and so both entail assumptions as to the similarity of past and present.[19] Such assumptions tend to be less problematic for 'what' than 'why' questions, as the following two sections illustrate.

ANALOGICAL REASONING, 1: INFERRING WHAT PEOPLE DID IN THE PAST

Excavated bones and charred grains, identified to species by *analogy* with their modern counterparts, may reveal which animals and plants people used in the distant past. Most staple plants and animals have broad ecological tolerances, however, so this information alone tells us little about how each species was managed or exploited. The conditions under which crop plants were grown may potentially be identified in two ways: by isotopic analysis of crop grains; and by analysis of the ecological characteristics of suites of weed species whose seeds are found contaminating samples of charred grain. The potential for isotopic characterization of crop growing conditions is still being tested and one current project, involving analysis of broad beans grown recently under various degrees of intensive and extensive cultivation in central Evvia, is exploring the viability of isotopic recognition of manuring.[20] Earlier analogical research in the same area of Evvia established that intensively cultivated broad bean gardens can be distinguished from extensively cultivated fields of the same crop on the basis of their associated weed floras. The differences in composition of weed flora were not fortuitous, but could be attributed to the variable response of the constituent species to competition (and hence fertility) and to disturbance (and hence intensity of tillage).[21] This study formed part of a larger project, involving similar studies in other parts of Europe and the east Mediterranean, which makes it possible to distinguish such aspects of crop husbandry as sowing season, intensity of cultivation, irrigation and perhaps fallowing.[22] These methods have already been applied

13. Galli 2000; Koulidou 1998.

14. Krahtopoulou 1997.

15. Whitelaw 1994; Chang 1994.

16. Jones 1986, 849–80; Blitzer 1990; Day 2004; Kiriatzi in prep.

17. Isaakidou 2006.

18. Isaakidou 2008.

19. Cf. Fotiadis 1995.

20. Bogaard et al. 2007; pers. comm.

21. Jones et al. 1999; 2000.

22. Jones et al. 2005.

to Neolithic plant remains from central Europe and the north Balkans to infer an intensive 'horticultural' regime of early crop husbandry.[23]

One complication with the use of weed ecology to infer crop husbandry methods is that weed seeds are deliberately removed from the harvest by a series of crop cleaning measures (winnowing, coarse and fine sieving, hand picking) that selectively remove 'garden' in favour of 'field' weeds.[24] Samples of crop weeds must be assigned to a stage in the crop processing sequence, therefore, before any attempt is made to use them to infer husbandry regimes. Research on the threshing floors of Amorgos in 1981 showed that stage of crop processing can be identified reliably on the basis of the relative proportions not only of grain, chaff and weed seeds but also of weed seeds with aerodynamic or size properties that predispose them to removal by winnowing, coarse- or fine-sieving, or hand-picking.[25] This analogical model has been applied widely, from Britain to the Near East: as a prelude to exploring crop husbandry on the basis of weed ecology;[26] as a means of distinguishing 'granaries' for long-term storage of partly cleaned crops from 'larders' for short-term storage of fully cleaned crops at Late Bronze Age Assiros Toumba and Knossos, respectively;[27] and as a means of identifying 'deviant' samples derived from the dung — burnt as fuel — of animals that had been fed crop cleaning residues.[28]

In the case of animal husbandry, study of dental microwear on the teeth of sheep and goats from Greece — animals stall-fed on leafy hay (see below) and milled cereals in the Pindos Mountains and stubble-grazers in lowland central Macedonia — has helped build up a series of models for the recognition of animal diet.[29] These models have been applied to zooarchaeological specimens from the North Atlantic to Turkey and reveal, *inter alia*, that Neolithic sheep and goats in Greece and the northern Balkans had a more abrasive diet than modern stubble-grazers, suggesting that they were closely confined — perhaps on disturbed (cultivated) land. They have also shown that some animals consumed in large-scale feasting at Late Neolithic Makriyalos had had an unusually non-abrasive diet, perhaps because they had been fattened for slaughter on grain or the like.[30] Present-day herders in Greece played a vital part in the development of these models, because leafy hay, widely gathered even a century ago, is now rare in Europe and even stubble grazing is disappearing.

'Leafy hay' refers to leafy branches cut (or leaves stripped) from deciduous trees and dried for feeding to livestock over winter. In the mountains of northern Greece, beech and especially deciduous oak are preferred for this purpose, because their leaves are robust and survive storage well.[31] In Greece and elsewhere, branches collected for this purpose are usually cut on a fairly short cycle of 2–5 years, to maximize the production and transport of leaf rather than wood. The survival of this practice at the village of Plikati on Mt. Grammos in the Pindos provided the opportunity for a range of analogical research on the impact of branch cutting ('shredding') on tree-ring width and pollen production, on the pollen and beetle remains that accumulated in leafy hay barns, and, as already described, on the dental microwear found in animals fed with leafy hay.[32] For example, examination of annual growth rings in a series of recently felled deciduous oaks revealed frequent episodes of retarded growth that matched well the shredding histories gleaned from elderly local residents and also identified a period of uninterrupted growth around 1950, when the village was abandoned in the aftermath of the Civil War.

This potential for reading the management histories of individual trees was then exploited by a larger scale project around Plikati.[33] According to local oral histories, the land around Plikati, one of the highest (ca 1200 m) permanently occupied villages in the Pindos Mountains, used to be the estate of an Ottoman land-

23. Bogaard 2004*a*; 2004*b*.

24. Jones 1992.

25. Jones 1984; 1987*a*; 1988.

26. E.g., van der Veen 1992; Bogaard et al. 2005.

27. Jones 1987*b*.

28. Charles 1998; Charles and Bogaard 2005.

29. Mainland 2003; Mainland and Halstead 2005.

30. Mainland 2007; Mainland and Halstead 2005.

31. E.g., Halstead 1998; Ripoll 2003

32. Halstead and Tierney 1998; Smith 1998.

33. Hall 2003.

owner and was grazed in summer by large transhumant flocks of sheep that spent the winter in the lowlands of Thessaly. Probably in the late 19c AD, the estate was sold off to incomers who founded the mixed farming households that today make up Plikati. Other villages in the same valley, by contrast, are proud to have lived for centuries from a combination of mixed farming and seasonally migrant craft specialization,[34] a claim that is consistent with the antiquity of their churches. Mapping and selective coring of extant trees confirm the reliability of these local oral histories. Around Plikati, few trees bear signs of shredding before the late 19c AD, whereas trees around Gorgopotamos, located below Plikati in the same valley, indicate a tradition of shredding which is at least several centuries older — the lower limit is obscured by the rotten state of the heart of the oldest trees.[35] Moreover, while shredded oaks around Plikati have a relatively vertical growth form, because they grew up competing for light with neighbouring trees, their counterparts around Gorgopotamos have a much more spreading form and evidently grew in a more open landscape. This contrast also matches oral testimony that indicates the need for larger-scale provision of leafy hay in Plikati than in its slightly lower-lying neighbour, where animals are confined to their stalls in winter by snow for shorter periods.

In the examples described above, studies of modern crop weeds, animal teeth and tree-rings derived from *known* husbandry regimes have served to provide analogical models for inferring what people did — how they managed their grain crops, livestock and trees — in the past. In drawing these analogies, it has been assumed that the responses of weed species to disturbance or fertility, of sheep and goat teeth to dietary abrasives and of tree-rings to shredding were similar in the past to what is observed today. Of course, the physiology and ecology of plants and other animals do change in time and do vary in space, but much less so than the human behaviour that we seek to infer with such analogies. For this reason, bioarchaeologists have felt it safe to apply such models based on present-day

observations in Greece both to the distant past and to other regions. Significantly, such analogies have also served to identify forms of past behaviour, such as Neolithic cereal 'gardening'[36], which have no real modern counterparts.

ANALOGICAL REASONING, 2: INTERPRETING WHY PEOPLE DID THINGS IN THE PAST

This explosion of analogical models for recognizing past land use practices is timely, in that it has broadly coincided with growing awareness of the extent to which land use in the Mediterranean may have changed since prehistory and even since classical antiquity. 'Traditional' Mediterranean land use, in which the plains are given over to alternating cereals and fallow, the hills to olives and vines, and the mountains (in summer) to transhumant flocks of sheep, has been regarded as a more or less natural response to constraints of climate and topography by geographers, historical geographers, historians, ancient historians and prehistorians.[37] Closer examination, however, reveals considerable spatial and temporal variability in recent farming and herding regimes that undermines the notion that 'traditional' Mediterranean land use is dictated by climate and topography, or is a timeless feature of the landscape as in Braudel's less explicitly deterministic notion of a *longue durée*. On the other hand, recognition of this variability, and of the local and historically contingent factors that have shaped it, may help us understand *why* people in the past practised particular forms of land use. The following two examples may serve to illustrate this point.

One element of the 'traditional' model of land use underpinned Renfrew's argument that the emergence of Minoan and Mycenaean palatial civilization in southern Greece in the later Bronze Age was linked to the development of 'Mediterranean polyculture' — the growing of cereals, olives and vines.[38] He proposed that different parts of the Bronze Age landscape were devoted to

---

34. E.g., Makris 1981.
35. Hall 2003, esp. fig. 6.44.

36. Jones 1992; Bogaard 2004; 2005.
37. E.g., respectively: Grigg 1974; Semple 1922; Braudel 1975; Isager and Skydsgaard 1992; Jarman et al. 1982.
38. Renfrew 1972.

cereals or olives or vines, as has increasingly been the case in recent years, and that this local agricultural specialization favoured the development of a redistributive authority (the future palatial elite) to ensure consumers had access to the full range of produce. Specialization in one element of Mediterranean polyculture is often a very recent phenomenon, however, and a response to relatively ephemeral market conditions or to inequalities in land ownership rather than being a timeless outcome of environmental conditions.[39] Perhaps more widespread until recently was the strategy of growing 'a little of everything', that both promotes domestic self-sufficiency in a range of products and reduces the risk of subsistence failure.[40] There is some evidence, as yet far too sparse for certainty, that diversification was similarly the norm in prehistory and that specialized production was a consequence rather than cause of the emergence of a palatial elite.[41] The crucial point here, however, is that recent Mediterranean land use is variable and is historically contingent on medium-term factors (Braudel's *conjonctures*) as much as it is shaped by the *longue durée* of environmental constraints. Analogy at this level, therefore, cannot serve as evidence of *what* people did in the past, but it can be invaluable in offering alternative models of past land use and in suggesting possible reasons why one strategy might have been pursued rather than another.

Another element of traditional Mediterranean land use that has attracted widespread interest from ancient historians and prehistorians is summer grazing of mountain pastures by transhumant or nomadic flocks. Mixed farming communities like that at Plikati could be found until a few decades ago throughout the mountains of the Mediterranean,[42] however, making it clear that seasonal displacement is not inevitable for those herding animals at high altitude in this region. Of course, sedentary mixed farmers usually keep much smaller numbers of animals (because of the difficulty of stall-feeding over winter) than mobile pastoralists, while the latter were effectively tied to seasonal movement, until very recently, by the difficulty of finding sufficient good pasture for large flocks (either in winter in the mountains or in summer in the lowlands). The size and mobility of flocks, in turn, is to some extent shaped by environmental constraints: for example, Plikati has easier access to extensive summer pasture on the summit of Mt. Grammos and faces more severe problems of over-wintering livestock than the villages lower down the same valley that have a longer history of sedentary mixed farming. On the other hand, small-scale sedentary mixed farming apparently displaced large-scale mobile herding at Plikati just over a century ago in the context of changes in land ownership. The breaking up of lowland estates, and consequent restriction of winter pasture for transhumant flocks, had a similar effect on a national scale.[43] Moreover, as in the case of diversified versus specialized polyculture, small-scale mixed farming tends to be geared to domestic self-sufficiency while large-scale herding represents a strategy of dependence on the market. The fortunes of specialized pastoralists in the mountains of Greece have thus waxed and waned in the recent past as demand for their cheese, textiles and pack-animals has fluctuated in response to changing levels of urban prosperity, to international competition and to the development of mechanized transport. The absence or under-development of a market economy has also been cited as grounds for doubting the existence of specialized pastoralists in later prehistory and at least early classical antiquity.[44] As in the case of polyculture, therefore, recent mobile pastoralism is partly a product of medium-term historical contingency and so cannot be extrapolated to the past simply on the grounds of environmental necessity or timeless tradition. On the contrary, awareness of alternative strategies of animal husbandry and high-altitude land use has prompted ancient historians and prehistorians to re-examine their sources and to conclude that available literary, epigraphic and archaeological evidence[45] from classical antiquity and later prehistory is mostly compatible with diversified (and often small-scale) mixed farming rather than with specialized, large-scale pastoralism.

39. E.g., Psikhogios 1987; Forbes 1993; Halstead 1987.
40. Forbes 1976.
41. Halstead 1992.
42. E.g., McNeill 1992.

43. E.g., Vergopoulos 1975.
44. Halstead 1987; Cherry 1988.
45. E.g. respectively: Hodkinson 1988; Chandezon 2003; and Halstead 1991; 1996*a*; 1996*b*.

A recurrent theme in the preceding two examples has been the opposition between small-scale diversified land use, geared largely to domestic self-sufficiency, and specialized (and often large-scale) production intended for exchange.[46] Increasingly, archaeologists are able to distinguish between intensive and extensive and between diversified and specialized forms of husbandry and there is every reason to anticipate a steady increase both in the volume and resolution of relevant data and in the range of analogical models and analytical techniques to which these can be subjected. Deconstruction of 'traditional' Mediterranean land use suggests that intensity of husbandry is likely to be related inversely to scale of production, and degree of specialization related to level of market integration or redistributive control. These suggestions must be used heuristically, of course, as hypotheses to be tested, because husbandry practices are influenced, rather than determined, by systems of land ownership and exchange. Their heuristic value, however, depends on the likelihood of their shedding light on *why* people practised particular forms of land use in the past — and this in turn depends on the thorny issue of whether ancient and modern farmers make decisions in similar ways.

AGRICULTURAL DECISION-MAKING

Archaeologists (in common with ancient historians and anthropologists) have adopted a range of approaches to how farmers make decisions. These may be arranged on a scale of declining analytical convenience, but increasing (current) academic respectability, that is exemplified by the following three positions:

(1) decisions are determined by environmental constraints and so are highly predictable;

(2) decisions are shaped by 'rational' cost:benefit analysis ('practical reason'[47]) and so are fairly predictable;

(3) decisions are constrained by cultural considerations of identity, status and values[48] and so are only predictable to someone with a good inside knowledge of the particular (sub-)culture.

The first position has been widely discredited (including above), but the standpoints of practical and cultural reason deserve further consideration in the present context.

PRACTICAL REASON: RATIONAL FARMERS?

It must first be acknowledged that the success of cost:benefit-based decision-making is limited by the quality of available information; even today, farmers and herders always make decisions on the basis of incomplete knowledge of future weather, market conditions, and so on. In terms of access to relevant information, therefore, the difference between ancient and modern farmers or herders is arguably one of degree rather than kind, and the benefits to the latter of modern telecommunications and information technology are at least partly offset by the additional uncertainties associated with integration in a global market.

An issue of greater concern is whether or not cost:benefit analysis is restricted to market or capitalist economies.[49] Certainly, elderly farmers in Greece and elsewhere are more likely to offer quantified estimates of costs and benefits when these entail exchange beyond the household (e.g., the area tilled per day by a hired plough team or the number of sheaves cut per day by a hired harvest labourer) than when these simply involve the allocation of household resources (e.g., the area weeded per morning by a woman, in between performing other domestic tasks). Nonetheless, farmers do to varying degrees make rule of thumb estimates of many parameters that help them plan the allocation of domestic labour and other resources. For example, at Plikati and elsewhere in the Pindos, elderly villagers would never provide a quantified response to questions about provision 'in the old days' of unsown *grassy* hay, because its availability was very restricted and everyone collected whatever they could get hold of. When questioned about provision of *leafy* hay, however, they were invariably forthcoming and also fairly consistent (at least between villages at similar altitude) in their responses. Thanks partly to careful management of shredded trees,[50] the provision of *leafy* hay was limited

---

46. Cf. Halstead 2000.
47. Sahlins 1976.
48. Sahlins 1976.

49. E.g., Polanyi 1957; Finley 1973; cf. Jongman 1988.
50. E.g., Halstead 1998; also Moreno 1982.

primarily by the availability of (or willingness to commit) labour for cutting and transport and villagers usually had a fairly clear target for the number of bundles needed per winter per head of sheep and goats. Similarly, farmers in many parts of Greece were in the habit of keeping tally of the number of sheaves of cereals they had reaped, partly to avoid undetected theft and partly to give a first clue as to the size of the harvest, but also partly to aid in planning transport (e.g., how many cart-loads or trips with the mules) and threshing (e.g., how many times to fill the threshing floor). It is also noteworthy that, while some domestic planning was conducted with state-sponsored units of measurement (e.g., *strémmata* of land, *okádes* of grain, *drakhmés* of rent), much was based on 'practical' units — sheaves, barrels, days of ploughing, etc. — that sometimes varied according to local convention and sometimes were fairly standardized because so was the capacity for labour of human workers (FIG.18.1), draught cattle or pack-animals.[51] The etymology of many of these folk units of measurement, and of their ancient counterparts, suggests that Mediterranean farmers had coined means of assessing costs and benefits long before the emergence of capitalism.

The romantic legacy of classical 'bucolic' literature has undoubtedly led to some uncritical attributions of great wisdom to elderly Mediterranean villagers, but the converse suggestion that all wise Mediterranean farmers long ago sold up and moved to the towns[52] is equally unhelpful. On the contrary, after interviewing hundreds of elderly farmers and herders from Spain to Cyprus, and in many different parts of Greece, this author has been impressed by the range of variables (availability of land and labour, number of animals held, size of grain or cash reserves, weather, age and gender composition of the household, prices, etc.) that are routinely taken into account in planning what to grow/rear and where and how. Moreover, although these agricultural practitioners are (like academics!) more or less intelligent, more or less industrious, more or less risk-averse and more or less willing to innovate, it is striking how often they respond in a similar way to

Fig.18.1: Sofia Venianaki, Iraklio, Crete. 'As a girl in Aloides, I was a good harvester. In a day, I cut five mule loads of four sheaves each. Within the village, we helped each other in turn at harvest time in return for food. Outside the village, we were paid for reaping. When you were hired by outsiders, you had to cut 20 sheaves each day. My father kept a notebook in which he wrote down the size of our harvest and the amount of grain needed for the family, so that he knew how much he needed to buy in Iraklio.' Author's photograph.

similar problems or opportunities; unexpected answers are offered just often enough to make such conversations interesting, but responses tend to be remarkably consistent. Sometimes these consistencies can be attributed to the provision of similar advice by agronomists in different countries, but decisions are more frequently justified with reference to specific cases where the effects of alternative practices were experienced or observed. The frequency with which the same conclusions have been drawn from similar experiences in different parts of the Mediterranean suggests some success in discerning patterns of cause and effect. Lack of formal education means that these practitioners often express their knowledge in a manner alien to academic discourse, and to 'scientific' notions of cause and effect, but should not disguise the extent to which many are acute observers of the world around them and seek to use this knowledge in their day-to-day and year-to-year

---

51. E.g., Panaretos 1946; Petropoulos 1952.
52. Fotiadis 1995, 76 n.90.

Fig.18.2: Paliambela-Kolindrou, Pieria. Mitsos Boufos left Thraki (European Turkey) as an infant. His generation were taught to reap with the short local drepáni, making it easier to work as hired harvest workers in surrounding villages. Harvesting their own fields, however, Mitsos and his contemporaries had to reap, sheave and stook separately from their parents who used the longer Thracian leléki. The wooden palamariá on his left hand protected the fingers and gathered larger handfuls of crop. Its use was considered essential with the wide swinging movement of the leléki, but optional with the shorter cutting strokes of the drepáni. Author's photograph.

decision-making. Infallible decision-makers they are not (who is?), but desk-bound academics (especially those of urban and/or non-Mediterranean upbringing) are ill advised to ignore their experiences when trying to understand why past farmers and herders adopted particular practices.

CULTURAL REASON: WE FARM THIS WAY?

Although ethnic and regional identities are most obviously projected in different ways of dressing or speaking or cooking, they also find expression in farming and herding practices, as is well documented in the rich folklore or *laografía* literature from different parts of Greece. Across northern Greece in the mid–20c AD, Thracian refugees (*Thrakiótes*) were acutely conscious of using different plough animals (usually oxen rather than mules), different sickles (often the long un-toothed *leléki* rather than short toothed *drepáni*) and a different range of threshing-floor tools than their 'local' (*ntópioi*) neighbours.[53] Elderly farmers in Paliambela-Kolindrou and in Assiros further emphasized how Thracian and 'local' reaping equipment required different bodily movements, so that a Thracian could not easily use a 'local' sickle. It was also said that a man sowing could be identified from a distance as Thracian or 'local' by the way in which he moved around the field.

Farming practices were thus a means of expressing differences of identity and, as with more obvious markers, these differences were sometimes clearer in theory than in practice: for example, 'local' use of oxen for ploughing was by no means as rare as elderly Thracians claim. Moreover, as with other expressions of identity, husbandry practices were by no means immutable. For example, transhumant Vlachs often justify their pastoral specialization and mobile lifestyle with the normative statement that 'we Vlachs moved' or 'we Vlachs kept sheep', but it is notable that Vlachs from summer villages near the high Pindos pastures retained the normative lifestyle and distinctive identity longer than those in the lower-lying villages of the eastern Zagori who long ago became Hellenised, sedentary mixed farmers.

Many further examples could be presented that apparently demonstrate the triumph of practical over cultural reasoning or *vice versa*, but it is more interesting to explore the interplay between practical and cultural constraints on human decision-making.

53. E.g., Kizlaris 1938–48.

ENCULTURED PRACTICAL REASON?

The Vlachs and Sarakatsani are two groups of mobile pastoralists that remarkably have maintained distinct identities probably over several centuries, despite spending the winter half of the year widely dispersed among sedentary agriculturalists across much of the Balkans and despite economic dependence on urban merchants and lowland farmers of different identities.[54] It is arguable that the maintenance of these distinctive identities was essential to the viability of mobile specialized pastoralism, as shared identity ensured access to information about distant pastures, to economic assistance in the event of loss of a flock, to mutual defence against rustlers and brigands during the vulnerable seasonal migrations, to wives with the necessary skills and fortitude, and so on. A shared pastoral identity could also be mobilized in a repressive fashion, as when herders at Vlach Densko loosed their sheep into the crops of households that were attempting a transition to mixed farming and so threatening to undermine the collective land ownership that underpinned the stable and equitable exploitation of summer pasture.[55]

Returning to distinctive traditions of farming in the lowlands, Thracians and 'locals' describe the practical difficulty of working together at the harvest. The Thracian long-bladed *leléki* involved swinging movements of the right arm that were likely to injure a 'local' working alongside and making rapid sawing movements with a short *drepáni*. Moreover, the *leléki* cut lower down on the straw and so resulted in longer sheaves that could not be stooked in the field nor stacked at the threshing floor with their shorter 'local' counterparts without risk of collapse and exposure of the precious harvest to rain, wind and livestock. Accordingly, in Paliambela-Kolindrou, the first generation of Thracian refugees used the familiar *leléki* and, in time, reaped and stooked separately from their children, whom they equipped with the *drepáni* to enable them to work more easily as hired harvesters for the wealthier 'local' farmers (FIG.18.2). Distinctive agricultural tools and ways of doing things have been widely documented by folklorists in dif-

Fig.18.3: Metaxada, Messinia. The late Ilias Velisarios had a stock of sayings and parables, that seemed to cover most aspects of rural decision-making. He had acquired this library of mnemonics sitting around the fire in winter in his childhood home: 'there was no television in those days.' Childhood labour also gave him a broad practical education: 'I learnt to be a farmer, herder and butcher growing up in the village, but only learnt the profession of thief in the army'. (During the Civil War, his hungry commando unit had supplemented meagre rations by ingeniously robbing a guarded British army store outside Athens). Author's photograph.

ferent regions of Greece. These distinctive ways were perpetuated, because children tended to acquire tools and skills from their parents and, as described above, different tools often involved distinctive motor habits that were not easy to un-learn in adulthood. In the vast majority of cases, the alternative ways of doing things seem to have been equally viable, with no significant differences in practical efficiency. Where relatives and neighbours worked together, however, whether in mutual assistance or as hired labourers, there were significant gains in efficiency and even safety if all worked in a similar way. A man tying sheaves behind a team of reapers would not be able to keep up if the piles of cut cereal laid on the ground were of very variable size. And if sheaves of different size were loaded either side of a donkey or mule, they were liable to be shed on the way to the threshing floor, causing both delay and loss of grain. Distinctive ways of doing are often described as being superior to the alternatives, but the common refrain 'we do it this way' ('the grandfather

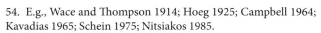

54. E.g., Wace and Thompson 1914; Hoeg 1925; Campbell 1964; Kavadias 1965; Schein 1975; Nitsiakos 1985.

55. Cf. Nitsiakos 1985.

response'[56]) arguably comes closer to the mark: shared ways of doing things improve efficiency.

Ways of doing things were often learned at an early age, thanks to the prevalence of childhood labour. A girl of eight or ten accompanying her mother to the harvest might initially help to gather the crop. At 12 years of age, she might be given her first sickle and be shown how to use it, but after watching her mother for several summers she might already know what to do. Likewise, teenagers who lost their father prematurely often knew how and when to plough or sow because they had long helped him with whatever tasks did not require adult physical strength. The stock of knowledge that underpinned flexible decision-making (e.g., which field to plough first after heavy rain) was sometimes explicitly taught by parents and sometimes learned from bitter experience (personal or of neighbours whose activities were followed closely). Much essential knowledge was also encapsulated in the stock of sayings, stories and parables that children heard on winter evenings around the fire (FIG.18.3).

These stories and parables often have a moralizing tone and, like Pacific Argonauts,[57] elderly Greek farmers often attach value to the clean and tidy products of (apparently needlessly) careful agricultural work. 'Locals' and Thracians alike in Paliambela-Kolindrou remember one (now dead) man for his ability to reap faster than anyone else, without dropping ears, and yet leave the field looking 'like it had been cut with a spirit-level'. Speed and lack of spillage are obvious virtues (hired reapers in northern Spain are said to have dropped as many ears as possible to improve the rewards of subsequent gleaning), but an even reaping height was also a sign that his sheaves would be of consistent size and so would make weather-proof stooks and stacks. Careful work also tended to save time and problems at a later stage in the agricultural cycle: a poorly ploughed field would produce a weedy crop, which would be difficult to harvest as well as lower-yielding, and would require more sieving and hand-picking to remove contaminants. Careful cleaning of seed corn, in turn, would reduce the weediness of the next crop. At Metaxada in Messinia, it was said that the farmer who took clean grain in carefully mended sacks to the mill could sell his grain at any time of year, while his children would be sought after as marriage partners. The miller saw the state of everyone's grain and so the whole district would learn who was a good farmer (*noikokíris*). In planning exchange or alliance with another household, it was important to know something of the quality of their work — the value attached to good workmanship is by no means as irrational as is sometimes suggested. (FIG.18.4)

CONCLUSION

Archaeologists are still very actively engaged with modern Greece and, focussing on examples related to contemporary land use, this paper has highlighted the growing volume of 'ethnoarchaeological' research intended to shed analogical light on the past. A key issue here is the extent to which present and past can be taken to be similar: dissimilarity makes the past interesting, but similarity is the basis of such use of analogy.

Similarity between present and past can be assumed with relative safety for the physiology and ecology of plants and animals and, on this basis, we can use present-day observations of weed ecology, tree-ring growth and dental microwear formation to identify aspects of *what* farmers and herders did in the past — how they managed their crops, woodland and livestock. Systems of land use cannot simply be extrapolated from present to past: recent Mediterranean farming practices are far more diverse than archaeologists and historians have often appreciated; and this diversity, in turn, betrays the fact that land use is shaped by historically and regionally contingent circumstances as well as timeless environmental constraints. Growing recognition of, and interest in understanding, the diversity of land use has yielded a wealth of insights into *why* particular forms of husbandry may have been practised in the past. In contrast to analogy-based inferences as to *what* past farmers and herders did, these insights into *why* they did so involve assumptions about human decision-making and so must be used heuristically — as suggestions to be explored.

These insights are more likely to be productive if present and past farmers/herders made decisions in

56. Forbes 1989.
57. Malinowski 1922.

Fig.18.4: Although pack-animals vary in size and strength, the 'load' was a widely used and fairly consistent unit of measurement. The size of sheaves varied according to local custom, and so too, therefore, did the number of sheaves per load, but both tended to be fairly consistent within a community. One advantage of such consistency was to reduce the risks of either overloading pack-animals or loading them unevenly so that the sheaves spilled. Author's photograph.

similar ways and this recalls the extended debates in anthropology, history and archaeology between primitivists/substantivists and modernists/formalists as to whether 'rational' decision-making based on the weighing up of costs and benefits is restricted to modern western economies. Of course, not even the most edentulous elderly informant in the remotest village of modern Greece (and likewise of highland New Guinea) is untouched by the global market economy. On the other hand, non-mechanized Mediterranean farmers and herders have the considerable analogical virtue of raising many of the same species of crops and livestock, under broadly similar constraints from the physical environment and with a substantially comparable technology, as did their ancient predecessors. Either way, engagement with elderly villagers in Greece and other parts of the Mediterranean offers some interesting perspectives on the issue of rational decision-making.

First, while money and the market provide a universal medium for comparing the value of goods and services, elderly present-day farmers and herders grew up with a wealth of rule-of-thumb measures for the likely costs and benefits of various husbandry practices. Such accounting was particularly common in (but by no means restricted to) dealings outside the household and even then often did not involve money: for example, a hired harvester was expected to cut 5 donkey loads of sheaves and received 20 *okádes* of grain per day. The etymology of folk units of measurement suggests that such accounting is probably very ancient. Secondly, elderly practitioners frequently weigh up a host of constraints and variables in making decisions, even if difficulty in imagining the ignorance of the interlocutor or in guessing what s/he is fishing for, may lead to a (truthful, if misleadingly minimalist) response such as 'we always did it that way'. Further discussion with such apparent slaves to tradition frequently yields a very different (more multivariate and more flexible) response. Overall, 'traditional' rustic agronomy is arguably good enough to be a useful heuristic aid to understanding the parameters that shaped past land use practices.

Nonetheless, culture-specific ways of farming are well documented in Greece and were perceived as markers of identity, much as were language, dress, cuisine and so on. To a great extent, these distinctive traditions are unlikely to be visible in the archaeological record, because they are simply different means of achieving a common end, but they may have considerable practical significance in two ways. First, in so far as they contribute to maintenance of a common identity, they may help to sustain essential bonds of mutual assistance and collaboration; this is perhaps particularly clear among mobile Sarakatsani and Vlach pastoralists. Secondly, and perhaps less obviously, the existence of commonly agreed ways of doing things is a pre-requisite for efficient and safe collaboration, both within and between households. This last point is of particular interest because it suggests that the polar perspectives of practical and cultural reason have scope for fruitful integration.

It also suggests that much could be gained from greater integration of the questions and methods of anthropology with the extraordinarily rich database of Greek folklore studies. In dispensing advice to other disciplines, however, this archaeologist's engagement with modern Greece perhaps risks *hubris*.

ACKNOWLEDGEMENTS

I am indebted to numerous, mostly elderly, residents of rural modern Greece, who have acceded with remarkably good grace to requests to sample their fields, barns, stables and kitchens and to questions about how they farmed and why. I also thank Valasia Isaakidou and Vangelio Kiriatzi for comments on versions of this paper.

REFERENCES

Binford, L.R., 1978. *Nunamiut Ethnoarchaeology*. New York.

—, 1981. *Bones: Ancient Men and Modern Myths*. New York.

Bintliff, J.L., and Snodgrass, A.M., 1985. 'The Cambridge/Bradford Boeotian expedition: the first four years', *Journal of Field Archaeology* 12: 123–61.

Blitzer, H., 1990. KORONEIKA: storage-jar production and trade in the traditional Aegean', *Hesperia* 59: 675–711.

Bogaard, A., 2004a. *Neolithic Farming in Central Europe: an Archaeobotanical Study of Crop Husbandry Practices*. London.

—, 2004b. 'The nature of early farming in central and south-eastern Europe', *Documenta Praehistorica* 31: 49–58.

—, Jones, G. and Charles, M., 2005. 'The impact of crop processing on the reconstruction of crop sowing time and cultivation intensity from archaeobotanical weed evidence', *Vegetation History and Archaeobotany* 14: 505–9.

—, 2005. '"Garden agriculture" and the nature of early farming in Europe and the Near East', *World Archaeology* 37: 177–96.

—, Heaton, T.H.E., Poulton, P. and Merbach, I., 2007. 'The impact of manuring on nitrogen isotope ratios in cereals: archaeological implications for reconstruction of diet and crop management practices', *Journal of Archaeological Science* 34: 335–43.

Braudel, F., 1975. *The Mediterranean and the Mediterranean World in the Age of Philip II*. London.

Broodbank, C., 1999. 'Kythera Survey: preliminary report on the 1998 season', *BSA* 94: 191–214.

Campbell, J.K., 1964. *Honour, Family and Patronage*. Oxford.

Chandezon, C., 2003. *L'élevage en Grèce (fin Ve-fin Ier s. a.C.): l' apport des sources épigraphiques*. Paris.

Chang, C., 1994. 'Sheep for the ancestors: ethnoarchaeology and the study of ancient pastoralism', in P.N. Kardulias (ed.), *Beyond the Site: Regional Studies in the Aegean*: 295–313. Lanham.

Charles, M., 1998. 'Fodder from dung: the recognition and interpretation of dung-derived plant material from archaeological sites', *Environmental Archaeology* 1: 111–22.

— and Bogaard, A., 2005. 'Identifying livestock diet from charred plant remains: a Neolithic case study from southern Turkmenistan', in J. Davies, M. Fabis, I. Mainland, M. Richards and R. Thomas (eds), *Diet and Health in Past Animal Populations: Current Research and Future Directions*: 93–103. Oxford.

Cherry, J.F., 1988. 'Pastoralism and the role of animals in the pre- and proto-historic economies of the Aegean', in C.R. Whittaker (ed.), *Pastoral Economies in Classical Antiquity. Cambridge Philological Society* Suppl. 14: 6–34. Cambridge.

—, Davis, J.L. and Mantzourani, E. (eds), 1991. *Landscape Archaeology as Long-Term History: Northern Keos in the Cycladic Islands from Earliest Settlement until Modern Times*. Los Angeles.

Davies, S., 2004. 'Pylos Regional Archaeological Project, part vi: administration and settlement in Venetian Navarino', *Hesperia* 73: 59–120.

Davis, J.L. (ed.), 1998. *Sandy Pylos: an Archaeological History from Nestor to Navarino*. Austin.

Dawkins, R.M., 1916. *Modern Greek in Asia Minor: a Study of the Dialects of Silli, Cappadocia and Phárasa, with Grammar, Texts, Translations and Glossary*. Cambridge.

Day, P.M., 2004. 'Marriage and mobility: tradition and the dynamics of pottery production in twentieth century East Crete', in P.P. Betancourt, C. Davaras and R. Hope Simpson (eds), *Pseira VIII. The Archaeological Survey of Pseira Island Part I*: 105–42. Philadelphia.

Finley, M.I., 1973. *The Ancient Economy*. London.

Forbes, H., 1976. '"We have a little of everything": the ecological basis of some agricultural practices in Methana, Trizinia', *Annals of the New York Academy of Sciences* 268: 236–50.

—, 1989. 'Of grandfathers and grand theories: the hierarchised ordering of responses to hazard in a Greek rural community', in P. Halstead and J. O'Shea (eds), *Bad Year Economics*: 87–97. Cambridge.

—, 1993. 'Ethnoarchaeology and the place of the olive in the economy of the southern Argolid, Greece', in M.-C. Amouretti and J.-P. Brun (eds), *Oil and Wine Production in the Mediterranean Area. BCH* suppl. 26: 213–26. Paris.

—, 2000a. 'The agrarian economy of the Ermionidha around 1700: an ethnohistorical reconstruction', in S.B. Sutton (ed.), *Contingent Countryside: Settlement, Economy, and Land Use in the Southern Argolid since 1700*: 41–70. Stanford.

—, 2000b. 'Dowry and inheritance: their relationship to land fragmentation and risk reduction on Methana', in S.B. Sutton (ed.), *Contingent Countryside: Settlement, Economy, and Land Use in the Southern Argolid since 1700*: 200–27. Stanford.

Fotiadis, M., 1995. 'Modernity and the past-still-present: politics and time in the birth of regional archaeological projects in Greece', *American Journal of Archaeology* 99: 59–78.

Galli, E., 2000. Earth Structures Deterioration Process and Patterns of Deposition: a Case Study from Macedonia, Greece on Natural Formation Processes. MSc thesis, University of Sheffield.

Grigg, D.B., 1974. *The Agricultural Systems of the World: an Evolutionary Approach*. Cambridge.

Hall, C., 2003. Leaf Fodder Management and Woodland History in the Pindos Mountains, Northwest Greece: a Dendroecological Study. PhD thesis, University of Sheffield.

Halstead, P., 1987. 'Traditional and ancient rural economy in Mediterranean Europe: plus ça change?', *Journal of Hellenic Studies* 107: 77–87.

—, 1991. 'Present to past in the Pindhos: specialisation and diversification in mountain economies', *Rivista di Studi Liguri* 56: 61–80.

—, 1992. 'Agriculture in the Bronze Age Aegean: towards a model of palatial economy', in B. Wells (ed.), *Agriculture in Ancient Greece: Proceedings of the Seventh International Symposium at the Swedish Institute at Athens*: 105–16. Stockholm.

—, 1996a. 'Pastoralism or household herding? Problems of scale and specialisation in early Greek animal husbandry', *World Archaeology* 28: 20–42.

—, 1996b. 'Μεσογειακή ορεινή οικονομία στην Πίνδο: μετακινήσεις ανάμεσα στο παρόν και το παρελθόν', in V. Nitsiakos (ed.), *Η Επαρχεία Κόνιτσας στο Χώρο και στο Χρόνο*: 63–73. Konitsa.

—, 1998. 'Ask the fellows who lop the hay: leaf-fodder in the mountains of northwest Greece', *Rural History* 9: 211–34.

—, 2000. 'Land use in postglacial Greece: cultural causes and environmental effects', in P. Halstead and C. Frederick (eds), *Landscape and Land Use in Postglacial Greece*: 110–28. Sheffield.

— and Tierney, J. (with S. Butler and Y. Mulder), 1998. 'Leafy hay: an ethnoarchaeological study in NW Greece', *Environmental Archaeology* 1: 71–80.

Hodder, I., 1982. *The Present Past*. London.

Hodkinson, S., 1988. 'Animal husbandry in the Greek polis', in C.R. Whittaker (ed.), *Pastoral Economies in Classical Antiquity. Cambridge Philological Society* Suppl. 14: 35–74. Cambridge.

Höeg, C., 1925. *Les Saracatsanes, une tribu nomade grecque*: 1. Paris.

Isaakidou, V., 2006. 'Ploughing with cows: Knossos and the "secondary products revolution"', in D. Serjeantson and D. Field (eds), *Animals in the Neolithic of Britain and Europe*: 95–112. Oxford.

—, 2008. 'The fauna and economy of Neolithic Knossos revisited', in V. Isaakidou and P. Tomkins (eds), *Escaping the Labyrinth: the Cretan Neolithic in Context*: 90-114. Oxford.

Isager, S. and Skydsgaard, J.E., 1992. *Ancient Greek Agriculture: an Introduction*. London.

Jameson, M.H., Runnels, C.N. and van Andel, T.H., 1994. *A Greek Countryside: the Southern Argolid from Prehistory to the Present Day*. Stanford.

Jarman, M.R., Bailey G.N. and Jarman, H.N. (eds), 1982. *Early European Agriculture*. Cambridge.

Jones, G., 1984. 'Interpretation of archaeological plant remains: ethnographic models from Greece', in W. van Zeist and W.A. Casparie (eds), *Plants and Ancient Man*: 43–61. Rotterdam.

—, 1987a. 'A statistical approach to the archaeological identification of crop processing', *Journal of Archaeological Science* 14: 311–23.

—, 1987b. 'Agricultural practice in Greek prehistory', *BSA* 82: 115–23.

—, 1988. 'The application of present-day cereal processing studies to charred archaeobotanical remains', *Circaea* 6: 91–96.

—, 1992. 'Weed phytosociology and crop husbandry: identifying a contrast between ancient and modern practice', *Review of Palaeobotany and Palynology* 73: 133–43.

—, Bogaard A.,Charles M., Halstead P. and Smith H., 1999. 'Identifying the intensity of crop husbandry practices on the basis of weed floras', *BSA* 94: 167–89.

—, Bogaard, A., Charles M. and Hodgson, J., 2000. 'Distinguishing the effects of agricultural practices relating to fertility and disturbance: a functional ecological approach in archaeobotany', *Journal of Archaeological Science* 27: 1073–84.

—, Charles, M., Bogaard, A., Hodgson, J.G. and Palmer, C., 2005. 'The functional ecology of present-day arable weed floras and its applicability for the identification of past crop husbandry', *Vegetation History and Archaeobotany* 14: 493–504.

Jones, R.E., 1986. *Greek and Cypriot Pottery: a Review of Scientific Studies*. Fitch Laboratory Occasional Paper 1. Athens.

Jongman, W., 1988. *The Economy and Society of Pompeii*. Amsterdam.

Kavadias, G.B., 1965. *Pasteurs-nomades méditerranéens: les Saracatsans de Grèce*. Paris.

Kizlaris, T., 1938–48. 'Ἀγροτικός βίος των Θρακῶν', *Λαογραφία* 12: 386–416.

Koulidou, S., 1998. Depositional Patterns in Abandoned Modern Mud Brick Structures. MSc thesis, University of Sheffield.

Krahtopoulou, A., 1997. 'Agricultural terraces in Livadi, Thessaly, Greece', in A. Sinclair, E. Slater and J. Gowlett (eds), *Archaeological Sciences 1995*: 249–59. Oxford.

MacNeal, R.A., 1974. 'The legacy of Arthur Evans', *California Studies in Classical Antiquity* 6: 205–20.

Mainland, I., 2003. 'Dental microwear in modern Greek ovicaprids: identifying microwear signatures associated with a diet of leafy hay', in E. Kotjabopoulou, Y. Hamilakis, P. Halstead, C. Gamble and P. Elefanti (eds), *Zooarchaeology in Greece: Recent Advances*: 45–50. London.

— and Halstead, P., 2005. 'The diet and management of domestic sheep and goats at Neolithic Makriyalos', in J. Davies, M. Fabis, I. Mainland, M. Richards and R. Thomas (eds), *Diet and Health in Past Animal Populations: Current Research and Future Directions*: 104–12. Oxford.

—, 2007. 'A microwear analysis of selected sheep and goat mandibles from Ecsegfalva', in A. Whittle (ed.), *The Early Neolithic on the Great Hungarian Plain: Investigations of the Körös Culture Site of Ecsegfalva 23, Co. Békés*: 343-8. Budapest.

Makris, K.A., 1981. *Χιοναδίτες Ζωγράφοι*. Athens.

Malinowski, B., 1922. *Argonauts of the Western Pacific*. London.

McDonald, W.A., and Rapp, G.R. (eds), 1972. *The Minnesota Messenia Expedition*. Minneapolis.

McNeill, J.R., 1992. *The Mountains of the Mediterranean World*. Cambridge.

Moreno, D., 1982. 'Querce come olivi: sulla rovericoltura in Liguria tra 18 e 19 secolo', in D. Moreno, P. Piussi and O. Rackham (eds), *Boschi: storia e archeologia. Quaderni Storici* 49: 108–36.

Nitsiakos, V., 1985. A Vlach Pastoral Community in Greece: the Effects of its Incorporation into the National Economy and Society. PhD thesis, University of Cambridge.

Panaretos, A., 1946. 'Κυπριακά μέτρα, σταθμά, μονάδες χρόνου και σχετικαί προς αυτά λέξεις', *Κυπριακαί Σπουδαί* 8: 61–82.

Petropoulos, D.A., 1952. 'Συμβολή εις την έρευναν των λαϊκών μέτρων και σταθμών', *Επετηρίς του Λαογραφικού Αρχείου* 7: 57–101.

Polanyi, K., 1957. 'The economy as instituted process', in K. Polanyi, C.M. Arensberg and H.W. Pearson (eds) *Trade and Market in the Early Empires: Economies in History and Theory*: 243–70. New York.

Psikhogios, D.K., 1987. *Προίκες, Φόροι, Σταφίδα και Ψωμί: Οικονομία και Οικογένεια στην Αγροτική Ελλάδα του 19 Αιώνα*. Athens.

Renfrew, C., 1972. *The Emergence of Civilisation: the Cyclades and the Aegean in the Third Millennium BC.* London.

— and M. Wagstaff (eds), 1982. *An Island Polity. The Archaeology of Exploitation in Melos.* Cambridge.

Ripoll, M.P., 2003. 'Preliminary study of pastoral activities among the Pomaks in Greek Thrace', in E. Kotjabopoulou, Y. Hamilakis, P. Halstead, C. Gamble and P. Elefanti (eds), *Zooarchaeology in Greece: Recent Advances*: 291–95. London.

Sahlins, M., 1976. *Culture and Practical Reason.* Chicago.

Schein, M.D., 1975. 'When is an ethnic group? Ecology and class structure in northern Greece', *Ethnology* 14: 83–97.

Semple, E.C., 1922. 'The influence of geographic conditions upon ancient Mediterranean stock-raising', *Annals of the Association of American Geographers* 12: 3–38.

Slaughter, C., and Kasimis, C., 1986. 'Some social-anthropological aspects of Boeotian rural society: a field-report', *Byzantine and Modern Greek Studies* 10: 103–60.

Smith, D., 1998. 'Beyond the barn beetles: difficulties in using some Coleoptera as indicators of stored fodder', *Environmental Archaeology* 1: 63–70.

Van der Veen, M., 1992. *Crop Husbandry Regimes: an Archaeobotanical Study of Farming in Northern England, 1000 BC–AD 500.* Sheffield.

Vergopoulos, K., 1975. *Το Αγροτικό Ζήτημα στην Ελλάδα, Η Κοινωνική Ενσωμάτωση της Γεωργίας.* Athens.

Vroom, J., 1998. 'Early modern archaeology in central Greece: the contrast of artefact-rich and sherdless sites', *Journal of Mediterranean Archaeology* 11: 131–64.

Wace, A.J.B., and M.S. Thompson, 1914. *The Nomads of the Balkans.* London.

Wagstaff, M., and S. Augustson, 1982. 'Traditional land use', in C. Renfrew and M. Wagstaff (eds), *An Island Polity: the Archaeology of Exploitation in Melos*: 106–33. Cambridge.

Whitelaw, T.M., 1991. 'The ethnoarchaeology of recent rural settlement and land use in northwest Keos', in J.F. Cherry, J.L. Davis and E. Mantzourani (eds), *Landscape Archaeology as Long-Term History: Northern Keos in the Cycladic Islands from Earliest Settlement until Modern Times*: 403–54.

—, 1994. 'An ethnoarchaeological study of rural land-use in north-west Keos: insights and implications for the study of past Aegean landscapes', in P.N. Doukellis and L.G. Mendoni (eds), *Structures rurales et sociétés antiques: actes du colloque de Corfou, 14–16 mai 1992*: 163–86. Paris.

Zarinebaf, F., J. Bennet and J.L. Davis, 2005. *A Historical and Economic Geography of Ottoman Greece: the Southwestern Morea in the Early 18th Century.* Princeton.

19

Epilogue

Roderick Beaton

This book has been primarily about an institution, the British School at Athens, and about many of the individuals who both shaped it, and were in turn of shaped *by* it. To that extent, *Scholars, Travels, Archives* builds upon two previous books about the School, *The British School at Athens: The First Hundred Years* by Helen Waterhouse, and *On Site: British Archaeologists in Greece* edited by Eleni Calligas and James Whitley. As all three books show, the School in its relatively short history has attracted some highly distinguished 'scholars and travellers'; as a result its archives contain rich material relating to a variety of disciplines and objects of study. As an institution, the BSA has often appeared endearingly idiosyncratic, an outpost of British academia that for years managed to remain 'more English than the English'. As several of the preceding chapters have shown, however, the School's influence was not invariably benign or even innocent; indeed, putting together glimpses that emerge in them, from different viewpoints, I find myself more than a little curious to know more about the character and temperament of Alan Wace. Perhaps that formidable wartime Director would be as deserving of a biography as the fascinating philhellene and forerunner of so much of the School's academic activity, George Finlay.

But as this book's subtitle declares, there is another, larger, story being told in its pages. In fact, I think there are two, interlocking stories, both of them much larger than the story of the institution that brings them together. One is the story of Greece as a modern nation, a story in which Great Britain was deeply involved from the time of the Greek Revolution up till at least 1947, and in which individual British scholars and travellers have often played a significant role; the same can even be said of archives, if one includes the card-index of spies concocted by Hasluck and Wace as described by Richard Clogg! The other story concerns the history of scholarship in a number of related disciplines: archae-

ology, anthropology, art history, architecture, linguistic study, folklore, Byzantine studies. In all of these fields, British intellectual encounters with Greece and with Greeks have had a formative part to play in the way that these disciplines are now practised internationally, and not least in universities today in both Britain and Greece.

BRITAIN AND GREECE:
A QUASI-COLONIAL RELATIONSHIP?

Renée Hirschon's anthropological fieldwork among former students of the School confirms that the BSA has often been experienced as something like a colonial institution. Other evidence is to be found in the foregoing pages to suggest that in the 'heroic age' of Directors such as Dawkins and Wace, attitudes that we would today describe as 'colonial' were taken for granted in the administrative organisation and social life of the School. Evidently this affected the institution's relationships with its Greek hosts at every level: whether with the local élite in the case of the Archaeological Service, with labourers on an excavation, or with locally recruited domestic servants. More surprisingly, perhaps, some of these attitudes seem to have outlasted the British empire, making the British School at Athens a kind of microcosm of colonial life almost until the end of the twentieth century. This prompts the reflection, implicit throughout much of this book and sometimes addressed explicitly, that perhaps for much of the last two centuries the wider political and diplomatic relationship between Britain and Greece had something about it of the relationship between coloniser and colonised.

The sovereignty granted to newly independent Greece by the London Protocols of 1830 and 1832 was, in legal terms, absolute. In practice, though, it is well known that throughout the nineteenth century and for much of the twentieth, the Greek state was often

Fig.19.1: *Students in the BSA Library, ca 1962; BSA Photographic Archive: BSAA6–51.*

reduced to client status *vis-à-vis* one or more of the 'Great Powers' of the day. That one of these should have been Britain was only to be expected: London had been the meeting place, between 1826 and 1832, of the standing conference at which the terms for Greek independence were negotiated; between 1805 and 1956, when the Royal Navy had a significant role in the Mediterranean, intervention in the internal affairs of Greece would often be motivated by British strategic interests in the region. Some instances of this have been touched on in this book; the 'big picture' of large-scale diplomatic, strategic, and military involvement has been well documented and studied.[1]

But it is only recently that a number of scholars have begun to approach the relationship in the context of British imperial history on the one hand, and of 'post-colonial' studies of the experience of the colonised on the other. This has been done, in different ways, by Thomas Gallant for the British Protectorate of the Ionian Islands, and by Robert Holland and Diana Markides in a comparative study of British 'decolonisation' in the same islands in 1864, in Crete after a shortlived mandate that began in 1898, and most traumatically in Cyprus in the late 1950s.[2] From a quite different perspective, and one that converges more obviously with the subject of this book, Yannis Hamilakis has investigated the history of archaeology in Greece in a way that consistently draws parallels

---

1. See, for example, Koliopoulos 1977 for the late 1930s; Papastratis 1984 for the period of the Second World War; Alexander 1982 for the years immediately following.

2. Gallant 2002; Holland and Markides 2006.

between archaeology as a 'western', rational science and the colonial adventures alongside which it developed in the nineteenth and early twentieth centuries.[3]

So it may be time to think about the historical relationship between Great Britain and Greece during the last two centuries as in some ways analogous to the story of colonisation, decolonisation and emancipation that has been more fully studied in other parts of the world.

THE GREEK EXPERIENCE AND THE HISTORY OF SCHOLARSHIP

It might possibly have come as a surprise to some readers of this book to discover how much of the scholarly work undertaken at the British School at Athens over the years has been in disciplines other than archaeology. Indeed one lesson that can be drawn from many of the preceding chapters is surely that archaeology, in its formative days, was not clearly marked off from a number of other disciplines that were often practised by the same people while 'doing' archaeology. As we now know, Dawkins, best known for his work on modern Greek dialects and folktales, was a good enough field archaeologist to be entrusted with the Directorship of the School. Hasluck came to anthropology through archaeology, while the opposite route had been taken by Arthur Evans (a figure of whom one might have expected to read more in these pages). Wace was as conversant with the language of contemporary Vlach shepherds as he was with that of Homer, on whom he would go on to publish an authoritative 'Companion', as well as being the excavator of Agamemnon's city. Arnold Toynbee, another figure of towering stature in his day, wins only passing mention here but also began his academic career at the BSA, from where he progressed to the Koraes Chair at King's College London and from there to Anatolia during the Greco-Turkish war of 1919–23; it was from his experiences there, as well as from the ensuing furore when he published his views in 1922, that the seed grew that many years later would become the monumental construction of the entire human past, *A Study of History*.[4]

It is salutary today to be reminded that not so long ago the boundaries separating these disciplines were much less rigid than they have since become. History, archaeology, anthropology, linguistics, and studies of Byzantine architecture all share a common intellectual descent; the underlying questions they ask about human beings and human institutions are very similar, only applied to different sorts of evidence. A rollcall of the British School on the eve of the First World War reveals a truly remarkable concentration of expertise and openness of intellectual curiosity. The intervening period of almost a century has seen a vast increase in professionalisation, as well as specialisation. But there is no reason, today, why archaeologists and anthropologists and folklorists and linguists, architects, Byzantinists, Ottomanists, and even — why not? — spies, should not talk to one another as they did in the Finlay Library a hundred years ago, even if no one now would expect to find so many of these scholarly identities combined in one and the same person.

It may have been archaeology that brought most of these scholars and travellers to Greece in the first place, but whether or not they went on to make a name for themselves in that field, all were deeply affected by their first-hand experience of Greece, and in particular of remote places in rural Greece. The importance of this goes far beyond the accident of history that much of the material they observed and recorded (language, folktales, embroideries, aspects of the rural economy, even the Church of St Demetrios in Thessaloniki, destroyed by fire in 1917) would soon be swept away in the aftermath of two world wars, as well as by more benign forms of modernisation. What these British scholars 'discovered' or experienced in Greece often had a profound effect on their own future careers, sometimes also on the future course of the academic discipline in which they worked.

This story begins, surely, with Finlay, whose early philhellenism brought him to Greece as a volunteer in the Revolution, and who later returned to spend the rest of his life in the country; it is perhaps no accident that a British historian living in Athens should have been the first to conceive of a continuous history of 'Greece' beginning in antiquity and ending (eventually) with the deposition of Otto, first king of 'Modern Greece', in 1862. It is beginning to be acknowledged

---

3. Hamilakis 2007.
4. Toynbee 1961; for this interpretation, see Beaton 1991. For the story of Toynbee's tenure of the Koraes Chair, see Clogg 1986.

Fig.19.2: The 'Palaiologoi', all at the time students of the BSA, performing at the 'Glendi', Menelaion, Laconia, 1977. Performers (Left to right): Paul Halstead (standing), Christine Donougher , Roderick Conway Morris, Roderick Beaton. BSA Photographic Archive: Members, O. Dickinson Album–38.

that the example of Finlay had a formative influence on the work of Konstantinos Paparrigopoulos, whose monumental *History of the Hellenic Nation*, published between 1860 and 1874, for the first time established the principle of continuity linking successive phases of Greek history, that has been a cornerstone of Greek national identity ever since.[5]

Similarly, Dawkins's systematic studies of the Greek dialects of Anatolia would prove a model for linguists who came after him; modern ethnographic methods were pioneered, if not quite invented, by Dawkins, Wace, and Hasluck. David Shankland, in his contribution here, even credits Hasluck with the invention of modern anthropology. Roger Just, in telling a story that I think has never been told before, that of Brit-

ish, American and French anthropologists in Greece since the Second World War, suggests that these scholars were pioneers who still await the credit for what in hindsight turns out to have been a remarkable 'paradigm shift' in anthropology.

And finally, let us not forget archaeology itself. It is probably a truism that archaeological science has been bound up from the beginning with the specific terrain and sites of Greece, along with those of Egypt, Mesopotamia and Italy. This book has not been concerned directly with the history of archaeology, a topic that has been treated recently elsewhere.[6] But one significant recent development in archaeological science, as

---

5. Koubourlis forthcoming.

6. Brown and Hamilakis 2003; Hamilakis 2007; Voutsaki 2003; cf. also, in relation to city-planning in Athens in the nineteenth century, Bastéa 2000.

we learn from Paul Halstead, is a direct product of the engagement of field archaeologists with the landscape, ecology and economy of remote Greek communities today. Ethno-archaeology, to which the Marc and Ismene Fitch Laboratory at the BSA has made a distinguished contribution, is a branch of scientific archaeology that has grown up since the early 1970s, much of it pioneered in Greece and subsequently applied to many other areas.

In conclusion, the story of the British School, of its scholars, travellers, and archives, is part and parcel of the story of modern Greece. The exploration of relatively recent Greek history, language and culture has enormously enriched British and worldwide scholarship, and may have been the touchstone for important advances in certain disciplines, with implications that go far beyond the Greek material from which they started. If so, these developments have not left Greek scholars unaffected either — as is evident already from the biographies of this book's contributors. From Leake in the early 1800s, and Finlay writing his history in the middle of that century, to those wonderfully self-made scholars of the twentieth, before scholarship became professionalised, William Miller and Philip Sherrard, all the scholars, travellers, and compilers of archives who feature in this book owed the greatest debt of all to the country from which they learned so much and to its people: Greece and the Greeks.

REFERENCES

Alexander, G.M., 1982. *The Prelude to the Truman Doctrine: British Policy in Greece 1944–1947*. Oxford.

Bastéa, E., 2000. *The Creation of Modern Athens: Planning the Myth*. Cambridge.

Beaton, R., 1991. 'Koraes, Toynbee and the modern Greek heritage'. *Byzantine and Modern Greek Studies* 15: 1–18.

Brown, K.S. and Hamilakis, Y. (eds), 2003. *The Usable Past: Greek Metahistories*, Lenham, MD.

Clogg, R., 1986. *Politics and the Academy: Arnold Toynbee and the Koraes Chair*. London.

Gallant, T., 2002. *Experiencing Dominion: Culture, Identity, and Power in the British Mediterranean*, Notre Dame, IN.

Hamilakis, Y., 2007, *The Nation and its Ruins: Antiquity, Archaeology, and National Imagination in Greece*. Oxford.

Holland, R. and Markides, D., 2006. *The British and the Hellenes: Struggles for Mastery in the Eastern Mediterranean 1850–1960*. Oxford.

Koliopoulos, J.S., 1977. *Greece and the British Connection 1935–1941*. Oxford.

Koubourlis, I., forthcoming. 'European historiographical influences upon the young Konstantinos Paparrigopoulos', in R. Beaton and D. Ricks (eds), *The Making of Modern Greece: Nationalism, Romanticism, and the Uses of the Past (1797–1896)*. Aldershot.

Papastratis, P., 1984. *British Policy towards Greece during the Second World War 1941–1944*. Cambridge.

Toynbee, A.J., 1961. *A Study of History* (12 vols). London.

Voutsaki, S., 2003. 'Archaeology and the construction of the past in nineteenth century Greece', in H. Hokwerda (ed.), *Constructions of Greek Past: Identity and Historical Consciousness from Antiquity to the Present*. Groningen, 231–55.

PLATE I

Plate I. Skyros Cushion — 1018; Wace Family Collection.

PLATE II

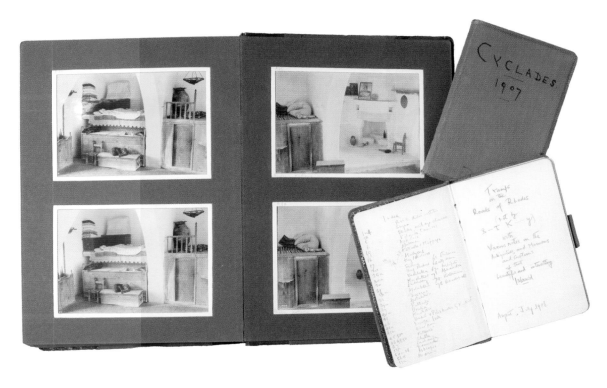

Plate II a. Pages from Photograph Album with two notebooks — Cyclades 1907 and (open) Rhodes 1908;
Wace Family Archives. b. Pages from Photograph Album; Wace Family Archives;

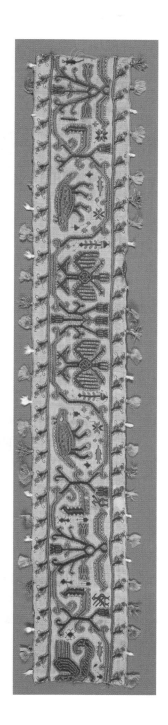
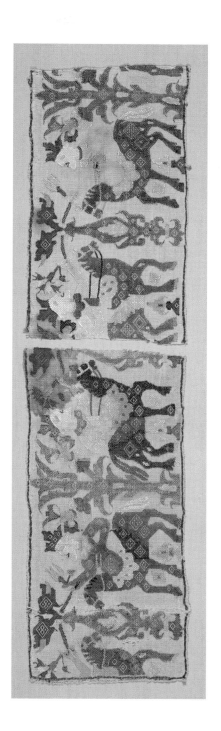

Plate III. Melos embroidery — 819b. This piece remains with Wace's family.
Plate IV. Fragments from Epirus; Wace Family Archives.

PLATE V

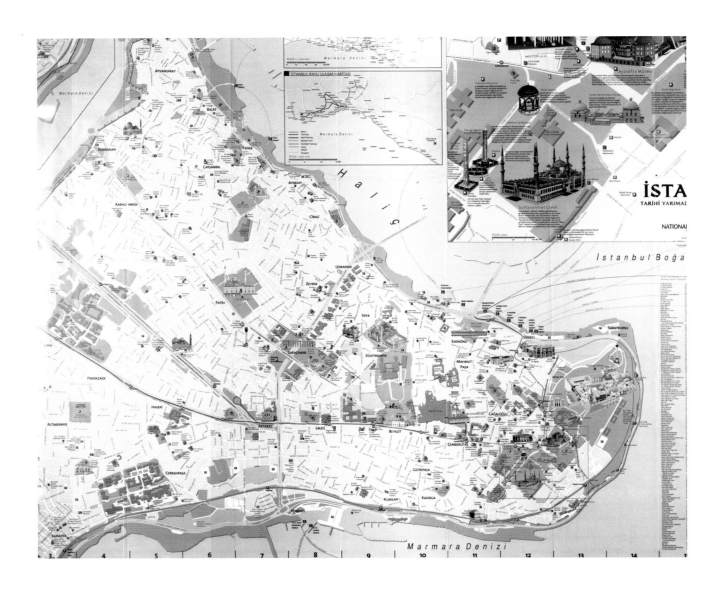

Plate V. Map of Istanbul.

PLATE VI

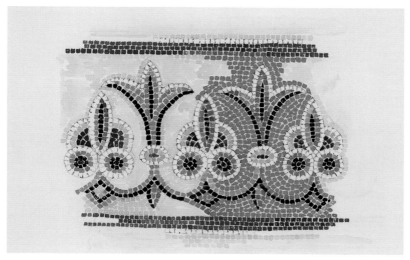

Plate VI a-d. Watercolours of various mosaics from Daphni monastery, 1888–90.
BSA BRF–01.01.01.170; BRF–01.01.01.176; BRF–01.01.01.172; BRF–01.01.01.168.

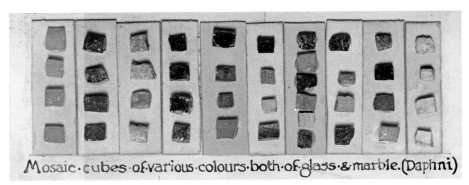

Mosaic·cubes·of·various·colours·both·of·glass·&·marble·(Daphni)

Plate VII. BRF mosaic 'swatch'.

:Church at Daphne near ATHENS:
Section looking East. ¼ Scale.

Plate VIII. Daphni monastery, Attica; BSA BRF–01.01.01.143.

PLATE IX

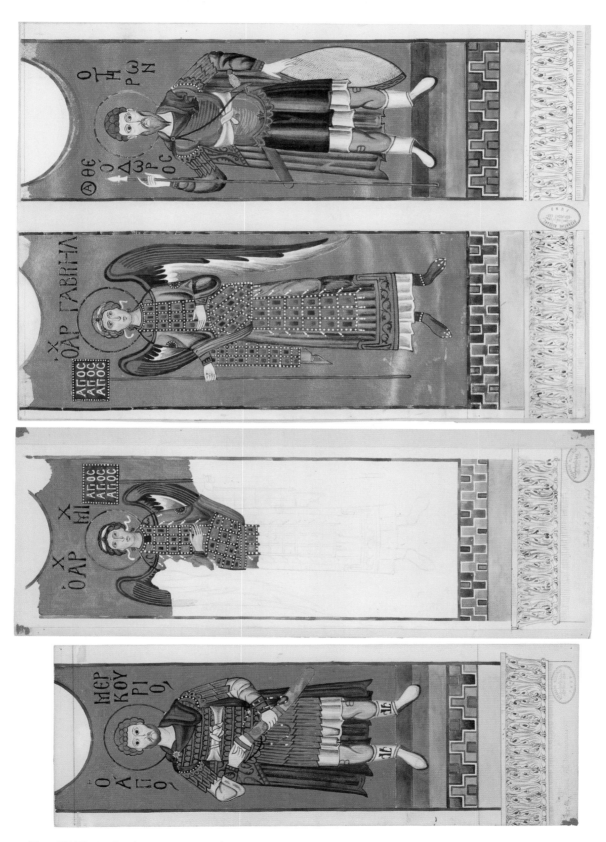

Plate IX. Hosios Loukas monastery, Phocis; BSA BRF–01.01.04.168; BRF–01.01.04.166; BRF–01.01.04.167.

PLATE X

Plate X. Hosios Loukas monastery, ca 1890; BSA BRF–01.01.04.135.

PLATE XI

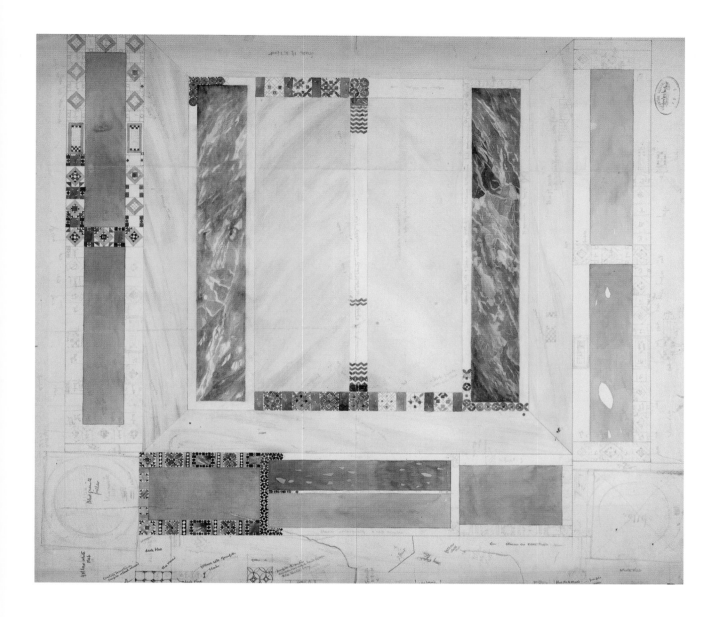

Plate XI. Hagios Demetrios church, Thessalonike; BSA BRF–01.01.07.314.

PLATE XII

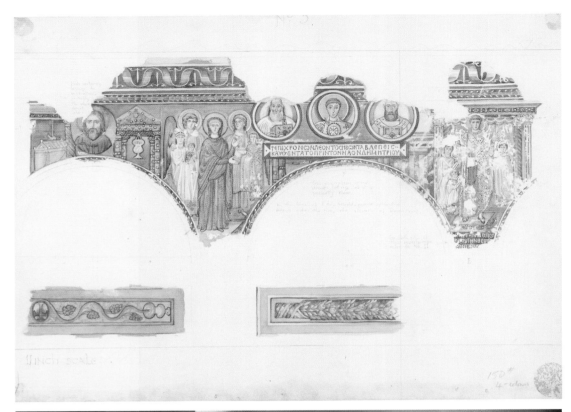

Plate XII a-b. Hagios Demetrios church, Thessalonike, 1909; BSA BRF–01.01.07.309; BRF–02.01.07.212.

PLATE XIII

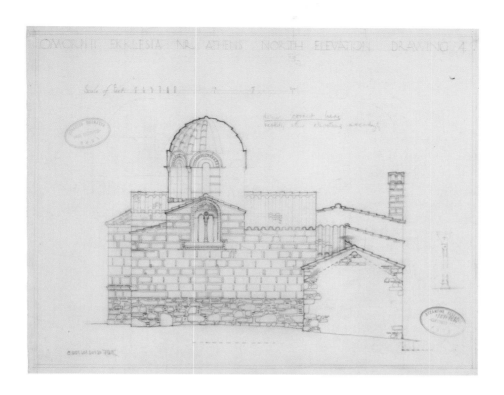

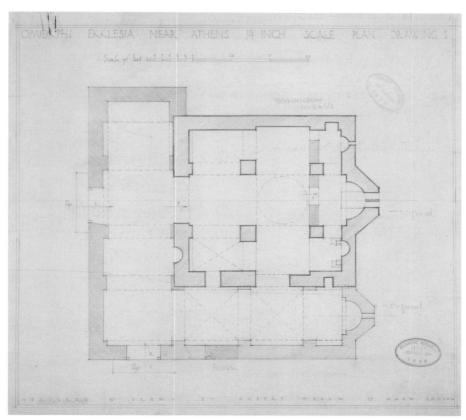

Plate XIII a-b. Omorphi Ekklesia, Galatsi, Athens, 1932; BSA BRF–01.01.01.222; BRF–01.01.01.225

PLATE XIV

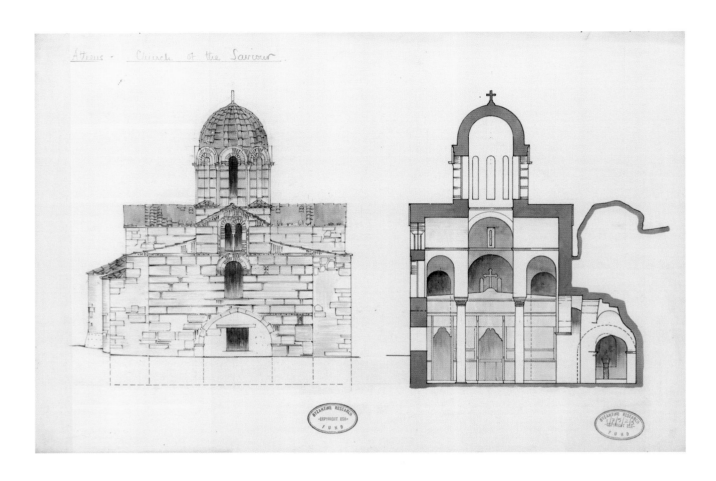

Plate XIV. North elevation and tranverse section, Metamorfosis church, 1888–90; BSA BRF–01.01.01.096.

PLATE XV

Plate XV. West elevation, Panagia Gorgoepikoos church, Athens; R. Weir Schultz & S. Barnsley, 1888–90;
ink, pencil, watercolour; 330mm x 490mm; BSA BRF–01.01.01.036.

PLATE XVI

Plate XVI. Katholikon, bema, marble wall revetment, Daphni monastery, Attica,
28 April 1888; BSA BRF–01.01.01.196.

PLATE XVII

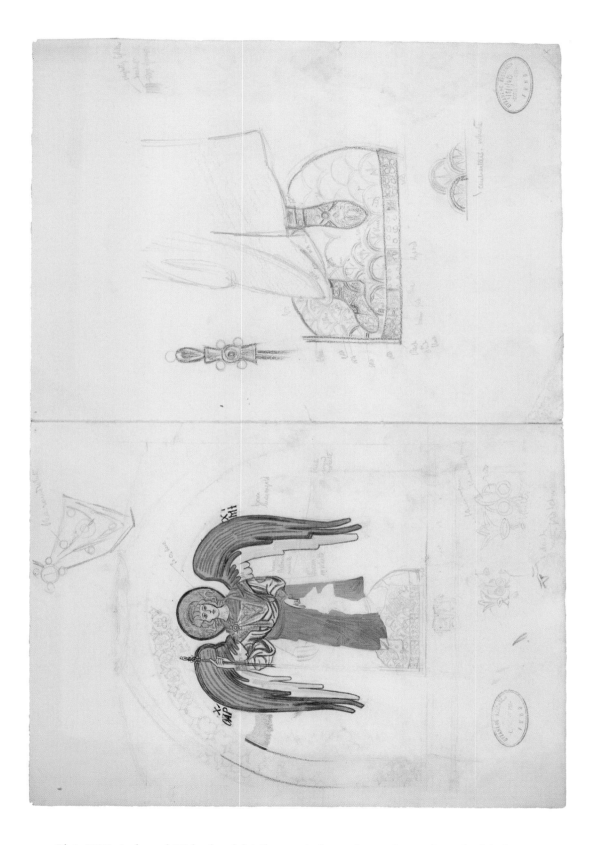

Plate XVII. Archangel Michael and details, mosaic decoration on the north conch of the bema, Daphni monastery, Attica, 1888–90; BSA BRF–01.01.01.185.

PLATE XVIII

Plate XVIII. The prophet Ezekiel, mosaic decoration in the dome of the nave, Katholikon, Daphni monastery, Attica, April 1889; BSA BRF–01.01.01.186.

Index of churches, monasteries and holy springs

Index of place names

General index

British School at Athens, Upper House, photograph by R.C. Bosanquet, ca 1902; BSA Photographic Archive: BSAA8–3 (SPHS–5028).